# Arlott on Cricket

David Rayvern Allen is a full-time radio producer with the BBC. Author of *A Song for Cricket, Samuel Britcher, the Hidden Scorer* and *Sir Aubrey* (a biograpy of cricketer, actor, film star, C. Aubrey Smith), and compiler of a collection of John Arlott's broadcasts and commentaries entitled *A Word from Arlott*, he has also contributed to *Wisden Cricket Monthly* and *The Cricketer* among other magazines. Married with two children, he lives in Hertfordshire.

# Arlott on Cricket

## His Writings on the Game

EDITED BY
### DAVID RAYVERN
### ALLEN

FONTANA/COLLINS

First published by
William Collins (Willow Books) 1984
First issued in Fontana Paperbacks 1985

Copyright © John Arlott 1984

Set in Plantin
Made and printed in Great Britain by
William Collins Sons & Co. Ltd, Glasgow

# Contents

# Author's Preface

The publisher's generous suggestion to publish a collection of 'occasional' writings about cricket was too tempting to refuse; especially since it would involve being paid a second time for work, first paid for long ago: how long ago – indeed in many cases long forgotten – was still to emerge. It seemed fair to transpose a filter between source and reader, in the shape of an independent editor – which is not too altruistic a decision if the editor is a friend.

David Rayvern Allen, honest cricket enthusiast, reliable critic and splendid archivist agreed. Have you, reader, ever been edited? At times, exhumed seemed a more precise word.

Pieces here – some of them written forty years ago – came back as startlingly as if they had been written by somebody else; yet – that idea *had* crossed the mind – that *fact* had been observed. Who, though, was it written for? Usually it seemed for benefit booklets; or as prefaces for club histories. (Delete that observation about being paid a second time!)

Many of these, of course, were written in series of essays for *Playfair Cricket Monthly*, *The Cricketer*, *Wisden Cricket Monthly* and during many happy years with *The Guardian*. This acknowledges those editors' kindness in allowing reprinting; and, even more, the pleasure of the opportunities they offered.

Except to correct outdated statistics – like, for instance, Ken Suttle's advance among batsmen's career records for Sussex – no attempt has been made to adjust in the light of hindsight.

David Rayvern Allen has made his choice with a sympathy which any author must regard with immense gratitude; and with a perspective of which no author is truly capable.

No writer can alter the history; but only reflect it: thus these pieces show the vast change – not for the better, nor the worst, but simply different – between the 1946 attempt to recreate the cricket scene of 1939; and that of 1984. Cricket has always changed in harmony with its social background; and this collection constitutes a salutary indication of how wide that change – or development – has been, over those forty years, while the world also changed – at times almost out of recognition.

It provides, too, perhaps, a reminder that not all cricket – certainly not all the cricket that matters – is played at Test, or even first-class level. The looks back into history and even more into the personalities of ordinary cricketers and ordinary clubs serve – thanks to understanding editing – to demonstrate that cricket is, above all, a vehicle of pleasure. This preface can but express gratitude to an editor who was offered, accepted, and never betrayed, complete freedom to choose or reflect as he wished; and who recalled for the writer poignant nostalgia for cricketers who have passed on; and the delight of years in, and about, the finest of all games.

JOHN ARLOTT
*Alderney*
*May* 1984

# Editor's Introduction

Every book-lover has had the alarming experience of stretching for an attractive title at the top of a library stack, only to bring down the spurned remainder in a cascading flood, with head and shoulders buffeted on their route to a spine-splitting landing on the floor. When John rang to inquire whether I would like to gather a representative collection of his writings on cricket, there was, of course, only one possible response: delight and a sense of privilege at being asked, excitement at the thought of finding more words of wisdom from sources perhaps unrealized, an assured knowledge that it was another typically kind and generous gesture from an old and dear friend, and yet mingling with all that, a growing feeling of apprehension at the sheer magnitude of the task. How does one cope with the mainstream of such a prodigious output over nearly four decades? Where do you start with the countless match reports in *The Guardian*, vignettes in the now defunct *Evening News* and *News Chronicle*, summaries in *The Observer*, essays in *The Times*, articles in *The Cricketer*, *Playfair Cricket Monthly* and *Wisden Cricket Monthly*, sketches in county yearbooks, written recollections in magazines, appreciations in benefit brochures and forewords . . .? It was time for those tremors in the library stretch once again.

John Arlott has written, co-authored or edited, around eighty books and booklets since 1943, when he chose an anthology of topographical verse for England and Wales with poet and epigrammatist, George Rostrevor Hamilton. About three-quarters of those books have been on cricket. It was as a youngster that he started to watch and read about the game, and once captured, his enthusiasm kept growing apace with the years of early manhood. In fact, John used to plan his annual leave from jobs in local government, with a sole view to taking in as much cricket as possible.

He had reached his early thirties, and was still a 'copper' on the beat in Southampton, when broadcast talks gave him a chance to relive for the general public some of those ineradicable memories of the players and matches from the years between Kaiser Bill and Adolf Hitler. Then, soon afterwards, in 1946, John was able to relay live the resurrection of cricket following the war, and carried out his commentary duties concurrently with his commitments as a literary programmes producer in the BBC External Services, where, incidentally, he had succeeded George Orwell. No doubt, the rich vocabulary and vivid phrase, until then gestating in relative seclusion within his own mind and orbit of acquaintances, had found a natural outlet in discourse on wireless. The words, both spoken and written, were well conceived but a spontaneous expression. The voice – a God-given bonus.

The young broadcaster's journalistic career began in earnest in 1950 when he started writing profiles, features and reviews for the *Evening News*, with also the occasional penned portrait for the *Daily Mail*. In 1955, he crossed the road to the *News Chronicle* and stayed until the demise of the paper some five years later, although by that time he had begun to report football for *The Observer*. His first outing could not have been more opportune – it was that incredible match in 1958 when Tottenham Hotspur beat Everton 10-4 at White Hart Lane. During the late 1950s and 1960s there had been the infrequent piece for *The Times*, and although he had written for *The Guardian* before, it was not until 1968 that he became the newspaper's full-time cricket correspondent.

John had the precipitous challenge of following Denys Rowbotham and Neville Cardus through the willow gate at *The Guardian*, and as Cardus himself with perhaps a pretence of conceit once wrote, 'it was as though a cricketer went in to bat after Hobbs and Sutcliffe.' More seriously, he went on: 'I have always admired Arlott's economy of words, his ability to depict a scene or character as though by flashlight ... Arlott can imprint on imagination by means of swift, accurately seen etching; he has a gift for the word photographic. He is never the literary Mandarin, yet he is one of our most civilized writers.'

John has always viewed and translated cricket with an eye for its inherent character. He is less concerned with the technique of the game and much appreciates its personality. Inevitably, the chosen pieces reflect that stance, with an emphasis placed on monographs of the players. They did, after all, choose him as President of their Professional Association. The twelve chapter-headings are devised with the idea of giving a convenient form to the book and, it is to be hoped also, some balance and shape. Each article should be treated as an entirely separate self-contained piece of work: overall though, can one detect a kind of stray pattern mirrored by the author's feelings at the given moment, the head and dipped lights perceived through a long career?

Specific mention perhaps should be made of the chapter on village cricket, containing a number of prefaces and tributes which, at first glance, might seem in themselves insubstantial. Another look, however, usually reveals time-consuming research of the game in each particular locality; an intriguing fossil of information dropped in to the narrative, and then casually thrown away within a sentence or two. The village club is surely the essence even now, the untutored 'hoicks' and 'tonks' representing the purest type of cricket. Historically as well, of course, the hallowed nursery slopes of the village Hambledon are part of John's backyard. Naturally, he feels a special affinity for the 'gallant and mighty men' depicted by Nyren in *The Cricketers of My Time*, and consequently, over a lifetime spent generating millions of words, the subject has found its way into much of his writing. Such a subject does not pall.

Other areas contain a certain degree of repetition – not surprising in a canon so colossal, and where most of the articles were written originally for monthly magazines, periodicals, or daily or weekly newspapers whose very nature condemns its material to a short transitory existence. Few of the pieces have previously found a more permanent status inside hard covers.

It is to be expected that time and events has altered the perspective on some comments and opinions since first penned. The advantage of hindsight has not been used within the 'body politic' as it were, except with the toast 'to the immortal memory of Madge' in 'At the Sign of the Bat and Ball'. The mystery of Madge perplexed so many for so long, and the story of the solution is such a tale in itself, that it would have been utterly unreasonable to expect any writer to resist the opportunity of revamping the *denouement*.

Any attempt to collate material from a multitude of sources involves the co-operation of others. Stephen Green, the curator of the MCC at Lord's, who naturally and deservedly has appeared in the acknowledgment lists of dozens of cricket books, performed many acts of succour with the help of his assistants Fay Ashmore and Michael Lucy, to whom my grateful thanks. Geoffrey Copinger and Geoffrey Whitelock, the former with the resources of his comprehensive collection and the latter with his invaluable bibliography of the writings of John Arlott, were a tremendous assistance. So was Tony Winder who acquired a major part of the Arlott cricket collection. Ken Murphy at *The Guardian*, the library staff there; Ray Smith at *The Times*; the staff of Manchester University library, where the files of the *Evening News* are kept; the assistants at Colindale Newspaper Library; the secretaries of most of the County Clubs; the Club Cricket Conference; David Frith, Editor of *Wisden Cricket Monthly*; Howard Milton, Tony Mitchener, Roy Oliver, the Editor of *Hampshire – the County Magazine* (hereinafter referred to as *Hampshire*) – all provided access to articles with great willingness and often at considerable inconvenience to themselves. There ought to be additional superlatives to 'thank you' in the English language, because sometimes it seems an inadequate response. There were several kindly souls who sent compositions by John, that, for one reason or another, mostly lack of space, failed eventually to find a place in these pages. Their ready assistance was much appreciated. Sue Dunford, my indefatigable secretary, performed remarkable feats of intuitive interpretation, and Tim Jollands of Collins Willow kept a check on exuberant excesses with charming tact and a twinkle in at least one eye.

Finally, the more one has contact with John himself, the more one explores his unequalled definitive contribution to the literature of cricket, the more one grows to admire and cherish the man. In this case, thanks are not enough, but he already knows my feelings on that score.

DAVID RAYVERN ALLEN
*Chorleywood*
*May* 1984

# I
# A Look at the Past

## The View from Elysium
### *Dr Grace in 1975*

*Dateline: Elysium, 1 April* 1975. I knew that eventually one of the newspapers, or some publication, would ask me if I thought I could succeed in the game of cricket today. The request would have come long ago, I suppose, but that people from the press do not often come to these exalted regions. Certainly C. P. Scott, the famous editor of the *Manchester Guardian*, was here for some years, but he spent most of his time with the statesmen and was never interested in popular sports writing. Anyway, he left when he heard the management had entered into negotiations for entry with Malcolm Muggeridge. So eventually this exclusive report was obtained by a 'ghost' with much experience of these ethereal deals who came here on a brief visitation that in no way foreshadowed his prospects of future permanent residence.

Some young readers may wonder why I should be consulted on the subject at all. Well, several people who ought to have known have said that I created modern cricket. That is not a claim I ever made for myself. My concern was with making runs and taking wickets and catches to win matches. It is a fact, though, that cricket was a vastly different game when I first scored a century at any worthwhile level, in 1864, from the one I left after my last first-class match – against Surrey, in 1908. Statisticians, who count these things – and several have paid me the compliment of counting mine – calculate that I scored 54,896 runs, took 2876 wickets and made 871 catches in first-class cricket; in all cricket, all but 100,000 runs, more than 7000 wickets and 1300 catches: and in my early days the opposition in what are now called 'minor' matches was often almost as strong as in the others.†

An old-un's view may be valuable now that England of the mid-1970s are struggling, not only against Australia but against the West Indies, Pakistan and New Zealand as well. This is certainly not the first time people have viewed the state of our cricket with alarm. In my time – when the Australians beat us at The Oval in 1882 – *The Sporting Times* actually printed an obituary of English cricket and announced the body would be cremated and the Ashes taken to Australia.

In case you think I am out of date, I can say that I have watched cricket all over the world in some detail ever since I came up here. The gods' eye view is a splendid one; we can see exactly what the ball does in the air and off the pitch and also the line of the batsman's stroke; a much better vantage point, for instance, than a mortal's press box. At one time it became somewhat monotonous seeing through the eyes of the celestial umpire all the time; but now we have television, we can vary the view when we feel like it, add to our information by lip-reading the players, and study the advertisements.

We play quite a bit among ourselves, too, which keeps us in touch with the new ideas. We have had some useful bowlers of the googly, the chinaman; inswing and offspin to a leg trap; we have tried the Carmody field and even – for two minutes before we abandoned it in disgust – a purely restrictive one. I have seen no development since my day that would stop me scoring as many runs as ever, though these fielders at short leg would mean that I had to give up my leg glance, which would slow my scoring rate a little.

We can whip up some historically strong sides, though it took the Australians a long time to raise an XI owing to the somewhat idiosyncratic language they used to Rhadamanthus at the gate. Our games, mind you, are not always as serious – nor the dedication so intense – as I would want. Last season the best of our lob bowlers, Simpson-Hayward, who is a botanist, went to the Garden of the Hesperides for a new flower. While he was away, Digby Jephson, his deputy, popped off to Parnassus for a poem. Charlie Fry, of course, is in too many of his elements; he misses at least a couple of matches a year through his visits to Helicon. Felix, too, the best of the mid-nineteenth-century left-handers and a key middle order batsman in any Gentlemen's XI, is constantly being called away to paint battle scenes from the Trojan wars.

† Subsequent research undertaken by G. Neville Weston and Maurice Alexander – the results of which were published in a limited edition, *W. G. Grace, the Great Cricketer, 1st supplement* (18 July 1980) – together with a later small amendment shown in a letter from Alexander, has revealed that, in his first-class career, Grace scored 54,904 runs, took 2879 wickets, held 871 catches and stumped 3. In all cricket, he scored 100,187 runs, took 7457 wickets, held 1528 catches and stumped 55.

The matches are interesting but, in this most perfect of worlds, almost too perfect. Dionysius looks after the drink, so the champagne is all vintage and, since the umpires are immortals, they never make a mistake. This means that some of the play is dull by comparison with my time, when every county had one umpire who travelled with the team and, to say the least, always knew which side was batting. The greatest change from my young days – both here and with you folk below – is the perfection of the pitches. I have had four shooters from Fred Morley – fast left-arm – in the first over of a Gentlemen v Players match at Lord's; and, while the crowd stood and cheered when I stopped them all, I should never have made the runs I did if I had not been able to stop more shooters than I missed. I must say all this celestial comfort makes it vastly entertaining to watch the troubles your young fellers are in now.

Two things the editor wants to know are why I had such a successful career and whether I should be as successful as I was if I came back now.

The first question is the more difficult. If you have the physical equipment, start early, study the techniques and practise hard, you can play any game fairly well. I certainly had all the original advantages. Ours was a cricketing family; my mother studied the game remarkably closely for a woman in mid-Victorian times; my father and my uncle Pocock were useful club cricketers, and my elder brother Edward – E.M., whom they called the Coroner – the youngest, Fred, and I, all played for England.

The background was there – the enthusiasm and the knowledge – and from my earliest memory there was a practice wicket worthy of a first-class club in the orchard of our house at Downend. So I was born into cricket; I was strong and tall, my reflexes were quick – or they became quick through constant training – and you could say that my eyesight was sharp; certainly I never abused it by reading a lot of books like some of the young fellers used to do. I suppose, too, I had unusual stamina. In 1895, when I was almost forty-seven years old, I was on the field, batting – 330 for once out – bowling or fielding all three days of a Gloucestershire match at Gravesend, when we beat Kent. That was the year I made the last 841 of my thousand runs in May, including my hundredth hundred, during the second half of the month.

You had to be fit then if you were going to enjoy everything that went with cricket. One August at Scarborough, Lord Londesborough asked four of us to shoot one morning. There was a ball the night before and no one went to bed until four. We were up again at seven – I had only time for a brandy and soda and raw herring for breakfast – we shot over sixteen miles on foot and were on the field sharp at twelve.

Even as a boy I was desperately keen: I played every moment I could, and if there was no one to play with, I just bowled at a tree trunk; if I did not hit it I had to run after the ball. From the time I was five, the family gave a considerable amount of thought to coaching. People used to joke about my brother E.M.'s pull stroke – he would pick up a ball pitching outside the off stump and land it over midwicket – but that was because he used too big a bat at an early age. My father never let me make the same mistake. Although I was tall as a lad he made me continue long with a small bat; and kept me bowling from eighteen yards until I was easily capable of a length on a full-sized pitch. We practised not only through the season but before and after it. Even in my fifties, I began in the nets at the start of April or in March if the weather was fine enough. Cricket was not easy for me. It is a difficult game for anyone and I practised like a Boycott at every chance. We ran, rode or hunted at times, but cricket was our life.

I enjoyed practice; I enjoyed fielding more; I enjoyed taking wickets more still; and I enjoyed making runs most of all. Above all, it is important that I enjoyed cricket so much that, for me, it was always fun. I never in my life grew tired of it: and, until I decided to give it up, it never occurred to me that I could not succeed. It was a long run: I was fifteen when I first batted for the All-England XI; and that year I scored a thousand runs in club cricket: fifty-one years afterwards, the bowlers could not get me out in my last innings.

In my last Test match, when I was fifty-one, I batted safely enough, if only for eight and twenty, but it was because I could not bend in the field that I knew I had come to the end of my international cricket. Then there was that 74 for Gentlemen against Players in 1906 when I was fifty-eight; and the final innings, eight years after that, 69 not out on a devilish wicket in a club match at Eltham.

I have no doubt that I could do it all again – or more – especially on these far, far easier wickets, without so much strain of travelling, and with better umpiring; no bowlers so fast as Ernie Jones, Charles Kortright – he left me black and blue about the ribs more than once – Tom Richardson, W. N. Powys or John Jackson. My dilemma would be whether or not I could afford to play cricket as things are now. I gave almost all my attention to it, and it paid me well: but I doubt if it would today. My brother E.M. and I were, and are, the only qualified doctors who ever managed to play anything like full-time cricket.

Because I gave so much attention to it, I never had real time for any other sport. On the last day of the Surrey v England match at The Oval in 1866, after I had scored 224, the England captain let me go over to the National Olympian Association meeting at the Crystal Palace to run in the quarter-mile hurdles which I won in the then good time of one minute ten seconds. I did not take to golf until my late fifties, but if I had played it earlier, I am sure I could have done well. So, if I were a young man now, I should have to consider the best living I could make. Would it be in cricket, I wonder?

For my medical practice in a working-class district of Bristol I needed an assistant during the winter and two locums during the cricket season. There were some fairly fierce disagreements with Gloucestershire over my expenses – including this help in the practice – and more than once I had to point out that, if they could not meet them, I could not afford to play county cricket. That, in a way, was the strength of my position and a factor in my success. I did not have to succeed at cricket; I could have made my living from medicine. Cricket was, in every way, a bonus.

I always had a weakness for champagne which, as I said, is wonderfully catered for up here. My father used to prescribe a pint of 'The Widow' as a stimulant for a bowler called on for a major effort: but you cannot drink Veuve Clicquot every day on a parish doctor's stipend. Through the 1870s, until I qualified in 1879, I used to run matches for the United South of England XI. The organizers were desperately keen for me to play in the games and there was never any pretence that I did it for nothing. By present-day standards my position was more like that of Pele than of any cricketer. The arrangements were conducted in a thoroughly businesslike fashion; there was a separate legal agreement for every match and it carried a heavy penalty clause if I failed to appear to play in person. There was not anything like a full first-class programme in those days and the professionals were happy enough to turn out for me for five pounds. It was a rewarding business and five or six matches brought me in enough to cover my living expenses for a year.

Cricket stood almost alone in importance and crowd appeal in the sport of Victorian England. Football began to catch up during my time: but it was then strictly a winter game, not your present ten-months-of-the-year affair. Perhaps nothing ever impressed me more as a compliment than when, one day, after we had beaten Middlesex at Lord's and their captain, Webbie – A. J. Webbe – came up to see me off on the Bristol train from Paddington. The station master saw me to an empty first-class carriage and stood at the door. Webbie had several things to say and suddenly I looked up at the station clock and saw it was five minutes after the train was due to leave. I turned and said to the station master, 'Is the train delayed?' He replied, 'Not really, sir, but we waited her – we didn't want to hurry you.'

That was fine for the ego; but it buttered no parsnips. I could not often spare the time to go overseas, but I did make a trip to Canada and the United States in 1872; and to Australia in 1873–74 and again in 1891. The American visit was short and the cricket not too serious, but it was a chance to see the country in as much luxury as could be mustered then, and in good company.

The first Australian tour was a business enterprise which stemmed from the United South of England XI matches. I was engaged to raise the team – which did not prove as strong as I wanted – and captain it. The match guarantees were high, but the agreements stipulated that, if play finished early, we had to fill out time with single-wicket games. Like most tours at that time, though, it was a considerable financial success. Conveniently and pleasantly, too, the promoters covered the expenses of my wife on the tour for what was, in effect, our honeymoon.

The second Australian visit, in 1891, was as captain of Lord Sheffield's team, at an agreed fee of £3000 – equivalent to £28,000 in 1974 – plus all expenses, including a locum for the practice.

When I qualified in 1879 a national testimonial raised almost £1500 – which would be worth £16,000 now – a clock and a pair of bronze ornaments.

Then, after that great season of 1895 there were three separate testimonials which produced a total of precisely £9073 8s 3d that was worth more than £80,000 by present-day standards. After the Bristol parish medical services were rearranged in 1899, I felt in honour bound to resign and, at almost the same time, I was invited to manage the new London County Cricket Club at Crystal Palace. Gloucestershire decided I could not take that job and captain the county as well; and, after thirty years, we parted. The Crystal Palace venture was only a partial success; but it paid me £1000 a year and expenses and when it ended, in 1908, I was able to retire and live on my savings.

The people near cricket knew well enough that I had taken some income from the game. It would have been odd if I had not. It is true that my young brother Fred was barred from a Gentleman v Players match because he had taken match fees for his games with the United South XI. He was by no means the only 'amateur' who accepted payment for playing. I could have been banned, too, and for the same reason. On the other hand, I was in a strong position. Cricket was the most popular and best-supported game in the country; and, without false modesty, I was by far the best player in the country. In several seasons my batting average was twice as high as that of the next player. More important, people came to watch me play. It was no uncommon sight to see outside a cricket ground:

CRICKET MATCH
Admission 6d
If W. G. Grace plays
Admission 1/-

If that was my value, I was prepared to accept it. No one *had* to offer me money – least of all the testimonials. It was proffered, and I took them in return for a moneysworth of performance. I am convinced that if I had my time over again I could do the same again in performance if I – and English cricket – could afford it. I must say that I find the reports of the financial rewards of Messrs Pelé, Mohammed Ali and Arnold tantalizing reading. So . . . who knows?

*Cricket, More than a Game (ed. J. Sheppard, Angus & Robertson, 1975)*

## At the Sign of the Bat and Ball

*Then fill up your glass, he's the best who drinks most*
*Here's the Hambledon Club! – who refuses the toast?*

It is a hundred and seventy years since that couplet by the Reverend Reynell Cotton set an absolute standard of drinking in pledging the first full flowering of cricket.

It was no accident that the first great cricket club grew up on those bare Hampshire hills above the Meon Valley. It was natural cricket country. Other fields in England grew grass more lush but, on Broad-Halfpenny Down, the alliance of nature and grazing sheep produced turf lively and trim as a convict's crop. That was the pitch on which the bowled ball would bounce true, to provide the foundations of length bowling and the art of batting.

The Solent winds still sweep freshly over the Hambledon Club's first ground. Still, too, the solitary building on its bald crown is the Bat and Ball Inn, where those legendary Hampshire village cricketers met on the first Tuesday in every May for more than fifty great summers.

The landlord of the Bat and Ball was Richard Nyren, the captain – indeed, 'the head and right arm' – of the club. His son, John, who, as a boy, was the 'farmer's pony' of the team became, many years afterwards, its chronicler in *The Cricketers of My Time*, still the finest study of cricket and cricketers ever written.

The yeomen – potters, publicans, bakers, builders, farmers and cobblers – who made up the Hambledon eleven might challenge the rest of the cricketing world of their day for a thousand guineas and win. 'Little Hambledon against All England was a proud thought for the Hampshire men,' wrote Nyren.

'Half the county would be present, and all their hearts with us. How those fine brawn-faced farmers would drink to our success! And then, what stuff they had to drink! – Punch! – not your new *Ponche à la Romaine*, or *Ponche à la Groseille*, or your modern cat-lap milk punch – punch bedeviled; but good, unsophisticated John Bull stuff – stark! – that would stand on end – punch that would make a cat speak! Sixpence a bottle: we had not sixty millions of interest to pay in those days.'

'The ale, too! . . . barleycorn, such as would put the souls of three butchers into one weaver. Ale that would flare like turpentine – genuine Boniface! This immortal viand (for it was more than liquor) was vended at twopence per pint.'

Those passages were written by an old man looking back nostalgically to the days of his youth. So we might suspect Nyren of wearing rose-coloured spectacles but that, by some village miracle, the Minute and Account books of the Hambledon Club still exist. It was E. V. Lucas who emerged from perusal of them with 'A wet day: only three members present: nine bottles of wine,' to which Lucas added drily – if the word may be pardoned – 'A wet day indeed.'

(What, we may wonder, was the tally on 15 August 1781, when the entry reads, 'Present at the Boys Match Hambledon against Petersfield and Buriton, Mr Jervoise, Rev. Mr Cooley, Mr Richards and Mr Leeke a fine Haunch of Venison. NB a very wet day.')

The first recorded meeting of the Hambledon club elected three members and passed two resolutions. The first ruled that every member proposing a candidate should pay for all dinners on the day of the new member's election. The second recorded, tersely, 'Ordered a Wine Cistern'. Throughout the club books, all the wines named and even the word 'Wine' itself are accorded capital letters. (While the accounts show that the club's wine merchants delivered thirteen bottles to the dozen, the committee could still rule, on one occasion, 'Order'd the Wine to be returned to Messrs Gauntlett not being approv'd.')

It was, clearly, a comfortable club. There were few restrictive rules. The earliest Minute book that still exists, however, recorded that in 1773 it was passed 'That for the future the Wicketts shall be pitched at half an Hour after Ten o'Clock in the Morn. and the players that come after Eleven are to forfeit 3d each to be spent amongst those that come at the appointed time of Eleven.' Was the hour too early? Or is it possible – surely not – that it was not understood how the threepences were to be spent? Or was a threepenny fine insufficient deterrent? Whichever was the case, the Committee of 1787 'Ordered that every Player who does not appear on the Cricket Ground by 12 o'Clock is to forfeit 6 pence to be spent in Punch for the benefit of the other Players.'

Clearly, penalties were designed to add to the comfort of non-offending members. 'Ordered nem con that Mr Jervoise be fined a Buck, for omitting to send Venison to Nyrens this day according to Custom, he being President of the Club.' 1774 – 'Ordered: that if any dispute shall arise amongst the Members should they not be silent after being desired to waive the subject by the President or in his absence by the Steward of Stewards The Gentlemen so disputing shall forfeit one Doz: of Claret to the Club.' In fact, while the accounts show many payments made to the steward for Port, Sherry and Madeira, there are none for Claret. It seems that, in civilized fashion, red wine was automatically provided with meals as, today, beer is in some clubs and, alas, water in more. (This is borne out by the minuting of the decision to pay to Barber, Nyren's successor as licensee of the Bat and Ball – 'the expence of his Wine Licence and sixpence per bottle for drinking the Club Wine.')

(In the same month it was 'Order'd that the Stewards direct a pig to be prepared for a Barbacue next Tuesday sennight.') One minute recurs throughout the book with only unsubstantial variations – 'That Mr Snell be requested to procure a Pipe of Port Wine immediately for the use of the Club.' A pipe of port is 115 gallons – or about 670 bottles. It was useful, apparently, to have such a stock in hand, for a minute of 1784 reads 'Order'd that Capt. Everett be allowed to take 20 Dozen of the Port Wine procured by Mr Snell for the Use of the Club, and that the same quantity shall be order'd from Mr Gauntlett by Capt. Everett.' It is strange to note that, although that minute stood, the line immediately under it runs 'Capt. Everett desires to withdraw his name.'

We may relish with the secretary of 1789 'Agreed and desired that Mr Nyren will send to Mr W. T. Thorn at the Blue Lion 75 Corner of Bagnio Court Newgate Street London for six pounds of the genuine Varinas Colaster Tobacco in a leaden case.' The word 'desire' is warmly more human than official.

The final meeting of the season of 1783 decided that the subscription should be increased from two guineas to three, but, characteristically, added the rider that the 'overplus' – not 'overplush' as the account-book says at one point – 'shall be laid out in Claret to be drunk on the day of passing the Accompts.'

It was a club which, while it dominated the cricket it had virtually created, could decide upon 'An Extra Meeting to eat Venison and drink Bonhams and Fitzherberts Claret'.

It is not surprising to find that for club meetings – 'Dinner on the table at three' – there was a list of standing toasts. Five of the six healths prescribed are those we should expect. They run:

1. The Queen's Mother
2. The King
3. Hambledon Club
4. Cricket
5. To the Immortal Memory of Madge
6. The President

E. V. Lucas, the outstanding Nyren/Hambledon editor, worried away at the problem for years; tireless, posing different possible solutions. He wondered who was Madge, that her toast preceded that of the President? Although pre-1770 scores are sparse, they could hardly have omitted all reference to some earlier Hobbs or Grace, surnamed Madge, if he had been so great that Hambledon deemed him immortal. In any case, there existed a minute to the effect that 'no Gentleman's health shall at any time be drank after Dinner except the President's and the King's. So, he had to assume that Madge was feminine. Some gifted pre-emancipation woman cricketer whose sex barred her powers from the great matches? he mused. A cook perhaps, who placed great dishes before them? But not, in that case, one to precede the President. Was Madge some Hampshire beauty of the day, so lovely that all who knew her adored her, but was doomed to obscurity by the Club secretary's damnable delicacy – or jealousy – which denied her surname to the Minute book? Was she, he might wonder, connected in any way with the entry in the Club book for 17 May 1785, which consists of two words only. There is no list of members present, no ballot, no decisions, only the cryptic inscription 'Dies Benedictorum'. The mystery long remained a mystery during modern times. It was a lady of extreme respectability who solved it, during the 1950s. In something of a dilemma about communicating the information, she asked Desmond Eagar one day 'Have you ever wondered who Madge was?' 'Wondered?' he said. 'I have been intrigued.' 'Then,' said she modestly, 'I am just going home. When I have gone you may look it up in this book.' She put the book on the table and left.

It was *Grose's Classical Dictionary of the Vulgar Tongue* (1785). He opened it, looked up 'Madge' and found it defined as 'the private parts of a woman'.

This was the club which decreed that in each season 'The last meeting of the Hambledon Club be in future of a moon light night.'

Its wind-swept, downland pitch was already empty when Nyren wrote of it in 1833; but he could still say 'the smell of that ale comes upon me as freshly as the new May flowers.'

*The Compleat Imbiber (ed. C. Ray, Puttnam, 1957)*

# The Impossible Victory

*June* 1964. Let it be admitted at once – I was *not* there. Sir Jack Hobbs once drily remarked that, on the historic day when he scored the century to beat W. G. Grace's record, there were only two or three hundred spectators at Taunton: but, he added, if all the people who subsequently told him they saw it had been there, they would have filled the ground twice over. So it is with what must justly be called the greatest cricket match ever played by Hampshire – and, surely, the most remarkable recovery in the entire history of cricket. It is dangerously easy to believe one was at such an often-related occasion.

# SCORE WARWICKSHIRE CARD
## • COUNTY •
# CRICKET CLUB

Commence first day 12, other days 11.30   Lunch Interval 1.30-2 10.   Stumps drawn 6.30

| WARWICKSHIRE | 1st Innings | | 2nd Innings | |
|---|---|---|---|---|
| 1 Bates | c Shirley b Newman ...... | 3 | c Mead b Kennedy ...... | 1 |
| 2 Smith | c Mead b Newman ...... | 24 | c Shirley b Kennedy..... | 41 |
| 3 Hn. F.S.G Calthorpe Capt | c Boyes b Kennedy ...... | 70 | b Newman ................... | 30 |
| 4 Quaife, W G | b Newman | 1 | not out ....................... | 40 |
| 5 F R. Santall | c McIntyre b Boyes ...... | 84 | b Newman ................... | 0 |
| 6 Rev E F Waddy | c Mead b Boyes ............ | 0 | b Newman ................... | 0 |
| 7 B. W. Quaife | b Boyes ........................ | 0 | c & b Kennedy ............. | 7 |
| 8 Fox | b Kennedy ................. | 4 | b Kennedy ............... | 0 |
| 9 Smart J. | b Newman .................. | 20 | b Newman ................. | 3 |
| 10 Smart C | c Mead b Boyes ... ... ... | 14 | c & b Boyes .............. | 15 |
| 11 Howell, H. | not out ....... ............ | 1 | c Kennedy b Newman ... | 11 |
| | Extras ... | 2 | ... ... | 10 |
| | **Total** ...... | **223** | | **158** |

| 1 wkt. for 3 | 2 36 | 3 44 | 4 166 | 5 177 | 6 184 | 7 184 | 8 200 | 9 219 | 10 223 |
|---|---|---|---|---|---|---|---|---|---|
| 1 wkt for 2 | 2 77 | 3 85 | 4 85 | 5 85 | 6 89 | 7 113 | 8 143 | 9 147 | 10 158 |

| Bowling Analysis | O. | M. | R. | W. | Wd. | Nb. | O. | M. | R. | W. | Wd. | Nb. |
|---|---|---|---|---|---|---|---|---|---|---|---|---|
| Kennedy ... | 24 | 7 | 74 | 2 | ... | ... | ... | ... | ... | — | — | — |
| Newman ... | 12 3 | ... | 70 | 4 | ... | ... | ... | ... | ... | — | — | — |
| Boyes | 16 | 5 | 56 | 4 | ... ... | | ... | ... | ... | — | — | — |
| Shirley | 3 | ... | 21 | ... | | | ... | ... | ... | — | — | — |

---

| HAMPSHIRE. | 1st Innings | | 2nd Innings | |
|---|---|---|---|---|
| 6. Kennedy | c Smith b Calthorpe .... | 0 | b Calthorpe ...... ...... | 7 |
| 5 Bowell | b Howell ........................ | 0 | c Howell b Quaife W. G. | 45 |
| 2 H. V L Day | b Calthorpe ...... ...... | 0 | c Bates b Quaife W. G... | 15 |
| 7 Mead | not out ...................... | 6 | b Howell ................... | 24 |
| 1 Hon. L. H. Tennyson | c Calthorpe b Howell ... | 4 | c Smart C. b Calthorpe | 45 |
| 4 Brown | b Howell ..................... | 0 | b Smart C. ................172 |
| 8 Newman | c Smart C. b Howell ... | 0 | c & b Quaife .............12 |
| 10 W R Shirley | c Smart J. b Calthorpe .. | 1 | lbw b Fox .................. 30 |
| 3 A. S. McIntyre | lbw b Calthorpe ......... | 0 | lbw b Howell ............... 5 |
| 9 Livsey | b Howell ................. | 0 | not out .......................110 |
| 11 Boyes | lbw b Howell ............. | 0 | b Howell ..................... 29 |
| | Extras... | 4 | | 27 |
| | **Total** ......... | **15** | | **521** |

Scorers-G. Austin & L. Sprankling   Umpires-A. J. Atfield & B. Brown.

| 1 wkt. for 0 | 2 0 | 3 0 | 4 5 | 5 5 | 6 9 | 7 10 | 8 10 | 9 15 | 10 15 |
|---|---|---|---|---|---|---|---|---|---|
| 1 wkt for 15 | 2 65 | 3 81 | 4 127 | 5 152 | 6 177 | 7 262 | 8 274 | 9 451 | 10 521 |

| Bowling Analysis | O | M | R | W | Wd | Nb | O | M | R | W | Wd | Nb |
|---|---|---|---|---|---|---|---|---|---|---|---|---|
| Howell ..... | 4 5 | 2 | 7 | 6 | - | - | 53 | 10 | 156 | 3 | — | 1 |
| Calthorpe ... | 4 | 3 | 4 | 4 | - | - | 33 | 7 | 97 | 2 | 1 | — |
| Quaife ...... | | | | | | | 49 | 8 | 154 | 3 | — | — |
| Fox .......... | | | | | | | 7 | ... | 30 | 1 | — | — |
| Smart J ... | ... | ... | ... | ... | | | 13 | 2 | 37 | — | — | — |
| Santall ... | ... | ... | ... | ... | | | 5 | ... | 15 | — | — | — |
| Smart C | | | | | | | 5 | 1 | 11 | — | — | — |

Half the twenty-two men are dead who took part in the fixture between Hampshire and Warwickshire at Birmingham on 14, 15 and 16 June 1922. But, though some of them left few other deep impresses on the game, they staked a claim to cricketing immortality merely by taking part, however obscurely, in that fantastic match.

There had been rain, the Edgbaston wicket was slightly soft and Lionel Tennyson, when he won the toss, decided to put Warwickshire in to bat. Tennyson was never a captain to hesitate about taking any worthwhile attacking chance; and, in any case, none of his elder pros demurred at the time – and they were never men slow to point out what they considered an error of judgement on the part of 'Lordship'. The ball turned, if only slowly: Newman and Boyes spun off a length and, significantly, while Santall and Calthorpe, whose main strength lay in driving, made 84 and 70, the other nine Warwickshire batsmen scored only 55 between them in the total of 223.

By the start of the Hampshire innings at four o'clock on the first afternoon, the pitch had largely dried out. 'A true, fair-paced batting wicket,' Alec Kennedy called it.

Yet in forty minutes – not quite nine overs – Hampshire were all out for 15. Only two lower totals have ever been recorded in County Championship cricket. To the end of his days, Philip Mead was baffled by it all. He went in at the fall of the second wicket and was six not out at the end. 'Nobody bowled me anything that I couldn't play in the middle,' he said.

'Tiger' Smith still believes that Harry Howell bowled faster that afternoon than at any other time in his career; and Calthorpe, in a sympathetic atmosphere, could make the ball swing sharply and late. In the first over Howell smashed Alec Bowell's middle stump and sent the fragments flying back to the wicket-keeper. With Bowell, Kennedy and Day gone, Hampshire were 0 for three wickets. It was Warwick's great hour: every ball the batsmen missed hit the stumps: every catch stuck. Howell took six for 7; Calthorpe four for 4, and Hampshire were 'invited' – gloriously ironic expression – to follow on, 208 behind: they lost the second-innings wickets of Bowell and Day that night.

In the pavilion after play, Freddie Gough-Calthorpe suggested that, as soon as the match was over next morning (!), the amateurs might play golf. This was enough to rouse Lionel Tennyson – that Regency buck misplaced in time – to peaks of defiant profanity and a willingness to bet – especially at long odds – on Hampshire winning.

On the second morning the Hampshire side received a considerable amount of mail – some humorous, some derogatory. But the item which stuck in the memory of all of them was the postcard addressed to Lionel Tennyson, and which he showed to the team, advising Hampshire to give up county cricket and take to painting spots on rocking horses.

Warwickshire went steadily about their work and, when Harry Howell bowled Philip Mead with a slow, swinging yorker for 24, the result seemed a foregone conclusion. Lionel Tennyson, in a flourish of heavy swings, made 45; but, when the sixth wicket – Jack Newman's – fell, Hampshire still needed another 31 to avoid an innings defeat. Now, however, that unpredictable giant of a cricketer, George Brown, was batting with that infinitely resistant, aggressive air which the bowlers of his day recognized with considerable respect.

W. R. Shirley – something of a copy-book batsman – stayed with him while they put on 85 for the seventh wicket, but Howell was altogether too fast for McIntyre and, at 274 for eight wickets, Hampshire were only 69 runs ahead with two wickets left and more than a day to play.

To hope to save the game was simply not reasonable: the history of cricket could show no example of a game being won from such a position.

Harry Howell was bowling at lively pace: two typical tailender's flicks and the game would be settled. At this point Walter Livsey came in to George Brown. Livsey was a capable wicket-keeper but, in those days, a nervous batsman who, apart from this occasion, scored only 181 runs in thirty-six Championship innings of the season. Only a man of George Brown's immensely passionate belief in his own powers could have thought the game might be saved. But he nursed Walter Livsey as if they were launching a match rather than facing its end. 'Tiger' Smith argues that it was at this point – when Warwickshire might have taken the new ball but did not – that the game was lost. George set out to 'farm' Harry Howell, to prevent him getting at Livsey. But he was looking for runs all the time and was particularly severe on Willie Quaife. On the third morning, Brown and Livsey were still together. When, at length, Charlie Smart – the seventh Warwick bowler – bowled Brown, who was trying to drive him through mid-on, the pair had put on 177 for the ninth wicket, and Hampshire were 243 ahead. Still, in terms of cricket logic, Warwickshire should have won. But now the game took its final and most fantastic twist. Walter Livsey assumed command of the situation. While the uncapped number eleven, Stuart Boyes, propped up the other end, Livsey – who had only reached double figures three times that season – went on to make the first century of his career. Once that was achieved Boyes, too, started to play strokes. The last wicket put on another 70 runs and, when at length Harry Howell bowled Boyes, Hampshire had scored 521, setting Warwickshire 314 to win. When Hampshire's second innings started eight of their batsmen had been 'bustling on a pair': every one of them avoided the indignity.

By now the initiative had passed to Hampshire. Warwick, both irritated and amazed, contemplated defeat. The combination of Kennedy and Newman was ideally relentless to rout an already unsettled side. To be sure, Boyes and Brown were given short, token spells, but the cold business of execution was entrusted to the old hands. Smith and Quaife (who went in at number three to act as sheet-anchor) made 75 for the second wicket. Then, in mid-afternoon, came the breakthrough – five wickets in an hour for 12 runs to Newman and Kennedy, bowling remorselessly on a length. The decisive blow had been struck. Hampshire won by 155 runs. The impossible had been achieved.

This was such a triumph as Lionel Tennyson loved. It was not merely that the odds were long, but that the manner of the victory had been so spectacular. His hospitality was always expansive: now, backed by his winnings and encouraged by the occasion, it overflowed. Memories of that night are, apparently, dim. At least one member of the Hampshire side stated categorically that the celebration party was given *en route* for Northampton, where the county was to play the next morning. But, according to *Wisden*, it was Warwickshire who played at Northampton the following day – did someone join the wrong party after the match? No matter: to have been there was enough: the manner of any man's departure from such a triumph is unimportant – especially since Hampshire's next match was four days later.

Sometimes I wish – sometimes I think . . . after all, no one can *prove* I was not there. *Hampshire*

# 2

# Legendary Figures

## Sydney Barnes

### *Cricket's Living Legend*

*May* 1963. The living legend of cricket that is Sydney Francis Barnes became ninety years old on 19 April 1963. Those who played with or against him, over a period of almost three normal cricketing lifetimes, had no doubt that he stood alone – the greatest bowler that ever lived. He played county cricket before the Boer War; he was still returning amazing analyses in club games during the Second World War. Yet he was perhaps the least seen of all great players.

He played in his first first-class match – for Warwickshire – in 1895; his last, for Wales, in 1930, when he was fifty-seven. Yet in that entire period of thirty-five years, he played only two full seasons and six odd games in the County Championship – forty-four matches altogether: he made more appearances than that for English touring teams in Australia and South Africa. But perhaps the most surprising comparison is that a man who played only forty-four Championship games, played in twenty-seven Tests.

Even if he had been an indifferent performer, the length of his cricketing life alone would make him remarkable. He played his first cricket match with adults for the third team of the local club in his native Smethwick in 1888: his last match was for Stone, in wartime Staffordshire league cricket, in 1940. That season, at the age of sixty-seven, he had such figures as six for 32 and four for 12 against Great Chell, five for 43 against Leek, and five for 22 against Caverswall.

More than six feet tall – he is still dominatingly erect at ninety – with high, wide, rugged shoulders, deep chest, long arms and strong legs, he was perfectly built to be a bowler. There was virtually no cricket in his family, and he was never coached. But he had a natural aptitude – and avidity – for the game, and, by application and determination, he made himself into a right-arm fast-medium bowler with the accuracy, spin and resource of a slow bowler, whose high delivery gave him a lift off the pitch that rapped the knuckles of the unwary and forced even the best batsmen to play him at an awkward height.

His usual pace was about that of Alec Bedser, with a faster ball and a slower one, in well-concealed reserve, and the ability to bowl a yorker. He himself is content that he was essentially a spin bowler, that his movement through the air was, in modern technical language, *swerve* – obtained by spin – rather than 'swing', which derives from the 'seam-up' method. Certainly he made the ball move both ways through the air, and – with a first- and second-finger application rather similar to that of Ramadhin – he bowled both the off-break and the leg-break. Indeed, he could bowl the googly at about slow-medium pace and where, in exceptional conditions, the pitch dictated it, he could be a fine slow bowler.

This is such technical equipment as no one in the history of the game has excelled. Barnes added to it a sustained hostility and remarkable stamina, which were reflected in constant, unrelenting probing for a batsman's weakness and then attacking it by surprise, each ball fitting into a tactical pattern.

A striking example of this aspect of his cricketing character comes from the 1913–14 tour of South Africa, where his combination of lift and spin was virtually unplayable on the matting wickets and he set up a record for any series by taking 49 wickets although, because of a financial disagreement, he did not play in the Fifth Test. H. W. Taylor was the only South African batsman who really resisted him, though Barnes took his wicket in five of the eight Test innings Taylor played against him. In the Fourth Test, Barnes, convinced that he knew how he might beat Taylor, bowled on and on at him: Taylor, content merely to defend against Barnes (thirty-two overs for 88 runs and seven wickets) scored 93 before Barnes had him lbw – as he had said he would do.

Both Sir Jack Hobbs and Wilfred Rhodes thought this one of Barnes's finest bowling spells, though they were both playing two years earlier when, on a perfect, hard Melbourne wicket, he produced his epic opening spell against a strong Australian batting side. Starting the bowling with F. R. Foster, he put out the first four Australian batsmen – Bardsley, Kelleway, Hill and Armstrong – for one run. He had Minnett's wicket, too, and after eighty minutes, his figures were 11 overs, 7 maidens, 6 runs, 5 wickets.

It is hard to believe that a player of such quality could be allowed to stay out of county cricket in modern times. As a straightforward fast bowler of nineteen, he was promising enough to play for Warwickshire in a two-day match against Cheshire, then an immensely strong Minor Counties side: he did not bowl in the first innings: in the second he was one of ten bowlers used by Warwickshire while Cheshire built up a big score: his eight overs cost 27 runs and he did not take a wicket. Still raw, he played in one match for Warwickshire in 1895 and two in 1896.

Three wickets at an average of 75 runs apiece, was the extent of his cricket with Warwickshire before he went to League cricket with Rishton from 1895 to 1899 and then for two seasons with Burnley. He played twice in the Championship for Lancashire in 1899 (four for 161), and then, in 1901, A. C. MacLaren put him in the Lancashire team for the last match of the season – against Leicestershire at Old Trafford.

Rain spoilt the last day but, in the first Leicestershire innings, Barnes took six for 70. Immediately afterwards MacLaren announced that the unknown bowler – with a first-class record of thirteen wickets, spread over seven seasons – would be in his team to go to Australia. Barnes began the tour with five wickets in the match against South Australia, twelve against Victoria and five against New South Wales. He was picked for the First Test (five for 65, and one for 74); in the Second he had six for 42 and seven for 121. Then he broke down with a knee injury but, although he himself believes he was still far short of his best, he had established himself as a world-class bowler.

He spent 1902 and – much over-bowled – 1903 with Lancashire: but then he left them because of a dispute about winter employment and became, for the rest of his career, a professional in League cricket and for Staffordshire in the Minor Counties competition. He was proud of the profession of cricketer and while he believed, uncompromisingly, that the labourer was worthy of his hire, it would have been foreign to his nature to shame it by giving less than his best.

But that best, outstanding on international level, was killing when directed at league players. Small wonder that many of them found themselves shaking at the approach of this glowering near-giant in physique, utter giant in ability. His professional honour, however, was satisfied by the fact that every league club that ever engaged him won its competition.

His first league engagement was in 1895, his last in 1938: in those forty-three years he earned his wages with over four thousand wickets for an average of about seven: seventeen thousand runs at roughly 25 an innings. For Staffordshire, in twenty-three seasons between 1904 and 1935, his record is 1437 wickets at 8.04, and 5254 runs at 22.45.

He continued to play for England, on and off, until 1914: in eight series (seven, if the Triangular of 1912 is counted as one) he played in twenty-seven Tests, all against Australia or South Africa, and took 189 wickets, at the rate of one every seven overs for an average of 16.43. In eight matches for the Players against the Gentlemen he took 45 wickets at 15.26: no other bowler in this century has taken so many in that fixture at so low cost. Otherwise his first-class cricket was confined to appearances for Staffordshire, the Minor Counties or Wales, usually against the touring side. In 1929, his figures in two matches against the South Africans were eight for 41 and one for 19 (for Minor Counties) and six for 28 and four for 62 (for Wales). That year, at the age of fifty-six, he was fifth in the first-class bowling averages.

His last season as a professional was for Bridgnorth in 1938. He was sixty-five years old; he played on every day except Friday of August week and finished top, not only of the club's bowling (126 wickets at 6.94), but of the batting as well (314 runs at 28.55).

Five wickets in five balls in a league match: four in four four times (including the first four of Durham in 1907): an uncounted number of hat-tricks but including two against major batsmen, one in a Test Trial, another in Gentlemen v Players: and, once, two in an innings: 'all ten' at least a dozen times.

Durham seem to have been his favourite victims: in 1909 he took fourteen of their wickets for 13 runs in a single day: the next year, eight for 16 and eight for 30: in 1911, nine for 37 in the first innings, eight for 46 in the second – and he himself scored 136 in his only innings of the match. In 1908, when the Minor Counties competition was arranged in four groups and played off between the four leaders in knockout form, Barnes won it for Staffordshire with 24 wickets at 3.25 each in their semi-final and final matches.

In all cricket he took over 6300 wickets at an average of nine. But one could go on and on quoting bewildering figures for him: and no one can hazard a guess at the number of times, even against the greatest batsmen and on good wickets, that he beat the bat and missed the stumps.

But certainly, with his peerless, flashing leg-break alone, he must have done so more often than anyone else in all cricket. So often the batsman could not even edge a catch. Hence the classic Sydney Barnes story of the day when two tailenders were playing at him and missing or, occasionally, snicking, and he stalked away at the end of the over with the comment, 'They aren't batting well enough to get out.'

It is an essential aspect of his cricket, however, that in the Second Test of 1907–08 against Australia, when he put on 34 for the ninth wicket with Humphries and 39 for the last with Fielder, his batting won the match for England by one wicket.

Indeed, there is good evidence that he could have made an extremely capable batsmen if his captains, MacLaren in particular, had not been so anxious to save him for his bowling that they even told him not to take batting practice! On the 1907–08 tour of Australia, when the MCC side was troubled with injuries and Barnes himself was only partly fit, A. O. Jones asked him, half-jokingly, to 'play for his batting' against Western Australia. After Hobbs, Fane, Hardstaff and Rhodes had all gone for less than 120, Barnes made 93, second-highest score of the innings and his own biggest score in first-class cricket, and with George Gunn put on over 200 for the fifth wicket. In League cricket, too, he often made runs at crucial stages of matches, batting very correctly and, from his appreciable height, getting well over pace bowling.

He was one of those fortunate athletes who, although very strongly built, never tended to run to fat. He kept himself sternly fit because he was deeply concerned *always* to bowl well: that guiding light to his life is important, for it explains the fact that no one records him bowling untidily, nor – amazingly – ever having an 'off day'. Even now, at ninety, his essential strength and co-ordination are reflected in an impeccable, copperplate handwriting and in his unhurried, but unwavering, movements at an age when most men are at least somewhat shaky.

Nowadays, among cricketers, it is a memory to cherish – like having bowled to W. G. Grace – that one batted against Barnes. It is sad, though, that he was so little seen. He did not play twenty first-class matches in the south of England and barely a hundred in all England. Yet the evidence is overwhelming, in South Africa, Australia and England, that he was the greatest of all bowlers.

His bowling in 1913–14 made the South African batting look abject: but it should not be forgotten that they had beaten England in the preceding series over there. In fact, too, more than half Barnes's seven-hundred-odd wickets were taken in representative games.

Simply to see him bowl – and he was over sixty on the only occasion I ever watched him in action – was to make the instant impression of majesty, hostility and control. This was, without doubt, a born bowler, who lived to bowl.

No batsman even dared to claim that he was Barnes's master. Asked which of them he found most difficult he answers 'Victor Trumper'. Who next? 'No one else ever troubled me.'

No cricketer who played with or against him has any doubt that Sydney Barnes was the greatest bowler the world has ever seen. Had Warwickshire, in 1896, or Lancashire, in 1903, thought differently and kept him in county cricket, the history of the game would be markedly different – and richer. *The Cricketer*

# C. B. Fry

## *That Most Variously Gifted Englishman*

*August* 1971. Every age has its totem figure and in the England of the 1890s it was C. B. Fry. Oscar Wilde may be the type character of the period but, in an age of initials, C. B. Fry was the hero. As *Vanity Fair* commented in presenting a caricature of him in 1894 – a rare and early degree of immortality for a young man of twenty-one – 'He is sometimes known as "C.B."; but it has lately been suggested that he should be called "Charles III".'

If he made an immense impact in the late-Victorian era, he became an eminent Edwardian, a distinguished figure between the wars and a respected one after the Second World War. He was the pre-eminent all-rounder, not merely of his own age but, so far as is measurable, of all English history.

At school, at Repton, he was captain of cricket and football, twice won the athletic prize, and was picked for the Casuals in the FA Cup: in the summer holidays after he left school he played cricket for Surrey. Meanwhile he had won an exhibition to Wadham College, Oxford, ahead of F. E. Smith (later Lord Birkenhead) and Sir John (later Lord) Simon.

As an undergraduate at Oxford he was best known to the general public as an outstanding athlete – with blues for athletics (100 yards, high jump, long jump), Association football and cricket (with a century against Cambridge in 1894 and eight wickets in 1895) in each of his four years: and missing a Blue for Rugby football because of an injury immediately before the University match: captain of cricket and football, and president of athletics.

As an undergraduate he played football for England and, putting down his after-lunch cigar in the groundsman's hut at Iffley Road, he went out and set a world record for the long jump – 23ft 6½in – although a damaged take-off board compelled him to take off nine inches short of it – and returned to his cigar. Moreover he took a first in Mods and an even more brilliant fourth in Greats.

It would be impossible for most men to live up to such a beginning. Charles Fry did so because he was – in the complete conviction of everyone who ever met him – a great man.

He continued an outstanding athlete after he left Oxford. He scored centuries for Gentlemen v Players and for England against Australia.

His great days as a cricketer were for Sussex – for whom he left his native Surrey – and in 1901 he scored 3147 runs at 78, with thirteen centuries, including a record which he shares only with Sir Donald Bradman – six hundreds were made in successive innings. Still, after he joined Hampshire he was top of the national batting averages and captained England – unbeaten – in the Triangular Tournament of 1912. Even as late as 1921, when he was forty-nine, he was playing so well in occasional matches for Hampshire that he was offered the captaincy against Australia but had to refuse because of a broken finger.

For many years in the pre-1914 era he was a first choice in the great Corinthian football teams; and in 1902 he played for Southampton in the FA Cup Final – the only amateur among the 22 – on Saturday and, on the following Monday, scored 82 for London County against Surrey at The Oval.

He was, too, a fine golfer, billiards and tennis player, fisherman and rifle shot. In many ways he was almost too good to be true – certainly larger than life size – over six feet tall, wide shouldered, superbly proportioned, fair-haired, blue-eyed, with a striking patrician nose, a sensitive voice and affecting a monocle he was said to be the most handsome and best dressed man at Oxford. He was not a prig because he was essentially one who did things on the large scale.

Until well into his seventies he was an original, perceptive and lively sporting journalist and an accomplished writer of Latin, Greek and occasional verse and splendid letters. He wrote some of the best books on cricket – *Batsmanship* – probably the finest examination of that department of the game – the two brilliant books of analysis of Beldam's action photos – *Great Batsmen* and *Great Bowlers and Fielders* – and he was substantially responsible for Ranjitsinhji's *Jubilee Book of Cricket*, the best seller of its day and still eminently readable. He collaborated with his wife – in name at least – in a novel called *A Mother's Son* which has two fine sporting descriptions which are undoubtedly his work: his autobiography, *Life Worth Living*, is a book of zest, character and originality; while he devised, founded and edited *C. B. Fry's Magazine* which was for some years in the early part of the century an outstanding periodical for boys.

He accompanied Ranjitsinhji – his partner for Sussex in many of the great batting stands of county cricket in their time – to Geneva where Ranji represented India in the councils of the League of Nations, and Fry prepared information, speeches and notes for him. He three times stood as a Liberal candidate for Parliament but, though he increased the Liberal poll substantially, he was never elected. In 1921 he was offered the throne of Albania. Ranji crucially prevented him accepting it, but it is absorbing to ponder how different the shape of European history might have been if 'CB' had been king of that unlucky country when Mussolini turned his covetous eye upon it.

In the event, Charles Fry's greatest achievement probably was as director, from 1908 to 1950, of the training ship *Mercury* on the Hamble River where he produced many highly esteemed generations of boys for the Royal Navy and the Merchant Navy. For his services there he was appointed Captain RNR but his best memorial is the affection and respect so many of his former pupils retain for him.

'CB' lived life more hugely than most men. He liked to eat well and drink well but he retained a shapely figure until his death in his eighties, and he carried his liquor superbly. He once told his biographer, Denzil Batchelor, that he was tired of cricket and proposed to take up horse racing. 'Oh, yes, Charles,' said Denzil, 'and what as, trainer, jockey or horse?' He was happy that his son – Stephen – also played cricket for Hampshire and he was sure that his grandson – also Charles – would do so, and he did.

My first recollections of him go back to the 1930s when, on his occasional visits to the County Ground at Southampton, I regarded him with considerable awe and listened to his pronouncements with due respect. In the 1940s when I was struggling to write and no one had ever heard of me, someone told 'CB' that I was trying to write poetry. He duly sent for me, commanded me to send my poetry to him at *Mercury* and to report to him there one evening a week afterwards. When I arrived I was given a hearty dinner during which he began with a treatise on poetry with special reference to the Greek and Latin poets but then quoted and analysed my verse pieces – which he had obviously read with more care than they were worth – and said, as no one had ever done before, that I had the germ of the matter in me. Did he, I asked, think I might become a poet? He thought for a moment and then said 'I think you are already – but you will be a better one.' A few years later we were broadcasting on cricket matches together. At the age of seventy-six he swung himself athletically over a tottering ladder on to a wrecked landing of the commentary box at Old Trafford which might well have frightened a man of half his years – and proceeded to make amusing, relevant and penetrating remarks about the game.

One evening during a Test match he again bade me to dine, ordered a splendid dinner and proceeded to expatiate on all subjects under the sun. He returned to his theme of the classic poets of Greece and Rome. 'They spoke their poetry, you know,' he said, 'and I suppose if they were alive now, they would broadcast; that is the poetry of the people now; and it is going to develop its own disciplines – I wish it had existed when I was a young man.'

He broadcast, as he did everything else, with character, originality and highly thoughtful skill. Most of his ability in all matters stemmed from the fact that he subjected anything he wanted to do to keen, analytical study in order to understand it fully and relate his actions logic-ally and scientifically to its problems.

Charles Fry could be autocratic, angry and self-willed: he was also magnanimous, extravagant, generous, elegant, brilliant – and fun: he was not simply the 'Admirable Crichton' of his time: he was probably the most variously gifted Englishman of any age.          *Hampshire*

# George Brown
## *The Amazing All-rounder*

*December* 1962. He is a Hampshire man beyond all but the quibble of birth qualification. He wore the county's rose-and-crown splendidly for a quarter of a century: indeed Hampshire never had a more zestful, brave, exciting, or variously gifted cricketer than George Brown. He made Hampshire his home, its accent has grown on him, and he still lives in Winchester, quietly busy, recalling the great men and burning days of his cricket. It was in the spring of 1906 that the eighteen-year-old country lad set out from his native Cowley on the now established track for the cricketers of that village, to the County Ground at Southampton. Hampshire has exerted a strange attraction for Oxfordshire cricketers: Neville Rogers's uncle, Harry, and Alec Bowell had known it before him: 'Lofty' Herman, Johnny Arnold, Neville Rogers, Jack Godfrey and Alan Castell were to follow.

George Brown was unique among them: unique, in fact, among all cricketers. There is no end to the talk about all-round players: this great batsman-and-fieldsman, people will say, would have been a truly fine bowler if he had cared to bowl: that batsman-bowler could keep wicket well at a pinch. But George Brown did everything, enough – and well enough – to be called the most complete all-round cricketer the game has ever known. He opened the innings for England, not as a stopgap but as a studied choice in 1921, when the best of England's batsmen were being swept aside by the torrent of the Australian fast bowlers, Gregory and McDonald. He held his nerve and his place, never failed, only once did either of the fast bowlers get him out; and he finished second in England's Test batting averages. Although he was not Hampshire's regular wicket-keeper, he kept for England against both Australia and South Africa: and he was chosen in the team which won back the Ashes at The Oval in 1926, but injured his thumb in practice and had to withdraw. That stern judge, Alec Kennedy, described George Brown as 'unquestionably the best wicket-keeper who ever took my bowling'. For Hampshire, however, he was more often a bowler: he took over six hundred wickets for the county at a pace which, in his early days, bordered on genuine fast, and he commanded sharp late outswing. Add to his batting, wicket-keeping and bowling the fact that the reference books before the First World War described him as 'the furthest thrower in first-class cricket', that he was fast and safe at mid-off or at mid-on, and the most fearless and spectacular silly mid-off or silly-point of his time, and you have the greatest width of performance ever achieved by one cricketer at the top level of play.

The records show that he scored over twenty-five thousand runs; made a thousand runs in each of eleven seasons and once over two thousand. But there was never, in all cricket, a player whose reputation was less beholden to statistics than George Brown. If every figure he ever set were surpassed a thousand times, that could not dim the picture he made.

First man in was right for him. Tall, with high, craggy shoulders, the essence of raw-boned strength, he personified aggression even in the act of taking guard. His face, heavily weathered and with high cheek bones, could have been that of a Red Indian chief: or some Roman sculptor might have carved it out of rock as the image of a gladiator. His stance was upright, militant; his backlift threateningly high. The opening bowler did not attack George Brown: he bowled, and George attacked him. Few batsmen play really fast bowling well: fewer still enjoy it. But George seemed positively to revel in it. In 1913, Kent came to play at Portsmouth with memories of an occasion when George Brown had rattled their batsmen's ribs with his bowling. 'Just you wait' one of them said, 'until Arthur Fielder gets at you.' Hampshire batted first: Jimmy Stone retired hurt; and George Brown came in at number three. Almost at once Fielder, one of the fastest bowlers of his day, let loose a bouncer. George dropped his bat, squared up and deliberately took it full on the chest. 'He's not fast' he said: and went on to make seventy.

This was his great gift, of standing up and attacking pace-bowling. He hooked and drove with furious strength, but his favourite stroke – discussed with awe by his juniors on the county staff – was one he called 'the whip'. A forward stroke played to anything fast and short, it was a strange and daring amalgam of glance, flick and hook, hitting the fast 'lifter' through a long curve, through square, round to fine, on the leg side: to execute it, he leant so straight into the line that to miss meant taking the ball straight between the eyes.

Some said he was less effective against slow bowling: certainly few could have been more dominating against any type than George against the fast bowlers. But at Southampton, in 1930, when Grimmett twice ran through Hampshire, George Brown made top score in both innings

– three times as many as any other batsman in the side – hitting that precise leg-spin with shrewdly controlled power.

He was at his best when the battle was at its hottest. In Hampshire's historic recovery against Warwickshire of 1922, when, bowled out for 15, they followed on 208 behind and, with six second-innings wickets down, still wanted 31 to escape defeat by an innings, it was characteristic that George should score the 172 that won the match. Characteristically again, he played the highest innings of his career (232 not out) against the traditionally toughest county opposition, Yorkshire; and easily his best record in touring side matches is against Australia. He thrived on challenge. That might have stemmed, in part, from the fact that, on his first experience of Championship cricket in May 1909, Surrey scored 742 (Brown two for 116). Once, after a run of poor innings, he opened the innings against Essex by striking the first ball, from as awkward a pace-bowler as Johnny Douglas, clean out of the Bournemouth ground. When a Gloucester fast bowler began with a short ball, he reached forward and deliberately spooned it straight upwards, over his own head, and the wicket-keeper's too, for six to the sightscreen behind him.

Cricket was and still is, for George Brown, a deeply personal matter, to be filled with all his native belligerence and gusty humour. On the South Africa tour of 1922–23, he and another pro bowled in the nets to a certain famous amateur for a whole hour of torrid heat. At the end of it, when George put on his pads for a knock, the gentleman remarked 'You don't think I'm going to bowl to you, do you? It's far too hot.' In the following summer, that same amateur, bowling at George Brown in a county match, found him in his most obdurate mood. Whatever temptation he framed elicited the same response – a calm, careful, defensive stroke, rolling the ball quietly back down the wicket. In the end he could stand it no more – 'What the hell is the matter with you, Brown?' 'There's nothing the matter with me: I'm just having that hour's net practice you owe me Mr. . . .'

One day at Taunton, a particularly trying stonewaller irked him beyond measure: so he measured out a forty-yard run, galloped up and trolled a slow, underarm all along the ground: the surprised batsman missed, and it hit the stumps ('Not out – failed to announce intention to bowl a lob').

George Brown was such a man as cause those who watched him to complain nowadays of the lack of 'characters' in cricket. Uninhibited, combative, physically superb, he *willed* life into a match. Nothing delighted him more than to field impossibly close to the bats of the great. In June 1919, he is credited by *Wisden* with causing the unexpected defeat of Surrey by catching Jack Hobbs (off one of Alec Kennedy's rare half-volleys) at silly-point. It was a catch so amazing that no one on the ground – not even, as he told me, the batsman himself – even saw it: they were looking to the boundary when George threw the ball up.

This was the titanic cricketer. George Brown could tear a pack of cards across in his huge bare hands; and, taking a fully-grown man by the coat front, lift him off the ground with one hand and hold him out at arm's length. His bowling, batting, catching and throwing could be equally violent: and quite unpredictable. One day, out of some twist of humour, he would refuse to play an attacking stroke at all, but make defensive cricket look childlike: the next, he would take an attack by the throat and shake it to pieces with vivid hooking, murderous driving and his own, unique 'whip'. Today, in Winchester, after recovering from illnesses only his mighty constitution could have survived, he is gently nostalgic, except when memory takes him back to those great moments of forty or more years ago. Then that squarely chiselled jaw stiffens again, the nostrils flare, the eyes light with the old unquenchable spirit and his listener shares with him the surging gusto of combat.

*Hampshire*

# The Late George Brown

The man to whom we, here, say farewell, George Brown, lives in the memories of many who watched him but did not know him, as a great cricketer – indeed a unique player of that game.

But we should do him less than justice if we did not think of him first of all as a man – a man, in ordinary life as on the cricket field, of infinite courage. Three times, in recent years, his great strength refuted the doctors' fears: three times he got up from a hospital bed and made his way home – back to the wife he called 'that good girl'; for his home and his family came first in his life, and I am sad to recall that, twenty-odd years ago, I shared in the greatest tragedy of his life when I was the last person to speak to his son, young George, before he was killed in an air raid. I am sure it would be George's wish that we should now remember his boy also.

Perhaps the most impressive aspect of George Brown's character was that he, who could make such violent impact on a game, had within him such depths of tenderness as he felt for his family.

When, at the last, even his mighty body was brought down, he faced death with an impressive mixture of courage and resignation. 'You knew me as I was,' he said. 'It hurts me for you to see me like this'. Characteristically he made up his mind: he looked ahead certain and unafraid. As the poet says, 'Why should we be so aghast you put off the whole flesh at last?' Life in later years had not been over-generous to him, but he lived it companionably, loyally and with immense dignity: and that dignity never left him to the end.

But, as he would expect us to remember him as a man, so, I am sure, he would want to be remembered for the legendary figure he was in the other half of his life – on the cricket field. The language of obituary, out of kindness, can be extravagant: but to over-praise George Brown would be to do him an injustice – the simple truth gives him an eminence that few games players have known. Greatness in cricket does not reside solely in figures but in manner, in character, in impact. This man was the only one to keep wicket for England and go in first for England against Australia: he was a considerable bowler, in his younger days genuinely and hostilely fast: his leaping pick-up and terrific, arrow-straight throw from mid-off made any run to him a risk; he fielded with extreme daring and speed at silly-point and, latterly at short leg: and was accounted in the reference books before the First World War, 'the furthest thrower in the game'.

Technically there was nothing in the game he could not do and do brilliantly. Yet even this does not do him full justice, for this was above all else a big man – physically superb, but big, too, in impact: just as he could pick up a split bat and tear it in two – as he once did, batting on aggressively with the spike – so he could take up a match and change its shape. He was one of the rare cricketers whose play was not dictated by the course of a game – he dictated the course of it. When a match was hopelessly dull and pointless, his humour or his practical jokes would rekindle it: but it was his glory that, when the game was hardest, when the challenge was highest, he rose to the moment. He looked a fighter – tall, gloriously strong and with the air of a warrior, and it was character-istic that in 1921, when the Australian fast bowlers Gregory and Mc-Donald tore open the England batting, the selectors should turn to George Brown; that he should be the one regular England batsman who never failed, and who was dismissed only once in the series by a fast bowler. It was characteristic, too, that the highest score of his life should have won a match against Yorkshire: that, when Hampshire beat the Australians in 1912, his bowling should create the breakthrough in both Australian innings: that when, in 1922, Hampshire were put out by Warwickshire for 15, compelled to follow on and stood on the brink of an innings defeat, he should play the cool, faultless innings which made possible Hampshire's win in the most amazing recovery in the history of cricket. He relished mightily the impossible situation, and he cherished his old enemies: it was ill luck for him that injury – injury to George, of all people – should have cost him his place in the team that regained the Ashes in 1926. But he was no man to repine or to rail at fate.

One of his colleagues once said to me, 'Most of us can work our way through against fast bowling, but we don't like it – only George Brown likes it; in fact, the faster they bowl, the better he seems to like it.' This was the man who, when a Test match fast bowler bowled a bouncer at him, stood up, deliberately took it on the chest, laughed and went on and made seventy; the man who drove the first ball of a match against the Australians out of the ground; who could lash a cricket ball so hard that it seemed a toy, without menace; or defend like one of the classic stone-wallers: a combative man – yet one with full capacity for the relish of life and humour.

He cared deeply for the game of cricket and, unlike some, he was generous and helpful to young players. Cricket itself, as distinct from his own play, mattered to him: to him – this Oxfordshire man who so happily made Hampshire his home – to him it was duty, enthusiasm, craft and challenge.

Now he has met the last challenge: he met it without flinching. We who remain, and who will never forget him, may know in our hearts that there can never be another cricketer like George Brown. And we might echo the poet's hope – 'Lightly lie the turf upon thee' – for this cricketer, too, was both kind and manly.

*Spoken at the funeral and reproduced*
*in the Hampshire CCC Handbook,* 1965

# The Master

The only *real* way into The Oval is through the Hobbs Gates. There is also the pleasant possibility that you may brush shoulders with Sir John himself, walking in characteristically unobtrusive fashion, into the manor of which he has been for so long the modest squire. But, for any cricketer, to pass through those gates is an evocative gesture of respect for one of the best-loved of all their kind.

If the world, and that microcosm of it which is called cricket, are spared nuclear destruction, future generations will ask why such a tribute still stands to the memory of this man, rather than on some hero of their own day. But the masonry and metal of those gates will outlast all of those who could answer that question from their own knowledge.

So it is a reasonable duty to Sir John Hobbs, and to the cricket of his time, to set down that evidence while we may. It has been done before; it will be done again. But weight of evidence never harmed any case; and even to marshal the ingredients stirs warm memories in a writer.

First we may say that, unlike some sports which are solely of their single moment, cricket never stands in isolation. Much of the game's richness lies in the depth of its tradition which, though it is such a small corner of the whole greater world, entitles it to its own immortals. Sir John Berry Hobbs is one of them.

There have been outstanding players of games whose public images were solely those of performers – two-dimensional figures whose impact was upon the record books, not on the imagination or the affection.

The cricketer who is still, to thousands, simply Jack Hobbs, or just 'Jack', is a person in the round, a full man.

Perhaps the simplest indication of his quality is implicit in the fact that, when he was knighted, the honour did not change him. Nor did he need to alter his manner in the slightest degree to carry it with as simple and easy a dignity as ever matched an accolade. Just as to see him play was to admire him as a cricketer, so to know him as a man has always been to hold him in respect and affection.

Much of Jack Hobbs's character is to be read in his face. The bony structure is firm and neatly chiselled; the forehead high enough to argue keen thought; the nose quizzical; mouth sensitive, its corners curled on the brink of a smile. But the main feature is the eyes, set in a nest of sun-and-laughter wrinkles; they are brightly observant, steady in regard, and quick to light with humour.

In play, the salient feature of his cricket was that it seemed so unspectacular; he batted perfectly because he was the perfect batsman. His strokes did not seem startling, but inevitable.

So, as a schoolboy, watching the famous cricketer for the first time, my immediate impression was of disappointment. He moved so unhurriedly, easily, forward or back, placing a single, smoothly powering a four, recognizing the good ball early and meeting it with impeccable defence. No violence, no hurry: the stroke rolled away like a well-cued billiard ball. It was only when I realized that his partner – a Test player of some standing – was in genuine difficulties that the utter perfection of Jack Hobbs's batting was borne in upon me.

Others have hit greater distances, scored faster, played longer innings; but no one ever batted with such consummate mastery over every type of bowling as this leanly built man who loved to bat but cared little for records.

Runs were to him the products of a craft which absorbed and satisfied him, but he never failed to see them in the perspective of winning or, at need, saving, a cricket match.

There have been arguments as to who bestowed his extra title on him. There should be no doubt. He created it for himself. Merely to watch him play a few strokes was to know that this was, indeed, 'The Master'.

No bowler ever seemed to hurry him or to disturb his laconic calm.

He himself says that, when he was in trouble, he played forward. But for thirty years it was extremely hard for his opponents to suspect that he was ever in any trouble at all.

He drove magnificently, to on or off, from the front foot. Unusually, among even the great batsmen, but like W. G. Grace, he was equally sound in forward and back play. Yet there is little doubt that he felt at greater advantage on the back foot.

Certainly he would rock on to his right foot and play a pace bowler who was 'moving' the ball off a 'green' wicket with quite amazingly fast, yet apparently casual, adjustments of stroke.

For thirty years bowlers sought to discover a flaw in his technique – a single weakness such as they could uncover, and hope to exploit in every other great batsman – but they never discovered one.

Yet his was no coldly technical perfection. His craftsmanship was warm, and mischief was never far below the surface of his cricket. Against some bowlers he would take considerable, but measured, risks when they first came on, because he knew that they bowled less well after they had suffered a few fours.

Others, old friends and rivals, he delighted to tease. There were at least two considerable leg-spinners whom, when the state of the game allowed, he would pick up from outside the off stump and hit to square leg against the spin – and then drily sympathize with them because they could not turn the ball!

Others, again, would set a deep field to him, whereupon he would ignore the bait and take walked singles off almost every ball he received. In that respect he was superb: he could check his stroke with such perfect control as to take a single to men who were 'saving the one' from a normally powered hit.

Profound technical understanding and tactical sense were at the root of his batting success. It has been said – as may, at first impact, seem trite, but actually with considerable accuracy – that most errors of batsmen stem from playing back when they should play forward, or forward when it would have been better to go back.

Jack Hobbs probably erred less often in that respect than any other batsman we have seen. Once in position, he seemed to harness pace, swing or spin to his strokes, hitting the ball with that sensitive sympathy – Sir Leonard Hutton much resembled him in that respect – which gave his play such a natural air. His study of the game made him the ideal senior professional: indeed he was effectively the captain of many England teams.

He came late to county cricket, lost four years of peak play to the 1914 war and most of another to illness, yet, between 1905, when he was twenty-three, and 1934, nearing fifty-two, he scored more runs, 61,237, and more centuries, 197, than anyone else has ever done in all first-class cricket.

His Test figures dominate those of all others in the period before the great widening of the field of representative play: in fact, all but two of his 102 Test innings (159 and 53 v West Indies) were played against Australia or South Africa.

He himself has said that he was never so good a batsman after the First World War as before it: yet, in that second, great period, *after he was thirty-six*, he scored another 132 centuries.

Pressed to play in George Duckworth's benefit match in 1934, he did so, though feeling out of form: and, at the age of fifty-one, made 116 and 51 not out against that year's county champions.

Sir Jack Hobbs was a cricketer who rose above figures. We shall long remember that excitingly fast swoop, balanced pick-up and shell-like, yet deadly accurate, throw, from cover-point. But most of all we shall recall the brilliant versatility of his batting.

He, who made runs in glorious flow on good wickets, played some of his best innings on really vicious pitches, where his thirty or forty runs were worth many a hundred taken in easier circumstances.

When in 1909–10, the South African googly bowlers were at their greatest, and won the series against England, only Hobbs mastered them: his average, 67.37, was more than twice as high as that of any other English batsman.

It is one of the riches of cricket to have watched him bat. Those who never saw him may find it difficult to imagine such skill as made all bowling seem easy; the unforced movement, on neat feet, into a flow of stroke which sent the ball away, placed to inches, and at the high pace of perfect timing. Here every man who had ever striven to bat could see the flowering of that craft, through perfect execution, into an art.

Jack Hobbs's cricket could never have been so complete if he had not relished it so much. He was always quick to appreciate the skill of others and (except when, naturally enough, in his fifties, he resented *persistent* bouncers) unrufflable: he was a cricketer of courtesy and humour.

In the dressing-room he was an inveterate, dry leg-puller and practical joker. One England captain could never quite *prove* that it was J.B.H. who substituted water for gin in his flask; while many of Jack's friends have been staggered when, completely unaware that he had picked their pockets, they have thanked him for the return of petrol-lighters, cigarette-cases and handkerchiefs they did not know they had 'lost'.

This poem was written for Sir Jack's seventieth birthday, but it belongs to any period of his cricket:

There falls across this one December day
The light remembered from those suns of June
That you reflected, in the summer play
Of perfect strokes across the afternoon.

No yeoman ever walked his household land
More sure of step or more secure of lease
Than you, accustomed and unhurried, trod
Your small, yet mighty, manor of the crease.

The game the Wealden rustics handed down
Through growing skill became, in you, a part
Of sense; and ripened to a style that showed
Their country sport matured to balanced art.

There was a wisdom so informed your bat
To understanding of the bowler's trade,
That each resource of strength or skill he used
Seemed but the context of the stroke you played.

The Master: records prove the title good;
Yet figures fail you, for they cannot say
How many men whose names you never knew
Are proud to tell their sons they saw you play.

They share the sunlight of your summer day
Of thirty years; and they, with you, recall
How, through those well-wrought centuries,
Your hand reshaped the history of bat and ball.

No poem is ever as good as its writer would wish. But those lines may be allowed to add to the weight of tributes already paid to 'The Master'. Certainly they cannot overpraise the greatest of modern batsmen, a happy, wise, modest, kind man and, surely, the best loved of all cricketers. *Surrey CCC Handbook, 1962*

# The Master's Club

The Master's Club is, surely, unique. Composed of former team-mates, opponents and friends of Sir Jack Hobbs, it met frequently during the last years of his life; and always on his birthday, to lunch with him and drink his health. Since his death the members have gathered regularly on his birthday to drink his health. For the past seventeen years that toast has been proposed by his old Surrey opening partner, Andrew Sandham.

The Master's Club was not planned. It simply happened. One day the writer was delighted to receive one of Sir Jack's cheerful telephone summonses to 'come over to Emil's and pull a cork'. Emil's – The Wellington Restaurant, next door to Sir Jack's sports-goods shop in Fleet Street – was kept by Emil Haon, an amiable Austrian who would always open a bottle of champagne in his cellar for our eleven o'clock refresher. Sir Jack, a strict teetotaller in his playing days, remained temperate; but he enjoyed a glass, perhaps two, of champagne in the morning; and perhaps a little claret with his lunch.

One day in 1953 Kenneth Adam, *Guardian* journalist and one-time Head of Television, and Frank Lee, Somerset left-hander and Test umpire, joined in the journey from Portland Place. That meant two bottles and, when the conversation became engrossing, it was decided to continue it over lunch in the restaurant upstairs.

That was the first of several such parties; Alf Gover was one of the earliest to join in. At one lunch, quite casually, it was suggested that we should form a club, with Sir Jack as its perpetual guest of honour. He modestly but clearly happily acquiesed. What more fitting title for it than that bestowed on him by his fellow players? So 'The Master's Club' came into existence. Then came Greville Stevens, Hugh Metcalfe – pre-war film star, actor and stage manager – Jack Ingham, who 'ghosted' for Sir Jack in his newspaper days; Alec – now Sir Alec – Durie, Stuart Surridge, Tom Pearce, Doug Insole, Morley Richards, John Bridges of the BBC.

It had – and has – only two rules: no speeches, and only one toast, that of 'The Master'. For years, with the port, it was customary to demand – and not to count it as a speech – Alf Gover's story of the day he went in first with The Master. Yes, it did happen, with only a few minutes left for play at the end of a first day at Northampton. Sadly, Alf tired of telling it at the point where the other members knew it so well that they recited it in unison with him.

The Club soon took positive shape. There was a spring lunch as someone used to put it 'to make sure we have all come through the winter'. On the Wednesday before the Lord's Test the guests invariably included the captain of the touring team: and there would be other meetings when someone thought it a good idea. Any member might bring a guest to a normal lunch but on 16 December, 'The Master's Birthday', soon recognized as the Club's great day, the members acted as hosts only to men who had played Test cricket with or against The Master. For many years they were an historic phalanx – George Gunn, Maurice Tate, George Geary, Bob Wyatt, Ian Peebles, Herbert Sutcliffe, Frank Woolley, Wilfred Rhodes, Herbert Strudwick, Tich Freeman, George Duckworth, Bill Hitch, Johnnie Taylor, Sir Don Bradman. Gradually, and to Sir Jack's obvious distress, one by one they dropped out; at best not well enough to turn up.

For all that poignancy, however, he cherished the occasion and on the birthday of 1962 he over-rode rule number one. Shyest of men that he was, he stood up after the toast of the day and said disarmingly, 'This is not a speech, it's just a thank-you.' Thereupon he proceeded conversationally to make a brief, apt, often funny, never malicious, comment about everyone at the table.

He was applauded delightedly and sat down saying, 'I always meant to do that.' Perhaps he felt it in his bones that he would never again come to the lunch of what he called 'My Club'. The next year his toast was drunk with acclaim and under a cloud of anxiety. A telegram was dispatched to him in Hove, where he lay gravely ill. Six days later he was dead.

The Master's Club continues in his honour. Many of the earlier members are no longer with us. New members, however, are recruited. In recent years Colin Cowdrey, Alec and Eric Bedser, Jack Parker. Most lately three immense admirers of The Master, Barry Reed, the former Hampshire opening batsman; Bob Carter, wine director of Devenish brewery, whose father played with Sir Jack on Parker's Piece at Cambridge; and J.A.D. – John – Hobbs, the Oxford Blue who at one time used to appear immediately above Sir Jack in the Births and Deaths section of *Wisden*. Thus the process of renewal goes on. Happily, too, the Club has been adopted and housed by the Surrey Club. The Birthday lunch now takes place in the Committee Room at The Oval; with The Master's Club guests acting as luncheon host to their host – the president of Surrey. Thus, it seems, continuity is ensured for the memory of – and there can be no real doubt about it – the greatest batsman.

*Surrey CCC Handbook*, 1981

# Maurice Tate

For years, simply 'Maurice' was enough. Everyone knew who you meant. His face was reddy-brown from the sun twelve months of the year; his grin was as broad as an autumn sunset, and he always had something to say. He had a million friends, many of them folk who had never been nearer to him than their seat at the match was from the start of his run to the wicket, but they made him their friend with true divination of the man he was.

Surely there never was a bowler who so often beat the bat and then missed the stumps by fractions of an inch. Then he would throw up his hands in wonderment, sometimes even in a fine fury, but never in the depression of a man who feels the world is against him. It merely meant that the next ball would contain every bit as much effort – if not more.

You would not, I suppose, have called Maurice Tate handsome. As a young man he was coltish; in his great years – a dozen years from the twenties into the thirties – his face was rustically cheerful, his strong shoulders drooped, his hips were wide, his legs thick, his feet spread. Yet the game of cricket has never seen anything finer than Maurice Tate bowling. Any sculptor of ancient Greece would unhesitatingly have taken him for a model.

There were only six strides to his run. Then came the delivery which he first used, without premeditation, one July day at Horsham when the defence of Philip Mead suddenly spurred him out of the slow off-breaks he had bowled until then. The eye retains across the years one point in that final swing when his left arm was stretched high, and his right, ball in hand, made a clear and splendid diagonal across the line of his arched body as it rocked back on his right foot. Then his right arm came over, wrist cocked, and he bowled with a fierce swing-over of his body and a mighty plunging thud of his left foot to the ground. Only hips as wide as his could have cushioned that jolt. His legs were strong from many years of following the beagles on foot and he was a good walker, but even his large countryman's feet could not stand that battering. It was the technician's ideal; wrist, arm, shoulder, back, waist, legs and feet all contributed their utmost to the ball he bowled. No one else ever has brought every item of that mechanism so effectively to bear. So it was that he seemed to contradict the laws of timing of a cricket ball.

Woe betide the batsman who did not play forward to him for the first half-hour or so of his innings, for the ball would leap from the pitch and be 'through' his back-stroke before the bat was half-way down.

In the autumn of 1924 Maurice Tate sailed to Australia. English cricket, plundered and disorganized by the war of 1914–18, was weak by comparison with that of the Australians who had so mercilessly defeated us in 1921. To be sure, England had the batting of Hobbs, Sutcliffe, Woolley, Hendren, Hearne: but the bowling, since Arthur Gilligan's injury, was Tate – with someone trying to shut up the other end. The Australian batting tactics were to defend against Tate until he tired and to take their runs off the other bowlers. In that Test series, Maurice Tate bowled almost twice as many overs as any other English bowler: he took more than twice as many wickets as anyone else, and at the lowest average. Once he bowled with the big toe nail of his left foot torn away and his boot full of blood. Still he could not be damped. Of his 38 Test wickets in the series – which set up a record – 30 were those of appreciable Test batsmen.

Some thought that that great sustained effort must have bowled the heart out of him. Not at all: he swept on and on until he had taken more wickets than any other bowler of his pace in all recorded cricket. Figures, however, are feeble outlines of Maurice Tate's bowling. For years, especially when the sea-fret was on the wicket at Hove, no batsman in the world was his master and, at any moment, he might sweep away an entire innings. He bowled both swings, but his outswinger was the sharper weapon: and, because his arm was so straight and high and because he 'hit the pitch with it', he made the ball move sharply off the ground. Many a batsman has covered up to Maurice's outswinger only for it to bite back and thump – in those days, before the 'new' lbw law, unrewardedly – against his pads.

He spanked many sound runs, many cheerful ones and not a few that were spectacular; and he held some very hard catches indeed. On figures, he must be called an all-rounder. But, in his day he was entitled to be called, like Mynn, seventy years before him, simply 'The Bowler'.

He was a warm man, Maurice Tate; a happy family man and a good friend. He loved cricket and, by some unique inspiration, he was so splendid a bowler that no one else can ever be quite like him. For many of us, the world is not quite complete without him. May the turf, which he bruised so often with his bowling, lie easy upon him.

*Official Sussex Cricket Handbook*, 1957

# Hammond

### *The Olympian Cricketer*

*July* 1981. The judgement of cricket history is that the greatest batsmen the game has known are – in order of appearance, only – W. G. Grace, Jack Hobbs, Walter Hammond and Don Bradman. Others may come close indeed to those four; but do not quite take place with them. It is, of course, coincidence that two of them played for Gloucestershire; but without doubt Hammond, although he was not a native of that county, succeeded by right and without question to the eminence there previously occupied solely by Dr Grace.

Wally Hammond was a most exciting cricketer, perhaps the more so for the hint of an almost Olympian aloofness. He was also – and the two do not always go together – a naturally-gifted athlete who could excel at any game he cared to play; today he would be bought up as a rising football star. He had that physical stamp; he moved easily, with an ease which yet promised that, at need, he could launch himself into a tiger leap. Even as late as 1951, when he made his last first-class appearance and after he had put on a considerable amount of weight, his movement was poised, assured, and graceful.

The instant he walked out of a pavilion, white-spotted blue handkerchief showing from his right pocket, bat tucked under arm, cap at a hint of an angle, he was identifiable as a thoroughbred. Strongly built, square-shouldered, deep-chested, with impressively powerful forearms, it seemed as if his bat weighed nothing in those purposeful hands.

His figures are convincing evidence of his quality. Between 1920 and 1951 he scored 50,493 runs, with 167 centuries and an average of 56.10; in Tests 7249 runs (22 centuries) at 58.45; as a bowler, 732 wickets (average 30.58); and he held 819 catches. Like Jack Hobbs, he might have achieved even more impressive figures if he had been able to play throughout his career. For instance, he first appeared for Gloucestershire (where he had been to school at Cirencester for five years) in 1920; but Lord Harris, piqued that he would not play for Kent, the county of his birth, quibbled about his qualification. So, effectively, he did not enter county cricket until 1923; he missed the entire season of 1926 through an illness contracted in West Indies (he came back to start the next season by scoring a thousand runs in May); of course, he lost the 1940 to 1945 seasons when he was on a high plateau of achievement: and played only two first-class matches after he returned from Australia in March 1947.

A natural player, he was virtually never coached until he had become a county player, when George Dennett used sometimes to advise him. Instinctively basically correct, he was sound in defence, but never defensively minded. Like most outstanding batsmen, he was primarily a front-foot player who, with the years, operated more off the back. His great power lay in his driving, which was pure textbook in style, clean, apparently effortless but, through the combination of innate timing and immense strength, often achieving immense velocity.

As a young man he was a dashing strokemaker; willing to tilt at all the bowlers of the world. He remained superbly stylish, his cover-driving, from front foot or back, utterly memorable. In those early days he cut, glanced, hooked and lofted the ball quite fearlessly. With his early maturity, he became a thinking batsman. When he went to Australia under Percy Chapman in 1928–29, although he was only twenty-five, he had worked out exactly how he would make his runs. Eschewing the hook altogether and, largely, the cut, he decided to score – off all but the obviously punishable ball – within the V between cover-point and mid-wicket. He succeeded with a new record aggregate for a rubber of 905 runs at 113.12 in the five Tests; which has still only once been exceeded (by Sir Donald Bradman, of course).

Even in his cricketing middle-age, his footwork flowed like that of a young man. He would be down the pitch – two, three or four yards – with unhurried ease and, as he reached the length he wanted, the bat moved with languid certainty through the ball, which flew, with that savage force which was the measure of his hitting, to the place he wished.

Of the four great batsmen he was physically the finest and most powerfully equipped.

He was a superb fast-medium bowler who often, as Sir Donald Bradman once remarked, 'was too busy scoring runs to worry about bowling'. When he was roused – as he once was by Essex bowling bouncers at the Gloucestershire batsmen – his pace could be devastating. 'I never saw a man bowl faster for Gloucestershire than Wally did that day,' said Tom Goddard, 'and he not only battered them, he bowled them out as well.'

At slip he had no superior. He stood all but motionless, moved late but with uncanny speed, never needing to stretch or strain but plucking the ball from air like an apple from a tree.

Statistics cannot tell all: but revealingly they show of Wally Hammond that he made 167 centuries and reached fifty without making a hundred 184 times; in Tests 22 hundreds, only 24 fifties without reaching three figures: in each case almost even money on 100 if he got halfway.

He became an amateur in 1938; and captained England as well as both Gentlemen and Players.

It is some measure of his quality that in 1946, at forty-three, he was top of the first-class averages with 1783 runs at 84.90 – 16 ahead of the next man. He had a sad tour as captain of England in Australia in 1946–47. He was miserably afflicted with arthritis, had acute personal problems, could make runs in State matches but not Tests, England were roundly beaten and, on his return to England, he announced his retirement. He mistakenly allowed himself to be persuaded to appear in one match in each of the 1950 and 1951 seasons. A quiet – some thought introverted – man, but a loyal friend, he retired, hard-up and unhappy, to South Africa. There he died in 1965, mourned by more admirers than he may have guessed. By then he was, unchallengeably, one of the cricketing immortals. *Wisden Cricket Monthly*

# 3
# A Dozen Game Characters

## 'Old' Clarke

It can be argued that William Clarke – 'Old' Clarke – was the greatest of all underarm bowlers: he obtained his twist and life from the pitch by spinning the ball out high from under his arm-pit. There can, though, be no argument about his influence on the game; he was the greatest missionary it ever knew, or ever can know.

His was an amazing, and amazingly long, career. He first played for Nottinghamshire when he was sixteen; did not make his first appearance at Lord's until he was thirty-eight; nor for England during the Canterbury week (in the pre-Test era) until forty-five; nor for Players against Gentlemen until rising forty-eight. Although he lost an eye in his twenties while playing fives, he stayed forty-one years in the first-class game and took several thousand wickets – 2385 for the All-England XI alone. Once, in 1834, he played single-handed against eleven on the Nottingham Forest ground, scored 39 in his single innings and bowled out his opponents in two for 27.

He was a bricklayer who once kept The Bell in Nottingham Market Place. In 1838 he married the widow who had inherited the Trent Bridge Inn, took over the licence and turned the meadow behind the house into Trent Bridge cricket ground. The locals, who had always watched their cricket free on the Forest ground, resented Clarke making an admission charge. Gradually, though, he made his ground a centre for the rising power of the county's cricket.

In 1846, too, he founded the All England Cricket Club which did, in truth, consist of the best players in the country. They travelled it, north, south, east and west, playing against local fifteens, eighteens and twenty-twos for a guarantee of gate money. Clarke knew precisely what he was doing. He once said to James Pycroft, 'It is going to be, sir, from one end of the land to the other; it will make good for cricket – it will make good for you as well as me.' Clarke, himself, manager, captain and stock bowler of the side, paid his players – fifty shillings, three or four pounds according to their eminence or performance – and pocketed the rest. He made a fine profit from it; but the All-England XI, playing in towns and villages which had never seen a first-class team and many of which have never seen one since, preached the technical gospel of length bowling and the straight bat through the provinces and villages of England. They gave provincial cricket playing standards.

Clarke would weigh up his opponents at practice before the match began and generally knew what to bowl them when they came in. During a match he would lunch off nothing heavier than a cigar and a glass of soda water. He dined, though, whenever possible, on a Michaelmas goose, of which he left little. He made a fortune out of cricket, and probably persuaded more people into playing the game, and understanding how to play it properly, than anyone else.

A lady anxious for her son to be invited to play for the 'Eleven' once said to Clarke, 'And, Mr Clarke, he's six feet in his stockings.' 'My word, ma'am,' said Clarke, 'what a lot of toes he must have.'

He was the first man to make a fortune out of cricket; he was, also, the first to see that a fortune was to be made out of it. He played it at competitive level for forty-one years; and – rare obituary note – took a wicket with the last ball he ever bowled.

*The Mike 'Pasty' Harris Benefit Souvenir Brochure*, 1977

# Sammy Woods
## *A Legend at Taunton*

All cricket grounds are rich with talk; but none, surely, richer than Taunton. Perhaps the Somerset accent makes it seem so; but, equally, it has been a ground of great characters. None of them was more relishable than Sammy Woods. Dead, now, these forty-seven years, he played his last first-class match in 1910; but stories are still told about him at Taunton, often by men who were not even alive when he died.

Australian born, he was a Test player for both England and Australia; and a rugby football international for England. A Somerset man by absorption, Sammy Woods was drawn into the life of the county so completely that he looked and, towards the end in his later days, even sounded, like a native.

He played cricket for the county for twenty-one seasons and captained it for thirteen, appreciably longer than anyone else in its history. He was a fast bowler of genuine fire, immense stamina with a well hidden slower ball; an increasingly capable batsman who drove extremely strongly: in Archie MacLaren's opinion, the finest of all silly-points, and an astute, enterprising captain.

In his youth he often kept wicket; indeed such was his all-round ability that he played rugby for England, soccer for the Corinthians, hockey, billiards and, of course, skittles for Somerset, and was also a fine hammer-thrower and shot-putter, as well as being a useful boxer.

Two stories about him still echo in conversation round the Taunton ground. Somerset were admitted to the County Championship in 1891, and, after their early performances, *The Sportsman* described them as 'first class in classification, at least for the remainder of the season'. They needed a major victory but could hardly expect it against Surrey, the county champions. Yet, when Woods began the last over Surrey not only had no chance of winning, but Sharpe and Wood, the last two Surrey men, were striving to play out time. After Sammy's second ball to Sharpe, Wood, the batsman at the bowler's end, said: 'Keeps his end up well for a man with only one eye, eh?' 'Which one?' asked Woods. 'The left' was the answer. Then, Woods related, 'I bowled the first roundarm ball of my life and hit his off stump.'

· Equally happily it is related how, during the winter, Sammy used to keep fit by following the hounds on foot, usually with a friend. Often when they paused for a breather he would say: 'Would you like a drink of good ale?' When the thirsty friend made a rude retort, Woods would go to the hedgerow and, from under the grass, in a hole or among the roots of a bush, produce a couple of bottles. He used to plant them on his country walks and it was said that he had dozens of such caches all over the Quantocks and never forgot one of them.

He left behind a characteristically simple piece of advice for those who followed him in the captaincy – 'Draws are only good for swimming in.' Once, as captain of the Gentlemen against the Players at Lord's – then the match of the season – he set the Players some 500 to win; and, when time ran out, they had two wickets left and the scores were level. Before the umpires could take off the bails, Woods seized the ball and insisted on bowling another over. The Players won; but Sammy had got his finish.

He made a game finish himself. Crippled by arthritis, he played games as long as he could move, and died in Taunton after a dour, uncomplaining struggle against a long illness. All cricketing England, it seemed, was at his funeral and unbroken crowds of people from his adopted county lined the route of the cortege. Two other Somerset cricketers, the

Reverend F. E. Spurway and Prebendary Wickham, conducted the service; and Sammy Woods was buried in St Mary's cemetery barely a a mile from the County Ground at Taunton, where he is still held in undying, affectionate, and admiring memory.

*Derek Taylor Testimonial Book,* 1978

# Rough Diamond

Tom Wass, the cricketer, died a week or two ago [27 October 1953] in Sutton-in-Ashfield, the village where he was born. He was seventy-nine. As a young man he played in Scotland and was once qualified for Lancashire, but he was always Nottinghamshire's man.

Wass's great cricketing days were long over when I first met him at Trent Bridge in 1946, and shook hands with a man whose third and little fingers were immovably fixed in the palm of his hand from many years of bowling what modern cricket terminology calls the 'leg-cutter', but which Edwardian players called, fairly enough, a fast leg-break.

Later that day, I turned to Tom Oates, for years the county's wicket-keeper, but by then their scorer, holding his pencil in fingers jerky as oak-twigs from the fractures of his trade.

'How good a bowler was Tom Wass?'

'He was *dam'* good.'

'Then why didn't he play for England?'

'Tom were a roogh diamond.'

'So were a good many of the Northerners of those days who played for England.'

'Ay, but Tom were roogher'n moast.'

'In what way, Tom?'

'Well, when he first come to play for t'county, skipper Dixon hisself goas down to meet Tom off t'train. Tom gets off wi' graat sheep-dog. "What," says skipper, "tha can't bring that wi' thee to t'ground, tha knows." "Then," says Tom, "if dog can't coom, Tom doan't coom," and goes over bridge an' back home on t'next train.'

When the weather was dry at Trent Bridge, the master batsmen of the pre-war years of this century took unhurried centuries from Wass's and his fellows' bowling on that green and regal wicket. On their own grounds, however, or at Nottingham, when there had been rain, Wass's leg-cutter would pitch on the leg stump and hit the top of the off or, taking the outside edge of the bat, fly to one of the five crouching slips or the prehensile A. O. Jones in the fielding position which he invented at gully. Wass had a reputation for bowling an extremely accurate first ball, and P. F. Warner and C. B. Fry fell to him only less often than the impeccable R. H. Spooner, who was beaten by that fast breaking ball for several ignominious 'ducks'.

He was christened simply Tom, which his friends 'shortened' into 'Topsy', but he was jealous of the right to address him thus, and one most eminent amateur batsman's amiable 'Hullo, Topsy' at the crease was answered with 'Tom Wass is my name, but I gi' thee mister, and I'll have mister o' thee – if tha must talk.'

That Nottinghamshire and Derbyshire coalfield on which Wass was born has been a breeding ground for fast bowlers for more than a century. They are men with the sloping shoulders and deep chests of the coal-miner, but few of them have been Wass's full six feet in height, for the narrow seams do not as a rule develop tall men. He had, however, the true miner's weight of body-muscle, and bowled long, tirelessly and eagerly at the cricket which brought him his days in the sun.

He belonged to that old breed of Lancashire, Yorkshire and Notting-hamshire professionals of the great days when the real cricketing strength of England was centred there.

They travelled third-class by rail – the motoring cricketer is a very recent phenomenon – and if they had been offered the writing of a gossip-column in a newspaper they would have been professionally indignant, even if they had been literate enough to encompass it, for they believed that cricket was a full-time job. In the winter, they put on their heavy, grey-tweed suits and their black boots, and drank beer and talked about cricket, for this time of bad weather was the well-earned holiday against which they had saved some shillings of the summer.

Good judgements among the players of his time confirm Tom Oates's opinion that Wass might reasonably have played for England. He took 1665 wickets for Nottinghamshire – more than any other bowler – and, in 1907, he and Hallam virtually bowled the county to the Champion-ship.

During one Lancashire v Nottingham match at Aigburth, where Wass was once the club pro, he and A. C. MacLaren, the Lancashire captain, met when they were both looking at the pitch after rain. 'Wass,' MacLaren said, 'you know this wicket; how do you think it will play?' The fast bowler looked slowly up at him, paused a moment, and said, 'We shall win.' Subsequently he took nine Lancashire wickets for sixty runs in verification of his opinion.

From 1897 to his bare two hours of post-war bowling in 1920, he bowled twelve thousand overs, running long and straight and often under punishment on batsmen's wickets. Most remarkably for a fast bowler, too, he came late to first-class cricket. The fast-bowler's effective period is usually regarded as the years between nineteen and thirty, but Wass did not have a full season – in which he bowled as many as five hundred overs – until he was twenty-six, while his best season came at thirty-three while, at thirty-eight, in the 'blood' match with Derbyshire, he had still the initial fire to take their first eight wickets for nineteen runs in fourteen balls.

The men who bowled at Trent Bridge have always had to take the task seriously, and Tom Wass's fitness was a pressing matter in his winter. He spent an hour with a punching bag every morning and he followed the hounds, often as far as twenty miles in a day, twice a week all through his 'off' season.

From the pavilion at Trent Bridge, he watched the county games as a forgotten player in the thirties until, during the past few years, he became something of a legend. Up there on the roof he held court in the eternal cloth cap set straightly upon his head, a collar looking two sizes too large for his neck which had become stringy with age, and wearing a loose jacket which drooped about his craggy bones.

The men who had played with him would climb slowly up the two flights of stairs to see him. As he came back into his heroic own, much of his earlier hardness seemed to drop from the old man, and, if he was never really expansive, there was perhaps more of social uncertainty than of unfriendliness in his silences.

'Tom were roogher'n moast,' said Tom Oates, and the bowler himself once told me, 'Ah feared nowt.' His batting was almost useless, and *Wisden* said of his fielding – when according him selection as one of its Five Cricketers of the Year in 1908 – 'When an easy catch goes to him the batsman has a feeling of hopefulness until he sees that the ball has been safely held.' So his bowling was his cricket and his living; perhaps that was why he gave so little away. In fact, his economy was always careful, like that of most of his fellows. The three pounds a week of the Edwardian professional left little room for extravagance, and in the effort to economise on their match money many of them had arrangements with the players of opposing counties to save hotel bills by housing one another on a 'home and out' basis.

It was a strange irony which brought together in such a bargain A. E. Knight, the Leicestershire all-rounder, who was a fervent Salvationist, and the big 'roogh' miner who bowled with such fury that he needed beer to give him something to sweat out, and who unloaded his emotions in words as hard as his bowling. For years, the dressing-rooms cherished the story of Albert Edward Knight, given a camp-bed in the Wass family bedroom, and, saying his prayers within the hearing of his host, closing with 'Please, Lord, let me make a century tomorrow. Amen.' There was, they say, a creaking of the springs of the Wass bed, Tom fell upon his knees, introduced himself to the Almighty as one whose voice might not be well known in those regions, but who was the Nottingham fast bowler and who prayed that he might be allowed, upon the morrow, to 'bowl beggar out for aught'.

He followed the hounds for many years in those strong black boots of his. He had a good run, and would, I fancy, relish the thought that, like many a fox of those distant winters, he has gone to his Nottinghamshire earth. *The Spectator*

# George Gunn

Legends of George Gunn abound, and justifiably. He was not only arguably the greatest batsman Nottinghamshire ever produced (though for that ranking he might have to contend with his uncle William) but one of the finest – and certainly the most impudent – player of fast bowling the game has ever known. He had a dry, wry humour which often concealed his genuine and deep humanity; and he was always wise enough to realize that cricket was only a game. 'What is wrong with English batsmen today?' Neville Cardus asked him, when England were being routed by Lindwall and Miller. George pondered a moment before replying 'I think they take too much notice of bowlers.'

It is credibly reported that, one match day at Trent Bridge, in August of 1920, George was handed an envelope; he slipped it into his pocket, forgot it, and did not find it and open it until he put on the blazer for pre-season practice in the following season. It had contained an invitation to make the Australian tour of 1920–21: he had never replied, and never went. So, the one man who, in the absence of Jack Hobbs through illness, might have coped with the Australian fast bowling pair, Gregory and McDonald, who wrecked the English batting in 1921, never played in the series at all. Nor, until he went to West Indies in 1929, did he ever play for England again. There was never a more tragic waste of great ability – and character.

In his playing days, during home matches, Mrs Gunn used to take him up a pot of tea, some toast and the papers about eight o'clock, and then go downstairs and busy herself about her household duties. Once – on the second day of a match when Nottinghamshire had gone in second on the first afternoon – she paused in her work, realized she had not heard George moving and went up to find him dozing over the paper. 'Ee, George,' she said, 'but its a quatter past ten.' 'Never mind,' said George, 'we've not enough runs for skipper to declare, he'll let us bat till lunch.' Mrs Gunn shook her head sadly. 'Nay, but, George lad,' she said, 'Tha's sixty-three not out.' George confirmed the information from his newspaper and slid unhurriedly out of bed.

*Frank Woodhead Testimonial Year*, 1979

# Jack Newman

## *A Hampshire Portrait*

*September* 1967. If you look at the railings in front of the pavilion on the county cricket ground at Southampton you will see, just above ground level, a number of dents, curving in towards the pavilion. Almost forty years ago, when I was an aspiring schoolboy off-break bowler, Jack Newman pointed to those dents and said to me, only half humorously – 'See those dents – all made by batsmen edging my fast ball through the slips.' Last year I pointed to them – 'See those dents, Jack?' 'Yes,' he said, 'made by chaps edging my faster ball.' Those lively eyes twinkled: a grin dawned, 'So I told you, did I? – must have been a long time ago – I haven't remembered that for years now.'

Jack was one of the greatest of Hampshire cricketers. He is the last survivor of the four great professionals – Philip Mead, George Brown and Alec Kennedy were the others – of sharply contrasted characters and gifts who, for years, carried Hampshire cricket on their strong backs and were, arguably, as fine a group as any county has ever possessed at the same time.

There are only ten performances of the allrounder's double of a hundred wickets and a thousand runs in a season in the county's records – five of them by Jack. Only Derek Shackleton and Alec Kennedy have taken more wickets for Hampshire than he did; only twelve men have scored more runs; and only seven fielders have held more catches. Only three bowlers have taken over two thousand wickets yet never appeared in a Test, and Jack is one of them.

He settled in South Africa over twenty years ago and for some years he was obviously homesick when, every March, he used to see off the MCC touring side or the English coaches leaving Cape Town for the English season. But lately he has made some return visits, staying in Southampton and with old cricketing friends around the country, watching cricket, talking cricket and, for all that he will be eighty this year, looking almost as lean, trim and upright as he did in his playing days. Last September he said goodbye with the air of a man consciously making a final farewell, and went back to the Cape. He has made a home there; he is used to the country and the sun warms his bones. But he wanted to relish a last look at England, especially Hampshire.

It is no adverse criticism of contemporary cricketers, but merely a reflection of our present social pattern, to say that it is almost impossible for modern English life to produce another such as Jack Newman. He lived in, and by, cricket for sixty years as few will ever do again.

The whole story of his career is something of a period piece. He was born in Southsea, but when he was quite small his parents moved to Bitterne, not then a suburb of Southampton but a village with a separate life, character and identity of its own. In due course, as a self-taught player, he became a member of the local Sunday School cricket team. One Saturday morning of his last year at school just before he was fourteen, he went, as something of an occasion, to a match at the County Ground. Watching the Hampshire players at net practice he picked up a ball that was hit towards him, and asked if he might bowl. Tom Soar, a senior professional, nodded and after watching for a few minutes, fetched the secretary, Fred Bacon, to look at him. Less than an hour later Jack Newman, surprised and happy, had agreed to join the county staff when he left school. The year was 1901: in 1963 he completed his last season as a cricket coach in South Africa.

In between those years, he played his first county match in 1906, his last in 1930 when, after a breakdown, he was told to give up active play; but immediately reappeared as an umpire and began the sequence of winter coaching engagements in South Africa which eventually became his regular employment.

For almost twenty years Newman and Kennedy *were* the Hampshire bowling, like Shackleton and Cannings in a later generation. Jack was primarily an off-break bowler. After the First World War, to adjust the balance of the side, he opened the bowling, with medium-paced outswingers until the shine was gone. His orthodox, determined batting made him a useful all-rounder but his outstanding value was as an off-spinner. From a springy eight-pace run-up, he bowled with a high action at almost medium pace and his lean, strong fingers applied such spin as turned the ball on all but the most unsympathetic wickets. His length was impeccable, his variations subtle, and he concealed well that waspish, faster ball which went with his arm to produce catches – and those dents in the pavilion railings.

Oddly enough, he was never happy bowling from round the wicket and probably was the less effective for that. He bowled in the old manner, pitching outside the off stump to hit middle-and-leg: but, in his day, the 'new' lbw law had not been introduced and batsmen often deliberately covered up with their pads against him. He was a sensitive, highly strung cricketer and once told me that he feared he had not made the most of his cricketing gifts. On the other hand, he was an artist, consumed with the idea of bowling, who spun the ball fiercely and delightedly. In his own words 'bowling is my second nature and I never tire of it'.

He was almost seventy when he wrote, 'I still bowl, but my friends say I bowl too much.' The records show that he took 2032 wickets, including those of all the best batsmen of two decades, a hat-trick against the 1909 Australians and sixteen – for 88 runs – in a match against Somerset. But they do not tell the quality of the spare, lean-shouldered bachelor who was at once generous and competitive, who sometimes suffered in his cricket but who also found much in it to make him laugh. Somewhere, however, there may be a balance and loss account of his unfailing belief that he could beat the bookmakers at their own game.

So many of the older generation look upon the cricket of today only as a whipping boy to be lashed by unfavourable comparison with the players of old. Jack Newman watched the cricket of 1966 and, those clear eyes bright with interest, warmed to it and its players. He enjoyed it; they recognized him as one of their own and, when he sailed from Southampton, he had not only seen old friends, but made fresh ones.

This will be printed in time to reach him in South Africa on his eightieth birthday to tell him that many of those friends will raise a glass to him that day. *Hampshire*

# The Man Who Loved Sixes

*March* 1981. Arthur Wellard, who died on the last day of 1980, at seventy-eight, was a cricketer to be relished. Undemonstrative, laconic in speech, he was a man of mighty gusto; inveterate hitter of sixes, capable of rising to immense peaks of effort, but firmly disinclined to discuss them. A late developer, but long-lasting, he was a better cricketer than his two Test matches would argue and, if his popular reputation was as a big-hitter, his colleagues and opponents regarded his fast-medium bowling with considerable respect. Like Sammy Woods and Len Braund, on joining Somerset he seemed to assume the character of the county's cricket; though he never lost his near-Cockney accent, uttered through the side of barely-parted lips.

Kent-born, at Southfleet, and brought up in Bexley, he was quite exceptional among first-class cricketers in playing no cricket at school, nor for several years afterwards. At eighteen some unexplained urge moved him to go to the Bexley club ground and field out to members batting in the nets until – in novelettish fashion – he was offered the chance to bowl. At once he showed sufficient native ability to be accepted into the club. In a match against Kent Colts he took eight wickets – including those of Leslie Ames, Alan Watt, 'Hopper' Levett and Jack Hubble – quite cheaply. For the seasons of 1924, 1925 and 1926 he was top of both the batting and bowling averages for Bexley; but, the story goes, when he wanted a trial for Kent he was advised to join the police force.

By the freakish kind of accident that shapes so many careers, at a Bexley match in August 1926, he met Archie Haywood, a former Kent ground staff player just back from coaching at Taunton School. Haywood wrote to the Somerset secretary so enthusiastically that Wellard was asked down for a three-day trial at the end of that season and engaged for 1927. He was twenty-five years old but, as could hardly have happened in any other sport, a performer of outstanding ability was not allowed to enter the first-class game for two more years. He spent his years of residential qualification playing with Weston-super-Mare with his subsequent bowling partner for Somerset, and boon companion, the irrepressible Bill Andrews. Of course there were convivial occasions and days of achievement – he strove desperately hard for success – in club cricket. In later years, though, he sometimes revealed his frustration at having played seasons of his young manhood away on a level so much lower than his ability justified.

At last, in 1929, he began his first Championship match – against Worcestershire at Bath – firing off some pent-up energy when he bowled Bernard Quaife with only his third ball; and before a run had been scored. Four wickets in that match; five against Glamorgan and seven against Hampshire – all of recognized batsmen – and he had put his team place beyond doubt for twenty years. At Whitsun he established himself in the history of the traditional Bank Holiday 'blood' match with Gloucestershire when, in the absence of Wally Hammond, he took the wickets of Alf Dipper, Reg Sinfield and Charlie Barnett in both innings – in all eleven for 175 – and scored 75 and 55. Against Leicestershire he performed the first – and only – hat-trick of his career; and, as he remembered wrily, 'bagged a pair'. He took 125 wickets at 21 in that first season: only ten bowlers in the country had more at a lower average; and he was in the top flight.

Memory recalls Arthur Wellard as he was then; eager to make up for the lost years. Over six feet tall, swarthy, invariably sunburnt and capless, his black hair parted near centre in the fashion of the 1920s and 1930s; he had well-formed, strong-looking features; and he was magnificently equipped to bowl at pace. Wide-shouldered and already thickening, deep-chested, with muscular, slightly bowed legs, he was an extremely powerful man; able to bowl at the livelier end of fast-medium, yet well within himself. At this time, in addition to pace off the pitch, his sharpest weapon was a splendid body-action breakback. He was, though, already developing the outswinger which he bowled as well as anyone in his time. Somerset wicket-keepers and slips of his period would tell you how, as soon as he released the ball and they saw the seam absolutely vertical and unwavering, they knew it was his 'outer'. It 'went' very late indeed and he suffered more than most from dropped slip catches; though generally he mumbled his discontent to himself.

In a later period, with his immense stamina, control and persistent hostility, Arthur Wellard would have walked into a Test team. In those pre-war days, though, he competed with Maurice Tate, Harold Larwood, 'Gubby' Allen, Bill Bowes, George Geary, Ken Farnes, Bill Copson, Alf Gover, 'Nobby' Clark, Morris Nichols, 'Hopper' Read, Jim Smith, Austin Matthews and – too often forgotten as a bowler, but a considerable performer – Wally Hammond, for the new ball in an English side. It is measure of Wellard's ability that, against such opposition, he forced his way in for one Test against New Zealand in 1937, and one against Australia in the next year. Four wickets (all in the first six) for 81; none for 30 on a turner, at first appearance; three (Hassett, Badcock and Fingleton) when Australia scored 626 for the loss of sixteen wickets in the two innings of the drawn match at Lord's – when he hit McCabe for six into the grandstand.

In his early days with Somerset, his somewhat unsophisticated batting was highly vulnerable to off-spin; but the guidance of Tom Young and Jack Lee, coupled with his own devoted practice, soon repaired the fault and he developed a sound basic style. Essentially, though, he was a hitter. At a pinch he could hook or cut; but he was by nature a front-foot player and, even in those days of unlimited boundaries, he would back himself to drive or pull any bowler over his deep field. Despite his limited backlift he struck with immense, clean power. In the fashion of that time, too, the spinners would set their men back and dare him to succeed. Twice – off T. R. Armstrong and Woolley – he hit five consecutive balls for six. His records for sixes in a season – 72 in 1935, 57 (1936 and 1938) and 51 (1933) – have never been exceeded in English first-class cricket. He was never a mere slogger. He three times performed the double; and at need he could, and would, defend orthodoxly; his hitting was a tactical asset.

To the end he exulted in bowling. When conditions favoured the method, he employed slow-medium to medium off-breaks to a precise length. His urge, though, was to bowl fast. Even in his last full county summer, in 1949 – at the end of which Somerset sacked him too soon, though he was forty-seven – he would bowl hungrily on and on: he sent down 1010 overs for 87 wickets and a report on the Somerset season said 'Wellard's pace at so advanced an age remained one of the wonders of cricket.' Then, at the end of a spell, he would stand, shirt clinging with sweat to his barrel chest, his heart visibly thundering against the rib-cage. Even at seventy he would bowl for sheer pleasure at a surprising pace.

His casual air in the field belied the rapidity of his reactions as an unflinching silly mid-off or short leg or slip; 375 catches were absorbed into those vast yet dextrous hands.

He was never one to hedge his bets, Arthur: and he was a born gambler. He never truly settled in Somerset because he was reluctant to give up his confectionery and tobacco shop in Sutton. So he took lodgings in Taunton, which his friends recall as so full of chiming clocks that only Arthur Wellard could sleep there. So all but Somerset's fixtures with Surrey and Kent were away games to him; and, although he was a steady and convivial beer-drinker, he loved to spend his evenings – like his spare time in the dressing-room – playing cards. He was astute at cribbage, brag, solo whist, bridge (a highly perceptive bidder): but, above all, he was in his element in a poker school: expressionless, all concentration, he had an extra sense for bluffing. A good man, brave – though never so tough as he pretended. Deadly honest, Arthur Wellard never took life – except, perhaps, the bowling part of it – too seriously.

*Wisden Cricket Monthly*

# Haydn Davies

Haydn Davies is one of the relatively few players in first-class cricket today to persuade us that character and the day of 'characters' in cricket is not ended. Because he thinks much of, and much about, the game, because he brings to it a good mind as well as considerable ability, he was bound to make an impression on the cricket of his time.

Although he was one of those whom the war robbed of years which were vital to their development, he has reached the top class as a wicket-keeper. Indeed in 1946 he was extremely unlucky not to go to Australia but in his case as, we may feel, in those of Watkins and Parkhouse, the selectors have demanded more than of others who were chosen. Moreover, Haydn Davies still stands high enough in his own branch of the game not to be out of place in a Test match.

Visual impressions have much to do with some non-expert cricket judgements. Thus, it used to be said that Philip Mead of Hampshire was a slow-scoring batsman, although figures showed that his speed of run-getting was well up to that of most of his contemporaries who scored a comparable number of runs. This judgement, I have always believed, was based on Mead's lumbering carriage. In the same way, many spectators are deceived into thinking that Haydn Davies is slow because of his heavy build and shambling movement behind the stumps. In fact, that shamble maintains him in perfect balance at far greater speed than that of some of his more acrobatic contemporaries.

Not only is he fast but he maintains his eagerness until the end of the longest day's play so that he becomes naturally an important cog in the eagerness and general outcricketing hostility which characterized Glamorgan's Championship-winning eleven. Few wicket-keepers of our time have made the leg-side catch or stumping with such speed – nor have they celebrated it with such an echo-stirring appeal. Moreover, week in, week out through the season he takes, with an impressive nonchalance, the hardest set of throws-in in the County Championship. That occasionally careless air is, of course, quite false for, such is his technical quality, that I remember his claiming while he was suffering from a broken thumb, that he could so adjust the point in his hands at which he took the ball that only the accident of his being blinded of sight of the ball could cause him to be hit on the injured thumb.

Perhaps my own most vivid picture of Haydn comes from Ebbw Vale where, against Worcester a few seasons ago, he played a ball pitching outside his off stump, off the back foot into the river at long-on. His hitting has now become so celebrated that small boys, not only in Wales but all through England, settle from chasing after autographs to watch his innings intently. His hitting is not, of course, consistent; such mighty swings cannot always meet the ball at the right place, but if in every other innings he gives us some of his strokes from Gargantua, we shall be satisfied. It would be a mistake, however, to think that Haydn Davies is crude in his approach. While his hitting has won matches for Glamorgan against time, his defence has shared in other matches won against the run of the tide – and he has opened the innings for the county in an academic manner which, if irksome to him, was nevertheless invaluable.

There used to be an old cricketing maxim – which has never been discredited even if it is sometimes ignored nowadays – that, in picking a cricket team, you should always pick the wicket-keeper first. Glamorgan have been fortunate for fourteen seasons in having their first choice automatically to hand. It is by this sound cricket-standard that I hope Haydn Davies's Benefit will be supported.

*Glamorgan CCC Year Book, 1951*

# 'Roly'

Some people spell his name 'Roley': he always writes 'Roly', and that is good enough for me. He himself is very good for all of us who watch cricket. In a day when the game cricket has threatened to become stereotyped, he is one of its characters, unique and to be relished.

I first met him when Hampshire came up to play Worcester in Bank August week, fifteen years ago. From the humble post of twelfth man, I looked up to one who had played his first county match two whole months before. He had scored only 1 and 4, had not bowled and he took no catches in that first appearance against Essex at Southend in the beginning of June 1938; but, as he would remind me, Worcester won. He did not get back into the side until that day in July when he bowled out the mighty Maurice Leyland at Bradford. *Wisden*, in its review of Worcestershire's season of 1938, commented tersely, 'Jenkins, a leg-break bowler, showed promise.'

He has come a long way since then. In Tests he has captured good wickets – including those of men who had promised to hit him out of sight. Scoring a thousand runs a season entitles him to consideration as a batsman also, but so, even more definitely, do two of his Test innings in South Africa – on a sticky wicket at Durban and at Port Elizabeth. There he played two fighting knocks which turned the course of these games, and led to the two narrow wins which gave us the rubber. I have heard unthinking spectators criticise his fielding and, certainly, his running and throwing are not up to Australian standards but, put Roly Jenkins close to the wicket and he will drop very little – and flinch from nothing.

Cricket history, however, is going to remember him as a bowler. In this post-1945 period of tragically slow wickets, he has been one of the few bowlers in the country to demonstrate that the man who flights the ball, bowls a length and really spins, can take the best of wickets. Watch him from sideways on and you will see how his arc of flight varies from ball to ball. Watch him from end-on and you will see that he turns the ball as much as any bowler in England. Play with or against him and you will see – and hear – how fiercely he loves his cricket and what a terrific trier he is.

Perhaps the fairest measure of Roly Jenkins, who has deserved well of Worcester cricket, is that, winning or losing, on all wickets and in all weather, he is always giving the best he has got, and that best is very good indeed.                                      *Worcestershire CCC Year Book*, 1953

# Tony Lock

*February* 1962. Graham Anthony Richard Lock – politely 'Tony' – is simply and expressively 'Locky' to the many friends who are his enemies on the cricket field. As a cricketer, he is guts incarnate: the ultimate enthusiast, cricket mad, a furious and never-flagging trier and as absorbed in the game as any man who ever played it. There are some, who, failing to understand the essential character of the man, regard him as an exhibitionist: but every one of his apparently theatrical gestures on the field is the spontaneous expression of the fierce and deep emotion he feels for the game. He lives every minute of every match with an absorption and dedication far too great to admit of impassivity.

He has been as deadly a slow left-arm bowler as cricket has ever known, a short leg who has caught the impossible so often as to make his fielding legendary, and a batsman who has aspired to success with such fixity of purpose that it was no more than his due when – at Headingley in 1961 – his innings tilted the issue of a Test against Australia.

Cricket is the abiding passion of Tony Lock's life. At fourteen he was playing for Surrey Colts: at sixteen – in 1946 – he joined The Oval staff as a professional: and in the same season he played his first county match, against Kent (1 not out: no wickets for 24 runs and a 'blinding' catch off Alf Gover's bowling when, for the first time in his life, he stood at short leg). He had to wait almost a year for his next first-class game – for Surrey against the South Africans. Then he delighted the present writer, as a bowler of mild, high-tossed slow left-arm, who fielded to his own bowling with such enthusiasm as warmed the heart. At that time he was purely a 'flight' bowler, his spin almost negligible. When he returned to The Oval in 1949, after two years of National Service, he won a regular team-place and took fifty-five Championship wickets. But he recognized that his main assets of flight and length were not sufficient: he knew he did not spin the ball enough to disturb good batsmen. With a typical whole-hog approach he went to work in an indoor school, hour after hour, day after day, through two winters. He achieved his immediate end: he learnt to spin the ball as sharply as any of his type. But, unhappily for him, the combination of a low beam in the indoor school – making it impossible for him to give the ball any air – and his own determination to spin, destroyed his former high action and left a sinister kink in his bowling arm. But he was now the ultimate 'killer' as a spin bowler: he could wrest turn from all but the deadest of wickets: on anything approaching a spinner's pitch his break was staggering: and his quicker ball came at wicked pace. His rise coincided with Surrey's. Year after year he swept aside county batsmen with sustained and eager hostility. In 1955 and 1957 he took over two hundred wickets and in 1958 – only his tenth full season – he reached his 1500th wicket in first-class cricket.

In 1952 he played his first Test – against India, at Old Trafford – but a few days afterwards, in a county game, he was three times no-balled for throwing: and he was 'called' again for illegal delivery on the West Indies tour of 1953–54. The principal cause of umpires' disapproval seemed to be his faster ball, and for some time afterwards he renounced it. But when, after the MCC's Australian tour of 1958–59 – with the 'throwing' controversy at its height – Lock moved on with the team to New Zealand, he was shown – for the first time – a film of himself bowling. He looked and, characteristically but with feelings which can only be imagined, he said, boldly, that he was now satisfied that his action was unfair.

So, rising thirty, he was faced with the tacit demand to scrap the action that had made him a Test bowler and build in its place another type of delivery which would pass the extra-suspicious scrutiny he would have to expect for the rest of his career. In 1958 he had taken 170 wickets at 12.08: in 1959 he had only 111 and at 21.38: for only the second time since in eight years he did not play in a home Test: he was not taken on that winter's tour to the West Indies: and Yorkshire ousted Surrey from the position of champions. Lock, with his new action, was fairly accurate; but the old devil was missing.

For some time he had been playing under the handicap of 'a Compton knee': 1960 was his benefit year and, in Surrey's first match of the season – against Cambridge University – he was again 'called' for throwing. 'Locky' – because he was 'Locky' – fought. Sometimes it was agonizing to watch him drive himself along on that wretched leg, as if forcing himself to his old pace. Surely, we thought, he will take his benefit and retire. 'Locky' – because he was 'Locky' – fought on. In 1961, against Yorkshire at The Oval, he bowled like one of the classic slow left-arm bowlers: through a higher arc than in his 'slinger' days but with a truly straight arm, artful variations of flight and pace and, once more, genuine spin. There were selectors watching and the next day his name appeared among those picked to play against Australia in the Second Test. He had done it – Lock-fashion.

Sandy – and now tonsured – stringy, angular, strong, enemy of batsmen when he bowls or fields, enemy of bowlers when he bats, quick to anger, never one to mince his words, loyal, still full of boyish enthusiasm, 'Locky' is a good man to have on your side: he is quite incapable of giving less than all he has in him to a game or cricket.

*Playfair Cricket Monthly*


# Ken Mackay MBE

*March* 1963. There is no truth in the report that, when Ken Mackay was told he had been awarded the MBE, he asked 'Waddya dew with ut?' He is, nevertheless, an extremely utilitarian and 'Australian' Australian.

The official citation noted that the honour was bestowed 'for services to cricket'. If a cricketer had been responsible for the wording, it would have gone further, and said: 'For guts, application, tactical acumen and effectiveness as an all-round cricketer'.

'Handsome is,' they say, 'as handsome does'. But even his most impressive figures cannot make Ken Mackay's batting attractive. Indeed, I have sometimes suspected that he hesitates to play a good-looking stroke for fear of shattering his public image!

He walks out to the wicket – or to any other place – with the slow-motion, mock-sinister walk of the villain in a mid-Victorian melodrama. He is the only athlete I have ever seen who, as he walked, sagged at ankles, knees *and* hips.

It has been said that his remarkable gait results from an attack of poliomyelitis in childhood. His reply – accompanied by a cold blue look and one raised eyebrow – is: 'the next illness I have will be the first'. He walks that way because he walks that way.

From time to time he carries his bat in his arms as if it were a cherished child that weighed a ton. In fact, it is a heavy bat – 2lb 5oz – which means that, with proper timing, it hits a cricket ball very hard without passing through the more elegant arcs of recognized stroke-makers using lighter models.

Kenneth Donald Mackay, Member of the Most Excellent Order of the British Empire and captain of Queensland Cricket Club, is the thirty-seven-year-old grandson of a certain Captain Mackay who, at the end of the last century, sailed from the Isle of Skye as master of the ship 'Bingera' and settled in Australia.

The atmosphere of Brisbane fostered skills foreign to the Hebrides: the sea-captain's son became a cricketer whose six children, in turn, were all outstanding games players. At the age of twelve, the eldest son, Ken, was using a bat too big for him to make scores too big for schoolboy opponents.

He was fourteen when he played an innings of 367 not out in a school match; which caused some hair-trigger Australian cricket reporters to trot out their favourite tag of the past twenty years – 'a second Bradman'. Not at all: this was the original Mackay. Incidentally, he took ten wickets in that same match.

Despite the apparent visual evidence of his batting to the contrary, Mackay is a natural ball-games player. If he had not chosen to concentrate on cricket, he had already done enough at squash, tennis and table-tennis to promise that he might have been outstanding at any or all of those games.

But he chose cricket, and succeeded by the hard method. He first played for Queensland in 1946, and had scored more runs than anyone else in that State's Sheffield Shield history before he was picked for Australia.

He made 223 in almost ten hours – four hours for the first fifty – against Victoria in 1953–54. His Queensland colleague, Carrigan, ironically dubbed him 'Slasher': and his home crowd barracked him off the ground. Meanwhile, the official voice of Australian cricket was calling for attractive batting; but such handsome strikers of the ball as de Courcy, Hole and Favell were proving ineffective at Test level.

In the end, results prevailed and Mackay came to England with Johnson's 1956 side. Anyone who watched that series has ineradicable memories of his sorry struggles against Laker, who put him out for 2 in each innings of the Leeds Test, and for a 'pair' in the 'sticky wicket' rout at Old Trafford; wherefore Mackay was left out of the side for the final Test at The Oval.

But he played a rigorously effective part in Australia's only win of the series, at Lord's, where he scored 38 in over two-and-a-half hours in the first innings and 31 in almost four-and-a-half hours in the second; in the same match he bowled eleven overs for 15 runs and Cowdrey's wicket.

It is usually forgotten that he was top of the Australian batting for that tour and, in fact, of the entire first-class averages in England that summer. Little more than a year later, he faced the other great off-spinner of the time – Tayfield – in South Africa and finished top of Australia's Test batting with an average of 125.

Mackay's batting is unprepossessing, not enhanced by being left-handed; and, against off-spin on a turning wicket, it can look abjectly vulnerable. But, apart from that important flaw, it is technically interesting and, in the last analysis, impressive.

Like most modern Australians, he is a back-foot player. Very early in the flight of anything short of a half-volley, his left foot moves across and his body comes round almost square. He holds his bat, at first sight, awkwardly, but the grip is fractionally more biased towards the fingers than in the case of most batsmen, as if he were feeling the grip sensitively.

He has mastered the slack-bottom-hand technique so thoroughly that, at times, he pulls his left completely away at the moment of impact. This gesture, though, is partly dictated by the bruising of his forefinger from the jar of the ball, which also accounts for his strange hand-wriggling gesture between strokes. His grip is so high that, but for the connotation, one would be tempted to describe it as 'long-handled'; but his backlift is negligible. When he must play forward, he invariably limits his stroke to a point safely behind his right foot.

As a general rule, Mackay scores by dabs behind the wicket, jabs square on the off and pushes in front of it. His most punishing stroke is the hook, with which, it is believed, he has scored all his few sixes in first-class cricket. But on his day he hits the ball very hard indeed through the arc between square cover and the right of mid-off. The absence of backlift makes most of these blows appear mild, even ham-handed, but their power is apparent to fieldsmen – and scorers.

He may move in an ungainly fashion, but his timing is so good that what seems to be a heavy-handed scoop is often a perfectly-made impact. Above all, he has the most remarkable eye. He often delays his stroke to a moment that seems too late; and he can set his partner – and the entire field – on tenterhooks by leaving unplayed a ball which misses the stumps by an inch, with a precision of judgement never excelled by the greatest batsmen.

Benaud recognized Mackay as an immensely valuable tactical weapon and – which was an additional advantage – one who understood tactics as well as himself. Accordingly, he moved him to the middle of Australia's batting order, where, at need, he could either shore up a collapsing innings, or keep an end going for hitters like Benaud himself, Davidson or Grout.

Soon, too, Benaud began to lean increasingly upon Mackay's right-arm medium bowling. Years earlier Mackay's Queensland team-mates had declared that he 'moved' the ball in the air more than any other bowler, apart from Lindwall, had ever done at Brisbane. It took time for his seniors at Test level to appreciate his skill. But it gradually became inescapable that Mackay with his grudging length and precise control of both swings, could both fret and put out the best of batsmen.

In the 1961 Test series in England, only Davidson of the Australian bowlers took more than Mackay's sixteen wickets. He bowled Australia to a strong position in the first innings at Edgbaston by taking four of England's best wickets; sustained the seam attack shrewdly at Lord's; and kept the game – as it proved – decisively tight, with forty overs in the first innings at Old Trafford. But technically his most impressive bowling in that rubber was at The Oval, where he dared England to attack him. Exploiting a humid atmosphere, he made his medium-pace right arm bowling curve so late and sharply, even with a worn ball, and pitched it so tightly short of drivable length that every batsman who tried to hit him lost his wicket in the process.

Because he observes and feels every ball bowled in any cricket match he plays, Mackay is already halfway to being a good fieldsman. He rounds off close-catching with a good pair of hands. This is the all-rounder: dour batsman, accurate swing-bowler, safe catcher, constant and acute cricket thinker.

Now the fact can no longer be burked! Ken Mackay chews gum in a strangely fascinating manner. Cricket statisticians can cite the vast number of runs Ken Mackay has scored – including more in the Sheffield Shield than any other Australian now playing. But, from careful – nay, more – compulsive watching, I am convinced that they would be amazed to know the number of miles of gum he has masticated! It seems that, during observable waking hours, he ceases to chew only at the moment of playing – or leaving – the turning ball. Certainly his jaws are in motion again before his bat is still.

Bowling – when he controls the tempo – it seems that he deliberately synchronizes the delivery swing with a positive crunch on the gum, thus preserving his jaw-rhythm.

Apart from gum and cricket, he has few addictions, except the cinema, and cards on long journeys. But he did agree that, if ever Queensland beat New South Wales in Sydney he would celebrate by drinking his first glass of beer. The win was duly achieved, after a gap of seventeen years, in 1956, and Mackay took his drink, savoured it critically, and decided 'Ut might be the laast'.

In an earlier age, less concerned with run-rates, Ken Mackay would have become one of the legendary stonewallers – perhaps, indeed, he has done so. But, nowadays he has learnt, when he judges the moment right, to push the score along at much more than his old rate. But still his defence remains sound, and still his body moves unflinchingly into the line of pace bowling.

The early reaction of the cricket watcher to Mackay is one of no pleasure. Gradually, though, respect grows – for his uncanny eye, his courage and his unadvertised skill. In time, he inspires a relish almost akin to affection as he stands there, bent-kneed, lean jaw unendingly rolling, forehead plaintively wrinkled, bat held unnaturally upright, perpetually undaunted.

This dry, wry man who, at thirty, after ten years of Sheffield Shield cricket had never been picked for anything resembling a representative game – and who phlegmatically offered odds of two to one that he would not be chosen for the 1956 tour of England – has now played well over thirty times for Australia – more often than all but three of their present team – and scored over one thousand runs and taken over fifty wickets in Tests. And he has been awarded the MBE. That must have made his left eyebrow rise higher than ever. *The Cricketer*

# Milburn the Cricketer

## Time has Confirmed an Irreparable Loss

Colin Milburn was the best liked cricketer of modern times. There was a simplicity and a zest in his batting, a humour and generosity about his behaviour which made a direct and irresistible appeal to anyone who cared for cricket and for people. So, when the news came, in May 1969, that he had lost the sight of an eye, many who had never met him felt the cruel wastefulness of that accident as a personal hurt.

He made instant impact on everyone who saw him play. There he stood, vastly rotund, apparently – though not actually – relaxed; left toe cocked in the manner of W. G. Grace; and unmoving. When the ball came, if he liked it – and he had a wide range of acceptance – he hit it.

Sometimes he seemed to do no more than twitch his forearms to send a short ball from his leg stump to the square-leg boundary; but when he punched his weight, as they say of boxers, his blows were often of amazing force. His legside strokes are frequently recalled – three times he hooked Wes Hall for six, which must be some kind of record – but his square cutting, cover and straight driving were also of crushing power.

Some critics – and, self-deprecatingly, he himself – have called his batting 'slogging': but no slogger ever returned such figures as his on the highest level. He was a clean, uncomplicated and, at the pinch, a straight hitter; intuitively right in the most crucial of batting judgements – whether to play off the front or back foot – with a superb eye, magnificent timing and high courage.

Neither should it be thought that his batting was an insensitive act. Lusty it may have been but, beginning in the middle of the order, and later seeming settled at number three, he had eventually to move up to open the innings, he could not bear the nervous stress of waiting.

It is an open question as to whether he or Ted Dexter was the hardest hitter of our times. They were, of course, completely different in style; Dexter struck the cricket ball like a golfer. Milburn like a woodman felling a tree. When Milburn middled a lofted shot the ball seemed to go on and on as if it had a velocity of its own. The combination of his size and the effort of his hitting combined to produce some spectacular effects and several times – at least once in a Test – he burst his trousers.

His gusto was unmistakable and infectious. When he grinned his eyes almost disappeared in the laughter folds and his teeth made a gay white curve in his round sunburnt face. So, long before he was a competent professional batsman, he was one of the few men who attracted spectators to the English cricket grounds of the 1960s.

Word of him had gone ahead of even his first county appearance. George Duckworth, scorer for the 1959 Indian side, had been insistently enthusiastic about the heavyweight seventeen-year-old schoolboy who, in his first and last appearance for his native county, Durham, had scored a hundred against the touring side.

No boy from those parts could have a more certain guarantee of respect in sporting circles than the name Milburn; and his father, Jack – 'he was a slogger, like me' – had been a professional in the Tyneside Senior League. The news of his potential ran round English cricket like a bush fire; and, in negotiations followed with mounting interest in other counties, Northants engaged him by the advantage of ten shillings a week over Warwickshire.

He went into the second XI for his qualifying summer and the start of the next season when 201 not out, in a total of 256 against Middlesex second XI, and three more centuries – one of them before lunch – took him into the first team. It was always a highly important aspect of Colin Milburn's cricket that he was not a taker of cheap runs. In only his second county game, at the age of nineteen, he made 63 with a six and eleven fours, of a total of 125 for a losing side against Surrey.

Soon, though, he was sent back to the seconds for a couple of faults to be corrected. He suffered from the healthy but not wholly justified belief that he could belt anything out of sight. In time he became more, but never completely, wary in his choice of the ball to hit. He was, too, vulnerable to off-spin. This probably was less a matter of technique than of physique; if, when he played a stroke, his arms passed over his stomach there was bound to be a wide 'gate' between bat and pads; he had to learn to close it by straddling rather than orbiting his midriff.

Cricketing authority could never bring itself to forgive his fatness, and undoubtedly his weight cost him a number of Test caps. Except in 1963, when he trained and fasted down to sixteen-and-a-half stone, he hardly ever played at much less than eighteen stone. He was fat for the only good reason – he enjoyed eating and drinking too much to deny himself either. This did not prevent him from fielding nimbly and bravely at short leg and, until back trouble precluded it, bowling usefully at medium pace: but, though he was a useful rugby player, he could not run.

In 1962 he established his county place with another innings played 'against the tide', 102 of a total of 182 – only one other batsman made double figures – against a strong Derbyshire bowling side at Buxton. When he was capped in the following season he was, by this time, almost everybody's favourite cricketer.

Figures began to emphasize the power of his attack: three times he scored the fastest century of the season: he hit seven sixes and fourteen fours in 123 against Yorkshire: seven sixes and fifteen fours in 152 not out (two-thirds of the side's total) off Gloucestershire: in an opening partnership of 157 against Notts he made 113 in thirty-eight scoring strokes: for MCC v Kenya Kongonis on the 1963 tour of East Africa he took an over from N. G. Shuttleworth, hit each of the first five balls for six and was caught on the long-off boundary from the last.

Statistically his best season was 1966 when, but for a broken finger, he would almost certainly have made two thousand runs (in the event he had 1861, averaging 49.47): he hit six centuries – three before lunch – and played four times for England against West Indies.

In his first Test innings he was run out for 0; in the second, when England followed on, he mounted a characteristic attack, went from 88 to 94 with a six off Gibbs and then hit across the line and was bowled. At Lord's he was lbw to Hall for 6 in the first innings but, when England needed 284 to win in four hours – of which one was lost to rain – were reduced to 67 for four and the injured Graveney came in to prevent a hat-trick, Milburn savaged the West Indian bowling. He hit Holford, Gibbs and Hall for sixes as well as scoring seventeen fours and made 126 not out in three hours.

In the Fourth Test a lifter from Hall damaged his left elbow but, batting virtually one-handed, he made 29 not out and the highest-but-one score, 42, of the second innings. Left out of the last Test he opened the Northants innings with 203, the highest score of his life until then, against Essex.

That winter, and again in 1968–69, he played for Western Australia for whom he scored his first century in seventy-seven minutes and his 243 (181 between lunch and tea) against Queensland was the highest score in the state's history.

Many of Colin Milburn's innings were played before small crowds; but the best was not. Chosen for the second Australian Test of 1968 after England had lost the first, he came in at number three on a lively wicket with the score at 10 for one. Although he was constantly and painfully hit – the ball thudded into him like a cannon ball into a sandbag – he held on with Boycott until Friday when the pitch had improved. When Lawry brought on Cowper, whose off-breaks had unsettled England in the First Test, Milburn hooked his first ball toweringly into the grand stand for six. In less than an hour and a half he made 68 before, in the attempt to hit off Gleeson, he was caught from a huge hit to square leg; his 83 was the highest score of the match on either side. Almost immediately afterwards he sustained a wrist injury and did not play again in the series until the last Test when, although he scored no more than 8 and 18, he undermined each Australian innings with an early catch at short leg.

He played only once more for England. In March 1969, on his way back from a season with Western Australia, he joined MCC in Pakistan and played an innings of 139 in the Third Test which was ended by a riot.

He began the English season of 1969 explosively with 82 not out – sharing a partnership of 95 in forty-nine minutes with Tony Greig – for MCC against Yorkshire; 158 – with five sixes and sixteen fours – in the Northants-Leicestershire match; and a shrewd beginning of 42 and two useful catches when Northants beat West Indies.

After that match ended, the meeting took place which made Colin Milburn financially secure if he remained with Northants; this was what he wanted. When we parted, after a last drink at the bar, it seemed all his foreseeable problems were solved. Next morning I woke in Manchester to read in my paper that he had lost the sight of an eye. After the sickening personal pain it seemed, trying to stand back from the event, that English cricket – in strength, image and attraction – had suffered a desperate and irreparable loss. Time has confirmed that impression. Milburn himself has confirmed what everyone always felt about him as a man, by putting up a front of uncomplaining even cheerful resolution in face of the cruellest blow he could have suffered.

*Testimonial Brochure*, 1971

# Derek Randall

## *He Reminds Us of Our Own Mortality*

*May* 1983. The recurrent complaint of the cricketing malcontents – 'Of course, there are no characters in the game today' – is conclusively rebuffed by the two words 'Derek Randall'. Not merely a character, but an engaging one; and a rewarding cricketer. There are many capable players; but few of whom it may be said, as of him, that the game, its image and its atmosphere, are the better for his presence.

We probably have not yet seen the best of him; he is still only thirty-two; and might yet add technical stability to his other assets. Meanwhile, for all his capacity to delight, he has never quite established himself firmly as a Test cricketer: a fact which has kept him, and his admirers, on tenterhooks for six years. Certainly, though, he has won respect, and even affection – not unmixed with humour – in several cricketing countries.

It is now eleven years since he entered the first-class game. He remains a refreshing person to meet in an age of generally accepted scruffiness, offhandedness and even cynicism. The Derek Randall of 1972, not so far different from his 1983 self, was boyish, fresh, well-scrubbed and trim; proud of the new Retford blazer he had bought to make his entry into the county game.

He already had the Pinocchio-type width of shoulder and extreme looseness of limb that he has exploited in superb movement in the field and much of his best clowning. All his flowing motion belies the handicap of his boat-like size elevens, which are, oddly, not obtrusive in one only 5ft 8in tall. He is a spontaneous character, above all in his eagerness in the field, where his enthusiasm, speed, sureness of grip, and fiercely flat and accurate throwing save runs and take wickets. By his immense élan, too, he so fires any team he plays in that even the pragmatic Len Hutton thought him worth his Test place for his fielding alone.

Randall's cricket is so obviously played from the heart, and for fun, that one rarely thinks of him as a record-breaker. Yet he has to his credit a number of achievements justly the pride of a native-born Notts cricketer. To begin – but not to end – with, he has played in more Test matches for England – thirty-seven – than any other Notts cricketer. Shaw, Shrewsbury, the two Hardstaffs, George, William and John Gunn, Larwood, Voce, Reggie Simpson; he leads them all. Moreover, his 174 against Australia in the Centenary Test of 1977 at Melbourne (what a stage to choose) was the highest Test score by a Notts batsman. His double-century and century (209 and 146) in the same match (against Middlesex, 1979) is also a county record, and the only occasion the feat has been performed at Trent Bridge.

Remarkably for one so dedicated to the game, he came relatively late to it. He played hardly at all in his schooldays, but afterwards, encouraged by his father, a keen club cricketer, he joined Retford in the Bassetlaw League. His captain there – and then of Notts Second XI – was Michael Hall, and in 1968, at seventeen, Randall was chosen for the county Colts side. The next year he stepped up an important level to the second XI. He made an unremarkable beginning, with 0 and 9, but the authorities were sufficiently impressed to take him on the staff for 1970. In that apprentice summer, with helpful guidance from Frank Woodhead and Garfield Sobers – both impressed by his keenness and talent – he learnt voraciously and well. He averaged 29; and took three wickets with his medium-pace seam-up. Surprisingly, that was virtually the end of his bowling career. One would have expected one of his bubbling enthusiasm to bowl furiously fast; or very slow with prodigious spin.

The next season his fielding took him into the first team for a single John Player match in which he was not required to bat. He came of cricketing age in 1972 when, at twenty-one, he entered first-class cricket. It happened at Newark-on-Trent, which is about as near a home Championship match as is possible for a young man from Retford.

He went in at number seven and *Wisden*, unusually expansively, reported 'a dazzling display by the twenty-one-year-old Randall from Retford, making his County Championship début. He showed outstanding maturity in an innings of two hours twenty minutes, during which he hit five sixes and four fours in his 78.' He could hardly have been expected to maintain that standard; but averaged 22 and scored his first century for the second XI. In a poor season for the county – they won only one match, and finished fourteenth – his spectacular fielding and frequent clean, free hitting made him one of the bright spots of the Trent Bridge scene.

A bound forward in 1973 brought his first Championship century; the imprimatur of a thousand runs in the season; and selection for Young England against West Indies at Old Trafford. He had made á 'pair' for Notts against the West Indians at Trent Bridge; and now, in his first selection at international level, he came in at 30 for four which soon was 38 for five, against Shillingford in full cry, Julien and Gibbs. Rising to the challenge, he put on 93 with David Bairstow before, at 47, characteristically, he went down the wicket to drive Willett and was stumped.

1974 proved his all but inevitable fallback year; but, of course, he always had his fielding to commend him; and he soon took up the thread of advance. Again he made his thousand in 1975; and the critics began to talk of 'maturity' and 'consistency'.

West Indies were again the touring team in 1976, and Randall was accorded the hint of selectorial interest when he was picked for MCC against the tourists; he made 1 and 5 in a well-beaten side, and was not picked for a Test. He was, though, brought in at Lord's for the second of the one-day internationals. West Indies had won the first all too easily. Now they made 221; and Andy Roberts, in a burst of high speed, had cut England down to 31 for four when Randall came in. He has rarely batted better. *Wisden* commented: 'England again found consolation in defeat in the performance of one of their young batsmen. This time it was Randall, who successfully challenged the West Indies fast bowlers with a thrilling innings of 88 which included a six and ten fours. He drove their fielders back to the boundary boards in a manner achieved by no other English batsman during the summer.' The next-highest English score was 22. West Indies won again; and in the third match, when Randall's 39, off 31 balls, brought him the English 'Man of the Series' award.

That took him to India, where 37 on his Test début proved his highest score of the series; his fielding – a valuable contribution to England's success – kept him in the side.

So, on to Melbourne; where the Centenary match was his first Test against Australia, and England were set an 'impossible' 463 to win. It was Randall's occasion: his clowning humoured the potential menace of the 'Ockers': and his quite splendid innings of 174 – impressive for its concentration, soundness, bravery and frequent handsome strokes – took England to within 45 runs of a stronger and more confident side.

That was, and remains, the high peak of his achievement, and it, plus his fielding, earned his Test place through 1977 when, at Headingley, he set his inimitable stamp on the winning of the Ashes by catching Marsh to decide the rubber and instantly celebrating by turning an exuberant cartwheel.

On the Pakistan-New Zealand tour of 1977–78 a run of ordinary scores filled him with anxiety – for he is essentially a modest man – reflected in fidgeting and, above all, the shuffle across the crease which so often found him off balance when the ball arrived. He played in the one-day internationals, though not the Tests of 1978; and, after a successful Notts season, was chosen for the following tour of Australia of 1978–79; there, under Brearley's captaincy, he played three valuable Test innings, a ten-hour 150 at Sydney the most valuable of them.

In 1979 he had a good county season but little success against India. Probably his good heart and fine fielding found him a place to Australia in 1979–80, but his two Tests – going in first in one and third in the other – showed an average of only 6.5. So – as some might have found a relief – there was no place for him against the West Indian pace battery of 1980; nor Australia in 1981. That sorely disappointed him; though Notts' Championship win was considerable consolation. One of only two men to score a thousand runs in their season, and second in the averages, he played a significant part in five of their twelve wins. Neither was he called on for the Indian tour of 1981–82, and it seemed to some that his Test career was ended.

Renewed opportunity came with the exclusion of the South African defectors. In 1982 he averaged 73 against India; but, despite a probably decisive century at Edgbaston, only 28 against Pakistan. These, though, were winning series for England and he went to Australia in Bob Willis's losing side last winter. At last – surely – steady on those mighty feet, and, once again, of great heart in adversity, he finished top of the Test averages (45.63).

He has, though, never felt truly secure in the Test team. He is the oddest mixture of uncertainty and hectic overconfidence. Somewhere between the two, and especially when his side is in peril, he is a balanced, shrewd player; a natural batsman whose judgement is reliable; his defence sound, his strokes flowingly appropriate to the bowled ball.

Some cricketers seem (whatever they may feel) above ordinary falli-bility. Derek Randall, like Denis Compton – or even more – reminds the ordinary spectator of his own mortality. When he overplays his hand, and falls into disaster, the watcher understands and feels for him. Sometimes he attempts, sadly, to rationalize his weakness. 'I haven't got a long reach,' he says, 'so I move across the stumps so that the ball is on my legs where my strength lies.' In fact he *has* got a long reach; and he is handsomely strong on the off side. When he hooks the bouncer off his chin, or drives through the covers with the power of perfect timing, then the average cricketer is delighted. When he comes racing in from cover (where his speed of reaction and movement allow him to stand appreciably closer than most), sweeps up the ball and throws down the wicket with the outwitted and outpaced batsman fatally stranded, then even an opposing crowd rises spontaneously in recognition of his particular brand of genius.

For, let there be no mistake of it, he has genius. He also has doubt, self-doubt; on the bad days, it, and the suffering, are to be seen in those large, honest eyes. He worries; and when he worries, his friends worry with him; when he exults, so do they. This summer in his native county the exultation and the sympathy will be reflected in his benefit fund.

*Wisden Cricket Monthly*

# 4
# The Village Game

## Village Cricket

Village cricket is a serious matter. Once it was considered clever to make jokes about it. A. G. Macdonell's extremely funny passage in *England, Their England* is generally described as an account of a funny village cricket match. That, though, is not true. It is the funny story of a team of what the villagers would have called 'toffs', coming down to make fun of village cricket.

Villagers do not think village cricket is funny; they do not play it for fun, they play it to win. Indeed, it may well be that they know more about cricket than anyone else, for the first cricket was the village cricket of the Kent and Sussex Weald. Hambledon was not the 'birthplace of cricket' as some have said, nor the first great club, but thanks to Nyren's studies, 'The Cricketers of My Time', it is the first cricket team of which we have any detailed knowledge. Between 1772 and 1881, Hambledon were strong enough to beat All England twenty-nine times out of fifty-one matches played for five hundred guineas a side. Nyren makes it clear not that this was a village club but that the players were village people – the potter from Odiham; the farmers from Thursley near the Devil's Punchbowl; the inn-keeper from North Chapel; the Hambledon builder and shoemaker; the off-break bowler who learnt his skill while tending his father's sheep.

They were not simple rustics but something – much – more; men with the manual dexterity not always demanded of a farmer or a publican nowadays, but necessary for their work in the eighteenth century.

For hundreds of years village life in England was virtually static. In the days before railways or motor cars many country people did not go more than seven or eight miles from the place where they were born in their entire lifetimes. The same names occurred in the parish registers generation after generation; and the cricket matches with two or three neighbouring villages – and with one particular rival – might well be the longest journey many of the players made in a whole year. These were important occasions with some grandsons and great-grandsons following the first player of the family into these matches which were the major sporting events of the local year.

A budding local cricket historian recently wrote to express his surprise at the low scores made in many village matches in the nineteenth century, and to demand reasons why teams were so often bowled out for twenty or thirty runs. No village cricketer of forty years ago would have been in the least surprised. The first reason, of course, was rough pitches. More than one village side in north Hampshire was reputed to spend the winter coaxing plantains or bents to grow about the length spot of their main fast bowler. Equally, though, the tenets of orthodox and, therefore, sound batting are more complex – and less natural – than those of accurate bowling. So, while batsmen tended to swing 'naturally' across the line there were always bowlers who bowled a length and line; and some who were in relation to the opposing batting (which is not a matter of strength) genuinely fast. Certainly between the two wars many village teams in the south of England had men who still bowled in the old, roundarm fashion of the days before overarm was legalized, in 1864. They could drop on a length, and, on the roughly mown and rolled turf, they would wear away a spot from which the ball might do anything.

Village life, though, changes. Most of the former villagers now work in towns and they live in towns where they find facilities and the trimmings of leisure more readily available. Meanwhile the majority of the former labourers' cottages are now splendidly white-washed, their gardens embellished with plaster dwarves, their doors with polished brass knockers and hand bells; carriage lamps and porticos: and they are occupied by the retired, weekenders or commuters. The people who need to live in the village – the few traders, farmers and farm labourers – occupy the shop premises, farmhouses and adequately modern houses built out of the money paid to the farmer-owner for the thatched cottage which the worker found inadequate and, often, insanitary.

Similarly, many of the people who play cricket in villages come from towns. The village teams no longer share three pairs of pads, and gloves, and two bats. The new villagers demand properly prepared pitches. It is all far more sophisticated than it was; but, then, so is all village life; and cricket reflects its background. Village cricket is not what it was: but nothing is. *The Haig Village Cricket Annual*, 1977

# Alresford's Famous Cricketers

'Alresford' wrote Mary Russell Mitford 'will always be famous for two things; first for that it was my birthplace, second, for its cricketers.' When the town's most illustrious native set down those words in the mid-nineteenth century, though, Alresford's great days as a centre of cricket were already past. Between about 1770 and 1795, however, it stood higher in cricket than any town of its size has done in the history of the game. It saw some of the finest matches, and all the most distinguished players, of the period. Indeed, in that period, Alresford was second in Hampshire cricket only to Hambledon, and Hambledon was second to none in the world. Hambledon, though, even in its finest days, was happy to include Alresford players.

Between 1772 and 1796, the club known sometimes as Hampshire, more generally as Hambledon, met All England in sixty-six matches and won thirty-eight of them. They played generally for five hundred guineas a side, and it has been estimated that Hambledon won £22,497 10s to £10,030 in match-stakes alone. Worked out in modern values, of course, those were fortunes but in the obsessional gambling of the Regency period, many times more money than that depended on side-bets.

Hambledon has been called 'the birthplace of cricket': it certainly was not. Organized, and highly skilful, cricket was played much earlier in Kent, London, Sussex and Surrey. Hambledon, though, was the first consistently great club, probably the greatest in the history of the game. It is, too, the earliest of which we have substantial knowledge, thanks to the recollections, entitled 'The Cricketers of My Time', which John Nyren, one of its players, set down in his old age.

It would be a mistake to think of Hambledon simply as a village cricket team. It was a private club of noblemen and country gentry. Some of them occasionally appeared in matches but, like their London successors, White Conduit and MCC, they employed professionals to carry out their main fixtures. That was the only possible realistic attitude when such huge stakes were involved.

The professionals were drawn from as far afield – by the standards of eighteenth-century communications – as Odiham, Alresford, North Chapel (Sussex), Farnham, Alton and, even, in the case of James Bayley, Mitcham. They were recruited by one of the earliest systems of athletic talent spotting and, in one of the first professional team operations, managed and trained to a high level of proficiency. They were paid travelling expenses not only for matches, but to take part in pre-season and regular weekly practice sessions.

The standing of Alresford in the cricket world of Georgian and Regency times is indicated by the fact that a number of the Hambledon matches – including even major fixtures with England – were played there.

In the latter half of the eighteenth century there were four cricket grounds in Alresford. The chief was Stoke Down, reached by a sunken lane from the road junction at Abbotstone. It is now part of Itchen Down Farm. Another used for important games was Tichborne Down where the ground coincided then with the racecourse, and, now, with the fifth (former fourth) hole of the golf course, and the field to the south of it. A report of 1780 refers to 'the new laid ground' at Alresford; that was The Nythe, on drained land between the Pond and the Bighton Road. Fourth of the old pitches was at Fob Down, now part of Fobdown farm; it, too, has been ploughed up. There was also a private ground at the Grange in Northington: but the present Old Alresford ground, in Bighton Road, is substantially later than any of the others.

Hambledon teams of the great period included seven Alresford men. Veck, Taylor and Andrew Freemantle appeared quite regularly in major Hambledon matches; John Freemantle from time to time; Cole, Hall and Thomas Skinner on a few occasions. An eighth was 'poached'. John Crawte had the reputation, as a batsman, of playing David Harris – the outstanding bowler of the day – better than anyone else. 'Silver Billy' Beldham of Hambledon related that Crawte 'was taken away from our parish of Alresford by Mr Amherst, the gentleman who made the Kent matches'.

Tom Taylor was ranked by Nyren in the finest eleven of Hambledon cricket history. A considerable allrounder, he constantly took useful wickets; was an attacking batsman and, at cover-point, his speed in gathering, and accuracy of return, ran out many men on what appeared safe singles. He was born at Ropley, in 1753, but lived for much of his life at Alresford where he kept the Globe Inn, and regularly appeared for Alresford in matches played for stakes. A brilliant cutter, he was said to take risks – and often lose his wicket – by playing that stroke at a ball too near the stumps. Nyren, in his summing-up, thought Taylor 'had an excellent general knowledge of the game; but of fielding, in particular, he was perfect both in judgement and practice. He was a short, well-made man, strong and as watchful and active as a cat; but in no other instance will that comparison hold good, for he was without guile, and was an attached friend.' He died in 1806 and was buried at Old Alresford.

Richard Aubery Veck, born in New Alresford, played in 'grand' matches for only nine seasons. A highly talented cricketer, he played for Hambledon – unusually early by the standards of the time – when he was barely twenty. He was a reliable and consistent batsman but at twenty-nine, entering the usual prime of a batsman's career, he married, gave up the game, and moved to Bishops Waltham.

There, in Haygarth's words, he 'engaged in mercantile pursuits'; and became the main draper, hosier and undertaker of the town. Obviously he prospered. His son, whom he was able to send to university, entered the church and became 'perpetual curate' of Alverstoke. Richard Veck died at Bishops Waltham but was buried, in a handsome vault, at Old Alresford.

The Freemantle brothers, Andrew and John, were born in Bishops Sutton, but they and their sons, nephews and grandsons played for Alresford for the better part of a century. The younger brother, Andrew, was, in the sporting 'cant' of the day, 'one of the cracks'. As a regular player for Hambledon, he had a remarkably long – twenty-three-year – career on the highest level as a left-hand batsman and safe deepfield. In the days before wicket-keepers wore gloves or stood back, he often fielded long stop – so well that the Reverend James Pycroft wrote: 'Freemantle brought the province of long stop to perfection, never suffering a ball to pass, and covering a great deal of ground.' Nyren wrote of him, 'a shortish, well-set man, he was an uncommonly safe as well as a good hitter; and few wickets that I could name were more secure than Andrew's. He would often get long hands, and against the best bowling, too; and once he had warmed into his hitting, it was a deuced hard matter to get him out. Andrew Freemantle could be depended upon, whatever he might undertake, whether in cricket or in his worldly dealings.'

In his early thirties he moved to Easton where he took the Bat and Ball Inn; and worked as a carpenter. After he died, his elder son, Henry, took over the inn and another, George, lived in Winchester; both played for Alresford.

Andrew's elder brother, John, early became a master builder in Alresford. Stoutly built and fairly tall, he was reckoned good enough cricketer to play at times for Hambledon. Nyren recalled that 'He delivered his ball high and well and tolerably fast; as a batter he would have been reckoned a good hand in any club. As a man, he bore a high character for straightforward, manly integrity; in short, he was a hearty John Bull, and flinched no more from doing his duty than he did from a ball in the field, and this he never did, however hard it might hit him.'

Some indication of Alresford's standing about this time can be gathered from the press, though usually through announcements – in effect, advertisements – of matches to be played than from reporting of the scores or even of results. For instance, in 1778 Hambledon announced home and out matches – on level terms and with no 'given' players – with Alresford for fifty guineas a match. In the next year, Alresford, with two Hambledon men given, met the combined sides of Farnham, Alton and Odiham (with one given man from Yateley) for a silver cup. In 1780, a match was made for twenty-two guineas between Odiham with Noah Mann of Hambledon against Alresford with Taylor and Veck. In 1782 Alresford and Odiham combined, played the County of Southampton. There were frequent matches between Old Alresford and New, usually won by the latter; but for some fixtures they joined forces.

A rare match report – though of 'news' rather than strictly cricketing interest – appeared in *The Hampshire Chronicle* of 29 August 1774:

> 'On *Friday, August 5th* – on Tichborne Down, Alresford v Alton and Chawton – only two innings and a part of the third were played. The game ran in favour of the united parishes. It is imagined it will never be decided, as the Alresford gentlemen would not conform to the custom coeval with the game itself, viz. of playing it out the next day on the same ground when it is not finished on the first; which the opposite party were very desirous of doing.
> 'The reason generally assigned is that, not having lost a match the whole summer, they were determined to preserve their fame entire throughout the season, and being now in danger of losing the day, struck upon the above expedient to evade the decision of it.'

Alresford's reply, published a week later, read:

> 'The Alton and Chawton party sent word on Friday morning that they would not come to play as the weather was bad, but they came afterwards, two hours past the time appointed, to the great surprise of the Alresford party who were so dispersed that it was nearly one o'clock before they could get their side.
> 'The other side should have forfeited their deposit money. The next day, Saturday, two of the Alresford mates could not play, but they offered to play it out on the Monday following or any other day.'

Alresford are rarely seen in quite such an unfavourable light. In 1775, according to *The Hampshire Chronicle*, 'On August 28th at Stephens Castle Green, New Alresford beat Bishops Waltham with two given men by nine wickets. This is the first match lost by the Waltham Cricketers these last two years.' Later that summer New Alresford beat 'Odiham with three picked men from Farnham and Bentley' by 26 runs. An even more impressive fixture was 'On Wednesday June 19th, 1776, on Tichborne Down, Alresford with three of Waltham and two of Warnford v Petersfield and Catherington with the famous Messrs Small, Brett and Barber and H. Bonham Esq.' Although no result is recorded, these matches, invariably played for wagers, were based on teams of more or less even strength; and to set three such eminent Hambledon players on the other side means that Alresford must have been immensely powerful.

These cricketers were the sporting heroes of a county; virtually of a country. Nyren wrote of a Hambledon match 'Half the county would be present, and all their hearts with us. Little Hambledon against All England was a proud thought for the Hampshire men.'

At the end of the eighteenth century, the wealthy gentry of the Hambledon Club, who had already left Broad-Halfpenny Down for Windmill Down – barely less bleak but conveniently nearer the village – finally decided London was more in tune with their social taste. So White Conduit and MCC came into being; and, soon, into control of the cricket world. The Hambledon and Alresford professionals – and the skill of many of them impressively withstood the sapping of age – went on to play on Thomas Lord's different grounds, and at White Conduit.

Of course, cricket continued at Alresford, as at Hambledon, but it no longer stood at the high peak of its world. It was symbolic of the passing of an age when, in 1835, the 'old' Cricketers Inn was advertised for sale. It was the building, subsequently a laundry, now a private house, at the corner of Sun Lane and Tichborne Down. The advertisement in *The Hampshire Chronicle* read: 'To be sold; CRICKETERS INN, NEW ALRESFORD. This spot is well known as the most favourite place of amusement in that part of the county; and has been in the present proprietor's and occupier's family upwards of seventy years. Apply to Mr William Freeman on the premises.'

The production of Taylor, Veck, Andrew and John Freemantle, Cole, Skinner, Hall – and, arguably, Crawte as well – by Alresford (Old and New) with a population of only eleven thousand, was equivalent, nowadays, to turning out eight Test players in thirty years: a prodigious feat.

On into the Victorian period, Alresford remained a strong cricket club; good enough to beat Southampton and Alton; even to stage, and win, single-wicket spectaculars on Tichborne Down; and there were still Freemantles and Skinners to play. Even then, though, it was clear that the great days – and history confirms that they were, indeed, great – had ended with the eighteenth century.

*Alresford Displayed*, Winter 1978–79

# Dicker

'Cricket at the Dicker' – the words have the ring of history about them. For, thanks to the patient researches of Dr H. F. Squire of Henfield, every cricket reader knows that, in June 1677 the Keeper of the accounts of Lord Sussex 'pd to my Lord when his LordP went to the crekitt match at ye Dicker 03.00.00'.

That is not the earliest reference to a cricket match – that was at Coxheath in Kent in 1646 – but it is unlikely that it was the first at the Dicker. Indeed, it is hard not to believe that many years, probably centuries, earlier, cricket was born in these very parts. On the sheep-cropped turf about the Weald and the Downs, surely, one shepherd boy bowled a ball of sheep's wool, gummed solid with the red ochre they used for marking the sheep, at another, who defended the hurdle gate of the sheepfold with his crook and, upon opportunity, hit the ball far away and laughed while the bowler chased it.

If cricket began in that way, it is the natural game it has always seemed.

Perhaps, indeed, to congratulate the Dicker Club on its three hundredth, and wish it well for the next three hundred, is a considerable underestimate.                         *Dicker Club Centenary Book*

# Mayfield

There are stronger cricket teams than Mayfield [Sussex], but none, surely, with a more lovely name, and few with a longer history than that which stretches back – at least – to 28 May 1750, when Mayfield played Burwash. May their next two or three – or more – hundred years be prosperous and, if this old cricketing chestnut contributes to their gaiety in 1966, it will be a small token of my good wishes:

The incoming batsman was resplendent in completely new gear and he bore a bat unblemished by ball marks. He took guard somewhat negligently, imperiously ordered the sightscreen to be moved – and then moved back to its original position – before he settled to a stance apparently loosely adapted from that of W. G. Grace. The first ball slipped from the laughing bowler's hand and bounced gently down the leg side untouched by any of the batsman's several efforts to hit it. The next was a full toss which he attempted to cut and missed; the next, a half-volley, at which he aimed the same stroke some seconds after his middle stump had gone down. For the first time he looked round the field, in valediction rather than enquiry, sighed and departed. As he did so, first slip turned to the wicket-keeper and asked, 'How do you suppose he know's he's right-handed?'

*Mayfield Cricket Club: A History* 1866–1966 *(R. Bradfield)*

# Caterham

Caterham Cricket Club is a remarkably lusty hundred-year-old stripling. Although it celebrates its centenary as a club in 1973, Caterham, under Henry Rowed – called 'the Golden Farmer' because he wore a gold-laced hat in the field – played against Hambledon, the strongest club in England, over two hundred years ago. A contemporary report of their third, deciding, fixture at Guildford in 1769 said: 'There were near 20,000 spectators and it was generally allowed by the best judges to have been the finest match that ever was played.'

That is a great legacy to have inherited; may this history cherish it and the club enjoy and sustain it for as long again.

*Cricket in Caterham: A Brief History*
*(N. Turk and G. Charman, 1973)*

# Kingsclere

Kingsclere Cricket Club is unique. All cricket clubs, like all gatherings of human beings, are unique because their members are individuals – all themselves and different. Kingsclere Cricket Club, though, is unusual – in fact doubly unique – as – surely – the only club to celebrate its centenary and its bi-centenary in successive years.

To be accurate, the playing of a cricket match by a team calling itself 'Kingsclere' and the creation of a club of that name, are likely to have been two separate happenings. What matter? Kingsclere played a match in 1774 – against Uffington 'for a silver cup' – and the Kingsclere club was founded in 1845. Both are events worthy of celebration, not every hundred years but every year – or every day. For a gathering of cricketers to have existed for two hundred years – or two hundred days – is something to celebrate, for it has made and given pleasure – and that is the purpose of any game.

May the Kingsclere members and their guests be as happy in celebrating their bi-centenary as they were the year before – when their history – though not their company – was a hundred years younger.

*200 Years of Cricket in Kingsclere*, 1774–1974
*(ed. C. Garrett and D. Sember)*

# Baldock

It is a pleasure to introduce this centenary brochure of the Baldock Cricket Club. Presumably it means the centenary of the present club: if not, Baldock is being at least forty years modest.

According to G. B. Buckley's researches, on Monday, 3 July 1837, Baldock played at Biggleswade, where they beat the local team most heavily. Baldock scored 153 (G. Stockton 48, W. Hill 30) and 131 (John Mead 30) and bowled out Biggleswade for 67 (Robert Bloom six wickets) and for 9 in their second innings – John Little took five wickets; there were two absentees and six other 'ducks'. A fortnight afterwards they went to Royston and beat them by an innings and 72 runs. Baldock made 130 (Thomas Harvey 27); Royston 32 (Robert Bloom five wickets) and 26 (John Little five wickets). In 1840 on the Thursday and Monday, 24 and 28 September – presumably evening play – they beat Welwyn at Welwyn: Baldock 42 and 98 (Thomas Harvey top scorer in each innings with 15 and 23) and Welwyn 43 and 49 (John Little four wickets). How many descendants of those players are still in Baldock?

A century of cricket is a great deal of fun and excitement. May Baldock's next hundred – or hundred and forty one – be as good.

· *Baldock Town CC Centenary Year (ed. R. Gazely, 1979)*

# Sturry

The compliment of being asked to write the foreword to another man's book is always pleasant. To write the foreword to a cricket club history is, too, rewarding. Big cricket is news; but, of its very nature, it can rarely be quite so warmly human as club cricket. The Sturry Cricket Club has not, by some standards, made cricket history. Yet Mr Butler can record some fine performances by the team. Above all he reflects, without needing, or heeding, to stress it, the human warmth of English club cricket, especially in the south.

In the counties of Kent, Surrey, Sussex and Hampshire, where the game was born and where it grew to strength, it retains a quality which is unique. In other counties – even in the north of England – there is often complete failure to understand it. Once, some Australians, pressing the case for their 'Grade' cricket, demanded to know what I considered the merit of English village cricket. There was only one possible reply: 'In village cricket, the poor player is not only tolerated – there are at least two places for him in every side.' They did not, I fancy, believe me. Cricket for them was essentially combative. My own experience of village cricket is that it, too, can be fiercely combative – but not only combative. Even in its Evening League triumphs, did not Sturry sometimes include a man because he was a good chap – and keen? (Though not, perhaps, against the Beverley in 1901!)

In this workmanlike and friendly history of his club, Mr Butler may not have written a source book for cricket historians of the future. But he has, by implication, shown his kind of cricket to be the most human in the world. The wider historians, of a later and more highly technical day, may well read the History of the Sturry Cricket Club with nostalgia, if not with envy. In short, it needs no commendation from me, only my thanks for being allowed to share in celebrating its centenary.

*100 Years of Sturry Cricket (D. R. Butler, 1963)*

# Oxton

It is a compliment to be asked to contribute the foreword to the centenary [1875–1975] handbook of the Oxton Cricket Club – and a pleasure for one of its long-ago visitors to write it. There must be thousands more club histories of cricket than of any other sport. That can only be because more people see the game as more memorable than happens in other fields.

It is understandable that the great clubs – the counties or such historic and formative-stage names as Hambledon, Sevenoaks Vine, IZ, or MCC – should have histories. The impressive aspect is the number of ordinary clubs with their own books. They may – invariably do – contain record team and individual successes. Above all, though, they evoke nostalgic memories, recall each local generation's heroes – and provide a record of the happiness the game gives. A cricket club is a nucleus such as no other sport possesses in comparable numbers; a boy may grow up in its shadow, to play in his manhood, and watch in his old age in a continuity he could hardly expect of other games. That, surely, is why cricket histories abound – and why it will be a sad day for cricket when they cease to be written.

May Oxton continue to flourish – and give its members the same continuity of pleasure – in its second century as in its first.

# Waterloo Park

By producing books, rather than plated trophies, cricket proves its high standard of civilization, and to be asked to write a foreword to a cricket book is for me an honour within my own field.

I reach my peak of delight in writing in honour of a club – in this case the Waterloo Park Club – planned and run for sixty years – to the end of giving ordinary people pleasure. Moreover, club cricket is the real, the essential, cricket; without it neither Test cricket nor county cricket could ever have begun.

Possibly there has never been greater cricket – certainly no cricket has ever been more gloriously recorded – than the eighteenth-century club cricket Hambledon played on the downs above the Meon Valley: that club of country craftsmen could – and often did – beat All England. I used to play with a club of men of the same Wessex blood: we once went a whole season without totalling 60 runs in any innings: we enjoyed our cricket, too.

The Diamond Jubilee of a cricket club is a great occasion, far more important than the winning of a Test match – if not so sensational – for it marks sixty years of giving happiness. The result of a Test match, on the other hand, may be *News*, but outside the world of cricket it is not of the slightest importance. Hitler, one understands, believed that the outrunning of an Englishman by a German in 440 yards proved the English to be a decadent race. Of course it proved nothing of the sort, and no human inference should be drawn from an English defeat – or victory – in a Test match. Cricket is a game: its purpose is enjoyment, not a form of nationalist propaganda.

The great triumphs of the Waterloo Park Cricket Club do not lie in matches won, or centuries scored, or wickets bowled down, but in the warming recollections of men now past their playing days when they recall old matches played and enjoyed even though the scores are forgotten. The great scores recorded here, the mighty performances of men who strove hard at their Saturday afternoon play after a week of work – these figures are only the greatest in the club's annals if they brought the men who produced them the greatest happiness.

For my part, I ask you to remember with this book the humblest, most occasional player the club ever had, a man who one day took a catch, or threw down a wicket, or scraped a ball off the inside edge of his bat to achieve double figures, and who remembers that moment as one of simple but unalloyed joy; or, perhaps, a small boy, who, like all of us when small boys, looked up to mere mortal club cricketers, such as ourselves, as his gods, and who grew up to play no better than we do, but to find that the divinity of club cricket lies not in the technical excellence of performance, but in the pleasure of playing a game with bats and balls in the sunshine – or even in the rain – and doing it only because we like it. Therein lies the real wealth – not to be measured in averages, but, in the days of dimming eyes and stiffening muscles, as a cache of simple and unmixed delight.

This, for the benefit of readers whose memories are short, set out to be a preface: if it fell into a sermon, it did so only in its attempt at self-justification before drinking the introductory toast of the Waterloo Park Cricket Club and all who ever played for it, or against it, or who watched it, or in any way shared in the pleasure which it is the true and only purpose of a cricket club to give.

*History of Waterloo Park Cricket Club* 1890–1950
*(J. Mathews and F. B. Davidson)*

## Wrea Green

Golden Jubilees in village cricket are both rare and enviable. Few of us will ever attain such a distinction. So there is the best kind of envy, as well as congratulation, in saluting Richard Wilson's half century with the Wrea Green Cricket Club.

May 27 August be the sunniest of days for his celebratory match. May he, too, long survive to enjoy that earliest and best kind of cricket.

*Goodwill Message*, 1979

# 5

# Some Counties and Grounds

## Watching Northants

For a small boy who lived in North Hampshire, where the local cricket club was called Basingstoke and North Hants, the earliest days of bumbling through newspapers produced an unexpected delight in the Northants scores. We all knew about Hampshire, of course – Mead and Newman and Kennedy and so on – but no one ever said anything about Northants. The puzzling part about it all was that none of our Basingstoke and North Hants players whose names were in the local weekly paper ever appeared in the scores in the dailies. When the truth was explained to me, it left me with a sense of deprivation – Thomas, Wells Buswell and Murdin had become part of my twice-removed cricket scene.

By the time I first watched Northants play, I was full of gossip and information about the players – Fanny Walden, who had been in the Tottenham Hotspur team that won the FA Cup; Vallance Jupp from Sussex, who had played for England; W. W. Timms had actually been seen at Basingstoke – a master at Charterhouse, he played for Blackwater, wearing his Quidnunc cap (the first I ever saw). Vallance Jupp was an awe-inspiring figure; he seemed perpetually busy and he made an unforgettable impression on me when I stood near him as he bowled in the nets at Southampton and, for the first time in my life, heard the spun ball positively *buzz* as it left the bowler's hand. At Northampton in 1930 he virtually won the match against Hampshire himself – with the two highest scores of the match and eleven wickets. It was all over in two days and I still recall the impact of the score read in the morning paper.

Bowlers 'Nobby' Clark and Austin Matthews had the second chance batsmen never get: but on some slow home wickets they worked hard – invariably better in double harness than apart. 'Nobby' was one of the most splendid of all fast left-arm bowlers. When he was in full cry he made the ball swing, cut back from leg and leap too savagely for the best batsmen in the world. He was three times the bowler when he was taking wickets. He could wilt when he was out of luck.

The post-war period was a story of missed opportunities. Dennis Brookes, that Yorkshire-modelled stylist had such ample batting support from Fred Jakeman, Jock Livingston, Raman Subba Row, Des Barrick and Brian Reynolds that if only the wickets at Northampton had been a yard faster, Frank Tyson, George Tribe, Jack Manning and Mick Allen must have won them the title at least once. That was the period of the most underestimated wicket-keeper of modern times, the unobtrusive Keith Andrew, whom bowlers as different as Frank Tyson and George Tribe both reckoned the best player who ever 'took' them.

One memory of Northampton lingers ineradicably: Brian Crump, most diligent of allrounders, is not on the whole renowned for hitting sixes. On the other hand, Mervyn Burden of Hampshire, while a useful off-spinner, never gained much respect as a fieldsman. Yet in the Hampshire match at Northampton in 1961, Brian Crump was twice caught on the boundary by Mervyn Burden – once at full stretch, once leaping high into the air – from strokes that would otherwise have gone for six. It has never yet been decided who was the more surprised – striker or catcher.

No aspect of English county cricket in 1971 was more interesting to observe than the spirit of the reshaping and reforming Northants side. They have the heart and the application to go far in the years ahead, and they will be the stronger for the recruitment of a world class slow left-arm bowler in Bishen Singh Bedi and Bob Cottam from Hampshire.

*Brian Crump Benefit Souvenir*, 1972

# Spectator in Sussex

To contribute to George Cox's benefit booklet [1951] is to do some little towards discharging a debt which I have owed to him ever since that day in 1935 when I watched him take a brilliant 162 off the Hampshire bowlers at Southampton. He was near to a run a minute through that innings: to watch it was to see the entire Sussex batting tradition flowering in its right setting of bright sunshine, and one stroke – a square cut – off Pothecary went down to the old scoreboard like a thunderbolt.

George, however, insists that, since so much is being written about him in this book, I write on some other subject; thus I have taken for a few lines the subject of his background – cricket in Sussex.

Although I am a Hampshire man, I am not unwilling to concede that, before Hambledon in Hampshire became the home of the 'first' cricket, there were cricketers down in Slindon capable at teaching cricket to the man – Nyren – who was to make the Hambledon club.

I remember, too, something of a cricketing beginning in my own mind when, at Eastbourne in 1927, Lancashire, at the top of the table and with the County Championship dangling before their noses, came to play Sussex. The game barely ran to the third day for, with 'Tishy' Browne at his best in their first innings, Lancashire made only 99, and then Maurice Tate rolled up his right sleeve and bowled down the wickets of that great batting side to put them out for 76 in the second knock. A win for Sussex by an innings was no more than cricketing justice. It was then that I came to understand what great bowling meant. Here, indeed, was a cricketer who could rise above anything the technician could teach. Tate bowled, the ball swung and, if the wicket was 'green', it might go the other way off the pitch, while always it leapt out of its bounce as if some explosive force were behind it.

From that match onwards, I was a Sussex supporter. Sussex folk were not the only ones in the country to regret that those vintage years under Duleep, Alan Melville and R. S. G. Scott did not gain at least one Championship.

Yet, perhaps, there was something more than performance to give my feeling for the county a quality it has never lost. It is the great virtue of cricket that it is a true reflection of the men who play it. Thus, the Weald, where cricket grew up, has always produced cricketers in the original mould. Thence come the men to whom a cricket bat or ball in the hand is as natural as any implement of any other Wealden worker.

They are men who tread considerately on good grass and play cricket with one eye on eternity. How could they do otherwise when they belong in a tradition as old as the Downs – a tradition of which cricket is a true, but a single aspect? When Jim Langridge pulls his sun-bleached cap over his eyes and resigns himself to bowling for hours at two well-set batsmen on the pacific turf of Hove, there is neither resentment nor question in his mind. Did Langridges of earlier generations begrudge the digging of the soil merely because the crop would not appear the same night? For every plumb wicket there is a more responsive one round the corner, and for every batsman who stays all day, there are five or six who relax for a second in their tenancy of the good wicket – and that moment of relaxation is enough for the flighted ball, bowled to a length and a plan, to take a wicket.

So, too, it is with their batsmen. A 'duck' today at Worthing? Ah, well, we shall try just as hard the next time and, four days hence, who shall say but that there will be a hundred good runs at Hastings?

The temper of the Weald, whether it has been bringing forth iron, coal, cattle, wool, crops, runs or wickets, has been that of the craftsman who does his job patiently and well every day. On some days the sun shines, the next, equally good work brings no reward. It is not what the scoresheet calls 'failure' that counts with your craftsman-cricketer, but a craft mastered and woven into the understanding. So long as such men play for Sussex, no cricketer will ever fail to recognize the county at the game which has its roots there.

# An Innings at Hove

Hove is pre-eminently the southern English cricket ground. It could not be anywhere else in the world; and for many Englishmen overseas it is a nostalgic memory of summer at home. Its trim whiteness and Edwardian style, the deck chairs and the drinking tables outside the Hotel can rouse north-countrymen to ire as aspects of the effete southerner; but the number of northern accents among the retirement-age members in the pavilion is a convincing counter-argument.

To the cricketers of the pre-1914 period and their followers, Hove was the batsmen's harvest field: Maurice Tate could not yet exploit the sea fret and with his glorious action, make that true turf his killing ground. There for several years about the beginning of the century, the strikingly contrasted C. B. Fry and Ranjitsinhji scored vast numbers of runs and, if they failed, there were Tim Killick, Billy Newham, George Brann and Bob Relf to build huge totals. It was said that in those days when Yorkshire or Nottinghamshire won the toss and batted, their last three or four batsmen went down to spend the day – at least until teatime – on the beach.

Hove was the scene of the most remarkable hitting innings in the history of first-class cricket – and hardly a soul saw it. 20 May 1911 was a Saturday, a 'grey day' and the last of the match between Sussex and Notts (county matches in those days were played on Monday, Tuesday and Wednesday or Thursday, Friday and Saturday). Notts, 176 behind on the first innings, seemed all but beaten on Friday evening. Certainly when Ted Alletson picked up his bat to go in fifty minutes before lunch on Saturday they were only nine in front with three wickets left. It did not seem worth anyone's while to set out on a precious Saturday after-noon to a match that was likely to be over by lunch. In fact there was only one reporter on the ground and there is fairly convincing testimony that one of the scorers lunched too well to be a reliable witness of subsequent events.

Alletson was twenty-seven years old; like his father before him, he had been a wheelwright on the Duke of Portland's estate and he was now a medium-pace bowler and lower-order batsmen who, in the six years since his first appearance, had not been able to win a regular place in the Notts side. He was over six feet tall, deep chested, wide shouldered and remarkably long-armed: his span from finger tip was six feet six inches and though the bat he used was lightweight at two pounds three ounces, its second and extra thick rubber grip meant that it could only be wielded by a man with huge hands like his.

In the fifty minutes to lunch Alletson scored 48 out of 75 and was dropped twice; Leach put out Lee and Oates. So when play began in the afternoon at the then usual time of 2.15, Notts, with one second innings wicket left, were 84 in front. What followed was never recorded or remembered with complete accuracy; but it is certain that in the forty minutes until he was out Alletson scored another 142 runs.

Although the bowling analysis is missing from the Sussex scorebook, and that in the Nottingham book has been inked over, there seems no doubt that he hit eight sixes and twenty-three fours. No figures are more significant than that, in the after-lunch period, 70 balls were bowled; Riley the other batsman played only 19 of them – six in one over – while Alletson scored his 142 off 39 out of the 51 balls he received. He took 34 runs off one over from Killick which included two no balls; and 22 from another of six legitimate deliveries. Killick was a slow bowler and the no-balls were said to be caused by his anxiety to avoid being struck by a return drive.

Most of Alletson's runs came from drives between extra cover and long on. George Gunn recalled years afterwards, 'The two Relfs and Joe Vine were in the long field and the ball fizzed through them as if they were ghosts.' 'Ted cut one ball over point,' he said, 'that smashed the pavilion window and wrecked the bar.' H. P. Chaplin, captain of Sussex that season who was unfit to play in this match and watched the innings from the pavilion, said, 'Once he just lay back on his heels and pushed and the ball went through the clock face.'

Bob Relf's memory was that 'He just hit firm footed. He made no attempt to get to the pitch of the ball, but unless it was right up to him, hit under it, straight off the middle of the bat. I was out at long off and some of his drives were carrying as far as the hotel or over the stand to the skating rink.'

Alletson was caught by C. L. A. Smith who leant back against the stand and with his foot breaking the boundary line – not, strictly speaking, out, as John Gunn said – but he 'walked'. After his 189 (152 for the last wicket) Sussex needed 237 to win, finished 24 short with eight men out and the match was drawn.

In his innings against Gloucestershire at Bristol he scored 60 in thirty minutes and with one huge hit struck the pavilion clock. His innings against Sussex won him a place in the Test Trial when he made 15 and 8; despite some big hitting in 1913, that season was virtually his last in first-class cricket. In one of his rare bowling successes he won the match with Kent, the county champions, with his newly developed, fastish leg-breaks; but there were complaints about his action and two matches in 1914 ended his career with Notts.

Ted Alletson remains the classic one-innings batsman. Few people saw that amazing piece of hitting and most of them, like Alletson himself, are now dead. Even the cold recital of its facts make it, in its way, the most remarkable innings ever played; and despite his subsequent disappointments, at the end of his life, Alletson himself deeply relished those minutes of immortality at Hove. *Sussex CCC: Hove 1872–1972*

# Inescapable Tradition

No one simply thinks about Nottinghamshire cricket topically nor in terms of a single year. There is an inescapable feeling of tradition about Trent Bridge which those who care for cricket cannot escape. Sir Neville Cardus is a Lancastrian by birth and true Lancashire in his cricketing heart, but he has always had a second loyalty and feeling for Nottingham. He grew up on the legend of Arthur Shrewsbury and one of his closest friends, and most humanly rewarding subjects among cricketers, was George Gunn.

Sir Neville, indeed, passed the most evocative and complete remark about Trent Bridge: 'a Lotus-land for batsmen, a place where it was always afternoon and 360 for two wickets.' Totals like that may not be frequent nowadays but they yet may be again for there is an inherent truth and pace in the pitch which was demonstrated so thoroughly by Frank Dalling in 1969 as to win him the award for the best groundsman of the year.

It has been called a batsman's ground, yet it has given enough to great bowlers for them to bowl out good batsmen – that prince of fast bowlers Harold Larwood, who moved in unforgettably at a rhythmic rock and bowled with arm straight as a hop pole at terrifying pace; Keith Miller, who angered the crowd there yet still compelled their admiration; Alf

Shaw, the ultimate master of length; Alec Bedser, in one of the mighty efforts of Test cricket; Bruce Dooland through some of the finest sustained leg-break and googly bowling of modern times; Frank Tyson at one of his historic peaks.

What now? In 1970 Garfield Sobers should come rested to a new season – an almost forgotten experience for him – and when he is fully fit and fresh we must speak of him in superlatives among all the cricketers of history. How much more does the side that finished fourth in the 1968 Championship need to win the title? Probably no more than that two of their players – preferably one batsman and one bowler – should step up one grade. Brian Bolus is a batsman of such natural gifts that he needs only self-trust to stand at the top. Mike Smedley is equipped to be among the dozen finest stroke-makers in the country.

Basharat Hassan, with a little less sparkle – though it is hard to fault a man for sparkling – could score many runs on good pitches. Mike Harris has already given the batting a strong core; if one other man could make an extra eight hundred runs a season, life would look prosperous for Nottinghamshire this summer.

The greatest urgency, however, is for one of the bowlers to step up. Bob White has been all but a first-class allrounder for several seasons; and, if he took a few more wickets with his off-breaks, he would almost certainly gain the confidence to make more runs, for his method is basically sound. Mike Taylor and Barry Stead have both in the past needed a responsive pitch to be effective against good batsmen; but both, last year, buckled to and did a thoroughly good season's work. Still, however, everyone at Trent Bridge must be scanning the county for their traditional fast bowler or a wrist-spinner.

Anyone who realizes the immense extent of the feeling for cricket in the county – and the strength of the Nottinghamshire Cricket Association is convincing proof of it – must feel that somewhere, close at hand, is the Nottinghamshire man who will appear upon his cue to complete a winning side.

Meanwhile the county may seek the opportunity, presumably in a match outside the Championship, to give 'Bomber' Wells a long enough bowl for him to take the two wickets which, by my probably unreliable calculations, are all he needs for a thousand in first-class cricket.

There are in fact many attractive side-issues and backwaters to Nottinghamshire cricket at the moment – not least, the best restaurant on any English cricket ground.  *Nottinghamshire CCC Annual*, 1970

# Memories of Trent Bridge

It used to seem strange that Trent Bridge was the most convivial of the Test grounds; that people stayed there longer at night – and perhaps, for all I know, got there earlier in the morning – than on the other great grounds. Then it occurred to me that, whereas in the case of Lord's and The Oval, the Tavern followed the cricket grounds, at Trent Bridge the 'T.B.I.' was there before anyone thought of making that field a cricket ground, and at Edgbaston, Old Trafford and Headingley there is no pub. When William Clarke the Nottingham bricklayer – who lost an eye at fives, and took a wicket with the last ball he bowled in his life – married the widow of the landlord of the Trent Bridge Inn, even he, shrewd as he was, cannot have foreseen quite the extent of its financial possibilities. It was a tiny pub then, and the public of Nottingham did not take kindly to being charged for admission to the cricket matches when they had always watched them free on the Racecourse.

The T.B.I. has changed over the years – as pubs, probably more than any other kind of establishment, do change through a whole series of fashions. At Test match time, of course, it is always crowded but it used to be a magnificent resort after play in a midweek county match. There that great man Charlie Harris used to tell his stories and his friend Arthur Jepson would pull his leg. Sometimes it was possible to lure George Gunn in, his more solemn brother, John, 'Tich' Richmond or Bill Voce, Harry Winrow and Joe Hardstaff, too, were always probables and, for a stranger their store of Nottinghamshire cricket lore – notably about 'Topsy' Wass, George Gunn or Charlie Harris himself – was rich meat.

In those days, only just after the last war, every group was entitled to its privacy. Then, too, cars were scarce and instead of simply jumping into the driving seat and motoring away, we walked home. Some went away towards Bridgford and the rest of us, unhurriedly, across the bridge, as the light fell in yellow bars across the river, talking of unimportant things. They still seem to me some of the most companionable, hospitable and illuminating days – or nights – I have spent at cricket in my entire life.     *Plumtree CC v Notts CC programme*, 1971

# About Essex

There cannot be in the whole world a longer bus-ride through houses and streets unbroken by open space than that from Cambridge Circus to the site of the old Essex ground at Leyton. That ride taught me, in my cub cricket-following days, how large London was. It was at the end of it, on the old Leyton ground, that I sat on an ammunition box and strove daylong to comprehend the utterance of a man with a pronounced East London accent who shouted 'OosezaniceiceWallses'. And that day Larwood and Voce took initial practice in the bowling method which was to alarm and defeat Australia – and Denys Wilcox and Jim Cutmore revelled in it. I remember, too, with glee, the Hampshire and Essex fast bowlers (two in each team, O post-war doubters) routing each other's batting twice in two days at Chelmsford. But it took war-time acquaintanceships and post-war oyster-charmed visits to Southend to show me that Essex were the best pavilion team in England. Whether the richly avuncular Tom Pearce, the jaunty Ray Smith, the drily faithful Tom Wade, or that misplaced Elizabethan, Douglas Insole, be your guide, life with the Essex team is fun – probably at its brightest at Southend where the marquees house each their own felicities. The sea, however, is a puritan and turns its back upon such festival delights.

Beware the Southend Festival at Southchurch Park, however, if you are superstitious:

### FOR THOSE WHO BAT AT SOUTHEND

Umpire or fieldsman or score-board clerk,
Bowler, spectator—oh! pause!—and hark!—
Above the crowd's cheers and the stray dog's bark—
To cricket-field birdsong—perhaps the lark
Or thrush or the magpie of piebald mark.
But batsman, oh batsman, be deaf to the dark
Ill-omened, cold-fear-breeding, run-killing, stark
Quack, quack of the ducks down at Southchurch Park.

But ducks or no ducks, Essex cricket is at its best when it holds festival. Dicky Dodds, the Smiths, Cray, Horsfall and Rist all assume twice the stature as batsmen when they can shed responsibility and bat freely – for they are by nature free batsmen. The spinners, Peter Smith and Vigar, too, are men who prefer to spin extravagantly – and extravagant spin and a steady length rarely go together – but hard hitting and wickets taken with snorting spinners make for the joys of cricket. In Essex the batsmen can bowl and the bowlers can bat. At times the batting order can almost be reversed, for nine Essex batsmen can press hard upon a thousand runs in a good season. This argues a cricket team bent upon cricket rather than the eleven specialists grimly hunting for points – cricket to be enjoyed rather than frozen into figures.

The follower of Essex cricket since the war has more than one problem. He must wonder why Tom Pearce was not picked for the Gentlemen of England against Australia. The skipper has made so many runs as to be on performance one of the most successful county captains of today – and many of his runs have been made when his side has been in trouble for he is no vainglorious taker of the easy century. In no other eleven in England would he look quite so right, quite so much himself, as with Essex.

After a successful batting run through 1947 the weakness of the Essex side was exposed on the damp slow wickets of 1948. Essex are a sunshine cricket team – at their brightest under the sun and on hard wickets where their batsmen can make their strokes freely and firmly, their leg-spinners can spin on the 'dusty one' and their pace bowlers come into their own.

Is it, I wonder, the keen breeze of the estuary, bracing a man into warming bursts of exertion, that breeds fast bowlers in Essex? Ray Smith with gusto at fast-medium, Trevor Bailey (now shorn of one cartwheel) at a yard faster and young Preston promising appreciably greater pace than either, were there to warm the sinking English heart in 1948 and to send the mind back to other Essex arms that scorned economy of effort. Maurice Nichols, Ken Farnes, 'Hopper' Read and H. T. O. Smith lead back to Charles Kortright – the first and perhaps the fastest of them all.

Charles Kortright is one of those rare men who become legends in their own lifetimes. 'Kortright,' the astonished cricket-follower says – 'Kortright – but – is he still alive?' And the amazed one must be told that Charles Kortright is probably much more alive than many who think him past history. It is not for me to reveal the geographical location of his kingdom. In fact, I have a superstitious fear that if I were to name it, it would vanish away the next time I went to visit it – for surely such a Utopia would be defiled by print. That King Edward who sported a beard, a de Dion Bouton and the affectionate nickname 'Teddy', died before I was born; but the adjective 'Edwardian' to describe an easier, more spacious day, lingered to nag at my brain. It nags no longer because I have seen and eaten and drunk and talked and heard that day. Charles Kortright recreates it about him today. Sample that lost day only once and you must ever want to wipe out the two wars that stand immovably between ourselves and it.

Perhaps, though, the spirit of the Edwardian day does not remain solely with the first Essex fast bowler, perhaps something of it resides still in Essex cricket. How else shall we explain away the fine faith of Tom Pearce as he goes staunchly forward 'down the track', Douglas Insole's willingness to 'keep wicket if wanted', Tom Wade in the role of the faithful retainer, 'Sonny' Avery's quiet devotion to the game of cricket, Ray Smith's cheerful labour in bowling until half-past six of a resultless third day for little but the sweat and the satisfaction of doing an honest job he relishes? Cherish these men, for they have that which threatens in a standardized age to disappear from some cricket. Batting averages and bowling averages will continue, and names will be at the top of them, but character gives colour to cricket beyond the black and white of statistics – and here, not so far from the far-retreating sea of the estuary, cricket has its characters – and character.

*Essex CCC Annual*, 1949

# A Weekend at Southend

It does not seem so very long ago – yet, indeed, it was the year before John Lever was born – that Don Bradman brought his 1948 Australians to play Essex at Southend over the Whit weekend. Not all of today's cricket followers will appreciate how – in an age before televized sport was general – people swarmed to that match in such numbers that, although it was all over in two days, it broke the ground records for both attendance and gate receipts.

It was something more than a nine days' wonder, for the tourists set a new record – of 721, which still stands – for the number of runs scored in a six-hour day in first-class cricket. (In fact it was not even a full day; the last wicket fell only moments after twenty-past six, not quite in time for Essex to bat that night.

According to which way one looked at it, either Trevor Bailey took the wickets of Bill Brown and Keith Miller with consecutive balls; or, alternatively, after Brown was out for 153, Miller simply took his bat away from his first ball and let it hit the stumps.

The innings was launched by Barnes (who 'failed' with only 79) and Brown with 145 in 95 minutes for the first wicket; Bradman (187 in 125 minutes) and Brown made 219 in 90 minutes for the second: Loxton (120) and Saggers (104 not out) 166 in 65, for the sixth.

Tom Pearce, that most amiable of captains, brought on Frank Vigar with his gentle leg-spin for the over before lunch; after all, he *might* lure Bradman into a reckless stroke. In fact not a single ball of the over touched the ground between bowler's hand and bat. The Don simply went down the pitch and cracked each of the first five balls over the boundary in various parts of the ground; and, such was his annoyance when he struck the last murderously, but straight at mid-off, that, even before the fieldsman had completed the stop, he was punching his fist into his hand at failing to hit it, too, for four. Since Frank Vigar also suffered a 'pair', it was not exactly the happiest match of his career;

though his eventual two for 66 was more bearable than Eric Price's nought for 156.

Tom Pearce, to his intense mirth, was made a 'Purchaser' for being the first county captain to get Bradman's side out in a day. Moreover, he won a good dinner for the writer, who backed him to make top score for Essex. He was not the best-looking of batsmen but he was a shrewd and dogged forward player and his 71 was comfortably the highest for the county. He and Peter Smith put on 133 for the seventh wicket before Australia won by an innings and 451, and left themselves a whole leisurely day for the journey to Oxford. There Bill Brown scored his third century in consecutive innings but that was not enough to keep him in Bradman's team for more than the first two Tests. No wonder it has been called the greatest of all Australian teams; few can have been more entertaining; and certainly none in any country ever averaged 120 runs an hour for a whole day.     *John Lever Benefit Year*, 1980

# The Image of Middlesex

The image of Middlesex is not clear. That is not to say it lacks definition; but that it has several definitions. For instance there is now, administratively, no such county. Even though they must have considered it impossible, however, the cricket authorities provided for such a contingency, in the last century. When the Championship was 'filled out' by the addition of five counties in 1895 it was decided that the boundaries of the first-class counties for the purposes of qualification – which really was a 'sacred cow' until relatively recent times – should be those defined by the Local Government Act of 1894, and they still are. For that reason, Somerset and Yorkshire do not have to worry about the recent truncation of their territory; which is, in any case, a trifling matter compared with the complete disappearance of Middlesex.

On the other hand, Middlesex, more perhaps than any other county, has changed its identity. It was for long the place of the separate gates; of an autocratic amateur establishment supported in the field by the highly trained and talented professionals of the 'ground staff'. That discipline is still basically in force; beyond doubt Middlesex have profited from the high playing standards of 'Headquarters'. Now, under Don Bennett, they probably have the finest nursery scheme in the game.

Lord's, where they are sub-tenants, has always been a place for authoritarians, of MCC, of course as well as – indeed, rather than – Middlesex. Though many of the great Headquarters figures – men like the Hon. Robert Grimston, Lord Harris and W. G. Grace – played elsewhere, the father figure of this century – 'Plum' Warner – was of both camps. He first appeared at Lord's as a schoolboy; played there for Oxford and Middlesex and with England as captain; as cricket writer, selector and administrator he saw more cricket there – or, for that matter all over the world – than anyone else who ever lived. He would find his Lord's much changed now; but there was always the streak of the cricket politician in him; he would understand – and support – anything to 'Benefit Middlesex'.                          *Middlesex Souvenir Brochure*, 1979

# Edgbaston

## *A Ground of Dramatic Event*

First impressions are usually deep. Certainly Edgbaston became for me, at first sight, a ground of dramatic event, even in a match heavily interrupted by rain and ending in a draw. It was the euphoric season of 1946 when to many people cricket was a symbol of the return to peace.

There was rain in the morning when the Indians came to an Edgbaston much more Edwardian in style than nowadays to play Peter Cranmer's cheerful, and often surprising side. Vijay Merchant, captaining the touring team in the absence of the elder Pataudi, studied the pitch at length and put Warwickshire in to bat. His estimate was right; Mankad's left-arm spin turned and lifted; and Amarnath's cutters moved sharply. Unfortunately for Merchant, his fieldsmen had an off-day.

Dick Sale, the tall, strong, Oxford left-hander, dropped four times, drove like thunder to make 157, his highest score; Tom Dollery, already looking a top class player, a characteristically poised 40; and Peter Cranmer a boisterous 48 before he declared at 375 for nine.

Tom Pritchard, the New Zealander, probably then the fastest bowler in England, was in his qualifying year and this was his only first-class match of the season. When play resumed after more rain, on Thursday afternoon, Merchant jabbed at his first ball and was dropped in the gully.

Hollies picked up three good wickets that afternoon and next morning, despite the bad footholds. Pritchard, working up high pace, clean bowled Hazare, Mankad and Gul Mahomed in seven balls. He and Hollies cut down India to 154 for nine before Merchant – who carried his bat for 86 in five hours after his early escape – and Hindlekar put on 43 for the last wicket. Cranmer enforced the follow-on; the same two batsmen came out again and Hindlekar was out to Robinson for the second time within eleven minutes.

Then the rain came again to draw the match: but not to end the events of a constantly shifting game. Before speculation could break out as to what might have happened if Merchant had been caught off the first ball, a tall bearded man came into the back of the old commentary box – which was under the Pavilion clock. 'Very unusual for this pitch to play like that,' he said, 'and I ought to know – I'm Frank Foster.' He was history: but that is another story.

*Neil Abberley's Benefit Brochure,* 1979

# Eleven of the Best!

The invitation to 'write anything about Warwickshire' rouses the cricketer's enthusiasm for team selection. The best eleven in the county's history?

The beneficiary is in: during the past four years Dennis Amiss has risen from uncertainty to maturity and he must open the innings.

Despite the claims of the under-rated Fred Gardner and that mighty striker John Jameson, his partner should be little Willie Quaife.

The remaining batting places are disputed by Bob Wyatt – also a useful medium-pace bowler – Mike Smith, Tom Dollery – who must surely captain any Warwickshire team from history – that magnificent left-hander Martin Donnelly, and Rohan Kanhai. Even that leaves out Canon Jack Parsons, Len Bates, Sep Kinnier, Frank Santall, Norman Kilner, Bob Barber and Norman Horner.

By common consent the finest Warwickshire allrounder was Frank Foster.

His bowling partner then was S. F. Barnes, six of whose few county matches were played for Warwickshire and, since he is generally accepted as the greatest of all bowlers, he goes in.

On that great tour the wicket-keeper was that elder of Warwickshire cricket, 'Tiger' Smith, who will keep wicket in this side – ahead even of 'Dick' Lilley.

Tom Cartwright – who also performed the 'double' – will be the stock bowler. So one place remains – for a slow bowler.

If the side is to play in England it will go to Eric Hollies, that uncannily accurate and effective leg-spinner.

If it plays elsewhere, despite the claims of Sam Hargreave and George Paine as finger-spinners, it must go to Lance Gibbs.

So the eventual team, which bats strongly to number ten, would be D. L. Amiss, W. G. Quaife, R. E. S. Wyatt, R. B. Kanhai, M. J. K. Smith, H. E. Dollery, F. R. Foster, T. W. Cartwright, E. J. Smith,

S. F. Barnes, W. E. Hollies: twelfth man, L. R. Gibbs – and it would extend most counties.          *Dennis Amiss's Benefit Brochure*, 1975

# Queen's Park
## *One of the Most Beautiful in the World*

First impressions are invariably deep. Certainly that first sight, in 1946, of cricket in its garden setting of Queen's Park, Chesterfield, remains sharp in memory. So, too, does the extremely tense finish to the match between Derbyshire and the Indian touring team; but, most enduringly, it saw the foundation of some friendships which have lasted until today; while others were ended only by death.

It was a convivial occasion, the hospitality most impressive in those days of rationing; and the incorrigible 'Simmy' – assistant baggage man to Bill Ferguson and seller of tour souvenirs – almost provoked a riot. The Indians batted and Bert Rhodes – bowling seam-up bareheaded, and putting on his cap for his leg-spinners – took five for 135; he had the Nawab of Pataudi senior stumped by Pat Vaulkhard; and clean bowled Rusi Modi when he had made 99. Bill Copson, deep-chested and rhythmically powerful – the fastest bowler in England that year – bowled well with no luck. They scored 380 for eight declared and Derbyshire replied with 366, their highest total of the summer.

Charlie Elliott made a determined 61 and Alan Revill a watchful 42, before Eric Marsh and Cliff Gladwin laid about them in a hectic seventh wicket stand of 127. When the Indians batted again the unlucky Modi was run out for 68 but, scoring at over 100 an hour, they could declare at 313 for eight and set Derbyshire 328 to win.

Again Charlie Elliott and Alan Revill defended stoutly, but six wickets were down when extra time was claimed. Amarnath senior had a remarkable match; he scored 17 in the first innings; a superb 89, at more than a run a minute, largely by splendid driving in the second; kept wicket in the first Derbyshire innings – when he stumped Arnold Townsend – but reverted to his usual immaculate medium pace in their second to take three for 33 and, after the Indian fieldsmen had changed over at a sprint, bowled the youngest Pope with the second ball of the last possible over to give India a win by 118 runs.

The view from the Queen's Park pavilion has changed much since those days; but it remains one of the most companionable – and most beautiful – cricket grounds in the world.

*Hendo–Mike Hendrick's Testimonial Brochure*, 1980

# Bramall Lane

The end of Yorkshire matches at Bramall Lane closes an aspect of the game which for many years seemed certain to last as long as county cricket itself. Certainly the ground was always one for Spartan spectatorship but it had an atmosphere and a tradition – after all there was a time when Sheffield, through Darnall, Hyde Park and Bramall Lane, virtually was Yorkshire cricket – which can never be replaced.

It was always a favourite of Fred Trueman's if only because it was the nearest Yorkshire ground to his home at Maltby, and his family could conveniently come to watch him play. It is sad that his father, who had been so stirred by some of his early bowling feats there, could not know his fine moment at Bramall Lane in 1968 when he captained Yorkshire to their first win against the Australians since 1902.

Fred knew the end of his county career could not be far ahead but he still was capable of lifting his performance, on isolated occasions, to what had been his high normal standard when he was younger and tired less easily. He was always an intelligent cricketer with far more tactical acumen than some suspected; and whatever jokes he may have made, to captain Yorkshire, even as a deputy, was a matter of emotional and professional importance to him. On this occasion, taking over because Brian Close was injured, he performed the first duty of any captain by winning the toss; and gave Yorkshire first innings on a good wicket.

Boycott, Sharpe, Padgett, Illingworth and, at the end, Trueman in a late foray with Stringer, had taken their score to 355 for nine on the second morning, when he declared to give himself and Richard Hutton half an hour before lunch with the new ball.

It was the last time many of us ever saw Fred Trueman bowl genuinely fast. His first ball screamed past Bill Lawry's nose; and immediately Jimmy Binks – standing back – took another full-toss on the arm. In the few overs to lunch his inswinger was too fast for Redpath who snicked it and was caught wide down the leg side by Binks; and he himself dived a long way for a thirty-seven-year-old to catch Walters at slip.

When Australia were all out for 143, he had taken three wickets, made three catches and run out Ian Chappell – and he enforced the follow-on. He wanted a wicket – one particular wicket – Bill Lawry's – that night and Richard Hutton took it with a swinging yorker. Next morning the acting captain of Yorkshire was cheerfully expansive. What would happen? He prophesied that Yorkshire would win at half-past three that afternoon. At one point Walters and Sheehan were batting together with such comfortable assurance that it was by no means certain the Australians could be put out – especially since

Stringer's pulled muscle had left Yorkshire a bowler short. Characteristically Trueman broke the stand; first he hit Sheehan's middle stump; and then, soon afterwards, bowled his best ball of the match to Walters who was compelled to play at it along the line of middle-and-off; it left him off the pitch and Illingworth caught him in the gully. That afternoon Yorkshire won, by an innings and 60 runs; the Australians are not often beaten by such a margin. As it happened, the church clock which has ticked away so much cricket at Bramall Lane, showed half-past three. Fred Trueman had made his point. *Twelfth Man*, 1973

# It's No Surprise Brian Close
# Went to Somerset . . .

No one, least of all Brian Close himself, would suggest that he is less than grimly delighted to be a member of a Somerset side that beats Yorkshire. In 1971 – his first season with his new county – he scored 102, Tom Cartwright took nine for 49 and Somerset won by ten wickets. In 1974, he and Mervyn Kitchen, with a second-innings stand of 90, effectively beat Yorkshire in a finish much closer than the eventual difference of seven wickets made it seem.

All this, though, is a repetitive pattern of history for, as soon as they first entered the County Championship, Somerset were known as 'The Team of Surprises' from their habit of beating the top counties – especially Yorkshire and Surrey. In that initial season, of 1891, the magnificent Sammy Woods, by an innings of fifty; five for 62 and six for 64, gave them a win – beyond the batting of Bobby Peel and the bowling of Ted Wainwright to avert – by six wickets. The next year Woods made 76, by far the highest score of the match at Sheffield when Somerset won by 87 runs. In 1895 at Taunton, the supreme stylist Lionel Palairet scored 165, the faithful Tyler took fourteen wickets and Somerset won again, this time by 29 runs.

The most historic win in these matches, though, was achieved at Leeds in 1901. Yorkshire had not been beaten for two years and they took a first-innings lead of 238, only for Lionel Palairet and Len Braund to put on 222 for the first wicket, Somerset to score 630 and win by 279 runs. That was the first time that splendid allrounder – forcing batsman, leg-spin bowler and slip fielder – and happiest of cricketers, Len Braund, proved a match-winner against Yorkshire. He was to do it again – and found the tradition of Yorkshire's vulnerability to leg-spin – at Sheffield in 1902 when Yorkshire were again Champions and his fifteen for 71 gave Somerset a narrow win by 34 runs; and the next year when his ten for 116, and 61 runs, took them in by six wickets.

It is always a refreshing experience for any county to beat Yorkshire; Somerset have achieved that feat historically and surprisingly; perhaps that is why Brian Close joined them.

*Brian Close Testimonial Brochure*, 1976

# Cricket at Taunton

*This piece for the players' yearbook comes with the gratitude and compliments of the club's newest honorary – and honoured – life member.*

Perhaps there are other English county grounds as completely central in their towns as Taunton. Portsmouth, Scarborough, Eastbourne and Hastings come readily to mind, but none ever seems so much at its urban heart as Taunton. No transport is needed to stroll from the Castle or the County Hotel to the ground enclosed between St James's Street, the River Tone, Priory Bridge Road, the Cattle Market and the Coal Market.

Once there, the tall new pavilion, its Edwardian predecessor, and the old Stragglers pavilion on the corner near the Coal Market; the school, and the main entrance through the J. C. White Gates emphasize the almost domestic intimacy of the place. Above all, the red sandstone tower of St James's occupying as it were one corner of the site and echoed, with subtle difference, by St Mary's, sets the cricket field in the very core of Taunton.

For many years at least one commentator used often to be late for the start of play there, delayed by the purchase of secondhand books, glass, china or, on occasions, even furniture, from Chapman's rambling old shop and warehouse almost immediately opposite the gates.

There is still much along the way to beguile the casual playgoer on his morning saunter. The idea of a picnic at the cricket has persuaded many to the County Stores who have emerged laden with something nearer an open-air banquet. Antique dealers, bookshops, restaurants, grocers, camera shops, off-licences; tug at the sleeve. Lately, too, most conveniently close at hand for the spectator's lunch, Dennis Noble has decorated the walls of the Ring of Bells with cricket photographs and souvenirs, and provides palatable lunch – hot or cold – and wine or beer to taste.

An early memory of the ground is of the lowing cows in the cattle market punctuating the applause from the crowd. It is the most companionable and pervasive of county grounds and, within its gregarious climate, men from origins as diverse as Sammy Woods, Len Braund,

Bill Alley, Arthur Wellard, Viv Richards, Johnny Lawrence, Ian Botham, Frank Lee have become as much part of the Taunton scene as the Somerset born Harold Gimblett, Horace Hazell, Jack White, Mervyn Kitchen, Peter Denning, Colin Dredge and Bertie Buse.

It is as if they had all been drawn into the same atmosphere, like the people converging on the market from the countryside for miles around. On a July Saturday market day, cricket and the weekly visitors and shoppers all merge together into a unique yet typically West Country warm, busy, relished – purely Taunton – summer's day.

*Somerset CCC Year Book*, 1982

# A Century in Gloucestershire

It is happy that Gloucestershire should go into their centenary year [1970] after as successful a season as any since they last won the Championship, ninety years ago, and in a year when Bristol will stage the first international representative match in its history.

Cricket is a game of tradition and of nostalgia; no men ever seem so big as the heroes of our youth – particularly, for many of us, the cricket heroes of that impressionable age. Thus cricketers, perhaps more than any other sportsmen, suffer constantly from the suggestion – if only by implication – that they are not so good as their predecessors. So it is warming that we can look back over the century of Gloucestershire cricket and say that it never had a better balanced side than that of 1969, with its all-purpose bowling of Procter, Smith, Brown, Allen, Mortimore and Bissex: and that W. G. Grace himself never captained a Gloucestershire team with six Test players in it. Indeed, but for the injuries to Geoff Pullar and David Shepherd – the two top batsmen in the county's averages – Tony Brown and Barry Meyer, the Championship might easily have come to Gloucestershire.

As one grows older, a hundred years does not seem an impossibly long time, certainly not too vast to be seen in perspective. When I first came to the county's grounds, there were men who had played regularly for Gloucestershire under W. G. Grace. There are many who have talked to Jessop, had the fortune to see some of Wally Hammond's finest innings, to watch Charlie Parker and Tom Goddard on their killing days and to relish Bev Lyon's captaincy. Billy Neale, Sam Cook, Andy Wilson and Tom Graveney helped to form the post-war pattern as Arthur Milton, David Allen and John Mortimore have done in later times. All this lies within the knowledge of many of the senior 'regulars': and there is always Reg Sinfield to appeal to for first-hand memory.

History is reflected from some unexpected surfaces. We might think the Grace era is most impressively recalled by the gates at Lord's or Bristol, by the Wortley portrait or the Memorial Biography. For me, however, it is most vividly brought home by the County Ground Hotel at Bristol. It is an impressive thought that it was built, with economic confidence, to accommodate the spectators of a few days of cricket: amazing to realize that they came in such numbers as to fill all those many and vast rooms which would take 800 people – and another 400 sitting for an 'ordinary' in the motorless street outside. There is no longer a captive audience for cricket in Bristol; but the county has more members than it had in W.G.'s day and, when the team pulled to the head of the Championship table in 1969, Gloucestershire men all over the world – as many as ever supported W.G.'s teams – followed them with proud interest through the press and radio. It has been a wonderful hundred years; and there is no good reason why another equally good and equally changing century should not lie ahead.

100 *Years of Gloucestershire Cricket*

# A Distant Memory of Gloucestershire

When, last September, Gloucestershire's spirited challenge for the Championship failed, it stirred sharp memories of another attempt that fell short. In 1931, when they finished second to Yorkshire, they were also inspiringly led, then by Beverley Lyon. It is hard to believe that there was ever a quicker-witted or more original cricket captain; nor one better able to – in the modern term – motivate his players. He ranked his own performance far less than a match won; but he was an extremely gifted batsman. Moreover, his fielding at first slip to Parker and, even more importantly, at short square leg to Tom Goddard, whom he virtually created as an off-spinner, were quite outstanding. He was a cricketer and a man of immense zest; a superbly amusing and convivial companion.

He regarded a drawn match as a bad match and, in May 1931, after much of the first two days of their opening fixture at The Oval had been lost to rain, he declared 83 behind Surrey on the first innings. Percy Fender, the Surrey captain – before the day of the habitual fourth-innings run-race – countered with a declaration which asked Gloucestershire 144 in 110 minutes, which proved to be 35 overs. They lost seven wickets in the process but a stand of 77 in 45 minutes between Wally Hammond and 'Cec' Dacre decided it. A month afterwards, when the first two days had been lost to rain at Sheffield, he suggested to Frank

Greenwood, the Yorkshire captain, that they should both declare their first innings closed after four byes and procure a result. Greenwood agreed, believing that Yorkshire could thus win in a day and, winning the toss, put Gloucestershire in to bat. Both sides duly declared at four for no wicket and, despite Verity's seven for 64, Gloucestershire made 171: and Yorkshire, going for the runs, were bowled out for 124 by Tom Goddard and Charlie Parker and lost by 47 runs. That was the year when Charlie Parker, most savage of left-arm spinners – and not so slow, either – equalled the record, which still stands and is unlikely now ever to be beaten, of taking one hundred wickets by 12 June. That led to the authorities at Lord's banning 'arranged' declarations: but nowadays, if the first two days are lost, a one-day – one innings – match may be played.

After that match, Bev Lyon had to return to business, and captained the side only twice more in the season. *Wisden* was of the strong opinion that 'If Lyon had continued to lead the side throughout the summer, Yorkshire would not have won the Championship by a margin of sixty-eight points because there were at least three games when a man of his enterprise must have made a bold bid for victory, and his inspiring example would have gone a long way to attain it.'

During May, at Bristol, he had sent Hampshire in to bat and Gloucestershire, striving for quick runs on a turning wicket, were beaten by 66. One of the two Championship games he was able to play in the latter part of the season was the return with Hampshire at Southampton, over the August Bank Holiday weekend. For a cricket-mad seventeen-year-old contriving to watch a rare three days of county cricket, the idea of Gloucestershire without Hammond seemed like short measure. Partisan feelings aside, though, it was a splendid cricket match.

This time, Ronny Aird, captaining Hampshire, sent Gloucestershire in to bat. Baring and Herman at fair pace and Bailey, slow left arm, all bowled usefully but, while Harry Smith hung on, Lyon made 65 of their third-wicket partnership of 85 in less than an hour and a half. After rain, the traditional Gloucestershire spin – the off-breaks of Tom Goddard and Reg Sinfield, and the slow left arm of Charlie Parker reduced Hampshire to 90 for nine: only for Philip Mead, the historic bulwark of Hampshire's batting for thirty years, and Giles Baring, to put on 82 for the last wicket, which left Gloucestershire with a lead of 81. With the wicket improving, time was now short, and Lyon drove his side on with another brilliantly quick-footed, impudent, innings, of 75 in an hour. That was capped by 'Cec' Dacre, the New Zealander, in a spectacular piece of batting. Nimble, strong-armed, heavy shouldered and possessed of splendid timing, he was not afraid to hit the ball 'on the up', as they say, and drove quite ferociously. He scored his first 50 in exactly as many minutes; and then, cutting loose, made another 51 in seventeen minutes. There were six sixes and nine fours in his 101 and one off drive, never more than about twelve feet above the ground, splintered the boarding at the back of the ladies stand. It rained again and Sinfield, Goddard and Parker – no one else so much as turned an arm – cut down Hampshire in an hour-and-a-half and beat them by 256 runs. Only the ingratitude of the young could have allowed me to say, 'But if only Hammond could have played . . .'

*Jack Davey and David Shepherd Joint Benefit brochure, 1978*

# The Hampshire Eleven

David White's benefit competition – choosing the best team from Hampshire's post-war players – lodged in my mind the nagging idea of attempting to pick the strongest eleven from the county's entire history. It is not simple; and the chief problem, of course, is not who to include, but who to leave out. Allowance must be made, too, for the fact that natural ability would enable a player to deal with technical problems which do not arise in his time. One day, after Philip Mead lost his sight, he was 'watching' Hampshire play Derbyshire at Bournemouth when he asked me to describe Cliff Gladwin's leg-side field – not only the angles of position, but their depth. He took it all in, thought for a moment, and then said, 'You know, I never had to work as hard as that for runs on the leg side.' No one who saw him, however, would doubt his ability to have scored many runs in any age.

Indeed, he probably would be everyone's first choice for an all-time Hampshire team; but we may stick to batting and bowling order. The two opening positions are in fierce dispute. Roy Marshall and Jimmy Gray held the county record for the first wicket; Barry Richards, in a couple of seasons with the county, has already played some superbly accomplished innings; C. B. Fry, John Arnold, Captain E. G. Wynyard and George Brown all went in first for England. Neville Rogers did not; but the county never had a more technically and temperamentally complete and reliable opening batsman, and he was at his best when his side was in trouble. If he and Richards – two utter realists – opened the innings, their opponents would be given no quarter.

On the 1950 West Indies tour, Roy Marshall several times made characteristically handsome runs at number three, four and five; and the sight of him coming in when the opening bowlers were tired would dishearten any side. So, too, would the appearance of the most run-hungry batsman in all history – Philip Mead – for number four is his place by right. He scored more runs for Hampshire than anyone else has ever done for any team in the history of cricket – 48,892 of them – and another 6168 for other sides: and only nine men have taken more than his 668 catches, most of them picked up with a misleadingly casual air at slip.

John Arnold batted happily and capably at number five in the later days of his career and would be a fine asset there for he can play either game; and he will give us a magnificent cover-point.

Number six will be George Brown, one of the most remarkable of all-round cricketers; he went in first and kept for England; took over six hundred wickets as a bowler of quite brisk pace; was described as both the best mid-off and the best silly-point in the country and, in his youth, was said to be 'the furthest thrower in England'. For this team he will keep wicket – ahead of Walter Livsey, Neil McCorkell and Leo Harrison – and bat – fearless against pace and a savage punisher of all kinds of bowling.

How arbitrary are these choices? A certain burden of responsibility is lifted by the argument that C. B. Fry's best years were spent with Sussex before he came to Hampshire. Others are not so easily omitted. In 1899, Major Wynyard and General Poore scored 411 together for Hampshire against Somerset – still the highest sixth-wicket stand by English batsmen; moreover, they made it in 260 minutes. In 1894 Major Wynyard's batting – he averaged 66 – was an important factor in Hampshire's acceptance into the County Championship for the following season. His average in first-class cricket was only 34 (for 7572 runs) but he was a member of the England side that won the Oval Test – and the rubber with it – against Australia in 1896. The other England batsmen were: W. G. Grace, F. S. Jackson, K. S. Ranjitsinhji, Archie MacLaren and Tom Hayward – illustrious company, indeed. True, William Gunn withdrew from the match because of a disagreement over payment; but Wynyard was chosen in preference to Stoddart, J. T. Brown, C. B. Fry, Billy Brockwell, and J. R. Mason. This ranks him high; but it is hard to see who to leave out for him. Incidentally, Wynyard was a member of the Old Carthusian team that won the FA Cup Final of 1881.

His partner, General R. M. Poore – whom some will remember coaching at the county nets at Bournemouth into the 1930s – was born in Dublin, but spent such time as he had free from his military duties in Hampshire. He was six-feet-four tall, built in proportion and handsome in appearance. He twice won the Lawn Tennis Championship of West India; was a fine rifle shot and, in a single fortnight of 1900, scored centuries in three consecutive innings for Hampshire, played in the winning team of the inter-regimental Polo Tournament and was adjudged the best 'Man at Arms' in the Royal Military and Naval Tournament. His army duties prevented him from playing much cricket and his reputation must rest largely on his phenomenal performance in the season of 1899. In the previous season he had gone in first against Somerset and carried his bat for 49 not out in a total of 97 on a difficult wicket at Bath, where his immense reach and correct forward play enabled him to cope with some difficult bowling from Tyler and Robson. He only averaged 34 for the county, however, and no one expected that a year later he would be the outstanding batsman in England. In his two months' leave from India he played nine Championship fixtures for Hampshire in which he had sixteen innings, never failed and, with seven centuries, scored 1399 runs at an average of 116.58, believed still to be the highest season's average ever achieved by anyone playing so few innings. He could play in only one other match for the county – against Darling's strong Australian team – when he made 29 and 71.

Perhaps modern prejudice prompts me to leave them out, and, surely, they must come in for subsequent matches of the eleven – like that other soldier, H. L. V. Day, who had such a brilliant season in 1922 that he was only one of the five Hampshire players invited to join the MCC side to South Africa in 1922–23 (Philip Mead, George Brown, Alec Kennedy and Walter Livsey were the others). He could not be released by the army and his promising career as batsman and fieldsman was regrettably brief at first-class level.

At this, though we have left out the phenomenally reliable Henry Horton, the batting is strong. The medium and fast-medium bowling will show no deficiency; it can be chosen from Derek Shackleton, Alec Kennedy, Victor Barton and Bob Cottam – all of whom played for England – Jack Newman, who was bitterly unlucky not to do so, Vic Cannings, George Heath, 'Lofty' Herman and T. A. Jaques (who was virtually the inventor of inswing to a leg trap). Of these, figures make Derek Shackleton and Alec Kennedy the automatic first choices; at need they will both bowl all day, steadily on batsmen's wickets, as killers when conditions help them. Each of them took more wickets than all but six other bowlers in the history of the game and Kennedy, who five times performed the 'double', will strengthen the batting.

The main question at this juncture is whether or not to include one bowler of genuine pace to provide variety from the immaculate length of the two medium-pace bowlers. If the eleven is to be balanced, there must be this contrast and the place must go to David White – the fastest of them all – ahead of Giles Baring, Rodney Palmer and Arthur Jaques.

So the question of the spin bowling: at once our generation thinks of the pairing of Jim Bailey – probably the best slow left-arm bowler in England in 1948 when he did the double for the first time at the age of forty – and Charles Knott, who had a Test trial as an off-spinner in 1946.

Yet neither can come in ahead of Charlie Llewellyn and Jack Newman. Llewellyn, recommended to Hampshire by General Poore who saw him playing in South Africa, was the first man to perform the 'double' for the county. He bowled orthodox left-arm spin with the ability to increase his pace to medium with appreciable cut, and could also bowl wrist spin. He was an attacking batsman, sound enough to score double centuries, and a fine fieldsman. His stature was such that, although he had already played for South Africa, he was one of the players summoned for England to the Edgbaston Test of 1902 when England are generally considered to have fielded the finest team in their history.

The other spinner must be Jack Newman; at his county's need he opened the bowling with accurate and often lively outswing; but he was at his best as an off-break bowler with subtle variations of pace and flight. It was always said that he lost many wickets he would otherwise have been given – lbw – because of his habit of running across in front of the umpire; nevertheless, only one bowler (George Dennett) has taken more than his 2032 wickets without playing in a Test match. Jack, too, was good enough batsman to score over a thousand runs in a season six times.

In the choice of captain, Charles Fry – who never lost a Test as captain of England – Lord Tennyson, of the amazing flair and equally surprising vagaries, Desmond Eagar – who built the post-war team – and Colin Ingleby-Mackenzie, who led it to the Championship, are not in our historic eleven. Hampshire's unbeaten captain was Neville Rogers; never appointed but, as a deputy, shrewd and capable and, like Desmond Eagar, a close fieldsman who kept the side's outcricket on its toes.

Richards and Mead will field at slip and Neville Rogers at short leg but Charles Llewellyn, John Arnold and Jack Newman, too, must come up into the close positions – and though all three were good catchers, they were not used to the specialist positions and this may be the weakness of the side; there is no other. So the eleven is:

N. H. Rogers, B. A. Richards, R. E. Marshall (E. G. Wynyard for the second match), C. P. Mead, J. Arnold (General R. M. Poore for the second match), George Brown (wicket-keeper), C. B. Llewellyn, A. S. Kennedy, J. A. Newman, D. Shackleton, D. W. White. *Twelfth man* P. J. Sainsbury. *Bowling* D. W. White, D. Shackleton, A. S. Kennedy, J. A. Newman, C. B. Llewellyn, B. A. Richards, C. P. Mead, R. E. Marshall. *Hampshire Handbook*, 1970

# 6

# The County Professionals

## Edwin Smith

### Pure Derbyshire

*August* 1966. Those who frequent the county cricket grounds of England
have long asked two rhetorical questions about Edwin Smith – what is
this off-spinner doing in the dourly seam-minded Derbyshire side? and,
secondly, how does he contrive to look so happy about it? Now, in 1966,
he can look happier than ever: the limitation of on-side fieldsmen has
been removed; all but one of the seam-bowlers of his early county days
have gone; he is taking a testimonial; and he has stood top of the first-
class bowling averages.

Edwin Smith – known as 'Tatt' – from the cricketing village of Grassmoor, just outside Chesterfield, first played for Derbyshire in 1951,
when he was seventeen. He does not look a day older now, at thirty-two,
than he did then. His cheeks are as rosy as ever, his grin as wide; he still
has the high, bony shoulders and lean frame of the youngster; and he
still comes in to bowl in a manner so modest as almost to be surreptitious
– as if a spinner had no right in a Derbyshire attack.

In his early days, Cliff Gladwin and Les Jackson opened, and often
maintained, the Derbyshire bowling: the second and third seam bowlers
were Tom Hall and Derek Morgan, while Bert Rhodes partly expiated
the intrusion of his leg-spin by, from time to time, taking off his cap and
bowling 'seam up'. Donald Carr barely got on with his rakish Chinamen:
but, if the wicket was a real turner, or the faster bowlers were unusually
tired, Arnold Hamer might be allowed to wheel up a few overs of off-
breaks.

Nevertheless, in that first year, Edwin Smith finished top of the county's bowling averages by dint of eight for 21 against Worcester-shire – though even that was not enough to keep him in the side for the next match. In 1952, 26 wickets in twelve Championship matches was meagre enough while, in 1953, eighteen matches for 22 wickets at 41 each was even less impressive. In that season, however, he made a con-siderable impression on the Australians: notwithstanding their besetting weakness against off-spin, his five for 36 marked another stage in his development. Now, too, Derbyshire desperately needed a new spinner, for Bert Rhodes, never really fit that year, decided to retire.

The place was not thrown open for Smith, however. Late in 1953 and at the outset of the 1954 season, he had to compete for it with Reg Carter, a young slow left-arm bowler. Both were promising: the decisive factor – in a team whose batting was sufficiently thin to demand economy from its bowlers – was Smith's steadiness. He was given his cap and, for the last dozen years, he has been a regular member of the side, and one of the steadiest slow bowlers in the country.

He has always turned the ball sharply and, given the opportunity, he can flight the ball with no little subtlety. His misfortune, like that of many another young spin bowler in a seam-conscious age, is that he has too often been used purely defensively, to close up the game for the few overs before another new ball became available. He carried out that duty efficiently and with his usual loyal good nature, tightening his length, bowling a careful line and lopping off the top arc of his trajectory.

Perhaps his most remarkable capacity is that for switching so tidily from a defensive to an attacking technique when a pitch offers help. He does not, however, need drying conditions to get batsmen out: in 1955, a season of, largely, hard pitches, he took over a hundred wickets for so far – the only time. That year, too, he produced – statistically speaking – his best bowling performance: nine for 46 against Scotland: he was himself the fieldsman who dropped the catch which would have given him all ten.

The 1957 legislation restricting the number of leg-side fieldsmen was aimed at the negative, inslant bowlers; but it proved a cruel handicap to off-spinners, especially on turning pitches. Batsmen, always alert to exploit new legislation, soon found they could hit 'with the tide' both safely and profitably through a field which was a man short: so a further burden of economy was laid on the off-spinner. It is salutary to read through *Wisden* for the past decade and see how many capable bowlers of the type lost their places and faded out of first-class cricket under the pressures of that era.

Edwin Smith has endured primarily because he is a first-class bowler. It has, though, been a help that he had a something to add as a batsman. He is not an outstanding player of pace, and he never looks more shyly boyish than when he comes out to bat: but he has a shrewd eye for spin and, if the ball is up to him, he drives it with quite surprising power. His partnerships with Cliff Gladwin used to provide some high – and by no means all deliberate – comedy: but he is not a rabbit: he has played some valuable late innings, and he once made 90 against Notts. Certainly no captain of Derbyshire will regard his 400 to 500 runs a season as negligible.

He has scored, altogether, over 5000 runs; and if his fielding is more dutiful than brilliant, nevertheless he has held over 150 catches. By the end of this season he will have taken almost 1000 wickets – and, given the opportunity, the figure would have been far larger. Now, at thirty-two, he is a better bowler than he has ever been before: thoughtful, controlled, thrifty and penetrative. He is, too, keen and fit enough to carry on for some years to come.

It might be said that Edwin Smith is pure Derbyshire – it would be more accurate to say that he is pure Grassmoor – sounds like it, is proud of it, and is a credit to a village that has always fostered and cherished cricketers.                                                                    *The Cricketer*

# Robin Hobbs

## *The Conscience of Essex Cricket*

Robin Hobbs has been called the conscience of Essex cricket, some might say that the county kept up an endless belt of 'seam-up' on its own grassy wicket, that Trevor Bailey shut up a game as a batsman or draw as a captain. On the other hand, there was always a leg-spinner to demonstrate that they were prepared to open up a match. Tom Pearce took pleasure in the leg-spin of Peter Smith, an allrounder who was one of the last English wrist-spinners to tour Australia. For some years Bill Greensmith practised the craft with philosophic diligence and often used Doug Insole's impatience to be on with the game; while Robin Hobbs came in time to provide an occasional velvet glove for Trevor Bailey's fist. Indeed in 1961, Essex often included both Greensmith and Hobbs, presenting the remarkable spectacle of an English county team of the 1960s with two leg-spinners – they bowled over seven hundred overs between them in Championship fixtures that summer.

In 1963 Robin Hobbs inherited the place; he was capped in 1964 and since then has been a regular and enlivening member of the side. In the 1973 season he once again took more wickets than any other English leg-spinner. He is widely respected, too, for his hard-hitting right-handed batting, which may not be particularly consistent – he averages only about 12 – but includes a century against Glamorgan (when he also took seven wickets and effectively won the match) – and which by sheer boldness and power has often turned a game.

He is, too, an exciting fieldsman at cover-point in the deep. No one who saw it will ever forget the occasion, in Jamaica, when he appeared virtually from nowhere, running at full tilt along the square-leg boundary to leap high and catch, one-handed, a square hook which seemed certain to be going for a very long six indeed.

If he represents the conscience of Essex, he has done as much for England and as the country's main – almost sole – wrist-spinner, he made four official tours, played in seven Tests between 1964 and 1971 and took a dozen wickets for England. In that period he came nearer than the figures might suggest to establishing a regular Test place. The selectors would have been delighted to have an effective leg-spinner capable of increasing the wicket-rate in Tests, while Robin Hobbs himself often seemed to lack only a fraction more confidence to dominate instead of concentrating on accuracy. Unfortunately for both sides – and for the game in general and English cricket in particular – the formula never quite worked out and Hobbs's place was given to finger-spin.

With Essex, where he is completely accepted, he is far more at his cheerful ease, far more his own man, far more likely to call the tune or to bowl a side out. He can claim, too, in an age when leg-spin has been unfashionable, to have taken more wickets – 953 – than any other current English bowler of his kind, or than any other in the world except Intikhab (1006) who plays virtually all the year round. He has earned a good benefit by immensely enthusiastic endeavour as batsman, bowler and fielder for many sides, but especially for Essex.

*Tollesbury CC v Essex CC Souvenir*, 1974

# Peter Walker

## *Glamorgan's Divine Discontent*

*July* 1966. Peter Walker, more than any other English cricketer of the present day, suffers from what Charles Kingsley called 'the divine discontent'. The victim of this 'appreciation' will be relieved to know – if he did not know already – that the phrase was used in a discussion of 'Health and Education', which is more or less his cup of tea (China, with lemon).

At different times Peter Walker has seemed to be discontented with his batting, bowling, fielding and cricket itself: but, in the end, usually with profit. He has been discontented with England, South Africa and the ordinary round of everyday life: but he returns regularly to the first two and frequently shows exuberant signs of enjoying the third. Sometimes he probably wishes he were a steady, established chap who never worried himself about anything. In which case he would be a vastly different person. He would be a consistent cricketer, perhaps; but once he descended into placidity he would cease to be the quickest catcher of a ball in the cricket of today.

Peter Walker was born in Bristol of Welsh parents in 1936. His parents took him to South Africa and, when he hitch-hiked to Cardiff to visit his grandfather in 1952, he slouched into the Glamorgan office, asked Wilf Wooller for a trial, was approved, and began to qualify for the county. Restless at the end of the 1962 season, he left Glamorgan with the intention of settling in South Africa, but county cricket had become both a hunger and a compelling problem for him and he returned part way through the next season. Since then, his visits to South Africa have been confined to the winter. The records show him as playing for Transvaal in 1956–57 and 1957–58, and for Western Province in 1962–63.

He is lanky (six-feet-four), long-armed and long-legged: but not *quite* so lanky, long-armed and long-legged as at times he sometimes makes himself look, particularly when he slowly uncoils himself for dramatic effect.

His height should help him as a bowler, and frequently does. He would not claim to bowl in more than two styles – orthodox, round-the-wicket slow left-arm, and medium, over-the-wicket 'seam up' and cutters: but he will insert one of either in a spell of the other, and has been known to introduce a Chinaman into both. He does not always bowl a length: sometimes it seems that he would be bored if he did: but he takes good wickets and will bowl all day if it will help his side.

As a batsman, his huge reach enables him to play forward and smother the danger of most kinds of bowling: this may explain why he so often plays back and hits with thunderous power. Strength and length of hitting, however, are characteristics of his batting: the long swing, at the full length of his arms, has a surging flow of power. Characteristically, he hit that most restrictive of bowlers, Trevor Goddard, for two sixes – and in a Test.

He has scored over 10,000 runs and taken more than 500 wickets at almost identical averages – a little above 28. In 1960, when he was chosen for three Tests, he performed the double – *and* took 73 catches, a figure only twice bettered in a season – by Walter Hammond and Micky Stewart.

A useful bowler who is never content to be negative, and a combative batsman who, on the attack, can win matches, he has, nevertheless, made his deepest mark on cricket as a fieldsman, formerly at short leg, nowadays usually at slip. Restlessly alert, and fierce in concentration, he has stood as close to the bat – especially to slow bowlers – as anyone in the history of cricket. This gives him – and his captain and the bowler – an immense psychological advantage which could not be maintained if Walker did not, with amazing frequency, take catches in these alarming positions. The highest comparative point of his success lies in matching his great Glamorgan predecessors – Maurice Turnbull, Arnold Dyson and Allan Watkins – at short leg, in a pattern of increasingly intense cricket.

He is a match-winner in county cricket: but that is not sufficient for him. Cricket is not the limit of his understanding, enthusiasm or ambition. He is capable in his business – a travel agency – but that does not fill the gap. His father and grandfather were professional writers and there is no doubt that he has an urge to follow them. He has already written about cricket with a fine determination not to fall into the old familiar grooves.

From time to time Peter Walker will win cricket matches without being fully satisfied. His humour may keep him free from frustration until his discontent is dispelled in wider – but probably more complicated – fields.                                                 *The Cricketer*

# John Mortimore
## *A Captain Who Relishes his Cricket*

*August* 1965. John Mortimore is not easily summed up in a few words: but then, he is not a man of few words. His character, in fact, contains a series of near-contradictions – quiet in manner, yet talkative: enthusiastic, yet cool: a man of serious approach, yet with a good sense of humour: unassertive, yet quite firm and a convivial teetotaller.

In 1964, when Gloucestershire, their playing strength virtually halved by injuries, were having a depressing run of failures, Ken Graveney had to miss a match, and John Mortimore deputized for him as captain. Then Martin Young, in a characteristic 'crack', could say, 'Meet our new captain, John Mortimore who, in a single match, led us from bottom-but-one to bottom of the Championship.' The measure of John Mortimore is that he could share the joke and that his appointment this year as captain was accepted happily by his team, and with every expectation throughout the county that he would hold the post for many years.

'Morty' relishes his cricket the more for the fact that he had to earn his team-place with greater difficulties, in his native Gloucestershire, than he would have met elsewhere. In any other county in England, except perhaps Yorkshire, he could have cruised easily to a county cap. But in his first few years he was fighting for a position in a side with the strongest spin-bowling resources in the Championship. Sam Cook was established as the slow left-arm bowler and there could never be room for more than two of the three highly capable off-spinners – Mortimore, 'Bomber' Wells and David Allen – while a fourth, Hawkins, good enough to be accounted an allrounder elsewhere, rarely had the chance to turn his arm.

Mortimore had always been a modest cricketer: he was, too, quick to appreciate the different and appreciable merits of Wells and Allen to an extent that once made him wonder whether Gloucester would keep him on their staff. In the event the county hung on to all three of them for seven years until Wells went to Notts in 1960; only then could Allen and Mortimore regard themselves as secure – and by then they had both played for England.

Those two, like Arthur Milton, were educated at Cotham Grammar School, Bristol, and, if an injury to Allen had not kept him out of the last Test against India in 1959, the school would have had a record unequalled by any other, of providing three players for England in the same Test series.

If Mortimore's chief talent is as an off-break bowler, he is nevertheless a genuine all-rounder. He was barely eighteen when he batted with an impressively cool and mature air against Lindwall. Indeed, he has scored a thousand runs a season five times. It may seem surprising – though it is understandable in a team where, until now, the bowling on turning wickets was shared between three spinners – that he has taken a hundred wickets in a season only three times.

His defence is orthodox and watchful; he plays spin understandingly, pace resolutely: and, from time to time, with an exuberance which seems, somehow, out of character, he hits with immense power: his long, high driving of other off-spinners can be quite spectacular.

His bowling is pre-eminently steady. His action, not unlike that of J. C. White in reverse, has a hint of the jerkiness of machinery about it, but it is soundly based. His line is utterly controlled and his spin, if not so great as Allen's, is appreciable; his main strength lies in the extent, concealment and subtlety of his variations in flight, length and pace. Tall, lean, pale and bony, he has a somewhat unathletic look but he is physically well co-ordinated, with a wiry strength and considerable stamina. He maintains long bowling spells not only without wavering but without ever deteriorating into the merely mechanical, and he is always likely to outwit good batsmen when they are well set on perfect batting wickets.

On a pitch that helps him he can be quite deadly: on seven occasions he has taken five or more wickets in a single innings for less than twenty runs, and in 1962, on that favourite killing-ground of Gloucestershire spinners at Cheltenham, he took four Lancashire wickets in five balls.

As well as being a member of the team in his own right, John Mortimore has the attributes of a captain in temperament and mental equipment. Although he is a sensitive and deeply involved cricketer, he is never over-tense at a crisis: under pressure, his bowling remains steady, his catching safe as ever and his batting shrewd. He observes play and players sharply, works out his problems and talks originally and well about the game – not without a dry, and sometimes striking, humour. Drawn one day into that perennial theme of cricketing conversation in Gloucestershire, the slowness of the Bristol wicket, he remarked, with a completely deadpan expression, 'The ideal bowler for Bristol is a fast-medium, round-arm dwarf.'

John has only been capped since 1954 yet he stands with W. G. Grace and Reg Sinfield as the only three Gloucestershire players who have scored 10,000 runs and taken 1000 wickets. But for David Allen, he must undoubtedly have played in more than his nine Tests. It is no easy matter to captain a team which includes his rival for the place as England's off-break bowler. There must be occasions when one end is far more suitable than the other for an off-spinner: times when only one of the spinners should come on while a seam bowler shuts up the other end. It is a high tribute to John Mortimore's quality as a man that there is no doubt in the Gloucester committee room or dressing-room that he is big enough to resolve those problems wisely.          *The Cricketer*

# Derek Shackleton

## *The Man Who Simply Bowled Straight*

*April* 1969. Derek Shackleton's retirement simply does not belong in the eternal fitness of things. No one could deny that he is entitled to stop bowling: he has bowled more overs and taken more wickets than any other bowler in post-war cricket. But the county scene will seem incomplete without 'Shack' tirelessly wheeling his arm at one end for Hampshire. Indeed, it sometimes seemed that only the Laws saved him from bowling at both ends.

In 1968 he completed the unique feat of taking a hundred wickets in each of twenty successive seasons. Wilfred Rhodes reached that figure twenty-three times, but not consecutively. Only seven bowlers in the history of cricket have exceeded his 2850 wickets, and all of them played first-class cricket longer than 'Shack' – if he really *has* gone.

Last September, at forty-four, he seemed to be bowling as comfortably within himself, as subtly and as accurately as ever. His figures for the season were 1086 overs: 451 maidens: 109 wickets: average 17.32. Only two bowlers in the country, Titmus and Birkenshaw, both of slower pace, bowled as many overs, and only three – Underwood, Wilson and Illingworth, spinners in a summer of wet pitches – took as many wickets at lower average: no one bowled such a high proportion of maidens.

'Shack' became a bowler by accident. At the beginning of the 1948 season Hampshire were so desperate for opening bowlers that the club chairman ordered the entire playing strength into the nets to bowl as fast as they could. (Desmond Eagar gave an unforgettable imitation of Bill Voce.) It emerged that Shackleton, engaged as a batsman and who was a mild leg-spinner in the nets, had bowled 'seam up' in club cricket. He played sixteen county matches in that season: 228 runs at 11.4: 21 wickets at 29.57: unremarkable figures, but it was apparent to those who watched him that he improved from match to match. Then, and all through his subsequent career, he pondered and practised his bowling. In 1949 he emerged as an allrounder and missed the 'double' by only 86 runs. Hampshire never afterwards demanded his batting except in emergency – when it often proved valuable. He needed all his strength for bowling.

The change in Derek Shackleton's bowling over twenty-one years was slight: his pace, never far above medium, declined somewhat but he compensated for that by increased variety, and he still, though less often, stamped his left foot on the delivery stride and made the ball snap through a half-completed stroke.

In appearance he ended as slim and spruce as he began: his hair was a shade greyer but still every strand of it was in place. His light, heel-and-toe twelve-yard approach still brought him, wrist cocked, to a high sweep of an arm which seemed lubricated at the shoulder joint. Still he had the straightness which comes from bowling so nearly over the stumps, and virtually every ball demanded a stroke. Still, too, he was a little faster than he looked. In his early days he bowled almost solely inswing but he soon added the outswinger and, working quietly away, evolved almost every possible variation on 'seam up', while the height of his arm meant that he achieved baffling movement off the seam when there was any greenness in the pitch. Only one of his innovations failed – a slow off-break, at the sight of which his short-leg fieldsmen used to groan and duck: he did not bowl it for long.

He disguised his intention artfully; never appealed without good cause; and accepted punishment phlegmatically. He unfailingly applauded anyone who hit him for six and he never seemed ruffled by dropped catches or any other misfortune. Only, at times, for a reason no one ever discovered, he would, during his run-up, break into a ditty which began: 'I'll slap thee on the belly with a big flat fish.'

Oddly enough he never performed the hat-trick or took 'all ten': though he once had five wickets in nine balls against Leicester and four times took nine wickets in an innings. In the first innings of the Somerset match at Weston-super-Mare in 1955 he had figures of 11.1 overs: 7 maidens: 4 runs: 8 wickets – and followed that with six for 25 in the second. But 'Shack's' most valuable piece of bowling occurred on the third afternoon of the match with Derbyshire at Bournemouth in 1961 by which Hampshire became county champions for the first time in their history. After lunch Derbyshire, needing 252 to win, were 11 for one wicket. 170 minutes remained for play on a typically slow, easy Bournemouth pitch. (The three previous innings had been 306, 318 and 263 for eight: and there was no deterioration.) The likeliest outcome was a draw; but, in four overs against careful defensive batting, Shackleton had Gibson lbw, bowled Oates and Johnson and reduced Derbyshire to 24 for four. He came back afterwards to take two more wickets but he had already made the decisive breakthrough in the most unpromising circumstances. Pressed as to what he 'did' he said: 'I did all I could – I just bowled straight.'

Some eminent batsmen were his rabbits and he was hardly ever collared. Trueman at times chanced his arm and hit him long distances: but of established batsmen Martin Young probably had the best record against him. A bowling average of 18 over a period of twenty-one years, however, is economic by any standard.

He might well have played in more than his seven Tests for, as he demonstrated as late as 1963 when he was rising thirty-nine, he could plague and beat the best batsmen in the world on the Lord's pitch, where his statistical record must be quite unparalleled. Nevertheless, he was arguably the best county bowler in England since the war; perhaps of any time: and so far as Hampshire cricket is concerned, he is quite irreplaceable – even, he fears, by his son, Julian.     *The Cricketer*

# David Halfyard

### *Bowling Was His Abiding Passion*

*August* 1965. David Halfyard stands sadly alone among cricketers who take benefits or testimonials this season. The others are established players with years of cricketing maturity still ahead of them. Halfyard, however, will never play first-class cricket again, unless his immense enthusiasm and determination defy – and defeat – medical opinion.

In the Kent practice before this season started, he showed that, despite the savage injury to his left leg he can still bowl – and bowl well. But the handicap is too heavy for him to perform the stints that daylong county cricket demands.

So the modern game loses one of its most devoted cricketers, and Kent the man who, in his last season, still took more wickets than anyone else in the side.

Halfyard has never been a lucky cricketer. When he joined the Surrey staff – in 1954 – Alec Bedser, Loader and Surridge were the pace bowlers in the first team, while Kelleher, Cox, Hall and Rodney Pratt made the competition unusually stern at second-eleven level. Nevertheless, Halfyard was top of the second eleven bowling averages that year, and took more wickets than anyone else except Kelleher in 1955.

Such was the extent of talent on the Oval staff, however, that this was not enough to win him even a single first-team appearance and, in 1956, he joined Kent. He was then a fast-medium bowler whose pace was at times extremely hostile – as more than one of the Norfolk batsmen of 1955 can testify.

He was, though, no more than a straightforward bowler, lacking in experience of the first-class game and, in his first season for Kent, his fifty wickets cost 33.76 runs each. But Kent were desperately short of bowlers and only Fred Ridgway, with eighty-two, took more wickets in Championship matches. In that summer, too, Halfyard learnt much. A single-minded bachelor, he lived cricket, thought and talked little else and worked untiringly at the craft of bowling. By 1957 he made himself into a valuable county bowler, and established himself with nine for 39 on a drying wicket in the first innings of Glamorgan at Neath.

For the next six seasons he was the backbone of the Kent bowling, with never less than thirty – once over fifty – wickets more than the next man in the county's averages. From 1957 to 1961 he was the only player in the side to take a hundred wickets: in 1962 his accident found him two short, with six matches left.

Gradually he made himself into two bowlers. He remained a serviceable opener who could swing the new ball a little both ways. But he developed the ability to cut the old ball both ways at brisk pace. His leg-cutter was quite deadly on turning wickets and he employed the ball that came in from the off as an unsettling variation.

This was virtually asking to be over-bowled, and – because for several years the Kent bowling was so limited – he often was: but that never seemed to distress him – rather the reverse.

A bear-like man, thickly built – his playing weight was over fifteen stones – with heavy shoulders, deep chest and powerful arms, he made his ponderous, tireless way to the crease for hour after hour. 'The Machine' they called him, and not without reason nor without respect.

His hair came to a peak over a forehead crinkled into a forbidding frown, and he bowled with an unfailing blend of hostility and hope. Year after year he worked his way through more than a thousand overs of undimmed devotion. When the wicket gave his cutter any help, he never wanted to come off. In contrast to the general trend in modern cricket, Halfyard was rarely – we might almost say never – a defensive bowler. He set out to take wickets. In the course of an opening spell – sometimes in the first over – he would slip in a googly, and, more often than not, drop it on a length and turn it. If it did not take a wicket, the expression of surprise on the batsman's face was reward enough for him. However strongly the scoreboard might argue to the contrary, he lived in a state of perpetual belief that he would take a wicket with his next ball. That faith was justified to the extent of two hat-tricks – against Worcestershire in 1957 and Leicestershire in 1958 – and, in Kent's remarkable one-day win over Worcestershire at Tunbridge Wells in 1960, when he had figures of four for seven in the first innings and five for two in the second.

Altogether he took 768 wickets for Kent at an average of 24.27. His batting was somewhat rustic but he occasionally struck some powerful and useful blows at a crisis: he fielded bravely and keenly at short leg, though his build restricted him in any position away from the wicket.

He was a massively impressive figure in the bubble car he was driving to the Somerset match at Weston-super-Mare in 1962 when he had the collision which fractured his leg. When the Kent players went to visit him in hospital a few hours afterwards, his first words were, 'I shall bowl again.' Surely enough, he was back in 1963, determined to bowl. He played in Kent's first two matches of the season and, at a cost in pain we can only imagine, he bowled thirty-one overs against Yorkshire and thirty-four against Essex. Kent won both matches but Halfyard's figures were one wicket for 179 runs. Kent backed his efforts to make his way back, and he plugged away in the second eleven, where he took twenty-two wickets. Then came the pre-season practice of 1965: the old quality and the eagerness were there, but not the sustained physical power: sympathetically but firmly, Kent had to say that this was the end of the road.

If David Halfyard's testimonial adequately recognizes the years when he carried the county's bowling on those huge shoulders, his devotion and his courage, it will realize a high figure. It must seem like a premature farewell, regrettable, and regretted, on both sides. Now he is down in Cornwall, working to earn his living with a small boat. Certainly such an injury as his would have ended any ordinary man's career beyond all question. But this is David Halfyard – and no one can be *quite* sure that he will not, one day, come shambling back to the bowling which is his abiding passion.

*The Cricketer*

# Peter Lever

## *A Man for All Seasons*

*July* 1972. The heart of English cricket is the county game; and the essence of county cricket is not the Test star who dominates it but the ordinary county cricketer who is there every day and gives it his constant and fullest effort. He does not, like the representative players, miss a dozen county games a year to play for his country. He is the man for all seasons; county cricket is for him an achieved peak and a fulfilment. He is a recognizable, respected and relishable person; in his way a representative Englishman.

Once in a rare while, when opportunity and a peak spell of performance coincide, such a cricketer plays for England; and when that happens, the body of the game is splendidly happy for him.

Whatever may be argued about the Rest of the World series of 1970, it afforded passage into the England team for two of the most diligent craftsmen in the county game, in Brian Luckhurst and Peter Lever. Brian Luckhurst was the least widely fancied of the three batsmen brought in to replace established men unavailable for the first match; but by the end of the rubber he had established his England place. Peter Lever had less room for manoeuvre. He replaced Greig in the last game of the series and, coming on as second change, after Snow, Old and Wilson, produced the best figures of his career – seven for 83 – in the first innings of the World XI. They were the worthwhile wickets of Barlow, Graeme Pollock, Mushtaq, Sobers, Clive Lloyd, Procter and Intikhab. It was also his achievement that, when the Saturday crowd turned up to watch Pollock and Sobers continue their spectacular partnership of the previous day, they saw, instead, Peter Lever tying them down, putting them out and bowling himself into the side for Australia.

Hardly any cricketer – least of all a pace bowler who has never taken a hundred wickets in a season – can hope to be chosen for England for the first time within a month of his thirtieth birthday and, when that happened to him, Peter Lever accepted it with the excitement and gratitude of a modest man. Since then he has rarely been out of the England side.

Omitted for the First Test in Australia, he bowled his way in for the Second; proved an admirable foil to Snow in the decisive breakthrough in the Fourth; was the most effective England bowler in the Sixth; and, with three good and economical wickets in the first innings and Chappell's in the second, played an important part in the winning of the

Seventh which gave England the Ashes. It was soon obvious, too, that he was a good tourist.

Left out of the First Indian Test last summer, he came back in the Second at Old Trafford when his five for 70 and an innings of 88 not out gave England the winning chance that was destroyed by rain. He has taken part in two valuable batting partnerships, both wicket records for those Test series; 149 – in 133 minutes – with Alan Knott for the seventh wicket against New Zealand; and 187 with Ray Illingworth for the eighth in the 1971 Indian Test at Lord's.

So he entered his benefit year on a far more exalted plane then he could have foreseen even two years ago. He belongs in the tradition of Lancashire professionals. Born in the 'border town' of Todmorden – since the 1890s legally in Yorkshire but Lancashire by virtue of being a cotton rather than a woollen town – he has the ancient gratitude for cricket as an alternative to the mills, after his dragging months there after leaving school. He first appeared for Lancashire in 1960 when he was nineteen; but he studied and served long and earnestly in the shadow of the England bowlers, Brian Statham and Ken Higgs. He was not capped until 1965 and even in that season he played in only fourteen of the county's twenty-eight Championship matches. Subsequently the more explosive Ken Shuttleworth appeared superficially a better prospect, and was chosen in the first of the England-Rest of the World matches.

Peter Lever – as he cheerfully recognizes – has come to his present standing through solid virtues rather than outstanding brilliance. He bowls at full effort: it may be argued that his run-up is too long but it is the approach of one set upon lifting his natural medium pace to the highest level consonant with control. His stamina – doggedly developed by regular cross country running – and application are such that he can, and does, bowl long spells without loss of control or enthusiasm.

Finally, the spark which lifts him above some others is his ability to make the ball – new or worn – which pitches on the right-hander's stumps leave the bat late, and with all the life the pitch will grant. These merits have made him an honest and respected performer on the highest level of cricket. He never expected so much – but he has earnt it – and he would not demand more.

His team-mates and his opponents like him for the basic virtues of integrity, modesty and diligence: and they do not miss his humour. To the spectator he is an engaging rather than an exciting figure with his wiry fair hair, pale, expressive face and angular, determined approach. He always bowls his best, trying, in the old manner, to get the batsman out with every ball.

Peter Lever belongs truly in, and to, the North Country; his travels make him the more appreciative of home, with his wife and three children, on the moorland edge of Rochdale. He took a three-year course at Leeds in physical education and has spent much time coaching young cricketers. Yet it is by no means certain that he will take that line after he leaves the county game. He has an alert mind, concerned with matters other than cricket and he could yet make a mark outside the world of games.                                      *The Cricketer*

# Jack Birkenshaw
## *A Flighter in the Classical Mould*

Jack Birkenshaw has always looked a cricketer. So trimly turned out as to satisfy even the most sergeant-majorly of the old time senior professionals, he is always 'in' any game he plays. Appropriately he is an allrounder in a team of allrounders; in their fine – and all but triply successful – season of 1972, virtually all the Leicestershire players bowled: even the wicket-keeper, Roger Tolchard, took one for four; at least fourteen others bowled usefully: and all the 'specialist' bowlers scored runs at a pinch.

This makes for healthy competition and Jack Birkenshaw, for all his modest, rather boyish look – it is difficult to realize that the youngster who played for Yorkshire at seventeen is now thirty-three – is a competitor. His figures may not be spectacular but he has performed a couple of hat-tricks, scored three centuries and is steadily approaching career records of a thousand wickets, ten thousand runs and two hundred catches: you must be a truly capable county cricketer to do as much as that.

He will improvise – or even uncharacteristically slog – quick runs in an over-limit game; or go in early to shore up a toppling innings in a Championship match: he will catch tidily close in, pick up and return tidily from the deep.

Essentially, however, he is an off-break bowler. Yorkshire recognized his ability while he was still at school and he is a natural – but now also a mature and highly informed – finger-spinner. His approach is light-footed, keen and springy, his delivery swing smooth but constantly varied. The accuracy of his line and length is a matter of professional pride and he genuinely spins the ball; but the best of his work is done through the air.

In modern times every spin bowler must learn at times to bowl economically flat in the over-limit game: but Jack Birkenshaw is a flighter in the classical mould. Wilfred Rhodes would have appreciated that inviting curve that disappears in a dip steep enough to produce the early, lofted and catchable stroke. This is the true art of the finger-spinner and Jack Birkenshaw has it; it is a major facet of his deep relish for the game of cricket. *Testimonial Brochure*, 1974

# Clive Radley
## *An Unmistakeable Lord's Product*

Lord's has always trained its cricketers hard. They are invariably neatly turned out, highly disciplined, diligent in the field, basically correct in method. Clive Radley is an unmistakable Lord's product – yet there is no doubt that, out of sheer enthusiasm, he would have been all those things even if he had never been near St John's Wood.

He is the ultimately dedicated cricketer. He bats with immense devotion. When he decides to defend, he is all orthodox forward defensive and determination; but you feel he would put his heart between ball and wicket to keep it out. When he attacks, he is not afraid to go down the wicket to the spinners, he uses his feet as nimbly as anyone in the game, improvises well and hustles the opposing field; while he is so fast between the wickets as often to leave his partner gasping.

He has some three hundred catches in first-class cricket as evidence of his superbly clean pair of hands – especially at slip – and his concentration, speed over the ground, quickness of pick-up and return, make him a splendid fieldsman anywhere.

Hertford-born, Clive Radley made his first appearance for Middlesex in 1964 when he was twenty; and in only his second season he shared with Fred Titmus the record Middlesex sixth-wicket partnership, of 227 against the South Africans. Capped in 1967, when he first scored a thousand runs in the season, he has done as much with complete consistency every year since. He has scored centuries in all four competitions; won three one-day match awards and been as near Test selection as a place in a Test trial. Among the new generation of young Middlesex players he now is an old hand, but he still plays with the eagerness of youth. Indeed, those who have played with him and watched him will always remember Clive Radley as the keenest and most whole-hearted of cricketers. *Beneficiary Souvenir Programme*, 1977

# Brian Reynolds
### *Northants' Northamptonshire Cricketer*

*June* 1965. The difference between post-war and inter-war cricketers is as clear as that between the two generations in any other field: it would be a contradiction of social history if it were not so. The amateur-professional distinction has been abolished but, in cricket, as in any other walk of life, the term 'a good professional' remains a compliment.

Brian Reynolds is cast in the mould of the traditional 'senior pro', that non-commissioned officer of the game whose duty it was to see that the side functioned efficiently. In fact he *is* the Northants senior professional, but he would be the same man if the appointment had never been made. He thinks in team terms, watches a game wisely, and is the kind of man any captain can turn to with trust. His turn-out – from well brushed cap and neatly trimmed hair, to freshly blancoed boots – bespeaks a respect for his work. His jaw and his steady look are those of a man of purpose. Fresh-faced and as honest as he looks, the word that best sums him up is 'reliable': let us say *utterly* reliable.

Brian Reynolds was good enough to play for Northants when he was eighteen, but then he went on two years' National Service, did not win a team place until 1953, and was not capped until 1956. Keith Andrew is the only remaining member of the Northants team that finished runners-up in the Championship of 1957. Reynolds lost the season of 1960 after he fractured his leg playing soccer for Kettering Town (that caused him to retire from playing football and he has, rather characteristically, become a first-class referee). He has scored over a thousand runs in each of seven seasons and he comes to his benefit year pressing on 14,000 runs and with a record of turning a good cricketing hand to any job the side needs done.

When Ken Fiddling left the county, Brian Reynolds took over as wicket-keeper and, in emergency, he can still fill that post capably. When Dennis Brookes retired, Reynolds, though by nature a middle-order batsman, stepped up to open the innings in his place. This year, when Mick Norman was out of action with scalded hands, Reynolds, normally a close fieldsman, replaced him adequately at cover-point.

His strength is his batting. He grew up as a front-foot player, scoring most of his runs by heavy-handed drives. As an opening batsman, he has moved more on to the back foot and, playing his strokes later, has developed his hooking, glancing and rather square cutting. Steady, unflinching before high pace and a careful watcher of the ball, he is temperamentally well suited to open the innings.

It is a reflection of his conscientious approach that he tends to be a 'nought-or-four' batsman. When his side is in trouble he can defend doggedly and, despite his inclinations, he will eschew all risks, rarely even taking a marginal chance to push ones or twos. But, when runs are wanted in a hurry, Reynolds's duty becomes his pleasure and he hammers the ball as if he hated it, with the full, impressive power of his strong arms and shoulders.

In the field he is a good close catcher, particularly at slip, while he anticipates well and, for all his four-square build, moves quickly and smoothly in the deep.

A modestly quiet man with an easy humour, Brian Reynolds has at least two prides. His bowling is not often seriously discussed but, if pressed, he will allow you to know that his four wickets in first-class cricket (at an average of 46) were all of Test batsmen. More seriously, he is a Northamptonshire man, whose Army service was in the Northamptonshire Regiment. His county has ranged the world to recruit the strongest possible team and, in Norman's absence, Brian Reynolds is the only Northamptonshire-born player in the side. In his own mind he is not only a cricketer, he is a *Northamptonshire* cricketer.

*The Cricketer*

# Brian Bolus

## *He Has Earned His Benefit*

My acquaintance with Brian Bolus is long enough for me to remember him taking his bowling seriously – and, indeed, you may find him in the 1956 bowling averages of Yorkshire second eleven with such names as Brian Close, Bob Platt, Bob Appleyard and ahead of Mel Ryan, Eddie Leadbeater and Philip Hodgson.

Nowadays we – like him – may settle for his batting and fielding; and relish the greatest 'I'll show them' act in cricket history when, not re-engaged by Yorkshire at the end of the 1962 season, he moved to Notts, and in less than a year, won a county cap, scored 2190 runs in the season, played himself into the England team and on the MCC tour of India.

He has played many brilliant innings but none more striking than in his first match for England when he opened the innings, hit his first ball in Test cricket – from no less a bowler than Wesley Hall – for four, and took ten off the over.

He was to find Test cricket increasingly hard going and, while it has never seemed to me that the amateur-professional distinction was one of general importance, in Brian Bolus's case I believe it was. A clear-minded man, he recognized that, for all his gifts as a stroke-maker, his living ultimately depended on runs. Therefore he went the certain way about making runs: but if he had had no obligations, many who know him believe he would have followed his inclination, matched himself against the bowlers, played attacking strokes and become one of the great forcing batsmen. Professionally turning to a more utilitarian game, he lost his England place – though he still has a Test batting average of 44, higher than that of many batsmen picked more often for their country.

Crucially, he has not surrendered. He is probably a shrewder player than he used to be, but he still strikes the ball magnificently, especially on the leg side – and on the off when bowlers are not bowling defensively to him, as they usually do – and he still clearly revels in the game.

He remains, like the young man I met fifteen years ago, bright, well scrubbed and groomed, quick of mind and with a perky sense of humour; one who, faced by challenge, rolls his already high-rolled sleeves higher still and goes out to meet it.

He has earned a generous benefit, for he has not merely enjoyed cricket but, from his very approach to it, he has helped spectators to enjoy it, too; and he has much effective and entertaining batting still to offer to Nottinghamshire cricket, and to the game in general.

*Nottinghamshire CCC Annual*, 1971

# Maurice Tremlett

## *Memories of Regal Purple*

The appointment of Maurice Tremlett to the captaincy of Somerset is a departure from that county's tradition. We may assume that it was not made without considerable thought, and those of us who know him will realize, too, that the appointment could redound immensely to the advantage of the side and of the player himself.

It was May, 1947; a Monday; and I went up to Lord's to watch the Middlesex–Somerset match in what was already emerging as a summer and sun, runs, Edrich and Compton. The first change bowler for Somerset was this fair-haired, athletic-looking young man with a sweeping run-up and a high, easy, natural delivery-swing. He swept away Compton – clean bowled – and four of the batsmen who followed him – five wickets for eight runs in five overs. It was as exciting a spell of bowling as I have ever watched and, in the poverty of our post-war game, the man responsible for it was a heady promise of resurgent greatness in English cricket.

Still, after Middlesex's first-innings lead of 97, Somerset needed 176 to win and, with five wickets down for 101 that night, they looked unlikely to get them. So it was socially, rather than in anticipation of watching cricket that I arranged to lunch at the Tavern next day. I went for a meal and found the stage set for drama – or anti-climax. Somerset's last two batsmen – Tremlett and Hazell – were together and they came out after lunch, needing 16 to win. *Wisden* says that Tremlett (in his first county match, remember) showed 'confidence and rashness'. Just one wicket to fall; surely, I thought, this must be batting of attrition. Then came that stroke that I have seen Maurice play many times since but never with quite the same astonished delight, nor against quite the same background – up went that great straight drive and into the seats before the pavilion. Twice again he drove past mid-on and, suddenly, the game was over. Somerset had won and, spontaneously, the Middlesex players cheered the two batsmen into the pavilion. Not often does cricket so stir the emotions. The only word for it was – indeed, *is* – 'splendid', with all that that great word implies.

No one has suffered more for those two days than Maurice Tremlett. I was by no means the only man impressed by them; folk in high office within cricket reacted in the same way. He was hustled into running before he could walk. He was swept too soon into representative cricket – and, greatest tragedy of all – he had too many captains. Now, at last, he has the chance to adjust the matter for himself. In that first season of his, he grew up as a fast-medium bowler who was, unusually among men of that pace, at his best with a worn ball, for his sharpest weapon was the classical break-back of the old fast bowlers, the men, like Charles Kortright, who rubbed the ball in the dirt to give their fingers adequate grip for the fierce breakback. He was, too, in that first season, developing as a batsman. During the very next winter, in the West Indies, he was given the new ball to open the bowling, and batted at number eleven.

He was to suffer again on the 1948–49 tour of South Africa, though, this time, from being underestimated. He was to suffer, too, from his own modesty and lack of confidence. Uncertain in his control of the swinging new ball, he was to be jeered out of his bowling gift by his own Somerset supporters. Certainly, cricket has not served him over-generously.

Yet always he has looked a handsome batsman. Like Sammy Woods, he looks a Somerset player although he is not a West Countryman by birth. Born in Cheshire, he might have gone to Middlesex and, in a 'fashionable' county, his Somerset friends may argue, he might have done better.

Let us, for the moment, forget his bowling, though I cannot help but believe that it needs only the smallest spark to fire that magnificent gift of his once more. Let us regard him as a batsman and close-fieldsman. In the latter role, he sustained a serious eye injury which, some thought, would put him out of cricket and even more believed must break his nerve. If any proof were needed of Maurice's courage, it lies in his un-flinching return, as soon as his sight was restored, to his old close-in position, where he still sweeps up the ball with the same lazy, yet im-pressive, ease.

At the crease, and in form, he can sometimes look like a man playing with boys as he leans comfortably forward to play a defensive stroke. Experience and swing bowling have developed in him the strokes essen-tial to the modern batsmen who has often to carry the main responsi-bility of his county's innings. Still, however, from time to time, his glorious lofted straight drive, the regal purple of cricket, bursts out, to lift a day of hard-fought cricket to a memorable moment. The batsman himself is at rest, bat hanging from his hand, before the mighty arc of the hit is ended beyond the ring.

He has always been a shrewd observer of the game, of his colleagues and his opponents. His criticism is friendly, but extremely well in-formed and he might easily develop into a considerable strategist if he is granted the reasonable due of a long run in the captaincy. Certainly any good cricketer should be happy to play under him.

Cricket memory will always retain the picture of Maurice Tremlett, a natural athlete, changed but still not destroyed, by the mechanics of contemporary cricket. Remember him, too, on many days when his duty to his side has meant hour after hour of batting in shackles when cricket has been a duty, instead of risk-riding pleasure to which his nature bids him.

Remember him, perhaps most fairly, as one who has given much to cricket, and particularly to Somerset cricket, with less return than some who have given less. And do not forget that there is greatness in him yet to be seen on our cricket fields.     *Somerset CCC Year Book*, 1955–56

# Micky Stewart

### *Batsman, Captain, Catcher and Enthusiast*

*July* 1965. The six-hour day and six-day week of routine of county cricket tends to slow down many men who, probably subconsciously, save their strength by answering the tempo of the play. Micky Stewart has never allowed himself to be reduced – mentally or physically – to plodding. He takes his benefit this year, rising thirty-three and with the responsibility of the Surrey captaincy, but still jaunty, alert, almost boyishly anxious to get on with the game.

Stewart is one of our more heavily battered players, but a whole series of injuries finds him still facing fast bowling, and fielding alarmingly close to the bat at forward short-leg, with the same lively enthusiasm.

In 1949 Stewart became the first boy of Alleyn's School to play for the Public Schools at Lord's. At that time he batted at number three or four, usually fielded at cover and was a change-bowler of off-˙ reaks. He had thought to go up to University after his National Service but, while he was still in the Royal Engineers, a suggestion from Kent that he should join their staff made him consider professional cricket as a career. When he asked his native county, Surrey, for permission to take up the offer, they countered with an invitation to come to The Oval, and he accepted.

An average of 41 in the second eleven after he was demobilized in 1953 brought him some county games the next year and his first century – 109 against the Pakistanis. In 1955 he made the positive advance to the top class; it was his first full season, he scored a thousand runs, finished third to May and Barrington in the Surrey averages, took 55 catches, won his county cap and, at the end of the season, moved up to open the innings.

Under the encouragement of Stuart Surridge, he had now left the covers to field at forward or square short-leg where, in 1957, he set a new record for all fieldsman – other than a wicket-keeper – when he caught seven batsmen in the second innings of Northants at Northampton. He ended the season with 77 catches – only one short of Walter Hammond's record. That year the Cricket Writers' Club elected him Young Cricketer of the Year by a large majority.

His batting has always been based on the urge to dominate the bowling – particularly the initial pace – though he has curbed the impetuosity that, too often, cost him his wicket in his early days. Nimble footwork takes him quickly into position for his strokes and, an eager, militant hooker and a strong cutter, either square or fine, he scores heavily and fast from anything short of a length. The more experienced county bowlers are careful to maintain a full length to him, but he is not slow to drive the overpitched ball.

On figures – 2045 runs at 44.45 – 1962, when he played twice against Pakistan, was his best season: but it is doubtful if he has ever batted better than in the first half of the 1963 summer. Once he is 'in the runs', he tends to reel them off in innings after innings and he did so then, so effectively and dominatingly as to win a place in four Tests against West Indies. His 87 was the highest score for England in the Old Trafford

Test where he played the spin bowling of Gibbs, Worrell and Sobers with considerable skill. As vice-captain of the MCC side in India during the following winter he seemed to have the chance to establish his England place but he twice fell ill, the second time so seriously that he had to return home part way through the tour. He remains a strong candidate, and rival of his team-mate, John Edrich, for the post as Boycott's opening partner and his claim is the stronger if the selectors insist on an aggressive approach to batting.

Stewart's footballing career was regrettably short. As an inside forward for Wimbledon, Hendon and Corinthian-Casuals, he was a fast mover, with the brain and dexterity to make openings, and he won an amateur International cap in 1956. Then he turned professional with Charlton Athletic and, though his ability was brightly apparent at that level, his light build coupled with his somewhat dashing style exposed him to injuries which threatened his fitness for cricket. Finally, the clash of overlapping seasons decided him that, since cricket was the game he most wanted to play, he must concentrate on it.

After two years as deputy captain of Surrey he succeeded to the full office in 1963, in what seemed to many likely to be a lengthy lean period after the county's great run. Now he has a team with as promising a group of young players as any in the country, and he has worked hard to imbue them with his own sense of urgency.

Stewart no longer bowls; but he enlivens the bowlers under him. As keen in September as in May, walking quickly and lightly from short leg at one end to short leg at the other, he is perpetually 'in' the game: and, from time to time, he lifts it by taking a full hit off the bat, or diving an improbable distance to make a catch which most men would not even have considered as a chance. *The Cricketer*

# Ken Suttle

### *'Useful' Stalwart of Sussex*

*July* 1966. Ken Suttle is the one constant figure in the Sussex cricket scene of recent years. Indeed, unless some remarkable catastrophe befalls, by the time this appears in print, he will have played in 345 consecutive Championship games for Sussex. He began the sequence on 18 August, 1954 and over that period, too, he has been the county's most consistent batsman.

Some have thought that he crosses – from slip at one end, to slip at the other – between overs, side by side with Alan Oakman – who stands almost a foot taller – as a deliberate contrast-comedy act. This is not so:

the careful observer will note that, as they walk – and while they stand in the slips – they are in conversation. To be more accurate, Suttle is talking to Oakman. It has been assumed, too, that Oakman's stoop betokens that he is listening. Neither is this the fact. Oakman's slouch is his natural attitude, and, while he may *hear* Suttle, he is rarely *listening*. But 'Oakie' is a kindly chap, and he cannot bring himself to such heartlessness as denying Suttle an audience.

It is fortunate for Suttle that he is a good enough slip to field there: for he feels desperately lonely in the outfield, and, when he stood at mid-off or mid-on, the bowlers used to complain that he talked to them as they walked back, and disturbed their rumination or concentration as the case might be.

From this it will be gathered that Suttle, K. G., is gregarious. It may be added that he is also game, friendly, cheerful, and that his shrewdness is tempered by charity.

His main – but not his sole – value to Sussex is as a left-hand batsman; usually, nowadays, as an opener, but, in other years at different positions in the top half of the order. The purists may take exception to some of his strokes. That does not worry him: so far as he is concerned he is paid to make runs for Sussex, not to be a model for text books. His justification lies in having scored over a thousand runs for Sussex for each of the last thirteen seasons. Superficially one recalls his penchant for the cut: he will often back away to play that stroke, with some impudence, to a ball very close to the line of the stumps – a number of aggrieved bowlers, indeed, have sworn that he has played it off middle-and-leg. Others remember his pull, which is quite impish in its defiance of the ancient canons of batsmanship – but profitable. His hooking – for all his lack of height he is an aggressive player of fast bowling – and his spanking drives are more orthodox, and these four strokes bring him most of his fours. It is less often noticed, however, that he is a busy, and virtually irrepressible maker of runs. He is extremely hard to keep quiet because his quick footwork constantly takes him into position to play the less spectacular, bread-and-butter shots with which he pushes the ball through the leg-side field, nudges or steers it to the off, for so many useful singles that often one can look at the scoreboard and be surprised that he has come so unobtrusively to a useful score against bowling which seemed to be restrictive.

Ken Suttle is a busy cricketer. Last season he was the only Sussex player to make a thousand runs in Championship matches: to be precise, he scored 507 more runs than anyone else in the side. He has shared in century partnerships for every Sussex wicket from one to nine: when he and Peter Kelland put on 119 for the ninth against Worcester in 1952, Suttle's share was 109. Of all the famous batsmen in Sussex cricket history, only one – John Langridge – scored more runs for the county.

His nearest approach to representative cricket was selection for the West Indian tour of 1953–54, when he was twelfth man in all five Tests, and made a remarkably deep impression on his captain, Len Hutton, by his unfailing diligence, good nature and consideration.

Because he can hardly bear to be 'out' of a cricket match, Ken Suttle has bowled orthodox, slow left-arm, the 'Chinaman', or little floaters hardly fast enough to be called 'seamers' – whatever his captain has asked or the situation has suggested. His length is tidy enough, his tactical sense bright and the outcome has been some two hundred wickets – including four for five (v Worcester, 1961), four for six (v Lancashire, 1959) and three for none (v Surrey, 1965). All these performances were achieved on the traditional batsman's wicket at Hove. Once at Edgbaston, however, the Warwickshire batsmen hit him for 72 runs from eight overs: his consolation lay in the fact that he took four wickets in the process.

He has been a spectacularly one-footed outside-left, of considerable shooting-power, for Chelsea, Brighton, Chelmsford, Tonbridge, and, as player-manager, Arundel; in other English winters he has coached conscientiously, and with characteristic good nature, in South Africa.

Many adjectives might be applied to Ken Suttle as a cricketer – cheerful, industrious, brave, alert – but he himself probably would prefer to be called useful. Certainly more impressive-looking batsmen have scored fewer runs; more spectacular fielders have taken fewer difficult catches and more esteemed bowlers have less often 'nipped in' with good wickets. Perhaps this is what he tells Alan Oakman as they walk across between overs.  *The Cricketer*

# W. J. Stewart

## *A Memorable Big Hitter*

*July* 1965. William James – Jim – Stewart is a large, likeable and unlucky cricketer. One of the biggest hitters of our time – not a slogger but a fine, clean striker of the ball – two operations interrupted his career at its peak.

Born in Carmarthen, Stewart played in a Welsh rugby trial and there was once some wishful talk of his leaving Warwickshire for Glamorgan, but he is a genuine Midlander by absorption. His parents brought him from Wales when he was a boy and he played rugby at Coventry, as a centre-three-quarter, at the age of sixteen, in the same year as he joined the Warwickshire staff. By coincidence his first Championship match was against Glamorgan and Willie Jones, recognizing Welsh blood as thicker than water – though to the anger of his captain – gave Jim 'one off the mark'. He won a regular team place and his county cap, and scored his first century (fifteen fours in his 104) two years afterwards – in 1957 – and began a run of five fine seasons.

Basically a front-foot player, he is correct enough in technique to have been an effective opening batsman. He always liked to go in first and he and Norman Horner were as aggressive an opening pair as any in post-war cricket. His main scoring range has always been in the arc between mid-off and mid-on, for he is a superb driver, not merely of the half-volley or full-length ball, but also, and valuably, of the ball taken 'on the rise'. As well as being immensely strong, he has a natural sense of timing and the power of his driving is such that his mishits – from which other men would be caught – often carry for sixes.

His defence is capable because it is correct, but his inclination is always to carry the fight to the bowler: and on his day he is a murderer of off-spin. He pulls powerfully, but rarely hooks: though he flicks the short ball down the leg side, he absorbed from Fred Gardner – an altogether different type of player whose technique he much respected – an almost masochistic willingness to allow fast short-pitched bowling to hit him on the body.

Stewart established a place in the record books in 1959 when, scoring a century in each innings of Warwickshire's match with Lancashire at Blackpool, he hit the record number of seventeen sixes, ten in his first innings. In that season he played a sequence of five consecutive innings for 155, 4, 156, 155 and 125. The next year he missed nine Championship matches through injury but nevertheless made nineteen scores of fifty or over and was chosen for the MCC tour of New Zealand in the following winter. He was troubled again by injuries in 1961 but still made more than a thousand runs: then, in 1962, he had statistically the best season of his life: going in regularly first wicket down, he had an aggregate of 2318 and an average of 43.73.

At this high point of his cricket life, by the same evil luck as brought the broken toe that kept him out of a final Welsh Rugby trial (his deputy won a cap), he had to have the big toe of his left foot amputated. Ever since, his batting balance has been, to the eye slightly, but for him crucially, affected: and his mobility in the field is impaired.

He did not find the way back easy but in 1965, on the whole a poor year for Warwickshire, he was their only player to score a century in a Championship match and finished top of their batting averages. Then, at the end of that season, he had an operation for an arthritic condition in the right hand, and played in only six Championship matches in 1966.

Although he began his rugby career as a centre, he played at full back in three of the outstanding Warwickshire teams that won the County Championship.

An amiable man, it might be argued that Jim has never disliked his opponents as the great competitors have done; sometimes, too, his modesty reached a point of sheer self-mistrust.

Still only thirty-two, but for physical troubles he should still be a major county batsman. He remains a friendly member of the Warwickshire party; he will be remembered as one who, even against modern restrictive bowling methods, was a memorable big hitter, and as an admirable trencherman with a genuine respect for good cooking and a fine capacity for it. *The Cricketer*

# Dick Richardson

## *A 'Genuine Competitor'*

*June* 1967. 'Dick' Richardson of Worcestershire is, in the language of the moment, a 'genuine competitor' – always, as batsman or fieldsman, a potential match-winner.

Christened Derek Walter, he is the second of the three cricketing sons – all left-hand batsmen – of Walter Richardson, a Herefordshire farmer. The eldest brother, Peter, who preceded him at Worcester and went on to Kent, opened the innings for England in 34 Tests: Bryan is on the Warwickshire staff.

Dick was only seventeen when he first appeared for Worcestershire – against Oxford University in 1952. Two more matches in 1953 and one in 1954 comprised his entire county career – though he had gained some useful experience with Stourbridge in the Birmingham and District League – before he made his rapid impact on the first-class game. He established his place in the Worcestershire side in the latter half of the 1955 season – when he completed a century against Gloucestershire with a broken thumb – won his county cap in 1956, and was chosen for England – in the same team as his brother Peter – in the Trent Bridge Test of 1957 with West Indies.

That match and that summer remain the high plateau of his individual achievement, if not of his contribution towards team-success. He scored 1830 runs (with five centuries) at an average of 32.67 that season, was chosen twice for Players v Gentlemen and, if some thought him lucky to be picked so soon for England, he was making his runs with impressive fluency. His Test innings of 33 was fashioned with an air of confident maturity and he was not among those who dropped the catches which cost England the win they seemed to have earned. But, apart from playing again for the Players in 1958, he has not since been selected for any representative match.

He has settled, however, into a notoriously awkward and combative number six for Worcestershire. He has scored a thousand runs in each of nine seasons and established the idea in the minds of his opponents that Worcestershire are never beaten until Dick Richardson is out. He is resolute, and generally correct, in defence, and never flinches from the highest pace. But he is at his best when he attacks; he cuts brilliantly and, out of wiry strength, drives to a remarkable length: it is usually when he makes his powerful pulled drive that he tends to play across the line of the ball which is his main technical fault.

He played a memorable innings at Dudley against Hampshire in that county's Championship year of 1961. White – at high pace – Heath and Shackleton all made the ball rear angrily from a difficult pitch and at one point Worcestershire were 107 for five. That was the cue for Richardson to mount a spectacular attack; disregarding some savage blows on the hands and body he hit both White and Heath high back over their heads, he scored 92, and with Booth his defensive partner at the other end, doubled the score and changed the entire feeling – though not the result – of the game. This was Richardson at his vivid and characteristic best.

He is a brilliant field anywhere, though he is rarely now seen in the deep because he is so valuable a catcher close to the wicket, usually at slip or in the gully. In 1961, he set a county record with 64 catches. At silly-point he has stood as close as any man in the history of the game – often, indeed, within swinging range of the bat – and, apart from the catches he makes there, he must give his bowlers a considerable psychological advantage.

To the beginning of this season, he had scored 16,147 runs, made 408 catches and, with his occasional right-arm leg-break or medium-pace bowling, taken seven wickets at the unimpressive average of 40.43. But the manner of Dick Richardson's cricket – aggressive and, at times, brilliant – transcends his figures. *The Cricketer*

# Jimmy Binks

## *The Best Wicket-Keeper in England*

*June* 1967. There is no doubt whatever in Yorkshire that Jimmy Binks is the best wicket-keeper in England – if not, indeed, in the world. His fellow-craftsmen in the other counties, though sympathetic towards one of their own hard-worked and underestimated kind, are quickest to spot a weakness: but, as one of the most experienced of them put it: 'Up or back, Jimmy is the most consistent wicket-keeper in the country.'

Consistency is a stern yardstick by which to measure him, for he has had little rest since he came into the first-class game. At the end of June 1955 Yorkshire's regular wicket-keeper, Roy Booth – now with Worcestershire – was injured and Binks was drafted into the side as his replacement. He caught the first three batsmen in the Northants second innings and kept so well that there was never any question of losing his place. Since then he has not missed a single Championship match for Yorkshire and, indeed, only one other – when he was picked for the MCC against Surrey, in May 1964. So, to the beginning of this season, he had appeared in an unbroken sequence of 334 Championship matches – second only to Ken Suttle among current players.

Yet if ever there was a refutation of the argument that our cricketers play too much cricket for their good, Jimmy Binks personifies it. He has a lively, boyish air, moves with an air of eagerness, retains his sense of humour – often valuably when nerves are on edge in a taut game – and never loses his zest for cricket or his fighting quality.

No one points to a particular strength in his wicket-keeping, rather they emphasize that he has no identifiable weakness. He has taken the varied pace of Trueman, the two types of spin of Wardle and almost every style of bowling in the game with uniform efficiency. It is usually considered that off-spin provides the most searching test of a wicket-keeper because he is so often blinded by the batsman: but Binks has handled it in the shape of Wardle's quickly turning 'Chinaman' and Illingworth's 'natural' break with its tendency to float away in the air. Compact in build like the classical wicket-keepers, he handles cleanly, takes spin bowling close to the stumps, and reaches some extremely wide deflections off the faster bowlers: but it is all done in a quiet fashion – except his appeal, which is more a triumphant statement than a question.

In his early days he batted last or at number ten, though in his first season he made 42 not out against Notts when his ninth-wicket stand of 92 with Illingworth changed the shape of the game and gave Yorkshire a first-innings lead. Since then he has graduated efficiently to number seven or eight, with all that position means in terms of responsibility – shoring up a collapsing innings or making quick runs according to the tactical situation.

It is surprising – in Yorkshire disgraceful – that his representative honours have been so few. He was flown out as a replacement when John Murray became unfit on the India-Pakistan tour of 1961–62, but took part in only two first-class matches. He was chosen in his own right for India 1963–64 – a tour on which his good spirits were much needed –

and he three times opened the England innings in Tests with Brian Bolus: at Bombay their stand of 125 averted the possibility of defeat. Few cricketers can have been so long or so justifiably in the minds of the selectors with such slight result.

Fresh-faced and merry-looking, Jimmy Binks comes from Hull – not as a rule a rich ground for Yorkshire players – but he is popular throughout the county as both man and cricketer. *The Cricketer*

# 7

# International Stars

## Barry Richards

*A Superlative Cricketer*

Barry Richards is a great batsman. Only his West Indian namesake Vivian and Greg Chappell challenge him as the finest in the world today. To say he is a great cricketer is not simply a technical assessment but a universally valid fact. Anyone who has watched him make a big score has felt a whole groundful of people, many of them completely unconcerned with technique, respond, from the heart, to the splendour of his batting. On the other side of the coin, when he is out cheaply the delight of the opposing side is matched only by the disappointment of the spectators.

Once in two or three generations there comes a batsman who beguiles even his opponents; such is Barry Richards; no one recognizes superlative cricket more clearly than an English professional cricketer. When he plays a major innings it appeals both to the savage and the artist in us. He butchers bowling, hitting with a savage power the more impressive for being veiled by the certainty of his timing. Yet, simultaneously, he appeals to the aesthetic sense because of the innate elegance of his movement, the sensitivity with which he harnesses the ball's course, such a princely case of style as makes the batting of some Test players seem workaday stuff.

He was seventeen when he first came to England as captain of the visiting South African Schools team of 1963. Against a number of adult sides he averaged 49.87 for the tour: an innings of 79 at a run a minute against Hampshire II caused Leo Harrison, then the county coach, to say, 'That is the best young batsman I have ever seen.' In 1965 Richards returned, with Mike Procter, to play a season on the Gloucestershire staff. He was not qualified for the county, but against the touring South Africans he made a handsome 59. Back home he scored a century for 'A South African XI' against the 1966–67 Australians but most surprisingly was not given a Test place against them.

When overseas players were admitted to the County Championship by special registration, in 1968, Richards negotiated with Sussex. He joined Hampshire because of Leo Harrison's unwavering belief in his genius. That opinion was justified at once when, in a dismally wet season, he scored 2395 runs at 47.90, an average bettered only by Boycott. He could not be kept out of the 1970 South African side against Australia; he was second to Graeme Pollock in the Test batting with 508 runs at 72.37. In 1970–71 he was engaged by South Australia and played a considerable part in the Sheffield Shield win with a phenomenal batting average of 109.86. Often in that season his performances diverted attention from the MCC tour. He is a cricketer of the jet age, fully conscious of the ease – and the danger – of playing too much cricket. By the end of the 1976 season he had scored 14,975 runs in English first-class cricket; 5868 in major over-limit matches; 9516 in South Africa where he plays for Natal; and 1538 in Australia. That is enough of his figures; although their number is prodigious, they have been surpassed by others; the manner of their making has been princely, even prodigal. Four or five times a year he plays innings quite unforgettable in their splendour. We are concerned with an almost unbelievably complete batsman.

Six feet tall and leanly but strongly built, Richards is a perfectly balanced right-hander. Basically his defence is sound and correct. When he sets out to play himself in, no one in the world has a straighter bat. His footwork then is unhurriedly fast; he is in position for his stroke so early that he has time to play it with an air of apparent boredom. Once he is set he will attack any bowling in the world; despite the curbs bowlers attempt to impose on him.

It is then apparent that whilst he has all the gifts of the great batsman, others match him in some of them; but his eye is quite incomparable. He sees and identifies the length and line of the bowled ball that moment faster than others which enables him to play at leisure where they must hurry. Thus, he often moves down the pitch to medium or fast-medium bowlers as assuredly as if they were slow spinners. Or, so sure is he of the ball, he simply does not bother to use his feet at all but stands still and throws his bat at it with such certainty as appals bowlers. Even then the consummate skill of his placing is apparent. He steers his strokes through a packed field with a precision which saves his legs and accounts for the high proportion of fours in his big scores.

Because of his brilliance, because he is capable of winning a match in two or three hours – an over-limit game in less – every captain and bowler in cricket plots to contain him. Few succeed. He is happiest in off-side strokes; most of all, the cover drive off the front foot; though with some affection for the square cut. For that reason, bowlers constantly attack his leg stump or bowl outside it to a defensive leg-side field. They can sometimes, by that means, fret him into self-destruction; and the sweep is by no means his strongest shot.

Often though, he improvises with the touch of genius drawing back outside his leg stump to cut against the spin or swing. His judgement and delicacy can be quite bewildering. For those who try him with the bouncer, he has a boldly powerful hook, controlled and kept down by a turn of the wrists. His timing conceals the force of his hitting; his straight and on-driving can be extremely long.

Runs probably come more easily to Barry Richards than to anyone else now playing, except perhaps the West Indian Richards. Some of his colleagues are inclined to think he can make a century more or less whenever he wants. Perhaps he does not always want. Certainly he thinks English cricketers play too much. Yet, face him with a challenge, a key match, a television audience, his mother's – or his own – birthday and he will rise to it. Then he plays himself in with clinical care, gradually unfolding his strokes until they flower all round the wicket.

Peter Sainsbury has kept one of the most observant of cricketing eyes on Barry Richards for the last ten years. He is not one given to extravagant statements about other players but he said, simply, 'If I had to pick one batsman to make a hundred for my life, it would be Barry.'

It is hard to select a particular innings of Richards as outstanding because, if he stays in long, he will either have given a rich display of stroke-making, or batted with consummate skill on a bowler's wicket. It is hard, though, not to believe that, against the Australians at Southampton in 1975, he spoke his heart in the idiom he commands most fully. Thomson, Hurst, Walker, Higgs and Mallett bowled; Richards played two innings of 96 and (retired hurt) 69, which declared his fitness to stand high on the level of Test cricket from which he is debarred by his country's racial policy. He played himself in with cold determination. Then, as soon as he was sure of his touch, he unleashed a fury of strokes, taking 34 from two overs of the fast bowler, Hurst; hitting Higgs twice for six; and tossing his wicket away to a bad ball when a century was his for the taking. He was repeating the performance with quite lordly command in the second innings when Thomson hit him in the groin and he retired.

He strolls where others must hustle. Sometimes he seems lack-lustre but never outclassed. He catches superbly at slip or anywhere else. He is a natural spinner who is reluctant to bowl, largely because he has taken considerable damage to his bottom hand while batting.

It has been said that Barry Richards cannot be called an absolutely great batsman because he has never passed the ordeal, such as Hutton, Barrington, Boycott and others suffered in Test cricket, of sustained battering by short-pitched fast bowling. His only answer is that he has overcome every challenge he has ever had to face. That he has the technique to deal with it, by cutting, or early judgement to take evasive action, cannot be doubted. In his heart he would welcome the chance to prove himself to the hilt against that ultimate attack. It can be said that he would not be satisfied with anything less than the finest performance on his own part. Although he sometimes seems withdrawn, Barry Richards is not an isolated player; he is terribly interested in Hampshire, their general strength and their team-building for the future. That is partly explained by his hunger for success; when Hampshire are battling for honours he will consider himself committed – so long, that is, as he maintains his own high standard. He will never be interested merely to earn his living from cricket as an ordinary player. As an extraordinary batsman he would not be satisfied to be less than great. Yet there are moments when he does not seem to enjoy it.

*Benefit Brochure*, 1977

# The Fast Bowler Tyson

*August* 1955. Cricket, perhaps from its very nature, has produced relatively few players who have been what Hollywood calls 'box office'. W. G. Grace was, because he was an Eminent Victorian, a figure whose importance extended beyond the field of sport to the social life of his time. Sir Donald Bradman and, in a less publicity-conscious age, Sir J. B. Hobbs must rank with Grace as institutions – with their knighthoods to indicate as much – but it should also be remembered that they broke records by attractive cricket.

The major 'draw' in the game today, attracting the non-cricketing curious and spectacle-seekers, is Frank Tyson, the Northamptonshire fast bowler. His Test match partner, Statham, a bowler of similar method, and whom experts reckon his equal by technical standards, lacks such sensational appeal. We may note, too, that Tyson himself has painstakingly avoided extraneous personal publicity.

The cardinal factor of this appeal is expressed, in 'shop' terms, as the 'extra yard' of pace. Simply, the fact spectators recognize is that Tyson is a 'pure' fast bowler. That is to say, without appreciable assistance from the pitch, or the employment of swing or spin, he can defeat accomplished batsmen by the sheer speed at which he propels the ball.

Tyson falls into the particularly modern pattern of the sportsman who, by taking thought, has added a cubit to his athletic stature. Like Roger Bannister, the runner, he has applied an academically trained brain to sport: he took a degree course in the arts at Durham University on scholarships. Beginning from the basic principles of bowling, he analysed his physical assets and exploited them to maximum effect.

By the standards of statistics, he is young in the game: he has taken a bare two hundred wickets in his entire career as a first-class cricketer. Yet, before and during his successes of the past twelve months he has constantly altered and developed his run-up and action. Physically unremarkable and well proportioned, he is sufficiently above average height to mask to some extent his considerable width of shoulders and depth of chest.

Between deliveries, he slouches back to his mark slackly flatfootedly, head down: arms hanging, body drooping, in such complete relaxation as marks the good boxer resting his entire body between rounds. There is, too, the probability that Tyson has consciously trained himself to the ultimate elimination of tension by severing himself mentally, also, from his bowling at this time.

Once turned at his mark, the spectator's eye can watch the process of tautening, implicit in the hardening of his face, the straightening of the body, as he scrabbles his spikes on the ground in a series of tiny steps which suggest a charging with nervous electricity. Then comes a run-in which accelerates as the strides lengthen into a series of leg-stretching leaps of an excitingly eager hostility. His body rocks back and, at the moment of delivery, swings forward and round, in a rhythmic wrench which sends the ball down the pitch at a pace beyond the experience – and faster than the normal reflexes – of any batsman in the world today who has not taken practice against Tyson himself. His follow-through takes him away to the off side, where he checks in an attitude of belligerence not normally to be distinguished in this quiet, thoughtfully bookish young man.

Technically speaking, he constantly endeavours to bowl – and frequently does bowl – the body-action break-back of the classical fast bowler, and he is steadily developing the full half-volley which, when it is effective, is called a 'yorker'. Every batsman against whom he bowls, however, is consistently beaten – if not dismissed – by the sheer *pace* of the ball.

It is as if he had a separate, fast-bowling self which canalizes all the aggression in his make-up into the action of bowling fast. In that act he undoubtedly finds satisfaction. The mind which relishes its effect must also recognize that the effective life of a fast bowler is short. If his body did not constantly tell him that such crescendos of energy cannot long be maintained, he has the history of cricket to remind him that the great fast bowlers – Larwood, Richardson, Kortright, Jones, Cotter – had lost their peak speed before they were thirty.

Many forms of sporting performance may be largely contrived out of good physique, application and practice. True fast bowling may not: it demands a rare, inborn synchronization of studied muscular effort. It demands, moreover, youth and strength, and the psychological urge to burn them up in the short-lived, but heady, glory of man-made pace beyond the power or timing of other men. That prodigality underlies and underlines the currently popular spectacle of 'Going up to the cricket to watch Tyson'.                                          *The Spectator*

# Geoff Boycott
## *Embattled Misfit*

*October* 1983. The only certain fact about Geoffrey Boycott's dismissal is that neither Yorkshire nor cricket in general has heard the last of it. The most obvious source of further distress is that, since the county has granted him a testimonial next season, he can hardly be banned from its grounds where his presence, plus that of his many supporters – and many critics – could lead to friction.

Moreover, if he and his faction do not effectively challenge the decision, it is unlikely that all the other sixteen counties will resist the temptation to recruit the services of a batsman who last season scored 1941 runs. His presence as an opponent of Yorkshire – especially if he were to be successful – could prove quite inflammatory.

The passionate partisanship engendered by the long saga is in itself evidence that it is not simply a matter of black and white; certainly not of right and wrong. The analysis of it all must lie in the philosophic concept that 'No man knowingly does evil' and its corollary that 'Each man does the thing he must.'

Significantly in explanation of Boycott's removal from the captaincy in 1978 the Yorkshire chairman said: 'It's not for what you have done; but for what you are.' Indeed, in that season, despite an injury and Test calls, Boycott had captained Yorkshire in half of the ten wins which took them to fourth position in the County Championship, and finished a close second in the batting averages.

In 1975, his fifth season as captain, and the only one in which he played a full county season, he was their most successful batsman with

1891 runs at 72.73 (the next man made 776 at 45.64) and they finished second; their best position between 1968 and now.

Many of Boycott's supporters will no doubt point to his service specifically to the county. Quite apart from his achievements in the international game, in eighteen of the past twenty-one seasons he has been top of the Yorkshire batting averages. In fact in 1979, the season after the captaincy was taken from him, and he declared himself happy to play for Yorkshire under any other captain, he was top of both the batting (with an average of 116) and of the bowling (nine wickets at 9.93).

By the usually pragmatic Yorkshire standard of figures, he could not on grounds of loyalty be faulted. Certain others, discontented or annoyed by committee decisions, have simply left the county: Boycott has always insisted: 'I want to play for Yorkshire.' It is not what he did, but what he is.

What he is has long been apparent. Some have described him as a solitary; which implies a deliberate state of mind. In truth he has generally been lonely, which is a different matter and explains much. In the mining village of Fitzwilliam, most youngsters accepted the life of a miner; Geoffrey Boycott did not.

Seven O levels and he went to work in the Ministry of Pensions; and most fastidiously he weighed that security of employment against committing himself to professional soccer; or for that matter, even cricket – although he recognized its potential for him – until he was sure of the situation.

The discovery that his eyesight was deficient drove him to even further effort to achieve his aim: adjustment to spectacles then to contact lenses. There was born the utter perfectionism which was to make him both the batsman and the person he is. Nothing could be left to chance; he must make all secure.

Every dismissal prompted practice to obviate error. All his gear, to the last strip of sticking plaster, must be laid out ready to put on. If others took a net, he would take two; four if possible. Bowlers became less fellow players than opponents; virtually enemies.

He did not fit into the mining, the village, or the cricketing societies into which he was born. Rather than the company of other boys or young men, he was devoted to a cricketing uncle; and, increasingly, to his mother with whom he lived until her death.

From his earliest playing days he was unfortunate – his critics would say culpable – in the matter of run-outs. Running, of course, is part of batting. Batting, though, can blind. Late in Bruce Mitchell's innings when he batted six and a half hours to save the Oval Test of 1947, he and his partner pulled up in the middle of the pitch as the ball went over the boundary.

Mitchell focused, puzzled, on the other batsman, Tuckett. 'Lindsay,' he said, 'but when did Tufty get out?' Mann had been out half an hour earlier. Such is the concentration of a batsman bent on utter security. That, too, can affect the entire perspective of an innings.

It is true that Geoffrey Boycott is a great batsman; but his limitation is that he is a great defensive batsman; often obsessionally so. He sees himself as embattled; the world against him. Then he goes into his shell, the cocoon of defence, and holds out.

Fiercely angry at his own weakness, he is utterly intolerant of other people's. 'Your ability, my brains,' he often said to members of the team he captained, and he saw it as the truth.

Had he ever considered the value of tact, all might have been different. Different, too, if he had not been so much alone; especially after his mother died. That happened at the same time as he lost the Yorkshire captaincy and the England vice-captaincy. It was the pit of his life. It was then, too, that he exposed himself on the difficult medium of television to the searching questioning of Michael Parkinson. He estranged much sympathy by seeking to justify himself – the embattled victim – by attacking the committee.

It is difficult to escape the conclusion that, if he had had a single close friend whom he trusted, so many errors of judgement, especially in personal relationships, would have been avoided. Friends, followers, he had, in scores; but no one – and, of course, no wife – whom he really believed he could trust. Many of his actions have amazed those closest to him, because he never even discussed them.

Why did the man who refused to tour India, and who put himself out of Test cricket for a year, return when he was older and the going harder? Was it simply to set the all-time record in India for Test run-scoring? Then, having achieved that, why did the man who had refused to join the Kerry Packer party go with the 'rebel' team to South Africa? Indeed will South Africa be his last refuge?

Why has he had recourse to law; bringing solicitors to his cricketing affairs? To attack others? Or to counter-attack – as a form of defence against those whom he sees as attacking him. What tortured nights of introverted thinking soured his achievements? *The Guardian*

# Ian Botham and Mike Brearley

## *Family Reunion*

To say that, at twenty-five, Ian Botham has a Test career which falls into three separate and distinct chapters may sound extravagant. It is, though, completely true. The three are, too, utterly different: and the latest – which is certainly not the last – is the most exciting of the three. All his cricket has been so episodic that it is not truly possible to appreciate Botham 1981 without knowledge of his previous phases.

Mike Brearley who must be seen as, until now, the major personal influence on his Test cricket has, characteristically, followed a far more logical and predictable path to success in, and retirement from, that sphere.

Those who had the good fortune to watch him regularly from the start have always relished – and sometimes feared for – Ian Botham. He was fifteen when he first played for Somerset Second XI in 1971; only seventeen, a cricket-mad, tousle-haired young giant when he turned out in their last two John Player League matches of 1973, and made little impression. When, at eighteen, he was picked for their Benson and Hedges quarter-final in 1974 against Hampshire which gave the first major impression of his quality, he had played only one match in that competition; and three in the County Championship. He shared with Burgess the initial break to 22 for four; and took two for 33 in his eleven overs. He went in to bat at 113 for eight – with 183 needed to win – and was instantly hit in the mouth by a savage bouncer from Roberts. That cost him four teeth: but, bleeding heavily, he proceeded to bat with a maturity far beyond his years and experience. Partnered by Moseley, and shielding Clapp, he struck two defiant sixes in his 45 not out – top score of the innings – to win the match with one wicket and one over to spare. He was cheered in like an emperor; and given the Gold Award for the match.

In 1975 he was erratically brilliant, constantly ending an innings of spectacular strokes with one of completely impossible exuberance. His bowling developed under the wise coaching of Tom Cartwright: to natural fast-medium outswing he added an inswinger, changes of pace and, out of his great strength, a genuinely fast ball and, as an emotional safety valve, the bouncer. The season of 1976 saw an advance; crucially in the Bank Holiday's 'blood' match with Gloucestershire, which means so much to the Taunton crowd. In the first innings, almost unplayable on a green wicket and under cloud cover, he took six for 25. In the second there was no such assistance and, if he often bowled too fast – and that was quite fast indeed – to employ his natural swing, he sent down thirty-seven overs and retained the stamina and control to knock down the last wicket for as narrow a win as eight runs; and an analysis of five for 125.

By the start of the 1977 season he was regarded seriously. He did little for MCC – under Brearley – against the Australians, though, and existed in a state of impatient frustration as twelfth man in the one-day internationals. Eventually his incontrovertible argument of runs and wickets took him into the English team – captained by Mike Brearley – for the third Australian match at Nottingham and bowled himself into Test cricket with five for 74 in his first morning. Nothing else to report on that occasion: on to Leeds where, in what became a familiar pattern, he scored nought in his only innings; took five for 21 in the first innings – and none for 47 in the second. He never, in his happy periods, allowed a Test to pass without making a profound – even decisive – mark on at least one innings. Injury kept him out of the Fifth Test but he has never been dropped by England.

No need for details of Botham in Pakistan and New Zealand in 1977-78; Australia 1978-79; Australia and India 1979-80; against New Zealand, India and Pakistan and at home in 1978 and 1979. It is enough to say that against all opposition, in a winning or, in Australia 1979-80, a losing team, he proved the most successful and exciting all-rounder England have ever had. As a batsman excelling in the drive, cut and hook he has moved crowds everywhere. When he came back from the Indian Jubilee match in spring 1980 he had played in 25 Tests; Mike Brearley, except when he was excluded by a broken arm in Pakistan-New Zealand and, in 1978, had captained him in all of them. By then Ian Botham had set impressive records with the achievement of the double – 100 wickets and 1000 runs – in Tests in the fewest matches (21), shortest time (2 years 33 days) and at the lowest age (23 years 279 days).

When Brearley, at thirty-eight, announced that he was not available to take the 1980-81 team to West Indies in the following winter, he had captained England in 27 Tests, of which they had won 15 and lost three, all in Australia, 1979-80; and had won six rubbers, drawn one (three draws in Pakistan 1977-78) and lost one. The selectors decided to 'blood' a captain for that tour. They chose their finest young cricketer, Ian Botham, for the home series with West Indies. He was twenty-four years old; had no experience of captaincy but was happy to accept the appointment and never, on the surface, appeared unhappy or uncertain in it. Of his twelve Tests, England lost four and drew eight.

It was a calculated risk. It is common knowledge that many – perhaps most – county players promoted to the captaincy lose performance for the first season or perhaps longer. Garfield Sobers, the finest allrounder in the history of the game, could not successfully nor happily incorporate the captaincy into his normal round of batting, bowling, and close fielding. Neither, as it proved, could Botham. No one should have been surprised. Happily no one – importantly not Botham – reacted unpleasantly to the decision – after his 'pair' and three wickets for 81 in the Lord's Test against Australia – to recall Brearley to the captaincy.

There is no good reason why an outstanding player should make a good captain. Although cricket is called a team game, the performer is alone. No one in any game is more lonely than the batsman facing a bowler supported by ten fieldsmen, with two umpires to ensure that he has no lucky escape. The bowler, too, is vulnerable; if he is to be effective he must bowl for himself. Successful cricket at the highest level must essentially be selfish: and demands concentration – concentrated selfishness.

So it is understandably difficult to think for, and about, other people while concentrating on matters not easy of solution even in complete single-mindedness. So it proved for Ian Botham. As captain, his hitherto glorious Test form disintegrated; his bowling lost its fire and control; his batting its splendidly aggressive command; perhaps most convincingly, his spontaneous and amazingly prehensile certainty in catching deserted him.

Happily he anticipated any action the selectors might have taken when he resigned the captaincy after his 'pair', and three for 81, in the disappointing draw at Lord's which left Australia one-up. There was no hint that he resented the recall of Mike Brearley as captain at Leeds.

Australia batted; Brearley held Botham back to second change, when, bursting for action, he took a wicket with his third ball. 'Leave it to me,' he said to Brearley; and his captain kept him at it to the tune of six for 95 – wholly admirable in a total of 401. It was the first time he had taken five wickets in an innings since the Test before he became captain. He batted, too, with much of his old assurance – and responsibly – to make 50 – more than twice as many as any other English batsman – but that was not enough to avert the follow-on.

At 105 for five – another 112 needed to avoid the innings defeat when Botham picked up his bat – the camp followers had booked out of their hotels, and the bookmakers were offering 500 to one against England. Brearley, with an easy grin, said, as he would have done in a game still open, 'Good luck, Guy' (Botham happily accepts being known in the dressing-room as 'Guy the Gorilla').

No one-innings nor even two-innings performance this. He proceeded to make cricket history of epic quality with 149 not out off 148 balls. Dilley made 50, and Old 29, opposite him, but Botham's innings turned the match in as violent a somersault as could be imagined; and wrested psychological advantage from Australia. When they batted again, needing only 130 to win, Botham took the early wicket of Wood: that was sufficient to trigger Willis into such furious action that (after none for 72 in the first innings) he finished with eight for 43. England won by 18 runs; the only side, apart from Stoddart's England at Sydney in 1894, to win a Test after following on. It was their first win for thirteen Test matches: and Botham was adjudged man of the match.

So to Edgbaston, where Botham made 26 and 3; took one wicket for 46 in the first Australian innings and Australia were left 151 to win. Again Brearley held Botham back; and they had an unusually long conference before he threw him in to take a quite amazing five for 11, to win the match by 29 runs, and, once again, to be declared man of the match. This apparently fictional story is, in fact, sane cricket history.

Botham had, by now, made – and, together with a number of originally sober cricket followers, come to accept – the incredible as normal. Who could be surprised at Old Trafford? Botham made nought in the first innings, took three Australian wickets for 26; and then, coming in at 104 for five, played an even more spectacular innings than at Headingley.

Even Dennis Lillee could not bowl at him. It was a splendidly extrovert display by a happy, and so exceedingly strong cricketer that at times – especially when he levered his gigantic hook strokes – he seemed like a man playing with boys: he made 118.

The Australian batsmen set up a game resistance; Botham took the early and valuable wicket of Hughes, and ended an ominous eighth-wicket stand by catching Lillee superbly off Willis. England had retained the Ashes; and who else should be man of the match once more?

At The Oval, with the rubber won and the Ashes retained (or, as Australians would argue, won), Brearley in one of his less successful moves put Australia in to bat. There Botham produced one of his mighty dray horse efforts, sending down 89 overs – far more than anyone else in the match – to take ten for 253, and hold Australia just within bounds. Brearley, for his part, when some commentators gave up England for lost, scored a workmanlike fifty in successful defence of his record of never having lost a Test in England.

'Take Botham out of our side' said Brearley 'and it would make us look very ordinary. We have an excellent relationship; he needs a father figure and I need a younger brother to help out.' Botham merely grinned.

The relevant figures are:

*Ian Botham, for England 1977 to February 1980* Tests 25: Innings 35: Not out 2: Runs 1336 @ 40.48: Highest 137. Wickets 139 @ 18.52.

*Ian Botham, as captain, June 1980 to 7 July 1981* Tests 12: Innings 22: Runs 276 @ 14.55: Highest 57. Wickets 35 @ 33.09.

*Ian Botham, after resigning the captaincy (last four Tests v Australia 1981)* Innings 8: Not out 1: Runs 365 @ 52.14: Highest 149. Wickets 28 @ 19.03.

Botham still happily believes it was all coincidental; but Fletcher was nominated to take the team to India.

Much of Mike Brearley's quality as a captain stems from his ability to stand back from cricket and observe cricketers as people. He was named Young Cricketer of the Year 1966 by the Cricket Writers; and took the MCC under-25 team to Pakistan where he once scored 312 not out in a day; and headed the batting averages comfortably ahead of Amiss, Fletcher, Ormrod and Abberley. Up to his invitation for The Oval, too, his county average was 45.45, in front of all but six English county batsmen. Importantly, in what should have been the formative years of his twenties, he left the game altogether for two years and played in only the latter weeks of three more. Perhaps that absence – or the attitude it denotes – prevented him from making quite the mark as a batsman that his early ability promised. On the other hand he did score nine Test fifties; and such a captain as he himself is might have motivated him, as he has done to others, over the crucial achievement gap. His triumph lies in equalling Bradman's record – far ahead of all others – of leading a winning team in twelve Anglo-Australian Tests. He is not a great batsman. It is difficult, though, to believe that Test cricket has ever known a better captain, strategically, tactically, above all, in psychological perception and consequent handling of men. He thinks – but does not consider it important – that it is not all coincidence.
*The Guardian Book of Sport* 1981/2 (*ed. J. Samuel, Secker & Warburg*)


# Greg Chappell
## *Matchwinner and Master Batsman*

*January* 1984. Greg Chappell's announcement of his retirement is less surprising than its timing. Only two months ago *Cricketer* – the Australian cricket magazine – conducted a poll among world ex-players, critics, and administrators which placed Chappell third among present-day batsmen.

The vast gap between him and the fourth man indicated the height of his standing but even that probably does him less than justice: for he is arguably second only to Bradman amongst Australia's batsmen.

His innings in the second Test of the current series with Pakistan demonstrated he is still capable of the peak performance at Test level. He is among the few truly great cricketers of modern times. Perhaps the most surprising aspect of his decision, though, is the fact that he needs only one little, above average, innings – in fact the figure is 69 – to overtake Bradman as Australia's leading scorer in Tests: and that has long been his cherished ambition.

Certainly he will have achieved that performance in over thirty more Tests than the 'little Master' but it would, nevertheless, represent an historic feat.

On the other side he has suffered much from the increasing stresses of modern cricket. The constant onslaught of high paced, intimidatory bowling, is only one aspect of that strain. Mounting and diversionary demands by the media; the sheer pressure of the increasing number of Test and international matches is cruel; not least, the savage atmosphere, especially in Australia, of the Packer operation – which distressed Chappell although he joined it – conspired to take much of the joy of the game from a man who never has the extrovert ebullience, nor even the animal health, of his five-years-older brother, Ian.

Indeed, especially during the 1970s, his batting was undoubtedly impaired by long and recurrent spells of glandular fever which made some of his performances even more impressive than their face value.

There were times in the late 1970s when he appeared quite exhausted at the crease. He has several times refused to make overseas tours; partly, no doubt, to continue business activities at home; but also to gain relief from the strains of almost unbroken top-level cricket. Had he made himself available for some of those series he would, of course, have passed Bradman's record long ago.

To evaluate him, he is a tall, upstanding, stylish batsman, splendid to watch, infallibly strong on the leg side; a brilliant hooker and a con- trolled stroke-maker through other lines; a powerful offside driver with an isolated weakness in playing outside the off stump. Above all, he has been a matchwinner in skill and temperament; batting decisively at crucial periods; often to win matches which otherwise probably would have been drawn or lost.

He went to England and Somerset in 1968 as a useful leg-spinner; returned as a bowler of medium-paced swing and cut, valuable enough to influence Test matches and win one-day games. A brilliant out- fieldsman, fast and safe-handed, he has preferred to captain his team from second slip; and has made more catches for Australia than any other player.

If he adheres to his intention – and he has changed his mind in such matters before – modern cricket will lose one of its most distinguished and finest performers: and one with the gift of rising to the great occa- sion. He comes of a cricketing family; his grandfather, Vic Richardson, was a fine and often spectacular batsman and close fieldsman for Aus- tralia during the inter-war period. As is well known, too, his brothers Ian and Trevor have also played for Australia.

In 1966-67 while Australia, including his brother Ian, were touring South Africa, Greg, at the age of eighteen, was first chosen for South Australia. He scored 53 and 62 not out and made a century in the same season.

He spent the English seasons of 1968 and 1969 with Somerset when he served the county valuably; striking a most spectacular Sunday League century – which was televized; and, with outstanding subsequent results, substantially tightened his technique against seam bowling on 'green' wickets and spin on 'turners'.

His first Test appearance in 1970 was also the first ever played at Perth; England had made 397, and Australia were 107 for five when Chappell came in to score a crucial 108 which saved the game. On, in 1972, to England where, batting with an impressive maturity for one of twenty-three, he was first in the tour averages with 1260 runs at 70.00; and second in the Tests to Stackpole with 437 at 48.55. His two centuries – at Lord's and The Oval – though, were decisive in the two wins which enabled Australia to draw the rubber.

In the season of 1972 all three Chappells appeared together for South Australia; but in the following season Greg joined Queensland, where he took over the captaincy. In the Wellington Test of the 1973–74 'out' series against New Zealand, Greg Chappell scored 247 not out and 133, and his brother Ian also made two centuries.

First appointed to the Australian captaincy in 1975–76 he began with 123 and 109 against the powerful West Indies team and led them on to a most impressive five-one win.

After the defeat of Packer disaffected sides of 1976 and 1977, he achieved an ambition in the three-nil Ashes win of 1979–80. He did not make the tour of 1981 when Kim Hughes's team was defeated.

His approach as captain, as in most other respects, has been quite different from that of his brother. He set his face against the permissive, sledging, sloppy-dressing and general bad manners of that era, to such a stern extent that he was dubbed 'the major general': and he strove to maintain high standards. It will, though, long be held against him that, after hours of superb cricket in the one-day international at Melbourne in 1981, when New Zealand needed six runs off the last ball of the match to tie it, Greg told his brother, Trevor, to bowl an underarm grub. He said he 'would never do such a thing again'. It was both an unhappy and uncharacteristic action.

Judged in his setting as batsman and captain, cricket history must see him as one of the great batsmen and at the age of thirty-five he is an asset the game cannot spare.                                                    *The Guardian*

# Dennis Lillee

## A Fast and Furious Foe

*January* 1984. Yesterday Dennis Lillee announced his retirement from Test cricket at the end of Australia's current match. He is thirty-four years old and already, with an innings to go, has taken, by a considerable margin – 351 to the 309 of Lance Gibbs – more Test wickets than any other bowler in cricket history. Despite missing three tours through a truly savage injury, the Packer banning and self-imposed withdrawal, he set that impressive record in 75 Tests spread over thirteen years.

A superb fast bowler with a classically flowing action, and fundamental hatred of batsmen, he had the capacity to move the ball either way in the air, and, in the latter half of his career, to cut it in extremely difficult fashion. His variation of pace and length was masterly; he commanded high pace, and a savage bouncer which he employed with delight as well as skill.

It must remain a major tragedy of cricket that a man of such gifts should have behaved premeditatedly as the Pom-hating 'ocker' of Australian yobbohood. His pantomiming over the use of an aluminium bat in which he had a financial interest; the kicking of Javed Miandad, the then Pakistan captain; his admitted betting on Australia to lose a Test in which he was playing; and his behaviour towards major English players such as Amiss, Randall and Brearley, were utterly distasteful.

Indeed, in any other country, his actions must have invited serious punishment. He was fortunate that his judges were a laughably pusillanimous and Packer-fearful Australian Board of Control.

None of that behaviour, however, can detract from his ability, his spirit, or his record as a match-winner. His talent was apparent as soon as he took 32 wickets in his first Sheffield Shield season for Western Australia in 1969–70 at the age of twenty. Immediately afterwards, included in the Australia B team which went to New Zealand, he took 18 wickets at an average of 16. Lillee spent the English season of 1971 playing, and learning, much of 'green' and slow-wicket technique, with Haslingden in the Lancashire League.

Here, in 1972 the stamp of a major bowler was unmistakable; he took 31 wickets in the series and an England side with some highly capable batsmen only narrowly held the Ashes.

Then, in Australia's immediately following tour of the West Indies, he broke down with stress fractures of the spine, and it was doubted that he would ever bowl fast again. But with immense determination and courage he undertook vast, difficult and punishing exercises which, to the surprise even of the medical experts, brought him back into the Australian team for the 1974–75 English tour of Australia.

It was then that he and Jeff Thomson established themselves as one of the greatest of all fast-bowling combinations. Extremely fast, utterly hostile and hugely effective in application, they established an immense psychological advantage over England.

Lillee took 25 wickets at 23.84 in the series; and 21 at 21.90 during the subsequent summer in England. A few months later he effectively won the Centenary Test at Melbourne with six for 26 and five for 139.

Tall, lean, wide-shouldered and rangy, with long, lank black hair, a Mexican-style moustache, and the satanic appearance of a latterday Spofforth, his rhythmic, menacing run-up ended in a high, sideways-on action. His appealing asked no favour – it stated – and his reaction when refused was often theatrical. He never sought to make friends on the field.

England were always his prime opponents, and he was all-but invariably successful against them. Although he arrived here with a virus infection in 1981, he went on to take 39 wickets at 22.30 in the six Tests.

He has seven times taken 10 wickets in a Test; 22 times five in a Test innings. Indeed, he has rarely been thwarted, though in the second innings of the last (Oval) Test of 1975, he flogged down 52 overs on a completely dead pitch to take four for 91. The match was drawn, but his main frustration lay in his failure to end it before the provided sixth day, thus missing the aeroplane he had proposed to take.

Now, his retirement, announced only a day after that of Greg Chappell, marks the effective end of one of the most powerful of all Australian teams. Lillee must always command respect for his immense talent (proved by the figures) and courage; but not for his manner or his manners. *The Guardian*

# Rodney Marsh

## *Soft Hand in Iron Gloves*

*February* 1984. The decision of Rodney Marsh to retire from top-level cricket marks the end of an important phase of Australian Test cricket. The 'gang of four' – Ian and Greg Chappell, Dennis Lillee and Marsh – formed the effective nucleus of power in the Australian side which between 1972 and 1980 inflicted upon England some heavy defeats. Their dominance was interrupted only by the upheavals of the Packer revolution. Effective as these players were, their methods and behaviour – especially the 'sledging' of opposing batsmen – proved often distasteful, sometimes more. In this respect Marsh could be dramatic, on occasions almost comically so. His dictum, 'never give a sucker a break', was belied by genuinely sporting gestures.

Marsh was at first dubbed 'iron gloves' because his gathering was frequently clumsy. He very rarely dropped catches, though, and his keeping improved steadily. Despite his vast, grizzly-bear-like physique he hurled himself vast distances to make catches with prehensile ability.

Hard though he strove to conceal it, he was also possessed of a teddy-bear amiability. His language could be aggressive but he liked to be liked and made far more friends in cricket than some of his associates. His record as a wicket-keeper stands in splendid isolation. In 96 matches he completed more dismissals in Test cricket – 355 – than any other keeper of any country.

He also batted capably. Indeed he first came into the Western Australian team in 1968–69, as a specialist left-hand batsman. His début was made against West Indies when he scored 104 in the second innings. He holds the record for most dismissals in an Australian season with 67 in 1975–76. Against Victoria at Perth that season he put out eleven, all caught.

He set another Australian record when he scored 104 and caught ten batsmen against South Australia in 1976–77. Against New Zealand at Adelaide in 1973–74 he made 132 and shared a seventh-wicket stand of 168 with O'Keeffe.

His batting ranged from the grimly and correctly defensive to the lustily spanking. He scored three Test centuries and made 50 in eleven scoring strokes (an Australian record) against West Indies at Perth in 1975–76.

When, earlier this year, Lillee and Greg Chappell announced their retirement Marsh said that he would not be available for the tour of West Indies but that he would expect to pick up his Test career subsequently. He had never previously opted out of an unattractive tour and this first gesture in that direction seemed uncharacteristic. Now, in a sense, he has assented to the passing of an era.

Marsh often looked an untidy wicket-keeper, even ugly in method, but he was of mighty stamina and ultimately splendidly efficient. It is a sad thought that a player of such integrity should, largely through the interests of others, have helped to instil an Ocker image into recent Australian Test cricket.

His brother is Graham, the international golfer. It is understandable that Rodney's comparison of his income, as arguably the finest wicket-keeper in the world, with that of Graham, who, though gifted, did not rank so high in his sphere, led to his support and in some ways instigation of the Packer operation.

In recent years he has given his occupation as 'professional cricketer'.

He could not have said that before the Packer revolution of 1977. He comes out of a cataclysmic event in cricket history with honest credit.

He is a genuinely earthy playing type, a steady smoker and beer drinker of some spirit. He is known as 'Bacchus', though, not because of his convivial habits but after the Melbourne bush town of Bacchus Marsh.

The Test cricketing scene will be the poorer for the loss of Rod Marsh's aggressive gusto and virile, sustained and often brilliant ability. *The Guardian*

# Walter Hadlee

On a Test match Monday morning in 1937 at Manchester, New Zealand went out to bat against England on a wicket made spiteful by weekend rain and in face of an English total 358. The English bowlers were Big Jim Smith, Arthur Wellard, Hammond, F. R. Brown and Tom Goddard – a powerful and varied attack supported by some brilliant fieldsmen. Half the New Zealand side was out for 119. Number six was a tall, lean, quiet young man of twenty-two – Walter Hadlee – who, in the words of *Wisden*, 'had accomplished little up to that stage of the tour'. Not always certain in playing Wellard early on, he went coolly about his rescue innings and gradually played himself in. Then he used his height and reach in fierce driving of any ball pitched up to him. He stayed to see the score more than doubled before, in turning a ball from Wellard 'round the corner', he slipped and kicked his wicket down. His 93 – more than a third of the runs scored from the bat in the New Zealand first innings – gave his side a fighting chance.

That coolness in trouble and courage to attack were characteristic of Hadlee's batting, and implicit in the New Zealand team he led in England in 1949. He captained that side by right, fitted as few touring captains have been for his post. He was worth his place in the side as a batsman, irrespective of whether he was captain or not – and was an experienced cricketer who had been playing Plunket Shield cricket for seventeen years. Only twenty when he first played for New Zealand – against G. O. Allen's side in the MCC team in 1936 – he came of age while on the tour of England in 1937. He was made captain of New Zealand against the Australians in 1945–46, and against Hammond's English team a year later. This experience, coupled with a thoughtful manner, made for real appreciation of the strategy of the game and an understanding of his men as men and players. He bridged the gap which has existed in some touring teams, between manager and players, so that his party was, in fact, a party. Here he was fortunate in having – in Jack Phillipps – a manager with a sense of humour who, like Hadlee, identified himself with the party rather than govern it from above.

If Hadlee needed to do more to establish himself among the members of his own team, he did so in the third game of the tour, against Surrey. New Zealand began their second innings on a crumbling wicket which might have been made for the Surrey bowlers. The pace of young Cox, the spin of Laker's and Eric Bedser's off-breaks and McMahon's 'Chinaman' were made doubly difficult, but most dangerous was the bowling of Alec Bedser. Bedser always has something in reserve for the wicket which really helps him, his pace seems to increase on a lively pitch, and every variation on the theme of fast-medium bowling is at his finger-tips under immaculate control. On that Monday at The Oval, his leg-cutter, pitched to a blind length on the middle or middle-and-leg stumps, was darting away outside the off stump – perfect slip-bait. Or his late inswinger would strike back at the wicket like a whip-lash. The ball was lifting – often waist-high from a good length – compelling a stroke, but investing the stroke with danger. Bedser conceded less than a run an over for thirty overs. Defence alone was a full-time job on such a pitch. Yet, his left side a mass of bruises from the rising ball, Hadlee made 119 not out – no other New Zealand batsman scored more than 20. To hear the New Zealanders speak of that innings was to realize that here was that unusual cricket captain whose appointment had the unqualified approval of all his team.

The captain who really captains his side is always reflected in the character of that side. Those 1949 New Zealanders, indeed, reflected their captain's power of fighting back. In the first match of the tour, against Yorkshire, the tourists had a narrow first-innings lead when they started their second innings. Aspinall and Coxon took the new ball to dismiss the first three New Zealand batsmen with only 30 runs on the board. Reacting as Yorkshire sides do when they scent the opportunity of bustling a side out, Yorkshire fieldsmen moved up close to the wicket. It seemed that they had only to break through this fourth-wicket partnership of Wallace and Donnelly to open the door of the hutch. Wallace and Donnelly appreciated their responsibility, but they proposed to shoulder it gallantly. Bat was put hard to ball, and they were still there as the clock-hand moved into the last ten minutes before lunch – usually the slow-motion period in a county game with the batsmen taking no chances, but batting for the afternoon. John Wardle bowled his slow left-arm breakaways from the pavilion end with no fieldsman in the deep. There were only a couple of minutes to go to lunch when Wallace stepped down the wicket and let go an old-fashioned straight drive which lofted the ball high to the pavilion rails. A minute later yet another towering hit went for four, and there, unmistakably, was the stamp of the happy cricketer which has been overlaid with care in much English cricket of recent years. In subsequent matches, not only Hadlee, Wallace and Donnelly, but also Reid, and – memorably against the MCC at Lord's – Rabone and wicket-keeper Mooney, played gallant rescue innings. Hadlee's consuming enthusiasm for cricket was also reflected in his team. At Leicester, Hayes, the young fast bowler – who was not playing in the match – went down to the Leicester nets, alone, just after nine each morning. He bowled six balls at full pace at the stumps, walked down, fetched the balls back to the end of his run and bowled another flat-out over. On and on he went, experimenting with his run and working up towards the pace whose promise had won him his selection for the tour.

These New Zealanders were a team of enthusiasts: none of them could show a financial profit on the tour – in fact, some actually lost money. The easiest point for us to overlook, accustomed as we are to full-time professional cricket, is that they were Saturday-afternoon cricketers and, while this accounts for the gaiety and spontaneity of their cricket, it could also lead to problems for their captain. Cowie, Wallace, Donnelly and Hadlee had toured England before, and Martin Donnelly had played at Oxford and in English cricket for several seasons. Apart from these four, any English pro has played, in a single English season, more three-day matches than any one of the younger New Zealanders had played in his entire cricket career until the English tour. In fact, Hayes, the young fast bowler of the party, had played only three first-class matches in his life prior to the trip. This fact, with the limiting of the party to fifteen players instead of the sixteen or even seventeen usually taken on tours, added to the menace of exhaustion and staleness.

A Saturday afternoon bowl of twenty-five overs is plenty for a pace-bowler, but it is also fairly unusual in New Zealand where there is a long Sunday morning in bed and a week away from cricket to put him back into trim. It is not ideal preparation for a tour of England with its twenty-five overs today, another twenty-five tomorrow, followed by a long train journey and, if the skipper loses the toss, another twenty-five overs the day after. No wonder such a trip seeks out the old strains and tears in Dominion bowlers' muscles.

New Zealand cricket is not rich, and it needed a financially successful tour. Moreover, because of its heavy expenses, a touring side must command larger gates than the average county match even to remain solvent. Coming after the Australians of 1948, Hadlee's men had to win their matches – and win them attractively – or seem like anti-climax, when the extra spectators would not come to see them. Meanwhile, players fresh from New Zealand had to be accustomed to the strain of week-long cricket and the vagaries of the English climate and wickets, even while they developed their strongest eleven for the Tests. At the same time, too, unsuccessful players had to be nursed back into form. Veteran pace-bowler Jack Cowie was a match-winner, but he had also to be rested against the Tests. These problems all tugged in different directions – yet a balance between them had to be struck. Perhaps it was fortunate that Hadlee is an accountant.

These problems have never been perfectly reconciled or solved, but, in Walter Hadlee, New Zealand had a captain as likely to solve them as all but two or three touring captains of this century. He did not solve them to the extent of winning the Test rubber – I think he would have been surprised if he had – but his 1949 New Zealanders tackled them with such tenacity that England could not beat them.

*The Echoing Green (Longmans, 1952)*

# Hanif Mohammad

## *Slow-Going Master of Defensive Batting*

*May* 1962. Hanif's team-mates on the 1954 Pakistani tour of England called him 'the Bambino'. Their successors now call him 'The Master'. In the interim, his captain dubbed him 'Mr Concentration'. Those names tell the story of his progress from a boy prodigy to one of the most mature and prolific batsmen in the world.

He was only sixteen, and still at school, when he opened the innings (in a stand of 96 with Nazar Mohammad) and kept wicket for Pakistan against Nigel Howard's 1951–52 MCC team; and at 16 and 300 days (by statisticians' measures) he played his first Test against India. Now, twenty-seven years old, he has played in thirty-five Test matches for 2754 runs (eight centuries) at an average of 46.46.

His 499 (for Karachi v Bahawalpur in the semi-final of the Quad-i-Azam Trophy, 1959) is the highest individual score ever made in first-class cricket: off the last ball of the day, he was run out, going for his five hundredth run. He has held other and less desirable records – for both the longest innings and the slowest century in all first-class cricket.

But these are reflections of the player Hanif has been *made*, not of the player he is by nature. When he came to England with the Pakistani side of 1954 he was a batsman with all the strokes. One by one the fast bowlers of England tried him with a bouncer. None, so far as I recall, gave him a second. His hooking was quick as light, and punitive as the sword. He would, too, drive through the covers in a gay flicker of forward-moving aggression. Neat and small-boned as he is – still with the physique of a boy – he hits with the full power of perfect timing and his footwork carries him back or forward into position against almost anything that can be bowled.

Hanif is, in fact, a superb cricketer. He was very young when his father died but his mother who 'has her own ideas on cricket' let her sons grow up in the game. Wazir, Hanif's eldest brother, has played for Pakistan: so has the last of them, Mushtaq, the youngest player to appear (before he was fourteen) in first-class cricket and in a Test: while Raees, yet another brother, is a provincial player. Hanif is not only a batsman and capable wicket-keeper: he is an adroit field close to the wicket or in the deep; while I have seen him, in a first-class match, bowl slow left-arm and medium-pace right arm in the same over!

When he first came to England, to be coached, in 1952 he was engaging, naive, a boyish figure with modesty and mischief in his eyes: seventeen years old, with, unmistakably, the germ of cricketing greatness in him. In those days he was determined to enjoy his batting and he rolled out strokes of impish yet impressive command.

He himself has probably expressed best the subsequent transition: 'They [his colleagues] have sometimes been very selfish in asking me to become the sheet-anchor whereas they have themselves continued to play aggressive cricket. But I do not mind at all.'

So the stroke-making prodigy has become as secure a defensive player as any in the world. Still his footwork and the wristy power of his punishing strokes stamp him as a batsman of all the gifts. But he has put the safety of his wicket first. Only just ahead of him lies a third and most glorious realm. His eye, concentration, balance, assessment of bowlers and range of strokes are those of a batsman who could take the bowling of a generation by the scruff of the neck and savage it, as Bradman did. The only barrier to that development is the defensive habit into which he has entered. It may, indeed, become intensified if, as was forecast eight years ago, he is made captain of Pakistan. He would make a highly informed captain, for he has played Tests against all the countries of the Imperial Conference – except, of course, South Africa – and in Lancashire league cricket: and he has noted – usually in writing – everything his quick understanding observed about his opponents. But the office could press the mantle of responsibility even more inhibitingly on his shoulders.

The shape of modern Test cricket; the Indian and Pakistani determination to tie cricketing success closely to national prestige, and the extent to which his team relies upon him may send him through the rest of his career as a slow-going master of defensive batting. But, even if that is so, we shall, from time to time, watch him, in the nets or in some half-day match, improvize and dominate, vouchsafing a glimpse of the great, glorious player he might have been. *Playfair Cricket Monthly*

# Mushtaq Mohammad

*A Stern Competitor*

*October* 1975. Mushtaq Mohammad is recognized as an outstanding cricketer, but not always for all the valid reasons. His public image is not completely exact. He is remembered as 'the youngest' – the youngest man to play first-class cricket (at 13 and 41 days); to appear in a Test (at 15 years 124 days); and to score a Test century (at 17 years 82 days). When he made his first major tour of England, in 1962, he was a lad of eighteen, but he did enough to become one of *Wisden*'s Cricketers of the Year. His chubby cheeks, 'cherubic' expression, white smile and modest manner emphasized the impression of youth. He could be a buoyantly attacking batsman and often would switch the bat in ·his hands to play a ball from a left-arm spinner, in effect, left-handed. So an idea was fostered that Mushtaq was a gay, boyish, carefree cricketer. In truth he is as stern a competitor as any of his competitive brothers – or as any cricketer in the world. That first Test century at Delhi in 1960–61 was played to save a Test and the rubber against India; his second, against England at Trent Bridge in 1962, lasted over five hours and drew the match.

He is, by nature and urge, a strokemaker, especially against pace bowling, which he hooks and cuts brilliantly and, at opportunity, will drive wristily. Yet, in many ways, he has inherited from his brother Hanif the role of anchorman of the Pakistan batting. He too is deeply conscious of his family's reputation. In 1962, when Hanif was troubled by a knee injury, Mushtaq, at eighteen, scored more runs than any other member of the team both in Tests and on the entire tour of England. In Pakistan's entire history as a Test-playing country, they have never taken the field without one of the sons of Ismail Mohammad and Amir Bee.

Born at Junagadh in India, but brought to Pakistan at the time of partition, all five of the brothers who grew to manhood – in order of age, Wazir, Raees, Hanif, Mushtaq and Sadiq – played first-class cricket; once all in the same match. All were Test players for Pakistan except Raees, whom his mother thought the most brilliant of the five and who was once told he would play against India, only to be made twelfth man.

Mushtaq is superbly technically equipped with a sharp eye, instinctive identification of length, nimble footwork, an innate sense of timing and the striking power of a compactly built and muscular thirteen-stone man. He is a fine, and frequently brilliant, batsman against any bowling. Under all his skills lies the determination, the concentration and the reluctance to get out which mark the good professional.

All this might suggest Mushtaq is a batsman pure and simple. On the contrary, there is barely a better leg-spinner in the world. He is more accurate than most of that kind, genuinely spins the ball, and hides his googly well. Only two current wrist-spinners, Chandrasekhar and Intikhab, have taken more than his forty wickets in Tests. His ability is such that often one wonders whether, if he were not a good batsman, he might not be substantially effective solely as a leg-spinner. While he has scored over 30,000 runs at an average of about 42, he has taken nearly 800 wickets at 23. When he first came to England – with the Pakistani Eaglets of 1958 at the age of fourteen – he kept wicket. Since then he has been a nimble fieldsman in the covers and a safe close catcher.

Mushtaq was already a mature cricketer at first-class and Test level when he joined Northamptonshire in 1964 at the age of twenty. While he was qualifying for Championship play he won the 1965 single-wicket tournament at Lord's. He has made two centuries in a match – and quite beguiling they were – and won a Gillette man of the match award. Now, still only thirty-one, he has played in thirty-six Tests, more than any other current Pakistani except the – sadly – deposed Intikhab. His Test batting average is 42.27, exceeded only among contemporary Pakistani players – by a mere .19 – by his younger brother, Sadiq.

Once the impression of Mushtaq as a light-hearted cricketer is dispelled, he becomes one to be savoured. Before he faces any ball he gives his bat the Mohammad family twirl and then, stern jutting, he is prepared to face whatever the bowler may deliver.

Whether he attacks or defends, he is an entertaining batsman to watch because he is so fluid in movement, so balanced, adroit and essentially aggressive. His resistance is never graceless nor lacking in imagination. In the most dogged innings he will identify the punishable ball and demolish it with a splendid punitive stroke.

Northamptonshire hired wisely when they engaged Mushtaq. Next year he has a benefit; from which, if his county's cricket-followers are just, he should do well. Yet, at thirty-one he still has at least ten years of effective cricket in him. Indeed, it may be that we have yet to see the best of him.

*The Cricketer*

# Abdul Qadir

## *The Master of Disguise*

*April* 1984. Nothing can be happier, healthier or more entertaining for cricket than the fact that Abdul Qadir has replaced Dennis Lillee as the cult figure of the game. His bowling is almost as hypnotically baffling to the spectator or the television watcher as to the batsman.

Even from the almost perfect position of the television camera, where everything might be revealed, nothing is; the harder he is studied the more impossible it becomes to 'read' him. Therein lies much of his entertainment value – though not for batsmen.

Abdul Qadir was only twenty-three when he was brought into the Pakistan team for the second of the three Tests against England in 1977–78. At once he took six for 44 to play a major part in dismissing Mike Brearley's side for 191, and finished with top Pakistani bowling figures for the series of 12 wickets at 25.41.

Even so, his Test place was rarely a foregone conclusion. Although Pakistan cricket has never turned its back on wrist spinners in the English fashion, they have grown accustomed to their being measurable batsmen, in the fashion of Mushtaq and Sadiq Mohammad and Wasim Raja.

Abdul Qadir's arrival in England with the touring side of 1978 aroused much interest, but a shoulder injury which dogs so many wrist spinners reduced him to six wickets on the tour. When he returned in 1982 he posed an altogether greater problem.

The experts who studied him closely – but by no means infallibly – came up with variants of the theory that, as embellishments of his leg-break – delivered with two different hand actions – he employed a googly, a Grimmett-style 'flipper' and, as one senior wrangler staunchly asserted, two different top-spinners, one of which looked like a googly.

Whatever may be the truth of that abstruse matter, Abdul Qadir savagely tormented normally good English batsmen inexperienced to the point of ignorance in wrist-spin. He took 57 wickets, but only 10 of them in Tests, where on slow pitches he reaped less than his due. As one old player put it, 'They didn't bat well enough to get out.'

Returning home, he played in the three Tests against the Australians, reputedly the masters of this type of bowling, and took 22 wickets – nine more than any other bowler on either side. In combination with Imran Khan, he was largely responsible for Pakistan's historic three-nil win.

He was less successful in the following rubber against India, but was twice Man of the Match with decisive bowling performances in last summer's World Cup.

He is a serviceable right-hand bat – indeed he scored a century in only his second first-class match – but his major contribution to cricket is as a bowler.

His unique approach is indelibly printed on many memories. He walks to the end of his run, stands for a moment, takes half a stride backwards, suddenly spins the ball across from right hand to left, peering along his knuckles as if he were 'drawing a bead' on the batsman, then shows him the ball and, in the course of four walking steps, pushes it back into his right hand then, taut as a coiled spring, bounds in four more strides, releases it in a wickedly spin-curved arc and seems only partly to check the urge to leap after it.

He had an unprofitable tour of Australia this winter, taking only 12 wickets at 61.08, for a well-beaten side, but seven of those wickets – including Greg Chappell twice – were in the first six of the order. That last fact indicates that he still has not been truly mastered. He still bowls so joyously and well that he must continue to surprise and delight.

He might have done more than that for English cricket, which must hark back to 1928 to find 'Tich' Freeman, of Kent, taking 304 wickets in a single season with leg-breaks. In the less distant past, England included four wrist-spinners in the second Test of 1946–47 in Australia, and they all bowled.

Since then, too, the Australians, Jack Walsh, George Tribe, Colin McCool and Bruce Dooland have practised the craft with considerable success in this country. English cricket, however, allowed it to die in 1980, when Robin Hobbs, the last true leg-spinner to play for England, was allowed to go out of the game.

It is sad that in the season of 1983 only three wickets were taken by English-born wrist-spinners. Certainly it was possible to watch Nasir Zaidi perform zestfully in that vein for Lancashire, but even he took only 16 of the season's total of 20. The solitary Englishman to make his mark was Derek Aslett of Kent, who captured all three of those English-claimed wickets, and, needless to say, he is employed as a batsman.

After the 1982 season Kent negotiated with Abdul Qadir to join them. What he might have done for young Aslett and English cricket can hardly be guessed. This summer though, in the event of their permitted overseas player, medium-pacer Eldine Baptiste, being wanted for the West Indian tour, Kent – the county of 'Tich' Freeman and Doug Wright – have taken an option on replacing him with Terry Alderman, an Australian of similar pace.                              *The Guardian*

# Sunil Gavaskar

## *Voracious Run-Maker*

*November* 1983. Sunil Gavaskar, who this week broke the individual record for most runs scored in Test cricket, looks likely to hold that distinction for a very long time.

He has achieved it in 96 Tests and 168 innings with an average of 52.40 by comparison with Boycott's 108,193 and 47.72. No one else is, or promises to be, within hailing distance of them. Boycott's voluntary withdrawal, of course, cost him thirty Tests between 1974 and 1977; and he has been suspended since his South African escapade of 1982. Crucially though, Gavaskar is thirty-four years old; Boycott forty-three and suspended until 1985.

There was never any real doubt that Sunny Gavaskar would be an outstanding cricketer. His father was a good, enthusiastic club player; his uncle, M. K. Mantri, a wicketkeeper-batsman, played four Tests for India and toured England in 1952. Enthusiastic from childhood, Gavaskar had all the essential attributes of a great batsman: basic correctness in defence; intuitively early footwork, unwavering concentration, a wide range of strokes, naturally good timing, fine temperament; and he invariably and unselfishly adjusts to his side's needs.

The fact that he is quite short – fractionally under 5ft 5ins – and extremely fast on his feet, enables him often to play attacking backfoot strokes to what a taller man would find a good length. However, he rarely hooks; he cuts well, but prefers to drive through the wide V between cover and mid-wicket. He strikes the ball with unexpected power.

He scored his first century at thirteen, another in his first representative match for India against London Schoolboys, and yet another in his first Ranji Trophy match. He had played only six first-class matches when, at twenty-two, he was chosen for India's 1970–71 tour of West Indies.

He missed the first Test through a finger injury. In the second, on his international début, he scored 65 and 67 not out; in the remaining three, 116, 64 not out, one, 117 not out, 124 and 220. He played the last of those innings, which almost won the match against all probability, in considerable pain from an infected fingernail; but refused pain-killing injections for fear they might dull his reactions. His 774 runs (at 154.80) remains a record for any batsman in his first Test series.

Gavaskar has generally had an undistinguished time against England. In 1979 though he totalled and averaged more than anyone else on either side and his masterly 221 saved, and almost won, the Oval Test.

In spite of a few unproductive patches he has, as his record shows, been successful elsewhere. He has never seemed in trouble against the Australian or the West Indian fast bowling. His latest achievement follows another unhappy visit to England when, completely out of form, he was actually twice dropped.

He has not only made more runs, but also taken more catches, than any other Indian in Tests. A fearless fielder close to the wicket, he suffered a broken leg in the Oval Test of 1982 standing silly-point to Botham's powerful drive.

Gavaskar's equable character has ridden out the idiosyncratic Indian switches of captaincy, in which his record is admirable if partly – understandably – defensive.

Thoughtful, studious, quiet (BA Bombay University, as they say), he may well have a considerable effect on Indian cricket in the future. Meanwhile, he is utterly content to bat for India.    *The Guardian*

# Sir Garfield Sobers

## *Cricket's Most Versatile Performer*

Sir Garfield Sobers, the finest all-round player in the history of cricket, has announced his retirement from full time county cricket at the age of thirty-eight. Circumstances seem to suggest he will not be seen again in Test matches. He was not with West Indies on their recent tour of India and Pakistan; and they have no other international commitment until 1976, when their full length tour of England might well prove too physically trying for a forty-year-old Sobers, most deservedly given a knighthood in the New Year Honours.

So it is likely that international cricket has seen the last of its most versatile performer. For twenty years – plus, to be precise, seven days – he served and graced West Indian cricket in almost every capacity. To review his career compels so many statistics as might mask the splendidly exciting quality of his play. Nevertheless, since many of his figures are, quite literally, unequalled, they must be quoted. Between 30 March 1954 and 5 April 1974, for West Indies, he appeared in 93 Tests – more than any other overseas cricketer: he played the highest Test innings – 365 not out against Pakistan at Kingston in 1958; scored the highest individual aggregate of runs in Test matches; and captained his country a record 39 times. His 110 catches and – except for a left-hander – his 235 wickets are not unique: but his talents in those directions alone justified a Test place.

Garfield Sobers was seventeen when he first played for West Indies – primarily as an orthodox slow left-arm bowler (four for 81), though he scored 40 runs for once out in a losing side. His batting developed more rapidly than his bowling and, in the 1957–58 series with Pakistan in West Indies, he played six consecutive innings of over fifty – the last three of them centuries. Through the sixties he developed left-arm wrist-spin, turning the ball sharply and concealing his googly well. Outstanding, however, at the need of his perceptive captain, Sir Frank Worrell, he made himself a Test-class fast-medium bowler. Out of his instinctive athleticism he evolved an ideally economic action, coupling life from the pitch with late movement through the air and, frequently, off the seam. Nothing in all his cricket was more impressive than his ability to switch from one bowling style to another with instant control.

He was always capable of bowling orthodox left arm accurately, with a surprising faster ball and as much turn as the pitch would allow a finger-spinner. He had, though, an innate urge to attack, which was his fundamental reason for taking up the less economical but often more penetrative 'chinaman', and the pace bowling which enabled him to make such hostile use of the new ball.

As a fieldsman he is remembered chiefly for his work at slip – where he made catching look absurdly simple – or at short leg where he splendidly reinforced the off-spin of Lance Gibbs. Few recall that as a young man he was extremely fast – and had a fine 'arm' – in the deep, and that he could look like a specialist at cover-point.

Everything he did was marked by a natural grace, apparent at first sight. As he walked out to bat, six feet tall, lithe but with adequately wide shoulders, he moved with long strides which, even when he was hurrying, had an air of laziness, the hip joints rippling like those of a great cat. He was, it seems, born with basic orthodoxy in batting; the fundamental reason for his high scoring lay in the correctness of his defence. Once he was established (and he did not always settle in quickly), his sharp eye, early assessment, and inborn gift of timing, enabled him to play almost any stroke. Neither a back foot nor a front foot player, he was either as the ball and conditions demanded. When he stepped out and drove it was with a full flow of the bat and a complete follow through, in the classical manner. When he could not get to the pitch of the ball, he would go back, wait – as it sometimes seemed, impossibly long – until he identified it and then, at the slightest opportunity, with an explosive whip of the wrists, hit it with immense power. His quick reactions and natural ability linked with his attacking instinct made him a brilliant improviser of strokes. When he was on the kill it was all but impossible to bowl to him – and he was one of the most thrilling of all batsmen to watch.

Crucially, Garfield Sobers was not merely extremely gifted, but a highly combative player. That was apparent on his first tour of England, under John Goddard in 1957. Too many members of that team lost appetite for the fight as England took the five-match rubber by three to none. Sobers, however, remained resistant to the end. He was a junior member of the side – his twenty-first birthday fell during the tour – but he batted with immense concentration and determination. He was only twice out cheaply in Tests: in two Worrell took him in to open the batting and, convincingly, in the rout at The Oval, he was top scorer in each West Indies innings. He was third in the Test batting averages of that series which marked his accession to technical and temperamental maturity.

The classic example of his competitive quality was the Lord's Test of 1966 when West Indies, with five second-innings wickets left, were only nine in front and Holford – a raw cricketer but their last remaining batting hope – came in to join his cousin Sobers. From the edge of defeat, they set a new West Indies Test record of 274 for the sixth wicket and, so far from losing, made a strong attempt to win the match.

Again, at Kingston in 1967–68, West Indies followed on against England and, with five second-innings wickets down, still needed 29 to avoid an innings defeat. Sobers – who fell for a duck in the first innings – was left with only tailenders for support yet, on an unreliable pitch, he made 113 – the highest score of the match – and then, taking the first two English wickets for no runs, almost carried West Indies to a win.

For many years, despite the presence of some other handsome stroke-makers in the side, West Indies placed heavy reliance on his batting, especially when a game was running against them. Against England 1959–60 and Australia 1964–65, West Indies lost the one Test in each series when Sobers failed. His effectiveness can be measured by the fact that in his 93 Tests for West Indies he scored 26 centuries, and fifties in 30 other innings; four times – twice against England – averaged over one hundred for a complete series; and had an overall average of 57.78. There is a case, too, that he played a crucial part as a bowler in winning at least a dozen Tests.

To add captaincy to his batting, different styles of bowling and close fielding may have been the final burden that brought his Test career to an early end. He was a generally sound, if orthodox, tactician but, after thirty-nine matches as skipper, the strain undoubtedly proved wearing. In everyday life he enjoys gambling and, as a Test captain, he is still remembered for taking a chance which failed. It occurred in the 1967–68 series against England, when he made more runs at a higher average – and bowled more overs than anyone else except Gibbs – on either side. After high scores by England the first three Tests were drawn, but in the fourth, after Butcher surprisingly had bowled out England in their first innings with leg-spin, Sobers made a challenging declaration. Butcher could not repeat his performance and Boycott and Cowdrey skilfully paced England to a win. Thereupon the very critics who constantly bemoaned the fact that Test match captains were afraid to take a chance castigated Sobers for doing so – and losing. The epilogue to that 'failure' was memorable. With characteristic confidence in his own ability, he set out to win the Fifth Test and square the rubber. He scored 152 and 95 not out, took three for 72 in the first England innings and three for 53 in the second – only to fall short of winning by one wicket.

Students of sporting psychology will long ponder the causes of Sobers's retirement. Why did this admirably equipped, well rewarded and single-minded cricketer limp out of the top level game which had brought him such eminence and success? He was only thirty-eight: some great players of the past continued appreciably longer. Simply enough, mentally and physically tired, he had lost his zest for the sport which had been his life – and was still his only observable means of earning a living. Ostensibly he had a damaged knee; in truth he was the victim of his unique range of talents – and the jet age. Because he was capable of doing so much, he was asked to do it too frequently. He did more than any other cricketer, and did it more concentratedly because high speed aircraft enabled him to travel half across the world in a day or two. Perhaps the long sea voyages between seasons of old had a restorative effect.

In a historically sapping career, Sobers has played for Barbados for twenty-one seasons; in English league cricket for eight, for South Australia in the Sheffield Shield for three, and Nottinghamshire for seven; he turned out regularly for the Cavaliers on Sundays for several years before there was a Sunday League in England; made nine tours for West Indies, two with Rest of the World sides and several in lesser teams; 85 of his 93 Tests for the West Indies were consecutive and he averaged more than four a year for twenty years. There is no doubt, also, that his car accident in which Collie Smith was killed affected him more profoundly and for longer than most people realized.

The wonder was not that the spark grew dim but that it endured so bright for so long. Though it happened so frequently and for so many years, it was always thrilling even to see Sobers come to the wicket. As lately as 1968 he hit six sixes from a six-ball over. In 1974 on his 'farewell' circuit of England he still, from time to time, recaptured his former glory, playing a lordly stroke or making the ball leave the pitch faster than the batsman believed possible. As he walked away afterwards, though, his step dragged. He was a weary man – as his unparalleled results do not merely justify, but demand. Anyone who ever matches Garfield Sobers's performances will have to be an extremely strong man – and he, too, will be weary.

An amazing man, he still insists, 'As long as I am fit and the West Indies need me, I will be willing to play for them.' Only time will tell if we shall see him in the Test arena again. In October last he joined the executive staff of National Continental Corporation to promote the company's products in the Caribbean and United Kingdom.

And now he has joined his lamented compatriots Sir Learie Constantine and Sir Frank Worrell with the title Sir Garfield Sobers.

*Wisden Cricketers' Almanack* 1975

# Clive Lloyd

## *Relish Him*

*June* 1983. For almost twenty years, Clive Hubert Lloyd – Clive to the press, Hubert in the dressing-room – has been one of the most exciting cricketers in the world. It comes almost as a surprise to recognize him as a setter and breaker of records. He has always played so spontaneously, so much from the heart, and with such zest, that his cricket has seemed all but beyond figures. Already, though, he has set a record for all Test cricket by captaining West Indies in 54 matches; he scored a century in his first Test against England and in his first against Australia, a year later. Before that he had made a valuable 82 and 78 not out on his début against India. With 201 not out in 120 minutes for West Indies against Glamorgan, he shares with Gilbert Jessop the record for the fastest double-century.

So much said, the quality of his cricket is most important. His early days were an odd mixture of handicaps and advantages. As a boy, trying to separate two friends who were fighting, he was hit damagingly in the eye with a ruler. Subsequent study in bad light made him permanently shortsighted, and he has always since needed to wear spectacles. Later he cut his leg; tetanus set in and he came near to death. Oddly enough, while he was lying in bed, he grew fantastically: six inches in a month. So he came through his teens a gangling 6ft 4ins; with a vast reach, hugely long legs and an absent-mindedly bespectacled look. As he gradually filled out, he became a very powerful man indeed.

His talent was obvious from his schooldays, when his batting, bowling – either fast or slow – and his fielding stamped him as a natural cricketer. He was first chosen for Guyana in 1964 – against Jamaica: he scored only 12 and was dropped. In the next season, scores of 2 and 17 against Australia cost him his place again. Such is the concentration of talent in West Indies that cricketers who do not succeed early receive short shrift. When, recalled for the match with Barbados, he was out for nought in the first innings, his chances of survival seemed slight. In the second he struck a powerful 107; since then he has progressed characteristically, steadily, unfussily, and unhurriedly.

He, surely, is the finest post-war fieldsman. His nearest rival would be the Rhodesian, Colin Bland, who was also at his best at cover-point. Bland was, superficially at least, more prepossessing to watch. Tall, slim and well-proportioned; whereas Lloyd, when not in urgent action, tends to shamble about like some amiable Paddington Bear; capable, though, of exploding into action like a roused panther. If Bland was more poised, Lloyd was crucially faster and, at the pinch, he would stop the ball which would have eluded Bland because, first of all, his legs and arms are longer but, decisively, because he has never hesitated to launch himself into as distant a goalkeeper-type dive as has been seen on the cricket field. The ball seems to settle as if by nature into those hugely certain hands; and his throwing is savagely flat and accurate.

When he first came to England – 'to develop my batting' as he modestly explained – with Haslingden in Lancashire League cricket, he was a leg-spin bowler who gave a ball a fair tweak. Unfortunately, pitch conditions, demands of the league game, and the twinges of fibrositis persuaded him – like Greg Chappell when he first came here – to switch from wrist-spin to medium-pace seam-up. He bowls in that manner now at a gentle piaffer, well within himself, accurately and often usefully. Still, though, it is possible to regret that he forsook the unusual for the all too usual.

Some of his run-outs have been the most remarkable pieces of cricket action of recent years. Some of his stops, though, have been even more spectacular; so rapid that the batsmen have been caught in only the first stride or two of the run, with time to be amazed – but not to make good their ground.

His batting has been a rare blend of brilliance and consistency. When he and Farokh Engineer first joined Lancashire in 1968, they represented imaginative recruitments for the one-day game. Both enterprising and fast-scoring batsmen, and brilliantly uplifting in the field, they contributed admirably to Jack Bond's intelligent approach to the limited-overs game. Both went on to assume considerable stature in the world game; especially Clive Lloyd.

Lance Gibbs, the great West Indian spin bowler, is his cousin and had a powerful influence on his development. If the negotiations through him had been successful, Clive Lloyd would have become a Hampshire player. In the event, his experience at Haslingden had given him, like Learie Constantine before him, a liking for Lancashire and its people, and he remained there to prove – on all counts – probably the most valuable of the modern players from overseas. As captain of both his country and his county, he has been strikingly calm, quiet, apparently relaxed – surely no-one could be *quite* so relaxed as he looks – but shrewd. At the same time he has been utterly pragmatic, at need, ruthless, especially in his handling of the West Indian pace attack.

He celebrated his Test appointment with 163 at Bangalore in his first match as captain; and decided that rubber with the highest score of his career: 242 not out at Bombay. So acceptable has his captaincy proved that he even survived that traumatic five-one defeat by Australia in 1975–76.

In addition to his Tests for West Indies he played seven matches for the Rest of the World XI, including membership of the side which went to Australia in 1971–72, when he had to return after two matches because of a back injury.

His batting has been valuable; entertaining, even exciting. His length of leg and reach enable him to go forward and drive 'on the up', as they say, bowling to which many men of average size would play back.

Sometimes, like M. J. K. Smith – and perhaps similarly because of eyesight problems – he used to seem at a loss in his opening at the start of an innings. More recently, while still not completely happy at the outset, he appears to have developed the capacity to 'soldier through'. Early on he had difficulty with the leg-spin of Chandrasekhar; and with the bouncer; in each case he applied himself determinedly to the problem, adapted his technique and lived profitably through. Once he has settled in, he goes forward or back with equal ease; and with the unhurried ease of the natural batsman.

His bat is an awe-inspiring weapon, with its several layers of grip and its added weight; so that, when he flings it at the ball at the full swing of those long arms, with his full weight and the muscle of an extremely strong man, the effect can be quite awe-inspiring. Once, at the Oval, he pull-drove a ball from Robin Jackman, from a wicket pitched on the gas-holder side, over midwicket into the yard of Archbishop Tenison's Grammar School on the far side of the road; a prodigious blow.

Not only is he magnificently physically equipped to hit the ball hard: but it is also his instinctive reaction to a cricketing problem. At need he will put his head down and battle, but his natural urge is to attack. The historic example, of course, was the Prudential World Cup final of 1975 when West Indies, pinned down by Australia, were 50 for three. At that juncture, Lloyd hooked Lillee's bouncer for six; proceeded to take a hundred off 82 balls and, with the highest score of the match – 102, 40 more than anyone else – and, importantly, steady bowling, gave West Indies the cup by 17 runs.

Next year he will be forty; and Lancashire must prepare to lose one of their most valuable assets. Lloyd is virtually irreplaceable; reliable, loyal, match-winner; glorious entertainer; thoughtful, humorous, modest and courteous man; they will miss him both on the field and off it. Meanwhile, they, and all the cricket world, should relish him while he is still there. *Wisden Cricket Monthly*

# 8

# Some Choice Books

## Fifty Years of Cricket Literature

*April* 1971. The past fifty years have seen an almost complete change in the course of cricket writing and publication, most of it for the better. The year 1921 was, in fact, the watershed. It was in 1919 that Neville Cardus was despatched to Old Trafford to write the first of the cricket reports for *The Manchester Guardian* which were to influence virtually every cricket writer who came after him. He introduced what may be called the literary-appreciative approach into the reporting of sport. He also forced cricket into a position where the literate had to notice it and, in doing so, compelled an improvement in the general standard of writing about the game.

It may be said that Sir Neville was merely the signal for an upsurge of cricket writing which would have occurred in any case, but which he now seems to have symbolized. Certainly since then there has been an immense advance in cricket history, reference, match reports – with which may be linked tour accounts – as well as appreciation.

### Pre-1921

Prior to 1921 there had been some faithful research – such as Haygarth's monumental *Scores and Biographies* but only one cricket history book of any pretensions – Charles Box's *The Game of Cricket* – and, since Nyren's *Young Cricketer's Tutor*, only one of any scope, *The Jubilee Book of Cricket* largely written for Ranjitsinhji by C. B. Fry who had produced the sole important technical analyses, of *Great Batsmen, Their Methods at a Glance* and *Great Bowlers and Fieldsmen, Their Methods at a Glance*. Suddenly, after the first World War, all these fields opened up, beyond the limitations of local pamphlets and boys' books.

In 1921 H. S. Altham began to publish his *History of Cricket* as a serial in *The Cricketer*; it appeared in book form in 1925 and subsequently, with additions by E. W. Swanton, until 1962, when it was divided into two volumes, with 1914 as their hinge, the first by H. S. Altham, the second by E. W. Swanton. Eric Parker produced his ambitious but rambling 'Lonsdale' *History* in 1950; Roy Webber the condensed *Phoenix History* in 1960; but the next significant step along this road was *Cricket: a History of its Growth and Development* by Rowland Bowen, which differs from its predecessors by being written from the outside looking in, not accepting earlier beliefs or values, criticizing not merely play but official attitudes and origins.

Also in the post-1945 period, A. G. Moyes produced his *Australian Cricket: a History*; Christopher Nicole, *West Indian Cricket*; Louis Duffus added *South African Cricket 1927–47* to W. M. Luckin's two previous volumes; and T. W. Reese his second volume of *New Zealand Cricket* (1914–1933) which has been followed by R. T. Brittenden's *Great Days in New Zealand Cricket* (1958) and *New Zealand Cricketers* (1961). The Indian coverage is divided between *Indian Cricket Cavalcade*, by Arbi, *The Encyclopaedia of Indian Cricket* of L. N. Mathur, *Cricket and Cricketers in India* by W. D. Begg and the brief but capable *March of Indian Cricket* by Professor Deodhar. Only *Compendium of Pakistan Test Cricket* (1947–67) has made any attempt to cover the span of the game in that country.

### Specialist histories

Histories of other and more specialized aspects of the game have come from Sir Pelham Warner (on *Lord's*, *Gentlemen v Players* and *Cricket Between Two Wars*), Gerald Brodribb, G. D. Martineau, F. S. Ashley-Cooper, Dermot Morrah and Geoffrey Bolton; the impressive symposium, *A Century of Philadelphia Cricket*; and *Cricket in Fiji* by P. A. Snow, and a number of studies – one substantial – of cricket in Scotland by N. L. Stevenson; numerous volumes on different facets of the game in Ceylon by S. P. Foenander; on English League cricket by John Kay; and works of authority and quality on various states, provinces and counties. Less well known are the many club histories – usually issued to mark a centenary or other anniversary – and invariably a faithful labour of love which will be of value to the ultimate historian of British club cricket.

The basis of history and scholarship has been immeasurably strengthened during the past twenty years through the development, by every first-class cricketing country, except Pakistan, of an apparently secure annual publication, covering its domestic and representative cricket. *Wisden*, too, continues substantial, wide-ranging, authoritative and, in 1963, reached its hundredth issue – of 1311 pages.

## Statistical works

The earlier statistical publications of F. S. Ashley-Cooper, A. D. Taylor, E. L. Roberts and Sir Home Gordon – who bravely attempted *Cricket Form at a Glance, 1878–1937* – have been followed by the more expansive works of Roy Webber, Arthur Wrigley, Bill Frindall and Irving Rosenwater who have covered the ground of cricket records widely and carefully. The two *Who's Who* books of the period are by S. Canynge Caple (1934) and Roy Webber (1952). The major reference book however was the often mooted, but never before genuinely attempted, encyclopaedia which emerged as *The World of Cricket* – by E. W. Swanton and Michael Melford – in 1966 at a length of 1165 quarto pages and, even at that, about half the length of the original compilation.

The outstanding advance, however, has been in appreciation, where the note sounded by Cardus has been picked up and, not simply echoed, but developed along the lines of their own character and style by Dudley Carew, Robertson-Glasgow, Alan Ross, J. H. Fingleton, J. M. Kilburn, Ray Robinson, Ralph Barker, Bernard Hollowood, Ian Peebles and A. A. Thomson – many of whom have also published histories or tour accounts. There has also been at least one volume apiece from such writers of distinction from other fields as E. V. Lucas, Robert Lynd, Edmund Blunden, Herbert Farjeon and James Thorpe; while, apart from his *History*, a posthumous collection brought together the best cricket writing and speeches of H. S. Altham.

## Sir Neville Cardus

If Sir Neville Cardus's *The Summer Game, Days in the Sun* and *A Cricketer's Book* were the outstanding works in this kind in the early phase – and his *Autobiography, Close of Play* and *Cricket All the Year* are major contributions in recent years – the most striking post-war achievement undoubtedly is by C. L. R. James. Like Sir Neville, he has a literary and creative background outside cricket and his *Beyond a Boundary* – perhaps the best book ever written on the game of cricket – is an amalgam of autobiography, appreciation, observation, reportage and, most intensely, a crystallization of the West Indian feeling for cricket.

Parallel with the romantic approach has been the illuminating, and sometimes salutary, writing of expert players of analytical bent, from C. B. Fry, through M. A. Noble, P. G. H. Fender, R. E. S. Wyatt and

Sir Don Bradman, Richie Benaud, Trevor Bailey with C. S. Marriott and Ian Peebles, while the prolific trenchant critic E. H. D. Sewell maintained a foot in either camp.

Instructional books have always been plentiful, but after the lavish Lonsdale *The Game of Cricket* in the thirties, there was nothing quite so thorough until the solid, thoughtful and authoritative communal production from Lord's, *The MCC Cricket Coaching Book*, and Sir Donald Bradman's perceptive and acute *The Art of Cricket*; though that experienced coach Alf Gover has published well-planned small manuals. *Cricket Umpiring and Scoring*, the official textbook of the Association of Cricket Umpires, has been kept up to date since it was first compiled by R. S. Rait Kerr in 1957.

## Autobiographies

Ever since W. G. Grace's 'ghosted' autobiography became a best seller in the last century, the 'amanuensis' has wielded increasing power in the field of sporting life-stories. Among the genuine autobiographies of cricketers, however, may be noted those of C. B. Fry, Sir Pelham Warner, Douglas Insole, Frank Tyson, Bill Bowes and Arthur Mailey.

Tour books proliferated from 1921 onwards and Harrap's *'Fight for the Ashes'* series provided a strong thread from its origination in 1926 to its final volume in 1961. Considerable contributions in this department were made by M. A. Noble, Sir Pelham Warner, J. H. Fingleton, Alan Ross, E. W. Swanton, R. A. Roberts, Peter West, Bruce Harris, R. S. Whitington and E. M. Wellings.

The chief pictorial publications were *The Noble Game of Cricket*, reproducing most of the cricket pictures collected by Sir Jeremiah Colman: it was issued in a limited edition and is now rare: *The Game of Cricket* with an introduction by Sir Norman Birkett, a smaller book also based on the Colman pictures: *The Book of Cricket* – 'A Gallery of Great Players from W. G. Grace to the Present Day' – compiled by Denzil Batchelor, with over two hundred reproductions of photographs of eminent players of all countries.

Cricket fiction has never been strong but the inter-war years saw two good novels in *The Cricket Match* by Hugh de Selincourt – who subsequently wrote some pleasing light stories but nothing more of such stature – and *The Son of Grief* by Dudley Carew; since 1946 the best have been *The Friendly Game* and *Malleson at Melbourne* of William Godfrey's unfinished trilogy, and Harold Hobson's *The Devil at Woodford Wells*.

Short stories about the game are best represented by the three collections, *Cricket Stories*, made by Howard Marshall (1933), *Best Cricket Short Stories* by E. W. Swanton (1953) and Denzil Batchelor (1967).

### The Poetic Muse

In 1925 A. A. Milne published *For the Luncheon Interval* a small book of mainly cricket verse; latterly Alan Ross has written some sensitive cricket poems and, in between, R. C. Robertson-Glasgow contributed some neat humour to the sparse field of cricket verse. We may note, too, R. C. Sherriff's play *Badger's Green* and *The Final Test* written for television by Terence Rattigan.

A number of anthologies have been *The Cricketer's Companion*; Gerald Brodribb's *Cricket Verse* and *The English Game*; *Six and Out* – 'The Legend of Australian Cricket' by Jack Pollard; two volumes of '*The Pick of The Cricketer*' and the symposium *Bat and Ball* by Thomas Moult.

### Cricket periodicals

Apart from the short-lived *Cricketers' Magazine* which grew out of *The South Wales Cricketers' Magazine*, *The Cricketer* had no competition as a periodical until 1960 when *Playfair Cricket Monthly* first appeared – edited by Gordon Ross and Roy Webber – and is now in its eleventh volume. *The Cricket Quarterly*, at once scholarly and trenchant, was founded by its editor Rowland Bowen in 1963. *Australian Cricket*, an ambitious venture by Eric Beecher in 1968 has proved healthy in that formerly infertile soil for cricket magazines, and in 1970 produced, at last, the kind of annual to do justice to its subject. *New Zealand Cricketer* edited by R. T. Brittenden began a year earlier and is now in its third volume. A South African magazine of the 1950s did not prove viable.

### County handbooks

County handbooks tend to be overlooked but many of them, since 1946, have made considerable efforts to add to their team records editorial material of historic and, often – for example, H. S. Altham's contributions to the Hampshire yearbooks – literary value.

It is hard either precisely to evaluate or to count the extent of cricket publication in these fifty historic years; but, including ephemera, it might well amount to some 6500 items. To pretend that all, or even a preponderant amount of it, is important, would be pointless; it does, nevertheless, contain vastly the greater proportion of important cricket writing in all fields.                                                    *The Cricketer*

# Books You Might Have Missed

*The Gusto and the Atmosphere of a Cricket Tour*

It is now more than thirty-five years since the two Cambridge Blues, 'Big Maurice' and 'Little Maurice' – M. J. C. Allom, the Surrey pace-bowler, and M. J. Turnbull, Glamorgan batsman and captain – published their account of the tour of Australasia by Harold Gilligan's MCC side in 1929-30. It is not easy for this reviewer to be coldly objective about it, for his copy was, at that time, the most expensive book he had ever possessed, bought with a schoolboy's carefully hoarded sixpences. Then it seemed something of a revelation, the story of a tour by 'two worshippers at the shrine of Cricket, making the most of the days before they place the halter of an established office-stool round their necks.'

Yet even the critic of today must see that it had the unusual merit, for a cricket book, of dealing seriously and expertly with the play, while catching all the gaiety of a tour which was important but not, by Test standards, *too* important. Its outstanding quality is its gusto – delight in cricket and uninhibited enjoyment of a tour.

It may be said that the humour is undergraduate humour: 'Are you "poor but honest"? We are poorer – but *honi-soit*. Are you lit up? Lead kindly light, for we are like Christmas trees.' But are there not less funny types of humour than undergraduate humour – especially for the young, or those who feel young?

The tour began with matches against each of the Australian States – and such opponents as Arthur Richardson, Victor Richardson, Clarrie Grimmett, Tim Wall, Jack Ryder, Bill Ponsford, Bert Oldfield, Stan McCabe, Alan Fairfax, Don Bradman, Archie Jackson, Alan Kippax and Bill Woodfull – the last four of whom made centuries against the touring side.

Then came the visit to New Zealand – seventeen matches, including four Tests, of which one was won and three drawn. The MCC side included Frank Woolley, Duleepsinhji, Fred Barratt, Maurice Nichols, Stan Worthington, Ted Bowley, Geoffrey Legge, Eddie Dawson, 'Tich' Cornford and the erratic but powerful hitter, Guy Earle. This was cricketing education – to see Jackson at his best, before illness reduced his stature, and the budding Bradman, to bat against Blackie and Ironmonger, neither of whom ever toured England – and to take part in the first Tests ever played by New Zealand. Yet no one seems to have made a deeper impression on these two – alertly impressionable – authors than Duleepsinhji: 'There are three things one should never tire of looking at – a two-year-old leaving his field; a slip of a girl dancing;

and old Duleep as he flashes his bat in the sun, moving gracefully the while, with heavy white silk buttoned over wrists of steel, the epitome of elegance combined with grim watchfulness.' The biographical notes are often astute, as this of Maurice Nichols: 'We are a side of triers, but in this direction Nick reached even more gigantic proportions than the rest of us. Clumsily built, with enormous feet, he is really good to watch on the cricket field, for in him seems to be concentrated the essence of purposeful endeavour.'

The match accounts are concise, and they include Turnbull's account – from a close-fielding position – of Allom's hat-trick in the first Test: 'Allom sent down an over which ranks on a level with the best ever bowled in New Zealand. It must have been a close thing that he did not get the decision when he yorked Blunt's foot first ball; with his second he knocked Dempster's off stump over with a break-back; Lowry struck at the third but missed; he was out lbw to the next; from the fifth James went, well caught by Cornford, standing up, off the inside edge; and to round the thing off, Allom completed the hat-trick by clean-bowling Badcock with an unplayable last ball. Four wickets in five balls with the score at 21 and including the hat-trick! Allom was whipping the ball back appreciably from the off and making tremendous pace from the pitch; his analysis at this point was four for 5.'

This book was followed by another – *The Two Maurices Again* – on the MCC South African tour of 1930–31. Maurice Allom did leave cricket for a business career but Maurice Turnbull, as captain and secretary of Glamorgan, played a major part in lifting his county's cricket – and keeping it solvent – until the last war, when, as a Major of the Welsh Guards, he was killed in action in Normandy.

There have been more profound and more polished cricket books but this is unique in catching, as no other has done, the atmosphere of a cricket tour.

The last word may come from the authors' 'Introduction the First': 'We are fortunate in that we have no axe to grind, no hare to start, no moss to gather; we bow and scrape to no one. Heaven forbid that we should give dirty linen an airing in public, even supposing cricketers have dirty linen.'

## Crusoe's Cultured Phrases Lodge in the Mind

Those of us who read *The Cricketer* in the twenties – turning those heavily print-laden pages of soft paper with its faint yellow-grey tinge – used to be vastly diverted by the writings of R. C. Robertson-Glasgow. In 1933 he made a selection of those pieces – prose and verse – in *The Brighter Side of Cricket* which was put out by that cricket-enthusiast-publisher, Arthur Barker.

There are more 'important' books on the game, many of which stand on cricketers' shelves impressively unread or to be used for reference. But every copy I have ever seen of Robertson-Glasgow's collection has a much-handled air. It is a book to be taken down for a couple of minutes or half an hour; it has phrases nostalgic, romantic, more often sheerly funny, which lodge in the mind so that one turns to it constantly for two or three lines that meet, and make, a point in cricket conversation.

The late Raymond Robertson-Glasgow – re-christened 'Crusoe' by Charlie McGahey – was a fast-medium bowler only just short of top level; four years an Oxford Blue and good enough to play for the Gentlemen at Lord's; and he became one of the most gracious of all cricket reporters. But his quality as a man is best to be inferred from the fact that he was in eager demand for festival matches and country house cricket. He felt too deeply for the game to play it at less than his best: but, as Ben Travers – the playwright of the Aldwych farces, and himself an enthusiast for cricket – wrote in his gay and perceptive preface to *The Brighter Side*: 'The fact remains (and to know "Crusoe" is to realize it) that the only reason for cricket is FUN.'

There have been many attempts to write 'funny' books about cricket, a number of which have misfired, so far as the cricketer is concerned, because they have lacked the basic human truth on which the best humour is based. Robertson-Glasgow did not simply try to be funny about the game – he had fun with it.

The first of these pieces – 'Puerilities' – deals with those schoolboy games played by closing the eyes (or, at least, *almost* closing them) and jabbing a piece of marked paper with a pen to produce such match-scores as the one he quotes:

> J. B. Hobbs, bowled Me.................................... o
> ME, not out (at the end of Latin)........................381

He ends that essay with a characteristic passage: 'It is a sweet disorder. For in boyhood the ball that hits the bottom of the middle stump is not a d—— shooter and the groundsman's fault, but a beastly grub and the action of wayward fate. The loss of a Test match is just a 'swindle', not the crash of an empire or the harbinger of national decay. In fact, *cricketomania* is never fatal, at least not to the young.'

Some of these pieces have become little light classics, almost current coin of cricket allusion – like 'The One-way Boy':

> ...*My boy is* always *caught at slip;*
> *It gives me one gigantic pip:*
> *Now can you give me any reason*
> *Why this should happen* all *the season,*
> *Instead of intermittently,*

*As it occurs with you or me?...*
*'Put on those pads,' his father said,*
*As if conversing with the dead,*
*'And show the gentleman the stroke,*
*Concerning which I lately spoke.'*
*He donned them filially resign'd.*
*I gave him guard, to leg inclined,*
*I bowled him long-hops free from guile,*
*Full-pitchers you could hit a mile,*
*Half-volleys straight, half-volleys wide,*
*Swervers, delicious for the glide.*
*He never swerved, nor lost his grip,*
*But snicked the ruddy lot to slip.*

'Crusoe' had a happy touch with light verse: 'First Slip', 'The Bowler's Epitaph', 'The Ancient Cricketer' and 'The Cricketer's Highway' all have their delights and cherished phrases. The series of parodies in 'The Poets' Limbo' are delightful, especially Tennyson's 'The Last Test' with its opening:

*Then rose Sir Woodstrong, moved his host by night –*
*(For fear of Autographs) and moving came,*
*Or seemed to come, to great Londinium . . .*

Robertson-Glasgow was to go on to become a major cricket writer; but this was the early fun of a man with a background of literature and the classics, and a true feeling for cricket, the writing which frothed up before he was visited by the cruel depressions which clouded his later life. His village Oracle, Aunt Emily, Charlie and The Fielder are genuinely comic characters. The drawings of A. Savory, who sat next to 'Crusoe' at a school, provide a happily light, slightly period accompaniment to the text. The essay 'Envoi' is the author at his most sincerely romantic; but he is probably at his best when he rends 'The One-Way Critic' with:

*Your fathers cursed the bowlers you adored,*
*Your fathers damned the batsmen of your choice,*
*Your fine, ecstatic rapture they deplored,*
*Theirs was the One-Way Critic's ageless voice,*
*And their immortal curse is yours today,*
*The croak which kills all airy Cricket Dryads,*
*Withers the light on tree and grass and spray*
*The strangling fugue of senile jeremiads.*

*I ceased, and turned to Larwood's bounding run,*
*And Woolley's rapier flashing in the sun.*

## Oh, those Shooters at Lord's!

*Seventy-one Not Out* sounds, and in some ways looks, a dull Victorian book. Its sub-title:

THE
### REMINISCENCES OF
### WILLIAM CAFFYN
MEMBER OF THE ALL ENGLAND AND
UNITED ELEVENS
OF THE SURREY COUNTY ELEVEN
OF THE ANGLO-AMERICAN TEAM OF
1859
AND OF THE ANGLO-AUSTRALIAN
TEAMS OF 1861 AND 1863

EDITED BY
'MID-ON'

must seem lengthily old-fashioned to those accustomed to the 'lively' production of the modern cricketer's own story. 'Mid-on', one of the earliest of cricket 'ghosts', was no great stylist. Yet, despite its literary limitations, *Seventy-One Not Out* is an essential book for anyone who wants to understand the history of cricket.

Caffyn, whose career in first-class cricket ran from 1849 to 1861, a major batsman of his time and often a valuable change-bowler, 'was known at The Oval,' he tells us, 'by the names of "The Surrey Pet" and "Terrible Billy".' He was the only man to make the first three overseas tours with English sides – one to America and two to Australia – and, between 1864 and 1871, as a coach in Melbourne and Sydney, he probably had a more profound effect on the development of cricket in Australia than any other single person. When he wrote his book he was one of the only two members of Clarke's All England XI still alive.

His book has two outstanding merits. It describes the players of the day with positive *definition*: and it gives us the feeling of the age. On the first page, he says, 'What a change in the history of cricket has been brought about by the railways! What a countless number of matches they have been responsible for!' Caffyn's own career began in the Railway Age.

In other respects he lived in an older time: 'My father was much averse to my taking up cricket as a profession, and when I was selected to play for the Players v The Gentlemen of Surrey at The Oval, he refused point blank to supply me with any money to get there. I managed to borrow half-a-crown, however, and received 10s. and my expenses for playing in the match, so I felt quite rich when I returned home.' Next came his first professional engagement – to play in Captain Alexander's country house matches at The Auberies: 'Often while the gentlemen were at dinner in the evening, I used to sit in the park and give them a solo on the cornet.'

There are absorbing and revealing flashes of conditions, as when the All England XI played at Worcester in 1851: 'The ground here was a very rough one, only a small square being laid, and the remainder ridge and furrow. Our first four wickets fell for 5 runs.'

Looking back from the 1890s he can write with feeling, 'There is one ball that is denied to the modern bowlers, which was a terror to all us old batters – the shooter. Oh, those shooters at Lord's! One or two balls as high as your ear, then perhaps one in the ribs, and then a shooter! No wonder that when we used to stop one of these we were greeted with a round of applause.'

Caffyn's close study of technique makes him a valuable guide to the development of the game, as when he writes of Lockyer: 'He was the first to adopt the modern attitude for wicket-keeping, and almost the first to take balls cleverly on the leg side. Few wicket-keepers had hitherto attempted to trouble about these balls.'

Or, of George Parr: 'His late cut was a hard chop, striking the ground at the same time as he struck the ball. We have seen as fine leg-hitters as Parr, but never one who hit so many balls in that direction. His method was to reach out with his left leg straight down the wicket, bending the knee, and to sweep the ball round in a sort of half-circle behind the wicket. There seems to be an idea sprung up of late years that Parr was in the habit of hitting straight balls to leg, but this is a mistake. In Parr's day to have attempted to make a deliberate leg-hit from a ball on the wicket would have been unpardonable.'

He is, too, absorbing on the old round-arm – and round-the-wicket – bowlers, such as Billy Buttress: 'A medium-paced bowler with a tremendous break from leg. I never saw a man in my life able to get more work on the ball. Woe betide the batsman who got playing forward to one of Billy's that was not right up to him. Sometimes the batter would simply play the air and the ball went into the slips, but more often he assisted it there with the edge of his bat, where short-slip anxiously awaited it.'

In passages like this, the methods of a hundred years come to life. Meanwhile, through little personal recollections, too, the players become rounded human beings: 'Tom Adams was a tall man with an exceedingly good-tempered countenance. He wore his hair rather long, with a curl which he trained down each side of his face. He was very fond of shooting, and declared he was so well known in one district as a deadly shot that every hare or rabbit he came across in the open never attempted to run away, knowing that it would be quite useless, but would sit quietly to be knocked over!'

In his closing section, Caffyn compares the great players at each end of half a century, a key period which began with some masters of lob bowling still in the first-class game and ended when the last of the round-arm bowlers had given way to over-arm.

The comparisons between the generations are made by a man who watched them through the eyes of an expert. 'The high, over-hand, over-the-wicket bowling by means of which the ball is almost invariably kept straight or on the off-side has entirely done away with genuine leg-hitting.' 'There is now more fast-footed play than formerly.' 'The bowling of today is straighter but not of such accurate length as formerly.'

On the outstanding players of the nineties he is also illuminating: 'Mr Lionel Palairet perhaps resembles Fuller Pilch in his graceful style of forward play and forward hitting more closely than any other batsman now living.'

In the course of his judgement of W. G. Grace he writes: 'We have been told that he invented modern batting. As a matter of fact, Dr Grace more closely resembles some of the old players than most of those of modern times resemble *him*. If it were possible to see Dr Grace and Mr Hankey at the wickets together, each well set, and each unknown to the spectators, they would in all probability pronounce Mr Hankey the finer batsman of the pair. What, then, has been the cause of Dr Grace's phenomenal success? He has been more consistent than any other player past or present. He is not so liable to be caught in two minds as other batsmen, and this, combined with his great science and splendid physique, practically allow him to have, so to speak, three innings to another batsman's one.'

## Inflatable Pads, and Coal Slack for Sawdust

There was once a man who sold books from a barrow in Lambeth Cut and was reputed to price his wares by weight – because, it was said, he had originally been a grocer. On the other hand, he may have observed the attraction that large books have for many people – with the corresponding tendency to overlook those of lesser size.

This might account for the fact that *Bat, Ball, Wicket and All* – by G. D. Martineau (Sporting Handbooks 1950) – is missing from so many cricket bookshelves which find room for much less admirable works. Little more than 30,000 words long, its slimness dictated by the paper shortage of its publication time, and with a modest dust-wrapper reproducing the pleasant, period engraving of Lewis Cage by Busiere, after

Francis Coates, it is unpretentious in appearance though, under the wrapper, the binding is of a gay *Wisden*-yellow.

The sub-title is 'An account of the origin and development of the implements, dress and appurtenances of the national game', which, though accurate, does not – and does not strive to – make exciting appeal to one who takes it up casually. In fact, however, it is a graceful, balanced, informative and often evocative, picture of an aspect of cricket history.

Mr Martineau has several outstanding assets as a cricket historian. He has read widely on cricket out of enthusiasm, so that he can write: 'I have been especially moved by cricket's romantic history. It has excited me to discover that the Civil War and the Restoration combined to make it an heroic spectacle, that a Jacobite rising gave Hambledon its "chosen general" and Lord's its title, that a cricket ball altered the succession to the throne and may even have helped America to her independence, that active feminism was the mother of round-arm bowling, and that the Victorian age gave the game its most powerful personality and made it imperial.'

*Bat, Ball, Wicket and All* was not the result of chasing the theme through the obvious reference-books but the result of specialized research, based on wide reading. Only the catholic reader would have had in mind for this book the story of Bill Worsley, of Lancashire – as late as 1903 – keeping wicket to the fast bowling of Walter Brearley in gloves so primitive that they had afterwards to be cut away from his battered hands with scissors.

No one before has brought together so extensive, so varied or so relevant a collection of historic facts and references on cricket gear – and it is difficult to believe that anyone could have arranged it more divertingly, or drawn sounder conclusions from it.

The section on the bat is a concise history – from John Chitty's broad-bladed, curved implement of 1729 and the 'Stonyhurst bats', through those straight blades which John Small made, and used, to revolutionize the game and the family tree of the Darks of Lord's, to rattans, malaccas, rubber springs and modern factory methods.

Some of the items, however, barely emerged from invention – for instance the inflatable gloves and pads (1865) of Henry Emmanuel and, in the 1770s, the use of coal slack to dry the ball – a somewhat grimy early variant of sawdust.

There are many discoveries – not a few from the Patent Office – but the scholarship is lightened by such anecdotes as that of the village batsman, on his first introduction to the 'abominable belt', going out to bat wearing it outside his trousers!

G. D. Martineau is never in danger of that besetting trap for historians which John Betjeman has called 'antiquarian prejudice' for, while he turns often – as he was bound to do – to Nyren, *Scores and Biographies* and the earlier works, he also uses – and acknowledges – the crisply factual researches of Colonel Rait Kerr and, if he is rather horrified by the idea of public-address loudspeakers at Lord's, he observes with an open mind the potentialities of the plastic-covered ball.

Some authors might have padded-out Mr Martineau's material to twice the length; he, however, has not only the sensibility but another, often disregarded, quality of the poet – conciseness. Even those who have read this minor classic of the game may have missed one of its gems, which occurs in the Preface – the place where so many delights of reading lie unnoticed. This consists of surely the briefest, but not least effective, anthology of cricket appreciation ever compiled:

'Of no other has it been said that it is "an institution and only a game incidentally" (Neville Cardus); that "the whole edifice of the Christian virtues could be raised on a basis of good cricket" (Lefroy); that he (Andrew Lang) has "had happier hours at Lord's or even on a rough country wicket than at the Louvre or in the Uffizzi"; that "it is surely the loveliest scene in England and the most disarming sound. From the ranks of the unseen dead for ever passing along our country lanes, the Englishman falls out for a moment to look over the gate of the cricket-field and smile" (Sir James Barrie); the game "That is battle and service and sport and art" (Arnold Wall).'

## Everyone Out, and Not a Ball Bowled

Thirty years ago almost every cricket book-case contained a copy of *Cricket Highways and Byways*, by F. S. Ashley-Cooper, which was published in 1927. Today it and its author are, apparently, forgotten – except by historians. Yet *Highways* is a diverting bedside book for any cricketer.

Ashley-Cooper – the Ashley and the hyphen were an affectation – though he described himself as an 'author and journalist', was more truly an archivist and editor. He was physically delicate: no one seems ever to have seen him so much as handle a cricket bat and he was little interested in contemporary play. In this book he wrote, 'Life is too short for one to be in the forefront both of active players and collectors. To be either is delightful; to be both would be "very Heaven" and a 24 hour day too short.' (Characteristically, his quotation is from Nyren.) It seems that apart from a – significantly? – brief period as secretary of the Notts club, he spent most of his life perusing documents rather, even, than watching cricket.

Certainly, he wrote a biography of E. M. Grace, the painstaking history, *Nottinghamshire Cricket and Cricketers*, compiled the monumental Volume 15 of *Scores and Biographies* – adding his own records to Arthur Haygarth's notes – and put together *Lord's and the MCC*, though sharing the credit with Lord Harris. But chiefly – sometimes under his own name but, as often, some *nom de plume* or unsigned – he contributed information, from full-length obituary notices to brief answers to enquiries to *Cricket, The Cricketer* and papers and magazines in many countries: and he would edit anything on cricket, however minor, with infinite care.

He clearly had enough money to subsidize his work, for it cannot have been profitable. He loved researching into cricket and, in his booklets and pamphlets – many of them printed in limited editions, and distributed among his friends – and his contributions to periodicals, there is a great weight of original research – in newspapers, diaries, manuscripts and correspondence, and by personal visits to those with worthwhile memories of the game – and an immense bulk of statistics.

*Highways and Byways* consists of fourteen essays, unpadded – he wrote everything by hand – orderly and informed and reflecting his studies : he was no plagiarist.

In 'A Girdle Round the Earth' he sets out the early records of cricket in France, Germany, Spain, Holland, Denmark, Turkey ('If a history of the game in Turkey ever comes to be written, the period dealt with will be one of well over fifty years'), Greece, Russia, the Canary Islands, Borneo, Manila, Java, Samoa, and twenty other places.

. 'Some Notes on Old Time Cricket' is an erudite piece of work which many a subsequent historian has used with gratitude, if not acknowledgement.

'Cricket and the Church' is a typical piece of scholarship: it includes a stanza from the poem with which the – subsequent – Cardinal Manning, thanked Charles Wordsworth for the gift of a cricket bat:

> *The bat that you were kind enough to send*
> *Seems (for as yet I have not tried it) good ;*
> *And if there's anything on earth can mend*
> *My wretched play, it is that piece of wood.*

He tells, too, the story that Manning – who in his day played for Harrow – once asked one of his priests: 'Would you like to enter Heaven with a chalice in one hand and a cricket bat in the other?' This essay is stored with such terse snippets as 'The Rev. T. A. Anson was in his day a wonderful wicket-keeper, who earned immortality at Lord's between Gentlemen and Players in 1843 by stumping G. Butler off one of Alfred Mynn's tremendous shooters, using the left hand only; E. H. Pickering, a celebrated old Etonian, was once called upon so suddenly to bat in a Gentlemen v Players match that he was obliged to go to the wicket in clerical garb; Canon McCormick held a curious record for one in Holy orders, for he could state that he once gained the verdict over Nat Langham, the only man who ever beat Tom Sayers.'

'Umpires and Umpiring' is full of anecdotes which must have been the result of many scores of conversations. 'A country umpire called "No ball" as the bowler stepped over the crease. "Wide", he added as the ball appeared to be so. But the batsman reached out and struck the ball. "Well hit!" shouted the umpire, and "Well caught!" as a fieldsman brought off a catch. "Hout! Hover!" And he strolled meditatively towards square leg.'

The practical cricketer and the story teller will be delighted by 'In the Kent v Sussex match of 1866, "Tiny" Wells of Sussex took guard within about an inch of the stumps and, as the bowler advanced, he also came forward. George Bennett pretended to deliver the ball from about a yard behind the non-striker's wicket. Wells became disconcerted and, moving his bat in his agitation, knocked a stump, causing a bail to fall. The umpire was right in giving Wells out, as he struck the wicket in the act of playing: the ball is in play as soon as the bowler commences his run. It is, therefore, possible for a match to be completed without a single ball being delivered. Another manner in which the same result could be reached would be for every man to be run out while backing up too far as the bowler is about to deliver the ball.'

From which it will be seen that Ashley-Cooper, if a non-player and something of an antiquarian, was not dry, except in wit.

## Dudley Carew Might Have Been as Well Known as Cardus

Many writers on cricket have had genuinely worthwhile contributions to make to our knowledge of the game – its technique, appreciation or history. There have been fewer, however, whose quality of writing would have been esteemed in a wider, and more consciously literary, field. Yet when style in cricket-writing is discussed, one rarely hears mention of Dudley Carew who wrote two books of cricket studies and a novel on the game in a limpid, smooth-flowing prose which conceals high skill.

The two books of studies – *England Over* and *To the Wicket* – appeared nineteen years apart, in 1927 and 1946; the novel, *The Son of Grief*, came between the two, in 1936. *To the Wicket* is composed of essays on each of the first-class cricketing counties, set between a masterly 'Dissertation' and a nostalgic 'Epilogue'. *The Son of Grief* is far removed from the usual 'hero wins at last moment' type of sporting story: it has its darknesses, but it is convincing, and its characters are rounded and credible. Dudley Carew was a special correspondent of *The Times* between the two wars, and an eminent film critic, with a strong literary background: all three of his cricket titles, it may be observed, are quotations from Housman. His childhood in the Edwardian period left a deep imprint on him so that, especially in his autobiography, he looks back to it constantly and nostalgically.

*England Over* was published by Martin Secker, at five shillings: it is slight, for the 204 attractively set pages hardly average two hundred words of large type. The preface explains the book: in May 1926 Mr Carew, young and exuberant, felt the urge to 'get away' – and, as so many of us have dreamt of doing, he decided to spend the summer watching cricket. In the four months that followed he saw a diversity of Englishmen: 'Each of them, amazingly dissimilar as they are in speech and habits, has a certain number of habits in common, not the least of which is their devotion to a game which does not pander to their cravings for money or sensation but which satisfies their unconscious need for beauty, and transforms them from men with rents to pay and children to feed, into boys whose whole happiness depends upon the hitting of a boundary or the fall of a wicket.'

If we except a single phrase of the preface which jars quite harshly – and seems far out of sympathy with the remainder of the book – this is a collection of vignettes written, we feel, as some other people in Mr Carew's situation might have drawn in a sketch book – the recording, for his own pleasure, of a series of delights.

The nine chapters are devoted not simply to a match apiece – but to a place and people and a match. They range through Oxford – The University v The Army; The Oval; Lord's – for Eton and Harrow; Bradford; Hastings; Nottingham; Canterbury – Kent's match with the Australians; Old Trafford and, finally, the Scarborough Gentlemen v Players.

It was, perhaps, unfortunate for Dudley Carew that his entry into cricket writing should have coincided with the rise of Neville Cardus. If there had never been a Cardus, how highly should we have ranked one who wrote: 'At the other end Gunn batted much as a man potters about a garden, digging his fork into a bed with an abstracted and absent-minded air, his thoughts far away. If Gunn had not got that curious kink of genius in him, the weary disillusion of young Alexander brooding over a tame and conquered world, he would, I think be as fine a batsman as Macartney.' Of H. L. Collins, the Australian captain of 1926: 'Collins withdrew deeper and deeper into the hard shell of his dour and invincible spirit. Cromwell would have welcomed him as one of his lieutenants; he knows how to watch and how to fight.' Again, on the course of play, – Yorkshire v Middlesex: 'Kilner, who cleverly pitched the ball a fraction short of orthodox good length, made it pop awkwardly, and Hearne gave two easy catches to a silly point that wasn't there. Kilner, supremely confident of his ability to make the batsman walk into the trap he had so clearly indicated, brought Holmes to that position and Lee immediately gave him the simplest of catches. Kilner, thoroughly pleased with himself, brought his field in closer, and before luncheon he accomplished the supreme task he had set himself – he caught Hearne in two minds and Robinson took the catch in slips.' As an example of his criticism – on Errol Holmes: 'His stand at the wicket, a certain naval rakishness about the fit of his cap, his expression as the bowler begins his run – all these combine to give one the feeling that the outer ring of fieldsmen will be hard-worked so long as he is in. Usually they are, but not for a sufficient time. Usually one is fortunate enough to see one or two of these splendid, free-swinging drives and then Holmes, getting impatient at that dangerous moment in the twenties when the ball is beginning to look deceptively big, hits out at the wrong ball and gets caught somewhere on the boundary.'

Such is *England Over*: a book of musings, appreciation and perception: it is, as I have warned, slight: it contains no scores – and needs none: one seems no sooner to have started it than one is at the end. But the flavour it leaves is lasting – and distinguished.

## The Best Written of All Books on Cricket

There have been few happier ideas for a cricket book than *Cricket All His Life* – Rupert Hart-Davis's collection and publishing of the cricket writings of E. V. Lucas. Happily, too, it was titled from one of Lucas's favourite quotations – from Mary Turner's letter – 'and wishd he had not anny thing else to do, he would play at Cricket all his Life'.

Lucas was one of the finest essayists of this century: a quiet, perceptive stylist, reminiscent, at times, of Charles Lamb, whom he much admired: he wrote felicitously on any of the wide range of subjects that engaged his lively mind. Cricket was one of many such enthusiasms but, although he was a prolific writer for some fifty years, it engaged only a little of his attention. The game is the richer for the work of a man who cared for the subject, who wrote with so certain and subtle a touch and who turned to it so rarely that, whenever he did so, he had something worth while to say.

In 1892 Lucas uttered an anonymous penny pamphlet of poems called *Songs of the Bat*, now one of the rarities of cricket literature. He reprinted some of those verses, in revised form, with some essays in his only complete cricket book – *Willow and Leather* – six years afterwards. In 1908 he produced one of the finest of all cricket books, *The Hambledon*

*Men*, in which he arranged, linked and commented on the writings of Nyren, Mitford, Haygarth and Pycroft on the early players. Finally, so far as cricket books were concerned, he edited, and introduced with a substantial essay, *A Hundred Years of Trent Bridge*, the book privately produced by Sir Julien Cahn to mark the centenary of the Nottingham ground.

Rupert Hart-Davis is a sympathetic editor: he selected *The Essential Cardus*, as well as doing some sensitive work on Hugh Walpole and Max Beerbohm. He made no attempt to collect everything that Lucas had written about cricket. For instance, he judged that much of his writing in *The Hambledon Men* was so closely connected with the edited material that only the biographical essay on John Nyren should be taken from it. Still enough remained to show, in some 60,000 words, that E. V. Lucas was, on cricket as on many other themes, one of the most felicitous of writers.

He began the essay titled 'The Incomparable Game' with: 'Having, the other day, once again spent an afternoon in watching a village cricket match, I am again perplexed by the passion for that game which is displayed by those who cannot shine at it. They cannot bat, they cannot bowl, they leave their place in the field, they miss catches, they fumble returns; and yet, every Saturday, there they are, often in perfect flannels, ready to fail once more.' This thought has been attempted so often: it has never been more clearly yet happily expressed: nor with greater subtlety: take, for instance, the phrase 'often in perfect flannels': there is the illuminating Lucas touch.

Consider the warm humour of this passage from Roderick's Pro's: 'Roderick also had a *Cricketer's Birthday Book*, so that when he came down to breakfast he used to say "Tyldesley's 35 today", "Hutchings is 24", and so on. And he knew the Christian name of every pro. That was not Roderick's only cricketing triumph. It is true that he had never succeeded in bowling out any other really swell batsman, but he had shaken hands with Sammy Woods and J. R. Mason, and one day Lord Hawke took him by both shoulders and lifted him to one side, saying "Now then, Tommy, out of the way." '

At the end of a piece about Lord's he dealt with W. G. Grace and says of the latter part of his life: 'Of late years, since his retirement, the Old Man was an occasional figure at Lord's. More than a figure, a landmark, for he grew vaster steadily, more massive, more monumental. At the big matches he would be seen on one of the lower seats of the pavilion with a friend on either side, watching and commenting. But the part of oracle sat very lightly upon him; he was ever a man of action rather than of words; shrewd and sagacious enough, but without rhetoric. That his mind worked with Ulysses-like acuteness, every other captain had reason to know; his tactics were superb. But he donned and doffed them with his flannels. In ordinary life he was content to be an ordinary man. Although sixty-seven, he did not exactly look old; he merely looked older than he had been, or than any such performer should be permitted to be . . . Almost to the end he kept himself fit, either with local matches where latterly he gave away more runs in the field than he hit up, not being able to "get down" to the ball, or with golf or beagling. But the great beard grew steadily more grizzled and the ponderous footfalls more weighty. Indeed, towards the last he might almost have been a work by Mestrovic, so colossal and cosmic were his lines.'

No finer prose has been written about the game of cricket. There is temptation to quote from the romantic light verse: even more to pick passages from 'The English Game', 'The Bats', 'A Rhapsodist at Lord's' (Francis Thompson). But to do so might hint to a reader that the best had been taken from *Cricket All His Life*. It is full of the best. It is written with perfect style (J. M. Barrie once said 'Lucas, unfortunately, has style' but he was referring to E. V. L.'s batting), human understanding, appreciation of cricket and its history. Anyone who reads it must be puzzled that it is not constantly quoted as the best written of all books on cricket.

*The Cricketer*, November 1965 to May 1966

# 9
# The Issues of Cricket

## The Bowling Called Bodyline

Thursday 27 April 1950 was a day of some sun, but along the Thames estuary a keen edge of wind carried the tang of the Essex salt-marshes into Tilbury Docks, where the liner *Orontes* stood at the quay with ropes of oil-smoke running from her thick yellow funnels.

On the tourist-class boat-deck I sat with Harold Larwood, who spoke of his great venture – the recent sale of his general store in Blackpool. He was off, with his wife and five daughters, who were sitting quietly near him, to make a new home in Australia.

Some old friends had given him a small farewell dinner in London on the previous night but, as sailing time approached, I was the only person there to see him off. He recalled the day, seventeen and a half years before, in September 1932, when he had set out for the same destination. He sailed then in this same *Orontes* and from this same quay as a member of Douglas Jardine's MCC team which was to win the Ashes from Australia in the Tests known to cricket history as the 'bodyline series'. That day, he remembered, there had been cameramen and photographers, reporters, friends, and well-wishers at the boat, and the dignitaries of the cricket world had given the tour their benison at a ceremonial luncheon on board.

Today, although it was now almost three o'clock, he had not yet had lunch. Somehow he had not felt like eating. I caught his straightforward look: we smiled thinly and went down to the tourist-class saloon for a cup of tea, passing through the family groups of emigrants whose view of the future was, for these moments, completely obscured by the concrete picture of a flat, uninspired Essex landscape which was the last some of them would ever see of England.

I took stock of him as we walked. Except for the horn-rimmed spectacles, there was little change in him. He had always been a slight man, with little sign, except his unusually long arms, to account for his being the fastest bowler in the world. His hair, though now thinner and with occasional grey strands, still stood up in short-cropped belligerence from his forehead. He wore a new sports coat, and I recalled that ordinary clothes had always seemed to sit uneasily on him; it was in cricket flannels that Harold Larwood looked at ease – in flannels and, I imagine, in the mining clothes he wore before his big cricket days.

While we were drinking our tea, my mind slipped back a month beyond the journey on the *Orontes* that my companion had recalled. On 3, 4, and 5 August 1932, Essex played Nottinghamshire at Leyton. I was in London with a fellow cricket student at the time and, since reports in Friday morning's papers showed the possibility of a good finish to the match, we took the long bus journey from Cambridge Circus to Leyton for the third day's play. It was a hot, sunny morning. We sat on the heavy grey ammunition boxes which formed the seating on the old Leyton ground and watched the Notts second innings grow to 203 for two wickets before Arthur Carr declared, and set Essex 298 runs in four hours to win. There was, I remember, an ice-cream man on the ground, whose cry we identified, after much study, as 'Oosezaniceice-Wallses'. We capped our sandwiches with one of his ices and settled to watch the Notts bowling – one of the strongest attacking combinations in the country on a hard wicket – attempt to put Essex out before half-past six.

Larwood and Voce began; Larwood bowling to the orthodox, heavy slip field of the fast bowler and Voce to the leg-trap he always employed for his fast-medium left-arm inswing. Voce completed his second over and the field changed for Larwood. Instead of going into slips, the close fieldsmen took up places on the leg side. I turned to my companion in surprise: 'But Voce can't bowl two consecutive overs.' Larwood was about to start his run-in. 'Good Lord, he's going to bounce them round his ears!'

The first ball of that over pitched well short of a length, lifted – but not very spitefully off that placid Leyton pitch – and Cutmore hooked it firmly over the short-leg fieldsmen. The remaining five deliveries were also what the schoolboy is taught to regard as long-hops, and Cutmore, standing straight up, had no difficulty in playing them and even hooking two of them very hard indeed.

Voce then had the opening batsman – the late Dudley Pope – caught by Lilley, the wicket-keeper, to let in Wilcox, who hooked Larwood's leg-stump attack unmercifully in the course of a short innings. By the end of the day Essex, even with O'Connor unable to bat, had scored 203 for four wickets, and the game was comfortably saved. Larwood had bowled all but his first two overs to a leg-side field, and taken no wicket for 43 runs in sixteen overs.

We two sixteen-year-olds discussed the matter until midnight. The trip to Australia was only a few weeks ahead. There, Bradman would be the problem – he had averaged 139.14 runs per innings against England two years before when Australia took the Ashes from us. Was this new method a preparation for the forthcoming Tests? Certainly it had been no help to Notts in the matter of beating Essex. If one of the weaker counties, without their best batsman, could treat such an attack so lightly, what would Bradman do to it? It would be no good, we decided, in our youthful omniscience, to bowl long-hops to Australian batsmen: they would hook them out of sight.

Notts then had a sequence of five matches in the North but, three weeks later, on 24, 25, and 26 August, they played Glamorgan at Cardiff. My curiosity led me to that game: Maurice Turnbull, finding Notts without one of the slow left-arm bowlers to whom he was so extremely vulnerable, proceeded to hook Larwood's leg-attack with an imperious power, heady to watch and, for me, conclusive proof that this bowling was a waste of time. I settled down to wait the reports of the tour matches for mention of fast leg-theory.

On 17 September 1932, the *Orontes* took the team out from Tilbury, and three weeks later they broke their journey to play a match against Ceylon at Colombo. Larwood played but did not bowl. In the first match in Australia – against Western Australia at Perth – he bowled only six overs and, on a rain-damaged pitch, took two wickets for 17 runs. No report made any mention of his bowling method. He missed the next match and then, against South Australia, merely sent down five unremarkable overs in the first innings and did not bowl at all in the second. 'Rested' again from the match against Victoria, he took six wickets against the side described as 'An Australian XI' at Melbourne. Reports said that he bowled at terrific speed. He did not play against New South Wales. Half-satisfied that my theory of a 'new' tactic was pure imagination, I awaited news of the First Test.

England included three pace-bowlers – Larwood, Voce, and Allen – and Australia, without Bradman, who was said to be unwell, were put out in their first innings for 360 – Larwood five wickets for 96, Voce four for 110; on that batsman's wicket, England had done well. There was praise for Larwood; the correspondents said that he had never bowled so fast before. There was no comment on his method. Then, with news of Australian objections to Voce's short bumpers on the leg side – his usual practice – it seemed to me that, if there had ever been any idea of Larwood using such an attack, it had been abandoned.

England led by 164 on the first innings. Australia batted again, and after his first two overs – a warming-up spell – Larwood was reported to have bowled to a leg-trap. He took five wickets for 28 runs, and Australia was beaten by ten wickets.

Jack Hobbs reported that Wall, the Australian fast bowler, 'tried to copy the leg-theory stuff of Larwood and Voce, but even at his fastest had not quite the pace and, more important than that, he could not find quite the right spot. Time must elapse before the Australians know how to direct this new form of attack; practice in England has given our bowlers a good start.'

I once played in a village match when a swarm of bees flew over the field. Their quick, angry sound, even when faint in the distance, struck startlingly across the mood of the game, and we all waited until they were out of hearing before we restarted play. The anger of Australians against Larwood and Voce, after that First Test, was apparent like a far-off swarm of bees.

Larwood played in only one of the three matches between the First and Second Tests, and then he did not bowl.

For the Second Test, England brought in Bowes, so that four of their five bowlers – Larwood, Voce, Bowes, and Allen – were of appreciable pace: Bradman played for Australia. On a wicket which helped the bowlers, O'Reilly bowled extremely well, and Australia won a low-scoring match by 111 runs. Larwood took only four wickets, but the Australian, Alan Kippax, was of the opinion that his fast leg-theory was so unsettling to the batsmen as to be responsible for a number of the wickets taken by other bowlers.

The sides were now level at one game each, and the noise of the 'body-line' controversy – not yet christened – was becoming intense. Ten days later, with only an up-country match intervening for the English players, the Third Test began – to bring cricket into practically every British home. People with no interest whatever in the game discussed the 'new' bowling instead of the latest murder-case.

England batted first and made 341. Larwood opened, as usual, to an orthodox off-side field. The last ball of his second over was short, and it rose steeply and hit Woodfull, the Australian captain, in the chest; there was a demonstration from the crowd. For Larwood's next over, Jardine, as usual, switched to the leg-trap, and the spectators howled with anger. From this point, wrote Kippax, 'all interest in the actual cricket had gone and there was a genuine feeling of relief when the last ball was bowled.' Oldfield was hit on the head when he ducked into a short but straight ball from Larwood, and he took no further part in the match. Larwood took three wickets for 55 runs in the first innings and four for 71 in the second. England won by 338 runs.

In the Fourth Test, Larwood took seven wickets, in the Fifth, five: England won both games and thus regained the Ashes by four matches to one. At several points it appeared improbable that the series would ever be finished. The Australian Cricket Board of Control sent a protest to the MCC about Larwood's bowling; and it was stated on good authority that there were consultations on high political levels between England and Australia.

Larwood, in his ten Tests against Australia before this tour, had taken thirty-one wickets at an average of 41.06 runs each; in this series he took thirty-three at 19.5 each. Bradman's batting average of 139.14 in England in 1930 was reduced to 56.5 against 'bodyline'. In April 1933 the MCC made a new Law of cricket, banning 'intimidatory' bowling.

It seems generally accepted that the bowling called 'bodyline' was a sudden and isolated piece of cricketing tactics, which the MCC outlawed and thereby made an end of the matter for ever. In fact, it was inevitable in the normal course of cricket history. The importance it assumed was due largely to the quality of both the man who directed it and the man who executed it.

I once discussed the methods of the fast bowler with C. J. Kortright, the legendary 'fastest bowler who ever lived'. Did he, I asked, ever bowl at the batsman? No, he said, he bowled as fast as he could on and around the off stump, and the batsmen of his time essayed to cut. If they succeeded, they were the better men on the day; if they did not, he took wickets.

In our time, however, it has been different. When Maurice Tate bowled his matchless away-swinger in the twenties, then, so long as he was fresh, Test batsmen played the straight ball defensively, but when it swung away outside the off stump they lifted their bats away and refrained from a stroke, covering the wicket with their pads (under the old lbw law) lest the ball break back. Thus the cut became almost an unknown stroke in Test cricket, and the finest of the pace bowler's energies were squandered against batsmen who did not care to join cricketing battle with him. Thus, too, the number of fast bowlers began to decline. What young man wanted to fight against an opponent who would not play him until he was tired?

The problem was to force the batsmen to play the ball. Douglas Jardine, appointed captain of England for the 1932–33 tour of Australia, was a Scot, naturally shrewd and quick-witted, and trained for the law. He had toured Australia under Chapman in 1928–29; he had observed Woodfull's team in England in 1930. It is probable that he consulted with A. W. Carr, captain of Nottinghamshire, who had directed the bowling development of Larwood and Voce. He was convinced that Bradman, the main strength of the Australian batting of his time, was vulnerable to *really fast* bowling along the line of the leg stump.

This reasoning was valueless unless he had the bowlers to put his plan into execution. It has been said that men do not make history from ideal material but from such materials, good or bad, as happen to be to hand in their time. It happened that Jardine had available, in 1932, four bowlers of pace. G. O. Allen, of Middlesex, did not, in fact, employ the fast leg-theory method but, as an orthodox fast bowler, he was valuable in maintaining the tension in the batsmen of having to play continual relays of fresh fast bowling. Voce and Bowes were, at the time, classed as fast-medium but, as Jardine exploited them – in short spells after adequate rest – they gave every inch of pace in the Tests.

Larwood, however, was the bowler who mattered. Without Jardine 'bodyline' *might* not have come as and when it did. Without Bradman it *might* not have been considered necessary. Without Larwood it would *never* have won a series of Tests, and might have passed almost unnoticed.

Unusually slight for a fast bowler – he was only 5ft 7½in tall and weighed less than eleven stone – Larwood had exceptionally long arms, and early days as a miner in the Notts and Derby coalfield – which has produced so many fast bowlers for the two counties – developed his chest and shoulder muscles. He took a twenty-yard run and accelerated through every stride of it, seeming to rock with speed, until he delivered, his arm very high, on a huge body-swing. He dragged his right toe as he bowled; and his boot was fitted with a steel toecap which became so highly polished by the friction that it winked back the sun like a mirror.

Larwood was an exhilarating bowler to watch, and he could make the ball rear amazingly for one so short. Batsmen said that when a ball from Larwood hit them it knocked them completely off balance by its terrific force and seemed to grind into the body. His pace was, perhaps, only a few degrees greater than that of some other bowlers we have known – such as Kenneth Farnes and Ray Lindwall at their fastest – but his accuracy was such that no other fast bowler in thirty years has even approached it.

When Larwood bowled from the edge of the crease and, as it were, *pushed* the ball into the line of the body, it was almost impossible to back away from it: the batsman was forced to play the ball off the line of his body as it came in at him. Moreover, Larwood could drop the ball on the precise length from which, at the pace of the wicket on which he was bowling, the ball would rise to the height he desired.

There were a fair number of reputable batsmen, players of average soundness against the other fast bowlers of the time, who were frankly afraid of batting against Larwood – and would admit it. Certainly, when he was fresh, no batsman in the world could guarantee to time the first few balls he received from him. There were some who have scored their centuries in county cricket who could not see the ball at all when they first went in against Larwood.

'Lol' they called him, and he was a legend in his own time. Even on the flawless batsman's wicket of Trent Bridge, he could make the ball hop, and when he hit the body he would raise a bruise even through padding. His 'bodyline' field was carefully worked out by Douglas Jardine, and varied according to the batsman, but it usually consisted of five short-leg fieldsmen in a regular arc round the batsmen and two deep fields out behind them, with a silly mid-off just in front of the bat. The side was fortunate in having six outstanding fieldsmen to fill those close positions; had they been less good, the plan might have collapsed.

Perhaps an equally important aspect lay in Australian conditions. The wickets there in the twenties and early thirties were much faster than in England, so that a good length was a foot shorter of the batsman than in England. Moreover, there was at the time a dearth of fast bowlers in Australia: their batsmen – like the English batsmen who faced Lindwall and Miller in 1948 – were completely out of practice against such speed.

On every village green since the game began, the fast bowler has tried a short ball at the batsman to see if he flinches: if he does, a yorker on the middle stump next ball may well find him drawing away and bowl him. In Australia, between 2 December 1932 and 28 February 1933, the state of the wickets, the particular make-up of Australian cricket, the strategic power of Douglas Jardine and his own great gifts enabled Harold Larwood to put that piece of rustic cricketing tactics into operation on such a level that he won a series of Tests.

Harold Larwood never played in another Test match after the 'bodyline' affair, and never again did he bowl against any Australian cricket team. He is still, as an honest man, a little bitter and, even more, puzzled, at what cricket did to him, for he took the game seriously and played it as hard as he could, for he relished its rigours.

I looked up at him across the table. We had finished our cups of tea and for some time we had not spoken. I do not know if our thoughts had been similar. The Tests of 1932–33 were not mentioned between us that day.

A little later we shook hands. As the *Orontes* stood out into the estuary at Tilbury, with Harold Larwood as one of its passengers for the second time, he waved from the rail. Then the man who had trafficked in thunderbolts, who had put bowling on top in an age of cricket which propagated batting records, went below, on his journey from the country which bred cricket to Australia.

*The Saturday Book (ed. L. Russell, Hutchinson, 1951)*

# Modern Cricket

*August* 1953. Perhaps no game has changed so much as cricket. Yet it might also be said that no game has *seemed* to change so little. The two statements may be reconciled by the defensible theory that the game has always reflected the community in which it is played and has, therefore, developed in unchanging relative sympathy with its followers and critics. The change from underarm to roundarm bowling came with the shift of the main centres of the game from rural Hampshire, Sussex and Kent, to London. The development from roundarm to overarm coincided with the growth of cricket in the still raw centres of the Industrial Revolution.

The batsmen of the Victorian day were not habitual strikers of sixes. Their spectators esteemed style above all. That William Guy of Nottingham who was said to be 'all ease and elegance, fit to play before the Queen in Her Majesty's parlour' was a member of William Clarke's Magnificent All-England XI which, in fact, consisted of the eleven finest players in the country but who often scored at no more than twenty runs an hour.

Jessop, Thornton, and Alletson – of the solitary but unparalleled orgy of hitting – were essentially Edwardian figures, like Bosanquet with his slightly improper googly, Jacques of Hampshire with his 'leg-theory', and George Gunn who teased fast bowlers. Inter-war cricket with its rich mixture of everything the game ever had, was contemporary with the palais de danse, ice-rinks, charabanc trips, holiday camps and all the symptoms of 'try everything once before tomorrow'.

'Modern' – or postwar – cricket is a planned, rationalized affair. In effect, the bowlers have created a trade union to adjust the balance between themselves and the batsmen. Once, most county teams were composed of amateurs – or members – who filled all but the sheet-anchor post in the early places of the batting-order, with professionals to do the donkey work of stock-bowling. Less definably, but equally definitely, batsmen blame the aristocrats of the twentieth-century game, the breakers of records whose cannon-fodder was bowling. The groundsmen, by their production of comfortable wickets, did much to perpetuate this situation.

The bowlers' revolution was the move labelled 'bodyline'; their masters' subsequent concession, the 'new' lbw law, under which a batsman could be out to a ball pitching outside his off stump. Bowlers and their captains took home the new law as lawyers take a fresh Act of Parliament, to probe it for loopholes. The batsman could no longer push a practised pad in front of the off-break or inswinger pitching outside the line of the off stump. This would mean more lbw decisions and the stumps would be hit more often. The bowlers, however, recognized the new law as capable of further exploitation.

Leg-theory had been bowled before, but not with outstanding success, except by Root, who coupled an exceptionally sharp inswing with a well-concealed ball which 'went the other way' to compel the batsman to play a stroke. Now, that compulsion was not required. Moreover, the ball moving in to the batsman could not, without in-artistic strokes – or, more compellingly, without danger of hitting a catch – be played to the off side. So B. H. Lyon recalled Tom Goddard, Gloucestershire's former fast bowler from Lord's where he had become a practitioner of the slow off-break. He posted legside fieldsmen in an arc a bare six yards from the bat – with a deep square leg to levy a catch on the bold man who hit over their heads – and then invited the batsmen to play the sharply-turning off-break without giving a catch. J. C. Clay, of Glamorgan, and the late George Macaulay of Yorkshire, at their different paces, used a similar method and, indeed, most counties carried a bowler capable of employing the method on a suitable wicket.

The real era of the inswing bowler began in 1946. Pollard, Pope, Gladwin, Bedser, Shackleton, Butler, Perks, Pritchard, Smith, Aspinall, Andrews, Gray, Clarke – every county had one, and six of them played for England.

They could not, however, work alone. They needed fieldsmen who could catch the betrayed stroke in positions from which the batsman's body blinded them to the ball until the last possible second. Upon their cue, these fieldsmen sprang up. The great tradition of slip-fielding began to die out in England until, today, good slips can be counted on the fingers of one hand. Meanwhile, such names as Watkins, Ikin, Lock, Geoffrey Edrich, Townsend, Clift, Wooller, Revill, became associated with acrobatic feats of catching a few feet from the bat on the leg side.

The initiative did not remain there, because batsmen began to perfect the technique – which had developed in the twenties and thirties – of the on-side push, steering the ball between the fieldsmen, or going in to drive wide of mid-on. The mastery of handsome strokes on the off became less a recommendation of a batsman than safety against the ball which 'comes on'. Even the leg glance was frowned upon. Did not Sir Donald Bradman himself fall three times in successive Test innings to leg glances played to Bedser's sharp inswing? The stroke was 'not business' and it must go. So, gradually, the inswing bowler had to develop variations: mere inswing could be played profitably and safely for runs, or, with an appearance of stoicism, was allowed to thump against a well-padded thigh.

All this the batsman could do – except on a fast wicket. Faithful still to his old masters, the groundsman produced yet slower pitches. After all, no groundsman has ever been dismissed for making a wicket on which a batting record was broken, but more than one has been in danger for creating a spin-bowler's pleasure-garden which ended a match in a single day. So the defensive field was developed. Like inswing, short-leg fieldsmen and leg-theory, it was not new, but it had never before been a general practice. With quick-moving fieldsmen deployed at a 'saving the one' distance from the batsman's wicket, the bowlers pitched the ball safely short of a length from which it could be driven, yet not short enough to be hooked.

In the case of inswing, the bowler's ally was the short-leg fieldsman. In defensive bowling, he is aided by the crowd with its new and antagonistically derisive slow hand-clap. The batsman may play orthodox strokes with all reasonable power along the ground: the defensively positioned fieldsmen will stop them. He may hit each ball of six hard and correctly, yet he will have played back a maiden over. Crowds notice maiden overs and, convinced of the batsman's supposed superiority over the bowler, they will resent such a passive state of affairs.

To such barracking, the batsman – other than the fortunate man who can shut out so consciously spiteful a sound – has two possible reactions. He can do his best to 'entertain his paying customers', hit out and be caught, or he can steel himself against it and relapse into even grimmer defence. If he waits long enough, the new ball will come again and the bowlers will begin to attack again, leaving gaps in the field for him to score runs. This very situation, at Old Trafford in 1951, cost the South African Eric Rowan his wicket and, subsequently, his chance of consideration for a place in the team to tour Australia.

The fact is that there is no consistent reply to accurate, fractionally short-of-a-length bowling to a skilfully placed field. The bowler is, for the moment, wielding a powerful weapon. Unfortunately, it is not exciting for spectators. They blame the batsman. The batsman blames the bowler. The bowler blames the groundsman, the spectator, the batsman, and history. *The Spectator*

# Cricket and Television

The conflicting arguments still being pursued by men with expert knowledge are proof that the effect of television on cricket is by no means yet fully understood.

To be sure, the television of any substantial proportion of a Test match will seriously affect even the first day – and certainly the second day – of a county match, while it would virtually kill the third day.

Cricket in this respect is probably luckier than football, for the smaller clubs which are its reservoir of players do not, like the soccer clubs in minor leagues, depend on gate money for their continued survival. It may be argued, too – and with good reason – that televsion has brought good cricket into the homes and minds of many who, previously, had neither knowledge of, nor interest in, the game. The vital question here is whether or not any substantial proportion of these will ever show their new found interest in paying admission to see 'flesh-and-blood' cricket. Thus, if when hundreds stay away from county matches to watch television, thousands of cash-paying spectators are being created, then there is a profit in TV for big cricket.

Again, we are told that youngsters will improve their own cricket by watching the great on the television screen. That might be countered by the suggestion that the really enthusiastic youngster will always go and find good cricketers to watch. That, of course, is not easy in some parts of the country and, for youths there, the model of a great cricketer could be highly beneficial to his play.

The question must arise, however, of the extent to which watching television during the usual hour from half-past-five to half-past-six does not, in many cases, stop children from playing themselves. There is no true substitute for the actual handling of bat and ball in the development of a cricketer. If the potential player, who without television would be out playing cricket, is turned into a spectator – however informed – at second hand, then cricket suffers on the deal.

It seems, indeed, that the eventual solution may prove to be the filming of major cricket matches for an edited version of the film to be shown at a time when it will not interfere with gates or with play. There must be no question of pro-TV or anti-TV: it is here and it will stay. It is an immense force and, if it can be harnessed to the service of cricket, cricket must not miss its chance. The principle is clear: the method of its application is the problem.

*Jock Livingston Testimonial Handbook*, 1955

# Stupid, Damaging, Unnecessary

*25 March* 1969. The sour difference between Lord's – the MCC Council – and the Cavaliers' Cricket Club of Rothmans, the most generous sponsors first-class cricket has ever had, was further and more acidly revealed at a press conference yesterday to announce the Cavaliers' fixtures for 1969. The matches and players have been worked out on the assumption that no registered English county or Australian players may take part in any televized match not arranged through the TCCB of the MCC Council.

In spite of the heavy overhead expenses involved by engagement of players from overseas, the Cavaliers propose to give 25 per cent of gross profits of every match to the club housing it, for donations to the local beneficiary. A fixture offered to Worcestershire for Tom Graveney's benefit was turned down by the county. Thereupon the Cavaliers went to the – private – Kidderminster club and offered a match on their ground. This week, however, Graveney was summoned to Lord's and informed that he would not be allowed to accept a donation accruing from any televized Cavaliers' match, whether played in Worcestershire or not.

Such decisions cannot benefit cricket or cricketers. The game has enough anxieties without internal strife between its main authority and the only organization which has succeeded in making money from it in modern times.

All the Cavaliers' matches, including one against the Welsh Cricket Association in Investiture week, were to have been offered to commercial television as a package. That intention has been altered because three fixtures involve Minor Counties cricketers whose absence would reduce local interest but who, like registered players of first-class counties, are forbidden to play in televized matches not arranged through the TCCB. So each fixture will be offered separately to local television contractors for regional or network showing.

The Cavaliers' playing strength will fairly regularly include Ted Dexter, Fred Trueman, Graeme Pollock, Bobby Simpson, and Saeed Ahmed among established Test players, and six young West Indians recommended by their territorial selectors – Colin Blades (wicketkeeper-batsman), Lawrence Maxwell (off-spin bowler), and Hallam Moseley (fast bowler) from Barbados; Lawrence Rowe (batsman), and Castel Folkes (batsman) from Jamaica; and Alvin Corneal (allrounder) from Trinidad. It is hoped that Keith Miller, Godfrey Evans, Trevor Bailey, and Brian Statham will play in occasional matches.

It must be debatable whether the banning of registered county players from taking part in televized Cavaliers' matches would be upheld in the courts if a case were brought for restraint of trade. Meanwhile, the paradoxical situation appears to exist in which Ted Dexter may play for the Cavaliers and England but not for Sussex. The situation is stupid, damaging, and unnecessary.                    *The Guardian*

# What Will the Players Think of Next?

*May* 1968. Those who live in what Brian Sellers once called 'the cricket circus' can recite the new County Championship points scoring system by rote, if not with conviction. But to the rest of the world it seems to be a deep mystery. 'I've read all about it in the papers, but I still don't understand it,' said a steward at Hove to an inquiring spectator.

This was, after all, a winter enactment and many readers must have felt that study could wait until the season began, so it may be worthwhile to outline the new system. Ten points are awarded for a win; five points to each side for a tie; nothing at all for a first-innings lead though, if play does not start until eight hours or less of the scheduled time remains, a one-innings match is played – for ten points. In addition, bonus points are won, *in the first 85 overs of each team's first innings only*, at a rate of one for every 25 runs scored over 150 and one for every two wickets taken.

Some will feel that such innovations destroy the essential simplicity of the issues at stake in a cricket match. The object of these incentives is to encourage enterprising cricket on the first day. The county captains, on the other hand, always examine new legislation in the manner of barristers, seeking to discover how they may exploit it to the advantage of their clients – in their case their clubs, which expect them to finish as high as possible in the table. So, in the first Championship match of the season to make a start, Marshall, the Hampshire captain, whose side had won five bonus points by bowling out Sussex at Hove well within the statutory 85 overs for 140, having nothing to gain by taking first-innings lead and with no real hope of reaching 175, declared at 135 for nine and thus gained an advantage of one point over his opponents.

There was always the probability that, as with the earlier bonus points award – for the faster scoring rate in the first innings – the captains might often find it tactically more effective to adopt the position of denying points to the opposition as distinct from setting out positively to win them for themselves. It must be expected, too, that if the championship grows close in August, there will be much weighing of the advantages of declaring – with, of course, an odd number of wickets down – to deny opponents bowling points which seem more probable than those for an extra 25 runs scored by tail-end batsmen.

It may also prove that the spin bowler, whose scant employment is deplored everywhere except on the harsh economic field of play, may be even less favoured by a captain whose side are losing a point for every 25 runs the opposition score. Some will ponder, moreover, the anomaly which allows a team to be completely outplayed and beaten, perhaps by an innings, but yet score five or more Championship points. One player asked of legislators who introduced this scoring system: 'What will they think of next?' By the end of the season those legislators may be asking the same question about the players.

The problems of next season are already being canvassed. Before a ball had been bowled in 1968, indeed, a number of players had voiced their discontent about the fixture list for 1969. It has proved difficult to fit the Sunday League fixtures into the pattern of the three-day weekend Championship fixtures. So some teams must travel to a match on Friday night, to the Sunday game on Saturday night or Sunday morning, and back again for the Monday of the first game – a pattern of five journeys a week. In some cases, if the finish of a Gillette Cup match were delayed by rain, it could bring a team something like a fortnight of unbroken play.

From time more or less immemorial the first-class fixture list has been compiled, out of experience and ingenuity, by the secretary of the Surrey club. Lately some members of the Sussex committee fed much of the relevant data into a computer, which produced solutions with such speed as to suggest it would welcome and swallow far more qualifications, snags and problems. In our age it can hardly be profitable to match a man – even the secretary of Surrey – against a machine. At least a computer should be given a preliminary run over the arrangements for 1970.

The most confirmed reactionary will find it hard to fault the new stand which has now been completed on the site of the old Lord's Tavern and Clock-tower block. It has a clean, light springing quality and, even in the dismal light of a wet Saturday afternoon, the long, simple, uncluttered bar on the ground floor, with its sharp internal lighting, had the bright air of an Italian piazza. It lacks only a name.

*The Guardian*

# Benefits Can Be Mixed Blessings

Most of us have been told at some time or another that 'We don't have benefits in Derbyshire -- only testimonials.' It is not for foreigners to argue the rights or wrongs of that decision but it might be pointed out that, especially for bowlers, benefits can be mixed blessings.

The classic triumph in this kind is that of Albert Trott, the Victorian who played for Australia with considerable success in their home Tests of 1894–95 but was left out of the side -- captained by his brother Harry -- which toured England in 1896. There upon he decided to set off for

England alone and qualify for Middlesex. At Lord's 'Alberto' became one of the most popular players of his day – and the only man to hit a ball over the top of the Lord's pavilion, a feat which he must have relished the more since he did it against the 1899 Australians.

He was good enough bowler to take 200 wickets in a season twice but, in 1905, he fell seriously ill and, though he played on for several seasons, he was only a fraction of the player he had been. In 1907, however, in his benefit match, against Somerset, he rose to the last high peak of his career. The first day was half ruined by rain and on the third, when a strong Somerset batting side might have made a fight, Trott took four wickets – of Lewis, Poyntz, Woods and Robson – with consecutive balls and only a few minutes later finished off the innings with a hat-trick. It was not a remunerative benefit.

The one man who stood firm in the Somerset innings was Len Braund, who appeared for England in more Tests than any other Somerset player; he went in first and was not out 28 at the end. For some years at the beginning of the century, Len Braund was the best allrounder in England, a superb leg-spinner and one of the best slip fielders the game has known.

Two years later he took his benefit – against Surrey. To honour an old promise to Braund, that great wicket-keeper, Harry Martyn, returned to play in the match; Somerset had, too, Sammy Woods, Lionel Palairet, John Daniell, Randall Johnson, Vernon Hill. For Surrey there was Jack Hobbs, Tom Hayward, Jack Crawford, Alan Marshal, and Herbert Strudwick: a collection of talent rich enough to fill any ground.

But the rain allowed no play until three o'clock on the first day and not a ball was bowled on either of the following two days. It was the practice in Somerset for the beneficiary to pay match expenses and take the profits. And when, after the First World War, Len Braund was offered another benefit he thanked the Committee respectfully but refused with the words: 'You see, I couldn't afford the first one.'

It was in Somerset, too – again at Bath, and on a newly-laid wicket – that Bert Buse, that game allrounder of artful, medium-paced outswing, took the Lancashire match of 1953. He himself was Somerset's most successful bowler, with six for 41, but Roy Tattersall had match figures of thirteen wickets for 69. Somerset were beaten by an innings and 24 by six o'clock on the first day: *Wisden* described it as 'financial disaster for Buse'.

At Bristol in 1922, Charlie Parker, of Gloucestershire, a left-arm bowler of too brisk pace to be called slow, but an immense spinner of the ball, had a remarkable spell in the first innings of his match – against Yorkshire. He bowled Norman Kilner with the last ball of an over. The first of the next hit George Macaulay's wicket but was called a 'no-ball' and went for a bye. With the next three balls he clean bowled Robinson, Waddington and Dolphin: so, including the no-ball, he hit the stumps with each of five consecutive deliveries. His nine for 36 – six bowled and two lbw – gave Gloucestershire a first innings lead of 106 – yet they lost the game by six wickets.

Bill Bowes, with remarkable prescience, chose the Middlesex match of 1947 – the season of Compton and Edrich – for his benefit and, given the privilege of tossing, won and put Middlesex in. He can hardly have expected to see them start their second innings on the same day. Middlesex 124 (Bowers four for 34): Yorkshire 85 (Young four for 28, Denis Compton four for 23): Middlesex 80 for three on Saturday evening. In fact the game was over – and Middlesex won by 87 runs – in two days. But an attendance of over 41,000 (£2817) more than compensated for the last day: and the eventual total – £8083 – set a record for a Yorkshire benefit.

Maurice Read, of Surrey, had the unusual experience of being dropped from his benefit match; but since it was the Oval Test match against Australia and raised the remarkable sum, for that time – 1893 – of more than £1200, he may not have felt unduly aggrieved.

There is luck and luck; but Harold Rhodes may at least contemplate that he is safe from the danger of bowling away his benefit.

*Harold Rhodes' Testimonial Year*, 1968

# The D'Oliveira Decision

29 *August* 1968. MCC have never made a sadder, more dramatic, or potentially more damaging decision than in omitting D'Oliveira from their team to tour South Africa. Fifteen players have been named. Jeff Jones of Glamorgan, if he is demonstrably fit after an operation on an elbow. If he is not, Higgs will probably be offered the place.

There is no case for leaving out D'Oliveira on cricketing grounds. Since the last MCC tour in South Africa, Test pitches have become grassy, ideal for seam bowlers, of whom South Africa deploy five. So England's tactical need is for a Test class batsman who is a reliable bowler at medium-pace, or above, to make the fourth seam bowler: only D'Oliveira, of our current players, meets that demand. He was top of the English batting averages in the series against Australia just completed, and second in the bowling. The latter may seem a statistical quibble, but when he bowled Jarman on Tuesday he made the breakthrough which brought England their close win in the Fifth Test.

He is a useful, if not great, fieldsman at slip or in the deep. Decisively, to the objective observer, he has the temperament to rise to the challenge of an occasion, as he proved against the West Indian fast bowlers, and in both his matches against Australia this summer. His behaviour in what might have been difficult situations has always been impeccably dignified and courteous.

If politics, in their fullest sense, now transcend cricket in importance, it might have been wiser to take D'Oliveira to South Africa though he were not good enough, than to leave him at home when he is not merely good enough but eminently suited for the tactical situation the side will face.

In the first place, no one of open mind will believe that he was left out for valid cricket reasons: there are figures and performances less than a week old – including a century yesterday – to refute such an argument. This may prove, perhaps to the surprise of MCC, far more than a sporting matter. It could have such repercussions on British relations with the coloured races of the world that the cancellation of a cricket tour would seem a trifling matter compared with an apparent British acceptance of apartheid. This was a case where justice had to be seen to be done.

Secondly, within a few years, the British-born children of West Indian, Indian, Pakistani and African immigrants will be worth places in English county and national teams. It seems hard to discourage them now, for, however the MCC's case may be argued, the club's ultimate decision must be a complete deterrent to any young coloured cricketer in this country.

After such an issue it seems anticlimax to discuss the remainder of the team. Cowdrey, Graveney, Edrich, Knott, Brown, Boycott, Underwood and Snow were automatic choices. His resource, stamina and accuracy make Cartwright the ideal bowler for the grassy wickets expected on the tour. Cottam has several values: he is a steady, direct seam bowler, who can also cut the ball effectively on turning wickets: and he catches well anywhere. Pocock was the obvious choice when Illingworth announced that he was not available. Murray, presumably on grounds of his batting ability and past Test performances, is somewhat surprisingly recalled ahead of the younger Taylor, or Tolchard, who had seemed in greater favour.

Prideaux made his case with a superb innings at Headingley, and Barrington must go as our most reliable compiler of runs overseas in the last decade: and in a side so short of spin bowling, his leg-breaks should be valuable.

The omission of Milburn deprives the team of character and attacking potential and, while Fletcher is a promising, attractive and responsible young batsman, he has no Test record to compare with D'Oliveira's.

This is a party mellow in experience, with a pleasing blend of solidity and enterprise in the batting, and its capacity for sustained attack in the bowling. The fielding is likely to be pedestrian, but that was inevitable.

The final thought on it, however, must be one of sadness and that in the selection MCC have stirred forces – for both good and evil – whose powers they do not truly comprehend.                    *The Guardian*

# Up to Players to Restore Cricket's Reputation

*April* 1969. English cricket has not wintered well. It, and its visitors, have never borne a heavier burden of reestablishment than they will do in 1969. The recurrent D'Oliveira affair (inescapably to be remembered by his name, even though he himself behaved in exemplary fashion), the cancelled tour of South Africa, the lamentable substitute series in Pakistan, and the deep and apparently unnecessary split between MCC and the Cavaliers have defaced the image of the game, to an extent that players, who must bear the responsibility, had done nothing to deserve.

The first three of these disturbing events are reflections of a single attitude – the failure of the administrators of cricket to recognize that politics can no longer be shut out of the game. Cricket, even on its most rarified strata, must now accept that it is, like every other aspect of human activity, a part of the human scene, of its nature interwoven with the thought of man, which is essentially – even and, indeed, perhaps most truly in the case of the self-styled 'non-political' – a matter of politics. Once that fact is recognized, the problem for the administrators of cricket becomes simpler; they must study to avoid such naive, politically-unconscious moves as were in the past their prerogative, but have now exposed them to suspicion.

Those near to cricket understand better than the politically aware non-cricketers that there can be two points of view about the involvement of South African cricketers with Apartheid. There have been gleams of hope, through multi-racial cricket matches – which have, in fact, taken place in South Africa – that this game was making gestures towards bridging the racial gap.

Cricket, however, will not be left to go its own way. The politicals, to whom it is no more than another facet of human relations, think in broad terms. But it remains the duty of cricket to satisfy them, and the widest public opinion, if its image is to be restored. There exists a feeling, which the game will ignore only to its own damage, that not all of those who control it are whole-heartedly in opposition to Apartheid.

If the MCC Council – the new and broader based controlling body of cricket – were to make a positive statement that its members were unanimously opposed to the principle of Apartheid, then any attempt it made to maintain cricketing relations with South Africa might be seen in a more charitable light from the outside. Until some such gesture is made, suspicion will persist. If the Council members are not opposed to Apartheid then, equally, let them say so, and, once again, the situation would be clear. It is the present equivocal attitude which has aroused mistrust of the motives of men whose friends must believe that they are nothing more sinister than politically myopic.

The virtual exclusion from television of the Cavaliers, who established and popularized the Sunday afternoon, over-limit match in the public mind and on television, is probably less susceptible even to partial resolution. It is not easy to believe that the tobacco firm – Players' – which has sponsored the Sunday League would readily admit the Cavaliers' team of rival firm – Rothman's. Yet it would be for the health and goodwill of the game, and probably of the Sunday League as well, if they and the Test and County Cricket Board could see their way clear to do so.

Meanwhile, the bad taste of the winter's skirmishing remains to be washed away, if possible, by the season's play. The two touring sides, West Indies and New Zealand, hold out no strong promise of being able to do so. After a decade of outstanding performances, West Indies have lost virtually a generation of great players, and they must excel even their record in producing unknown players able to step up to Test rank if they are to reestablish their dominance; with the qualification that any team with Sobers in it (especially on a short tour) could achieve the impossible.

New Zealand, for all their recent success against a disintegrating West Indies side, can hardly provide any real threat to England at full strength. They remain the most personally pleasant of opponents, playing hard, though not expecting to win at the highest level; they make steady, if slow, advances, and on a tour of England they invariably learn much that is reinvested in their domestic game and its younger players.

If the 1969 season is to succeed, however, it must be at county level. The Championship offers many interests: the Gillette Cup is an attractive and fixed part of the calendar, but, above all, the Sunday League must strike the public imagination. If it does not do so, it will represent the greatest failure – if only because it carried the highest hopes – of all cricket's attempts to revive public interest. The counties have already invested their probable profits from it in increased payments to their cricketers. The challenge now lies with the batsmen, bowlers and fielders to draw in the lost, or fresh, thousands of spectators from the other attractions of a summer Sunday, and, having drawn them, to satisfy them. *The Guardian*

# Facing up to the Modern Margins of Cricket

*March* 1971. The Test and County Cricket Board, when they meet next week, will have scope and responsibilities out of all proportion to those of their predecessors of even a decade ago.

In 1960 the rulers of English cricket – notably the County Advisory Committee – were still dealing with matters of detail, revision of laws, changes in the County Championship scoring system, arrangements of tours, appointment of Test selectors, tour captains, and managers. Occasionally they admitted another country to Test play, but generally they worked within what seemed an immutable pattern.

Those committees had not to handle anything like the introduction of the Gillette Cup; televised Sunday cricket; dual-Test tours of England; six-match Test series; one-day Test matches; the instant qualification of overseas Test players for English counties; commercial sponsorship; the political implications of Test matches with a country of conflicting philosophy.

Although many of these problems existed previously, they were not considered within the councils of cricket until 1962. They demand an entirely different kind of brain from that which decides when an umpire should retire, or whether the new ball should be available on the basis of overs bowled or runs scored. A decision to change the allocation of Championship points may be wildly, but harmlessly, wrong; it can be changed for the following season. Most of the changes being made in cricket now are irreversible.

If it is decided next week to alter the form of the County Championship, it is highly unlikely that it will ever revert to its present shape. More importantly, shifts in economic balance among the clubs and the players will introduce influences the game has never known before. Such matters might be better considered by barristers, politicians, sociologists, economists – so long as they have interest in cricket – or professional players, than by some more knowledgeable on the technical aspects of play.

This emphasizes the somewhat cynical fashion in which the 'switch' was made from control by MCC, plus the 'Advisory', to the Cricket Council. What was asked was a broadening of the base of government of cricket, with financial grants from central Government as the inducement. What has happened is that former peripheral figures have been added to the names on the committees. Absolute control remains where it always was – in the hands of MCC committee members, except that there are now more of them.

If the Council had in fact been broadened, to include varying viewpoints and knowledges – along the lines of the Sports Council – much goodwill and sound guidance would have been gained. For the present decision-makers error means damage to their hobby; for others, who have no control over the situation, their living can be impaired.

Cricket, like much of industry – and cricket is part of the entertainment industry – ought now to extend its government. It ought follow a system of including, in effective numbers, those for whom the game is their livelihood – players, umpires, coaches, groundsmen – instead of the present method, which is in effect that of governing with an upper chamber alone: the power of the Lords may have been reduced, but not that of Lord's.

The main question immediately at issue is whether to retain the County Championship in its present form or to reduce it by four matches – twelve days – to be replaced by a Saturday regional league, eventually decided between the top clubs on a knock-out basis. That is a compromise between a 28-match Championship (in itself a compromise between 32 and 16) and virtually jettisoning the championship by reducing it to sixteen mid-week fixtures.

It would be unwise to overlook the regional feeling involved. There is a strong wish in the northern counties to retain a full County Championship as a first priority in English cricket. This is not a fresh point of view: the Hon. F. S. Jackson withdrew from a Test match against Australia to play in a county fixture for Yorkshire; A. E. Stoddart did as much and played against him – for Middlesex. History, too, points to the Football League – which sprang from the Midlands and North – and the Rugby League as indications that the North is not content for the shape of its sport to be dictated.

Thought should now be given for the future of the county clubs in the light of what is going to happen to the counties themselves if, as is likely, the White Paper on local government reform is accepted. Neither area 18 – Warwickshire without Birmingham, Coventry, West Bromwich – nor area 15 – Birmingham without the present Warwickshire County Council district, but with Wolverhampton, Walsall, Dudley, and Stourbridge – can compel the same support as Warwickshire at present.

Meanwhile Gloucestershire without Bristol and its outliers (area 27), and Somerset without Bath and Weston-super-Mare (area 25) would simply not be viable. Hampshire without Bournemouth would be hard hit. So would Derbyshire without Chesterfield.

This may be the cue for the amalgamation of some counties. Although current feeling might reject the idea, the bond that binds men in Stratford-on-Avon to those in West Bromwich is not likely to endure after a generation in which they share nothing, and the boundary drawn between them applies to all aspects of their life. A West Midland Club or a Western Club or a Southern Club, in which a London county and a neighbouring provincial one were merged, could ease present acute financial difficulties. Six such partnerships would make a twenty-match championship ideal.

The appointment of selectors has not been difficult in recent years; the problem generally has been to find people with time, knowledge, and standing to undertake the duties. Now there are seven candidates for four places: last year's committee – Alec Bedser (Surrey), who was chairman, Don Kenyon (Worcestershire), Alan Smith (Warwickshire), and Billy Sutcliffe (Yorkshire) – plus G. O. Allen, Stuart Surridge, and Cyril Washbrook.

The nomination of G. O. Allen will surprise some. A former England captain and allrounder, he was chairman of selectors from 1955 to 1961 and is now sixty-nine years old. He is free to devote the necessary time to the duties, as most of his juniors are not. Presumably, if he is elected, he will become chairman of the committee – a thought which caused one observer to remark that Alec Bedser would lose office for the offence of picking a team that won a series in Australia, as only five England sides out of sixteen have done in this century.

Bedser has taken his duties seriously. He has felt himself involved with his team and applied high standards of behaviour and technique. His own county, while renewing his nomination, has also proposed his former county captain, Stuart Surridge. Although Bedser and May, of Surrey, and once previously Sir Stanley Jackson and Brian Sellers, of Yorkshire, served together on the committee, the counties do not like such a weighting. Given a choice of candidates, they are unlikely to choose two from the same county.

It used to be said that English cricket was run by the treasurer of MCC – and Mr Allen holds that post. It will be interesting to see if the old order has indeed changed.

While the meeting of the TCCB is in progress, Ray Illingworth's England side will return from Australia with the Ashes, recovered after twelve years. Len Hutton's team of 1953 performed the same feat, at home, after an interval of nineteen years. In the following summer the full MCC tour committee confirmed Hutton in the captaincy for Australia by a majority of only one vote.                    *The Guardian*

# The Contortions of Modern Cricket

*May* 1971. The most remarkable fact about English first-class cricket in 1971 is that it will be the same, in shape and organization, as it was last year. A decade ago no one could have passed such a comment: the game in the country of its birth and development was stable, hallowed by age and custom. Since then it has changed to the point of somersaulting so that, though this summer would have seemed odd to the cricketer of 1960, those of the younger generation may see it as the end of an era.

To the players and administrators of 1961, one-day, over-limit cricket was 'bun fight stuff', suitable only for the uninformed crowds who, on Sunday afternoons, drove their families out to village greens to watch games played for benefit funds. Bowlers served up half-volleys; batsmen slogged; the finish was cynically 'fiddled' to appear close. It was a huge piece of fun; everyone laughed, contributed to the fund, and went home entertained. But the professional hard core of the game regarded it as a tea-party, not seriously related to the real business that culminated in Test matches.

In 1972 there will be more competitive one-day than three-day fixtures. The counties will play twenty Championship matches each; sixteen in the John Player Sunday League: the least successful in the regional league-cup, three: and even those eliminated at the first attempt, one in the Gillette Cup. There will even be one-day 'Test matches' between England and Australia.

For many years cricket was the immutable sport; time-hallowed fixtures held fixed spots in the almanack; at one time the counties regarded Test matches as interference with the Championship: great amateurs turned out for their counties in preference to playing against Australia in a Test. The domestic calendar was sacrosanct. Since the war, however, the game has bent over painfully – almost suicidally – backwards in the attempt to lure back the retreating and diminishing crowds.

Bonus points: the limited-over first innings; restriction of the leg-side field; abolition of the follow-on; revision of the lbw law to stamp out deliberate pad play – all these expedients were tried, with the pathetic anxiety to please of an out-of-work acrobat. Did no one understand that regular cricket-watching is an addiction? That anyone who wants to watch it will watch it? While those who do not are unlikely to be attracted by minor adjustments?

The introduction of one-day, over-limit matches, especially in the Sunday games established by the Cavaliers on television, hauled in some of the former Sunday afternoon village green watchers, made an apparently well-received programme on BBC2, and drew large crowds to watch the winning counties. Instant registration of overseas players brought most of the world's finest players into the County Championships. Still, however, turnstile receipts and membership are below the levels of the days before the innovations. Last year Northants received a bare £10,000 from gates and subscriptions: their match expenses were £33,000.

Test match grounds may be full; television and wireless – especially car radio – audiences are high among those who discuss the game with authority and heat in bars, but do not go to matches and contribute nothing to the game in cash. Cricket now subsists largely on supporters' club football pools, television and radio fees and – now the last hope of solvency – commercial sponsorship. If the four projected competitions of 1972 are backed by firms who feel that the resultant publicity and goodwill are worth somewhere in the region of £200,000 the game should continue to exist: the asking figure would increase, though, with inflation.

If there is no great optimism among county treasurers for the season of 1971, it should show a far better on-paper situation than 1970. Then there was no full tour; television did not cover the first Test, nor the early days of the second. This year government compensation is due for the cancelled South African visit and, as there are tours by both Pakistan and India, there will be six Tests. Balance sheets are likely to show a deceptive improvement.

Neither of the visiting sides promises great excitement nor important challenge. Only the elderly remember the days before India enshrined the batsman, when they brought a genuine fast bowler to England: and, unless the Test wickets are unusually slow, both the Indian and Pakistani batsmen are likely to prove vulnerable to the high pace of Snow and, as everyone hopes, the returning young man, Ward. They may also be disturbed by the men of lesser speed who exploit the seam-movement granted by English pitches but virtually unknown in the domestic conditions of the sub-continent.

Among the counties, the Champions will probably come from the first five in last year's table – Kent, a side of attractive method and marked talent but unlikely to improve; Glamorgan, unpredictable and depending much on a dash of imported ability; Lancashire, a high-riding, well-led side, basically competent, with a flash of brilliance and promise of improvement; Yorkshire, not, on the surface, as well equipped as some of their predecessors but always likely to win because of their application; and, finally, Surrey, richer in talent than any other county (though they will be without Intikhab for half the season), but handicapped by deadly slow pitches at The Oval where often it seems only a miracle will produce a finish within the three days.

Lancashire must again be the likeliest winners of the over-limit competitions: last year they took the John Player Sunday League with, remarkably, three of the first twelve men in the batting averages and three of the first four in the bowling for the competition. They won the Gillette final from Sussex, who have shown marked facility for this kind of cricket from its introduction on a serious level. Lancashire have batsmen to make runs quickly and to maintain ability; bowlers to keep a game tight and, transcendentally, a fierce eagerness and unity in the field which makes them stronger than the sum of their individual talents.

English cricket has been unlucky in late years to lose – for completely different reasons – its two most attractive batsmen, Ted Dexter and Colin Milburn. Dexter has said that he will return for Sussex in the Sunday League. The resultant attendance figures, even in Sussex where there has always been a hunger for this kind of play, could prove revealing.

It may be true that English cricket is dying: that, although schoolboy cricket is more highly organized than ever – an English schools team has lately toured India – a smaller proportion of pupils play the game. It is true that fewer people come to matches, though a vast number watch Test matches on television. The three-day match, except one likely to settle the Championship, is not an appreciable public attraction, even though more people have more leisure than in the more prosperous days of the county game. There probably is no assurance of the continuation of the county game without large-scale subsidy, presumably by commercial firms. Only one possible alternative course has not been followed in the years of decline. Despite harangues and pleadings there is still a dearth of the true fast wickets which are the one absolute prerequisite of good cricket. It may be that the groundsmen have the solution; what, we may wonder, is their price?

*Illustrated London News*

# Merits of the Over-Limit Game Are Clear

The debate about one-day, over-limit cricket has continued fiercely for almost ten years and shows no sign of ending. There is, however, no argument on one point – it is here to stay. When, at the end of August 1970, about 32,000 people – 27,549 of them legally – crowded into Old Trafford to watch Lancashire play Yorkshire in the decisive match of the John Player Sunday League, it was obvious even to the extreme die-hards, that this type of cricket represented the main – perhaps the only – hope of English county cricket remaining solvent through public support.

For the rest it remains, as a generalisation, the form of the game that spectators like most and the players least. Of course there are some who prefer to watch the greater profundity of the three- or five-day game; similarly there are players more suited to the 'sudden death' tactics and high fielding standards of over-limit play than others: but these are the minorities in either sector.

Yet it must be said that, as the extent of public attraction is an un-answerable argument in favour of over-limit cricket, so it has one unjustifiable deficiency – it must be a negation of the idea of cricket when a fielding side does better to restrict the opposing batsmen to 150 for no wicket than to bowl them all out for 151.

The merits of the over-limit game are obvious, even apart from the fact that, barring bad weather – in Sunday matches, exceptionally bad – the crowd will see both sides bat and a result achieved in a day.

Bowlers who have only eight – or twelve – overs to bowl need not conserve their morning strength for the last spell down to half-past six: they can put in every effort. Fieldsmen who know they have no more than a two or three hour shift of duty can sustain peak pace and keenness as they cannot do over a full, hot, six-hour day.

One-day matches can be decided in minutes, often by innings which would barely create a ripple on the surface of a Test match. A brief sustained peak of activity will decide an issue. Lancashire twice won the John Player League by team work, splendid fielding and some brave individual performances. Those same aptitudes brought them the Gillette Cup and almost the County Championship of the same period, which is convincing proof, if it were needed, that good cricket is valid in both forms of the game.

The arguments for retaining a substantial proportion of the estab-lished forms of the game are less uperficially striking, but they are im-portant; and they go to the roots of first-class cricket.

Batting is a technique. Such precise – almost hair-raising – calcula-tion of risk as Ron Headley's in effectively winning the John Player League of 1971 is only possible for one who has learnt his craft in a game where batsmen build their innings, study bowlers, assess safety margins, develop techniques of placing and pacing strokes, anticipating a bowler's tactics and countering field-placings. Only a man with that background of experience can calculatedly force the pace in limited-over play.

Similarly, only the bowler who has developed his skills in a form of the game where he must be able to switch from attack to defence and back again with the changing shape of the match has the skill and the authority to contain both a forcing batsman and – which is a completely different matter – a slogger. The cricketer who grows up in the instant demands of one-day matches simply does not acquire this depth of understanding. This is to say, in short – but crucially for the whole future of the game – that the skills which make one-day cricket so exciting are only to be learnt in the longer forms of play.

It is obviously necessary for the technical and financial health of English cricket that these two forms should exist side by side. It is not so certain that all county cricketers are equally capable in both types of play. The counties may have to form cadres from which outside the top level of performers some players are one-day, and some three-day specialists. Thus the argument will be perpetuated.

*Cricket Spotlight,* 1972

# Growth of the Cricketers' Association

*March* 1979. The Cricketers' Association will be twelve years old in November. It is, simply enough, the body formed by English county cricketers to protect their interests. Until 1967 cricketers were virtually the only group of workers in Britain who had no voice in their own affairs or conditions of employment. Since then the Cricketers' Association has grown from an officially suspected and penniless minority to a respected body with a 100 per cent membership of every registered player in the country, solvent and increasingly effective in the counsels of the game. The Association functions through an annual general meeting of all members, held in April, which reaches the main policy decisions – except those so unforeseen and urgent that they demand a postal referendum – and, in day-to-day matters, through an executive composed of the officers and one elected representative from each county, which meets monthly from September to April.

It organizes insurance for all its members; obtains legal advice for them; represents them, if wanted, at disciplinary or qualification enquiries; co-ordinates benefit funds, and negotiates on behalf of individuals or entire county staffs. On major issues it has campaigned successfully for cricketers' freedom to speak publicly in their own defence against allegations made about them; for a more sympathetic approach to re-registration; and for a minimum wage.

The Cricketers' Association was conceived by Fred Rumsey, the Worcestershire, Somerset and England fast bowler, who canvassed the idea through the county dressing-rooms during the 1967 season. He found enough support to call a meeting in the following October. It was sponsored by the *Daily Express* and held in their Fleet Street offices.

Only forty people turned up; Jim Parks agreed to take the chair for that meeting only. Cliff Lloyd and Jimmy Hill, secretary and chairman of the Professional Footballers' Association, spoke, and it was agreed to form the Association, with membership confined solely to active, first-class county cricketers. Some who attended the meeting apparently did so to express pointed opposition to the idea of forming a trade union; and the Association has never been affiliated to the TUC. Roger Prideaux was elected chairman, Jack Bannister treasurer, and Fred Rumsey secretary.

A number of county administrators and executives were openly opposed to the entire concept; and their attitude was reflected by a number of players. At the first Annual General Meeting, in April 1968, the attendance was 52; the entire membership was reported as 135. Roger Prideaux resigned the chairmanship; Jack Bannister was elected in his place and Mike Edwards became treasurer. Billy Griffith, secretary of MCC, addressed the meeting, virtually the first demonstration of approval from the Establishment. Probably the most influentially enlightened early attitude towards the Association from the official side was shown by Cecil Paris, chairman of the TCCB, who recognized it and its potential even before many players did so.

Recruiting was slow. The subscription, tied to a players' insurance scheme, was barely sufficient to cover the premium; and the Association's only income was £750 a year from Lord's.

Frank Russell generously lent the homeless Association a room in his Cricketers' Club in London for its meetings. Edward Lincoln, a public relations' consultant, gave crucial help in the negotiations with John Player which eventually set the Cricketers' Association on a sound financial footing. The Warwickshire team have always been strong supporters and their county club housed early meetings free of charge at Edgbaston and still provide admirable accommodation.

Reg Hayter, managing director of Hayter's Agency and now editor of *The Cricketer*, was a good friend from early days. He released the conscientious and kindly Bob Moore from his office duties to act as secretary to the Association in its difficult early phase. He also gave the annual Hayter Award for the Cricketers' Association member elected Cricketer of the Year. The first winner, in 1969, was Mike Procter.

Harold Goldblatt was invaluable as financial adviser, and, through the growth pangs, such executive members as Arthur Milton, Ian Buxton, Ron Headley, Barry Reed, Roy Virgin, Peter Lever, John Murray, Mike Smedley and Norman Graham were loyally diligent.

Some business errors proved financially damaging; and efforts to raise funds had little success. A one-day match between a strong CA team and the 1969 New Zealanders barely covered expenses.

It was something of a landmark, and also a disappointment, when, in January 1970, the CA held a widely publicized referendum on the projected South African tour of that summer. Only about half the country's cricketers bothered to vote – by 123 to 27 – in favour of the tour. Membership, 220 in 1969, reached 250 in 1970, and, by 1971, some 99 per cent of those qualified to join (a few independents opted out – and some in-and-out) but since 1976 it has been 100 per cent, a steady 303 to 309 according to the size of county staffs.

The 1970 AGM elected Mike Edwards chairman, John Murray treasurer, and Bannister secretary. In the following year, the negotiation of a substantial donation from John Player made it possible for Bannister to be engaged as an (under- rather than over-) paid secretary. A sound middle-of-the-road thinker, a founder officer of the Association, and a player of long and varied experience, he was the ideal man for the job. It was, though, impossible for him to carry the weight of the day-to-day affairs and correspondence unpaid. His appointment meant that Bob Moore could be released from his generous and efficient service.

In 1971 the CA mediated successfully in the first of several disputes between the players and committee of Somerset. In the following year the subscription – which still included full injury and sickness insurance for the season – was fixed at £10 for capped, and £5 for uncapped, players. Since the premiums accounted for virtually all that revenue, the need to raise funds was urgent.

Accordingly, and optimistically, a one-day match was arranged against the Australian touring team for 24 June 1972 at Trent Bridge in aid of the Association's funds. The CA team – John Edrich, Barry Richards, Brian Close, Clive Lloyd, Basil D'Oliveira, Tony Greig, Farokh Engineer, David Hughes, Tom Cartwright, Fred Titmus and John Price – was, surely, as strong an over-limit combination as has ever been mustered – and they won most handsomely. Yet, despite the quality and attractiveness of the two sides, fine weather and local support, when the Australians' guarantee had been met and petrol and accommodation provided for the Association players – not one of them asked for more – the event showed no mentionable profit. As a result, the fixtures arranged with West Indies and New Zealand for 1973 were regretfully cancelled.

A CA referendum was held on applications by Bob Willis and Bob Cottam for registration with Warwickshire and Northamptonshire which were opposed by their counties. They were supported by the Association; though a subsequent poll of members showed a strong – 82-19 – majority in favour of some control of movement being retained.

In 1973, the six-year-old Association, for the first time, flexed its muscles. Its demand for a share of the radio and television fees (which included unpaid interviews with players) was backed by a threat of action to the point of disrupting Sunday matches. Peter Walker had become chairman when Edwards resigned after a majority decision to accept a donation from the Transvaal, consequent upon a Derrick Robins tour of South Africa. He, Mike Brearley – a stalwart at this crucial juncture – and Bannister negotiated successfully for a share of TCCB revenue. The Establishment, wisely and in dignified fashion, acceded.

When Walker retired from county cricket and, therefore, from the chairmanship, David Brown succeeded him. Mike Smedley – last survivor of the original members of the executive – now is treasurer. Recently Bob Stephenson, Malcolm Nash and Barry Dudleston have rendered sound service; and Geoff Cope has striven diligently to maintain the Yorkshire connection. Obviously elected representatives tend to be senior players, who are therefore soon lost. So it is pleasing to note the election to the executive of David Graveney, Cedric Boyns and Giles Cheatle.

The CA was now recognized. If hostility still lurked in some backwaters of the Establishment, it was no longer overt. Representation on the Registration Tribunal, the discipline committee and the right to sit in on Chairmen's Advisory meetings, strengthened its position as an effective voice in the government of English cricket. Following representations by the CA, TCCB discipline regulations were altered to allow any cricketer the right to reply to any allegation made against him by his employers. For that reason the Yorkshire committee had, in fact, no redress against Geoffrey Boycott for his protest at their 'disloyalty' on the Parkinson programme. That was his right of reply negotiated by the CA. It was able, too, to bring measurable influence to bear upon the ICC-Packer dispute. Motions before the extraordinary general meeting of September 1977 (when there was an attendance of 278) were left upon the table.

They are to be debated and voted upon at this year's AGM in April. They call for such action against Packer-contracted players as could wreck the World Cup due to be played in England this year. Officers of the Association were invited to talks with Packer and ICC representatives and, in consequence, wrote urgently to both sides pressing for rapid negotiations to reconcile the official ruling that Packer-signed men might take part in the World Cup with the known attitude of the majority of CA members. Unless some agreement is reached between those two sides, the issue of the 1979 World Cup is likely to be decided by the AGM of the Cricketers' Association. Thus historic could be the role of a trade association only twelve years freed from feudalism.

*The Cricketer*

# The 'Packer Business'

*June* 1979. All at once the air over our cricket grounds is sweet; free from the smell of war. The wrong in war lies not on either side, but in war itself. Cricket, too, is ill-equipped to endure hostilities. Already we have seen a potentially highly capable team – the 1977 Australians – dragged below their potential and beaten simply by their anxiety about the impending strife.

Now, if the establishment–Kerry Packer civil war is not over, at least there is a truce. It has been an unhealthy two years between the day in 1977 when Kerry Packer was told he could not have exclusive television rights of Test matches in Australia, and the day last month when he was told he could. The effect of the matter has not merely been to keep every cricket correspondent constantly looking away from action on the field and over his shoulder for the stirring of events on the second front; but, wherever one went, on any ground or in any pavilion, among players and spectators, the 'Packer business' dominated conversation in the most depressing fashion.

By the methods of big business; foreign to the world of cricket – but upheld in a British court as not only legal, but beneficial to the game – Mr Packer won his battle. He used primarily the tactic of divide and destroy; forcing the West Indian and Pakistani administrators to his side by weight of public opinion, winning a nod of approval from New Zealand, and making progress with India. Thus he virtually isolated Australia and, meanwhile, signed such an unnecessarily large number of their best players as to leave them so bankrupt of strength that they were beaten by West Indies, lost Test matches to India for the first time in Australia and then, cruellest blow of all, took that five-one hammering from the 'Poms'. The Australian Cricket Board not only lost the support of the other members of ICC on their flanks, but in the back areas where its public savagely resented such humiliations. They registered their disapproval in gestures of support for Packer but, primarily, by staying away from official Tests.

The truce will be devoted to peace negotiations in which Packer–WSC are in a strong bargaining position. They have the opportunity to swap television of their never-quite-convincing 'Supertests' for the real thing; which, in the long term, must be their best financial solution. On the other hand, if their other conditions are not met, they still have the players under contract; could continue the 'Supertests' and the evening floodlit games which proved so attractive to the public, to the continuing damage of official teams, finances, and revenue.

The outcome probably will be some kind of guarantee that Mr

Packer's Channel 9 will not again suffer such injustice over its bids for television rights as in the past. No doubt the floodlit matches will continue, at least until the end of the players' contracts; and subsequently, perhaps, with the co-operation of the Board. Kerry Packer will insist that his players are not victimized; and, so far as Alan Knott, Derek Underwood, Bob Woolmer and Dennis Amiss are concerned, there now seems no danger of that. What, though, of Tony Greig, who swept out of English cricket in indignation? Still hurt by public reaction to his decision, his pride will hardly allow him to return, and he has always believed that WSC and his other contacts would maintain him in Australia.

The Pakistanis and West Indians, of course, are already back in favour and will take part in the World Cup. Despite the clause in the competition rules which allows them to take part, none of the estranged Australians have been chosen and it is difficult to believe that their Board will now change its named party. Yet that must mean that, with their potential first team, and better part of a second, on Packer's books, they face another resounding defeat.

Not all the problems can be handled by the committee. If lasting peace is achieved, the character of the cricket world is such that the question of loyalty to the loyal will assume considerable importance. In England, for instance, the matter may well sort itself out; but it would be a mistake if the selectors appeared to forget the spirit of Bob Taylor. The Australian mood is not easy to forecast. For instance, was Wood omitted from the World Cup cadre because of his woeful tendency to run himself out or because he was understood to be about to sign for WSC? Where stand not merely Yallop and Hogg, but the faithful Higgs, Hurst, Hughes; such promising players, swamped in a losing side, as Toohey, Border and Darling? Essentially, of course, the Australians are pragmatists before disciplinarians; eventually they will pick their strongest side. Yet a lingering doubt remains that they may still employ a yardstick of degree of disloyalty.

Peace may be proclaimed; but still resentments, the feeling of having been let down, will persist in many dressing-rooms. There can be no questioning the fact that, traumatic as it has been, the 'Packer affair' has improved the financial lot of professional cricketers. Equally certainly the atmosphere of cricket is clearer without it. If the truce is not extended to a complete – even if compromise – peace, someone has failed the game of cricket.                    *Wisden Cricket Monthly*

# Cricket's Momentous Changes

*December* 1979. In 1970 cricket was controlled almost feudally – as it had been throughout the modern period – by an unpaid establishment. Subscriptions and gate money, its traditional forms of income, were inadequate to sustain it and, certainly in England, it was in acute financial difficulties. Indeed, the balance sheet at the end of 1969 showed all the first-class counties, except Lancashire with a winning side, as making losses, nine of them of over £10,000; and the possibility of several of them becoming insolvent and forced to leave the championship was seriously canvassed.

One-day play was being doubtfully and, at some levels, hostilely, examined. A number of influential figures had misgivings about its effect on first-class standards. It was sadly apparent, too, that the reservoir of talent was drying up. There was no longer any measurable flow from the universities; while, as soon as football abolished the maximum wage, it swept away cricket's former margin of attraction as a career, and swallowed up a majority of the young with measurable games-playing ability.

The experiment of admitting overseas cricketers to domestic competition was at an experimental stage. The Cricketers' Association, founded by Fred Rumsey in 1967 to protect the players' interests, was regarded with such disfavour in some high places that many were reluctant to join it.

By the end of 1979 and the 'Packer Revolution' all that was changed. Radio and television fees had been forced extremely high and the authorities had eagerly embraced commercial sponsorship, most obviously in one-day play, with the two Prudential World Cup competitions, of 1975 and 1979 in England (both won by West Indies) outstandingly successful.

The support by Schweppes for the County Championship and by the Wrigley Foundation for coaching young players, although less publicized, were probably of deeper significance.

Recognition that over-limit matches, with their instant-result appeal, were attracting an altogether fresh and profitable English cricket-going public, led to the introduction of the Benson and Hedges Cup in 1972.

In Australia, the presentation, packaging, exploitation, and various other aspects of salesmanship, of first-class matches recently passed most firmly into the hands of Kerry Packer, the television and press tycoon. His organization, with the Prudential World Cup and its own promotion of floodlit matches in 1978–79 in mind, is now apparently seeking to elevate the one-day game above the first-class to the high peak of television entertainment.

Meanwhile, in England, the gulf between the Cricketers' Association and authority was bridged, largely by Cecil Paris, the first chairman of the TCCB. By the end of the decade, the association had a voice in many affairs of concern to its members; and the principle of a minimum wage had been accepted. Moreover, outstanding as many of their performances had been, moves were afoot to phase overseas players out of the county game.

Less definably, but sadly, there has been a change of mood and attitude on the field, especially at Test level. It is reflected most sharply in the increasingly intensive employment of intimidatory bowling, which has caused a majority of the batsmen exposed to it to wear protective helmets – for many the most disturbing development of all. Others are equally distressed by the mounting practice of 'sledging' – offensively aggressive language and behaviour towards opponents – such as lately caused the Australian Board to suspend Ian Chappell.

The era opened with the cancellation of the South African tour to England. Two years before, South Africa had refused to accept an MCC team which included Basil D'Oliveira, formerly classified there as a Cape Coloured, but by then a British citizen. The threat of anti-apartheid demonstrations persuaded the Government, despite some sabre rattling by the establishment, to demand that the tour be called off. The Cricket Council reluctantly concurred but announced that they would not undertake further Test cricket with South Africa 'until a measure of multi-racial cricket was introduced'.

It is hard to escape the conclusion that, in the eyes of future historians, these events will overshadow even the most stirring performances on the field.

Appreciable changes took place in technique, too. Fewer spin bowlers were used and the survivors were forced by the demands of the over-limit game to 'push it through', flat, rather than practising the craft of flight. On the other hand, as a consequence of one-day cricket, the standard of fielding has never been higher.

Both Australia and West Indies produced outstanding fast bowlers. In 1974–75 Jeff Thomson and Dennis Lillee, coolly directed by Ian Chappell, so routed Mike Denness's England as to end the Test careers of all its specialist batsmen except John Edrich. Michael Holding, Andy Roberts and Wayne Daniel of the 1976 West Indians were the three fastest bowlers ever to play in the same team.

West Indies had Viv Richards, one of the most exciting of all stroke-makers, and Gordon Greenidge and Clive Lloyd, both magnificent punishers of even the best bowling; while the Chappell brothers, Greg and Ian, were the best of the Australian batsmen.

For England, Boycott's batting and Underwood's left-arm bowling, although interrupted, spanned the decade; and David Steele became a folk hero for his resistance to the great, fast bowling combinations. They had, too, outstanding captains in Ray Illingworth and Mike Brearley.

Two of the leading performers of the period in English county cricket were Barry Richards, the batsman, and Mike Procter, the allrounder – fast bowler and attacking batsman – both South Africans, barred from Test play. Geoffrey Boycott – in the Headingley Test that gave England the rubber of 1977 against Australia – and John Edrich, reached a hundred hundreds.

In 1977 two Australian journalists 'broke' the remarkably well-kept secret that a substantial number of Australians, some West Indians and a few Englishmen, including the captains of all three countries, had signed contracts with the Packer Channel-9 organization.

Packer, not unreasonably, resented the action of the Australian Board in denying him television rights to Test matches in Australia. Now he proposed to stage what he called 'World Series' matches there between the leading players of the world (a number of Pakistanis subsequently joined him). When the English TCCB sought to ban their defectors, they were challenged in the High Court where Mr Justice Slade found for Packer on all counts.

A state of fierce hostility persisted for two years until 1979, when the Australian Board – almost ruined by sustaining their 'official' Tests – surrendered to WSC in the hope that their former enemy might save them financially. England, as well as the scheduled West Indies, sent teams there this winter to assist in the rescue operation.

Of 24 Test rubbers in the Seventies, England won 12, lost 6 and drew 6; against Australia, they won three (two under Brearley), lost two (plus the Centenary Test) and drew one. For the first time they lost a Test to New Zealand and a home rubber to India.

In the English domestic game Kent, the first county to appoint a manager (Leslie Ames), and Leicestershire, the second (Michael Turner), were most successful. Kent, with their immense resources of discovered talent, had nine outright wins and one shared in the four competitions; Leicestershire, astutely directed by Ray Illingworth, also won five. Jack Bond, brought from the second team to the Lancashire captaincy at the age of thirty-six, drilled and led them to four of their five one-day titles.

The cricket of the coming decade is almost certainly being shaped in the current, crowded, completely novel, and utterly unpredictable, Australian season, with its plethora of one-day games – many under floodlights – and Australia's three-match rubbers against West Indies and England.                                                *The Guardian*

# Declining Over-Rates

A major problem now facing the cricket authorities of the world is that of the increasingly low over-rate, especially at Test level. It is not the less important for being less spectacular than, for instance, the bowling of bouncers, or perilous field-placings made possible by the wearing of helmets.

The simple fact is that, unless decisive steps are taken soon, the entire shape and character of the game could be radically altered. Indeed that change is already far advanced. Fortunately it has not yet reached the fundamental level of club and school cricket; but it is an insidious growth. It is, too, dangerously complex; for it has economic, ethical, tactical and strategic aspects, all of which are significant in their different ways.

Simply expressed, the over-rates of the two teams in last season's England–West Indies series were England 14.5 per hour, West Indies 13.5. Of the two rates the English probably is in some ways the more reprehensible for, of their 559 overs, 138 were bowled by slow or slowish bowlers; while, of the West Indian 886, all but 43 were delivered by the faster men.

The fact is that the lowering of the over-rate may have one of two purposes. In the case of the 1980 West Indies, as with Len Hutton's English team in Australia 1954–55, it was done to keep shock bowlers fresh and able to operate over a considerable period of time, as distinct from a large number of overs. Alternatively it may be employed to deny the other side enough bowling to build an effective score in the time available to achieve a finish. The first example, obviously, often provokes the second in the opponent's play.

Significantly the first Test of the series – the only one to yield a positive result – lasted four-and-a-half-days with an hour and a quarter lost to rain. In that time the two sides bowled 362 overs and five balls. In the epic England–Australia match at The Oval – three-day match – in 1902, England won by one wicket an hour before the close, after 311 overs.

Other examples of high, attainable over-rates come from the 1926 England–Australia series of four three-day matches, plus the last 'played to a finish'. At Trent Bridge and Old Trafford prolonged rain stoppages distorted the shape of play but at Lord's 410 overs were bowled (and 1052 runs were scored); at Headingley 379 (1042 runs) and, at The Oval, on one and a half hours less, an often difficult wicket, for 1143 runs. The 1930 England–Australia rubber consisted of five four-day matches (first day six hours, subsequently six and a half). At

Trent Bridge in five hours less than the allotted 25½, 397 overs were bowled; at Lord's, in 24 hours, 505 (1691 runs). Then, most remarkably, at Headingley, where a little less than three full days was possible, 394; for 1052 runs. This was the occasion of Bradman's 334. The English bowlers were Larwood – fast – Tate, Geary and Hammond – fast medium – and Tyldesley and Leyland (only 11 overs) slow. Between them they bowled 168 overs in the 7 hours 22 minutes (22.8 an hour) during the Australian innings of 566. At Old Trafford, 14 hours 15 minutes, the figure was 275; and in the final match, played to a finish at The Oval, when, though spread over six days, only four days' play was possible, 526 (1351 runs).

There were impressive returns, too, in England v South Africa, 1947 (four days, totalling 25½ hours). At Trent Bridge, 587 overs were bowled; at Lord's, 498; Old Trafford, 439; Headingley (three days only), 346; The Oval, 539. In almost comical contrast with that of 1980 is the rate during the England–West Indies series, the first West Indies ever won in this country, of 1950 when the allocation was of four five-day (six hour) Tests, though none ran anything near the distance. Of course it was the series of Valentine and Ramadhin who probably bowled their overs more quickly than any other pair in the history of Test cricket; and Berry, Hollies, Hilton, Jenkins, Laker, Wardle, Wright, Brown and Compton bowled for England. Still the figures are amazing.

At Old Trafford where there was 18½ hours play, 445 overs were bowled; at Lord's – West Indies first Test win in England and Ramadhin and Valentine's remarkable triumph – an amazing 687 were sent down in 25¼ hours; at Trent Bridge 556 overs in 25½ hours; and finally, at The Oval, 443 in 23 hours. Of course these are the contrasting poles of over-rate; almost 27 an hour at Lord's in 1950 compares with 14 in 1980.

This is inescapably a debasing of Test match cricket by almost half its possible number of overs. It means that the spectator, now paying a vastly higher admission charge than thirty years ago, receives less for it. While inflation is inescapable, a halving of the number of balls bowled should not be. That is the economic aspect. To give a full-dress performance with a probability of a positive result, this would argue that a nine- or ten-day match is necessary. Ethically, the spectator is being deprived of an honest moneysworth.

The tactical employment of a deliberately lowered over-rate has become inescapably prevalent in English county cricket ever since the post-war acceptance of the practice of the third-day declaration and the run race began to produce positive results from games which previously would have been left drawn. Where the batting side was apparently winning, the bowling side would slow its over-rate, if only by employing faster bowlers who, in the normal course, bowled their overs more slowly than the spinners. On the other hand, when the fielding side was winning, they tended to hurry across between overs, while the bowlers themselves reduced their time to a minimum.

At Test level this tactic – as distinct from strategy – was employed by Len Hutton in Australia in 1954–55 when he would often walk back to talk to the bowler at the beginning of his run-up for a few words of consultation or advice which spaced out deliveries and kept Tyson and Statham fresh enough to go on through most of a session.

The West Indian series in England last season, however, was the first in which the lowered rate was employed as part of a planned strategy. The West Indian method depended upon four fast bowlers being kept so fresh that each could bowl at full pace for an hour of a two-hour session of play. In one of the few cases where West Indies bowled through a full six-hour day without interruption (in fact 362 minutes) – in the Third Test at Old Trafford – they delivered 74 overs – a rate of 12.2 to the hour, or one ball every 45 seconds.

The first question to be asked is how many overs should spectators expect in a day of Test cricket? The 72 of Old Trafford 1980, or the 162 – more than twice as many – of Lord's 1950; or even the 132 general until only a decade ago?

Secondly, and most crucially, the International Cricket Conference must consider how many overs should be adequate to complete a Test match. Is it to be the optimum 420 of the 1980 series; the 548 of Headingley 1948, or 526 of The Oval 1930?

In the past the deliberate slowing of the rate has been occasionally employed for an instant tactical reason. West Indies, though, consistently leaving out their specialist spinner, put themselves in a position where they could only carry out their bowling operation effectively at the lowered rate. If that is to be accepted then, presumably, the ICC must allow six or seven days for a match. That arrangement is already under consideration from the viewpoint of time lost to bad light or weather; with consideration of a Wednesday start and/or Sunday play; or even an extension into the following match period. Yet a low over-rate has precisely the same effect as bad weather. Certainly to make an extra time allowance to ensure an adequate number of overs being bowled would appear to condone the slow rate. The alternative, however, is a strict enforcement of a minimum rate; and if authority is not prepared to legislate for that they ought to accept the other course.

*The Guardian*

# 10

# The Crafts of Cricket

## The Case for Teaching Cricket

*March* 1950. Few parents or teachers would forbid a boy to play cricket in his spare time if he wished to do so. On the other hand, the decision to *teach* cricket in schools should be taken only where there is reasonable conviction that a boy will leave school the better for having been taught the game. Cricket, as an item of a school curriculum, may occupy ten hours a week in the summer term, with enthusiasts voluntarily devoting another six or even eight hours a week to it. This time, obviously, should not be wasted. For some parents and teachers the emotional argument of their own feeling for cricket is sufficient justification for having their charges taught to play it. Such illogical advocates, however, do the game a disservice by their failure to state the considerable case which can be made out for teaching cricket in schools – a case, moreover, which does not regard proficiency at cricket as an end in itself.

In the first place, the slight physical barriers to playing cricket allow of a greater proportion of boy-players than most school games, such as the two footballs, which place strength and speed at a premium. At cricket, skill will always dominate sheer strength. Indeed, even acute eyesight is not necessary, the wearing of spectacles not an insuperable handicap. The modern Test match cricketers, A. J. Richardson, W. A. Hadlee, N. B. F. Mann, P. A. Gibb, T. B. Mitchell and W. E. Bowes, all played in spectacles, while E. P. Nupen of South Africa – mainly a bowler, but good enough batsman to score 50 in a Test match – had only one eye. Cricket does not *demand* bodily strength, but it *develops* it, as surely as physical training and, at the same time, it attracts more enthusiastic practitioners than supervized P.T.

My argument is concerned with 'organized' cricket because organized cricket produces, certainly and rapidly, those qualities necessarily lacking in haphazard play. Because the spirit of the game has come down to us unchanged from the day of the village craftsmen who imbued the sport at its inception with the inherent characteristics of their work, it both demands of its players and develops in them the qualities of craftsmanship. Woodwork is not taught in schools with a view to turning out all the pupils as carpenters, but to develop directed manual dexterity. Cricket demands a comparable dexterity, under similar mental control, but with greater variety of direction. Of all games, cricket is the most technically profound. Fortunately, it is the game for which most, and the most highly skilled, coaches are readily available.

The young player soon recognizes the importance of practice, and the competitive urge causes many to persevere in obscure labour at cricket who would rebel against the same monotony in the field of, for instance, chemical experiment. Out of such practice comes the skill necessary to bowl a cricket ball to a precise length and to make it break or swing at will or, in a batsman, to play the bowled ball safely in a desired direction. But, beyond this skill of hand, batting, bowling and fielding demand balance and co-ordination of limbs of as high an order as in the most advanced eurhythmics.

Once the basic principles of technique are mastered, the young player takes part in matches, and match-play leads to appreciation of two important human aspects of cricket. The established methods of batting, bowling and fielding when first encountered in instruction may appear ritualistic, but practical experience infallibly shows them to be the most efficient methods of play. There follows the realisation that the laws of cricket are by no means restrictive, but that, having grown with the game, logically, they control it to the end of giving skill and good play the fullest scope to achieve a just result. Thus the schoolboy's quick sense of justice finds both the technique and the laws of cricket satisfyingly reasonable.

Every cricket match, within the dramatic framework of runs–wickets–time, differs according to the relative strength – and direction of strength – of the two teams, the state and changes of the wicket and the weather. From this 'given' data the cricketer works out his plan of campaign – a task rendered more difficult by the human element – and the result of the match is the verdict on his solution. Thus the player is involved in a strategy which must alter with every change in the course of the game. This strategy is as involved as that of the army cadet on manoeuvres. But the schoolboy infallibly recognizes cadet manoeuvres as 'make-believe'. He sees that their end is not the end of real war, but academic 'points', and that they ignore individual gallantry – the very element of war which appeals most strongly to the boy-mind. His cricket-match, on the other hand, holds out opportunities for heroic single-handed efforts in the team interest and, in the end, it gives a result, clear and final and real.

Although match strategy is usually the responsibility of the captain, every player must employ psychology in the application of his playing skill. The good bowler must have more than pace, flight, length, swing or spin: he must also be able to gauge the batsman's reactions to a particular delivery or sequence of deliveries. Because the great slow bowlers knew their fellow-men as cricketers, they knew them also as men.

Because of the game's element of chance, the epic stories of cricket are of lesser players winning or saving a match after the great have failed. Each player must accept personal responsibility: the shyest boy must present himself at the wicket; the most enthusiastic slogger, at need, must play a defensive innings; the most self-seeking batsman sacrifices his hopes of a century to his side's need for forty quick runs. This dual demand – for initiative and discipline – is acceptable, even attractive, to the schoolboy, because of its immediate return in terms of success.

The extent to which cricket models character has been less exaggerated than distorted. It has been credited with producing prigs: in fact, it merely provides a sound basic training in good manners. Because of the close human contact involved in cricket, it both evolves and morally enforces a code of reasonable consideration for others. The home captain, as a matter of course, settles such factors as boundaries and hours of play with the visiting captain, warns him of local hazards and conditions.

The fact that it is unusual for a player to lose his temper or to question an umpire's decision is not due to an exceptionally angelic disposition in cricketers, but derives simply from the need for maintenance of mutual respect and a reasonable attitude being self-evident to all in a cricket match. The game affords a perspective in which the petty or childish attitude is so disturbingly conspicuous that no reasonable person is prepared to maintain it. The players are interdependent: the bowler depends upon fieldsmen to make catches; the batsman depends unquestioningly upon his partner in calling for a run; and no batsman, however great, can save a game without a partner at the other end. This inter-dependence and the good fellowship and sympathy which every cricketer asks of his fellows, produce a standard of practical manners much less easy to achieve by dictation.

The good games-master will produce in his cricket pupils a degree of physical fitness, dexterity, bodily control, strategic reasoning, discipline and self-reliance, comparable with those developed by woodwork, eurhythmics, geometry and military training. More, his charges will develop some knowledge of practical psychology, a respect for patient application, and a standard of manners which will make them acceptable in any reasonable company. The chances of education over so wide a field are good because cricket, sympathetically taught, compels a greater degree of enthusiasm in a larger proportion of boys than any other school activity. Training in cricket develops many valuable qualities – and it can also, and quite fortuitously, be its own reward.

*The Schoolmasters and Woman Teacher's Chronicle*

# On Wicket-Keeping – and Andy Wilson

The hero of a cricket story never seems to be a wicket-keeper. He may be a batsman who – back to the wall, or by terrific hitting – carries his side to victory with only one wicket to fall. He may be a bowler who takes the crucial wicket just when it seems that the batting side will coast comfortably home. In the last resort, he is a fieldsman who makes the catch which turns what would have been the winning six into defeat. But he is never a wicket-keeper.

Fiction is, here at least, a mirror of life. Go to a cricket match, and you will hear discussion of the bowler's run-up, his action, his flight or swing, his length, his spin. Of the batsman, there will be his preference for forward- or back-play, or for a particular stroke; his over-caution or his recklessness. Some will go so far as to analyse his footwork, his back-lift, or his follow-through. Once the ball is played, however, or has passed the wicket, interest is apt to disappear. Who, among the pavilion critics, is heard comparing two different wicket-keepers in terms of the relative closeness of their work to the stumps, how late they start to move, the angle of their hands, or the point at which they 'take' the ball? How often, on the other hand, there is applause for a throw-in which, although fast, was only converted from an untakable half-volley or a violent wide by the quick judgement and movement of the wicket-keeper.

It is not unfair to say that a large number of spectators – largely unconsciously – regard a wicket-keeper as a kind of field-piece into which all deliveries which pass the bat, and all returns from the field, ought to pass as if into a sandbag. Only when he misses a catch or a stumping do they move themselves – to grumble.

The conclusion to which all this is leading us is, inescapably, that the wicket-keeper, above all other players, is 'the cricketer's cricketer'. The old classical standards of team-selection, for instance, always called for the wicket-keeper to be picked first. Indeed, he is more vital than is always recognized, even by the experts, from the ring. The great wealth of available statistics does not – in fact, cannot – tell us some of the most important points of all. Thus, we cannot discover the number of instances in which a Test has been virtually decided by the taking or dropping of a catch behind the wicket in the opening overs. Perhaps the wicket-keeper's major ration of luck lies in the fact that such a chance often goes to him edged so finely that the spectators do not know it is a catch at all until he appeals, which means that, if he does not catch it, he *may* get away with it.

Yet, if the main spotlight rarely falls upon the wicket-keeper, he is the one player who is *never* out of the game. I once heard a well-known captain tell his fieldsmen, as they went out, to *bang* their throw-ins into the wicket-keeper's gloves, because he believed – rightly – that the smack impressed upon the batsmen a feeling of fierce fielding. It used to be said of Jack Hobbs throwing in from cover that, if Herbert Strudwick had missed one of those returns, it would have broken his ribs. He never did miss one. I have seen Struddy's hands, though, after thirty-odd years of keeping wicket: the fingers are bent like oak-branches from their many fractures.

If wicket-keeping yields more bruises than benefits, it is still not without its glories. It was the Honourable Alfred Lyttelton who, in that dim Test match of 1884, when Australia were past the 500 with six wickets down, handed over his pads and wicket-keeping gloves and took the last four wickets for 19 runs. Occasionally, too, a Duckworth, an Evans or a Tallon, startles a whole ground into applause with a sudden dive to turn what appeared a leg-glide for four into a catch. The hard standards of first-class cricket, however, demand of a wicket-keeper, *above all*, neatness and soundness, all day long. Let a wicket-keeper, who has been in the field since half-past eleven in the morning, stand up to a fast-medium bowler at twenty-five past six when a batsman edges a ball off a back stroke. With a foot in which to make the catch, the wicket-keeper has to make that vital adjustment in minimum time. But, if he drops it, who remembers his fatigue? It is reckoned 'a chance behind the wicket'.

It was, I believe, Prebendary A. P. Wickham, of Somerset, who told how he kept while W. G. Grace made a double century – and how 'The Old Man' only let three balls past his bat all day. Fancy shaping to take five hundred deliveries that never reached the gloves. A bowler can only bowl half the balls bowled: a batsman has his 'on' days, but the wicket-keeper must go through all the motions for everything bowled from either end, whether or not the ball comes through – and take the fieldsmen's returns as well.

All this would be an immense strain, even if it were easy. In fact, and as every cricketer knows, it is by no means easy. We have all of us, at some time or other, tried to keep wicket – and all been baffled by that last yard or two in which so many deliveries are lost behind the batsman's body. Yet, when the late inswinger moves just before pitching and passes closely behind the batsman's pad, that rare bird, the natural *and practised* wicket-keeper, takes it as if he had seen it all the way. You may watch Andy Wilson doing it twenty times a day.

It is the hall-mark of a good wicket-keeper that he should be unobtrusive. Andy Wilson has always been that: unobtrusive and sound. Tom Goddard and Sam Cook making the spun ball whip off a 'sticky'; George Lambert making his 'quickies' rear rib-high past the batsman on a 'green one'; or Colin Scott moving his swingers dangerously late in a responsive atmosphere – he takes them all in the normal run of every day of his faithful service.

Only once have I seen Andy *plunge* into the limelight. That was in Gloucestershire's last match of 1947 against Essex. Ray Smith was playing one of his inspired innings and he had driven Sam Cook's fieldsmen out in a great arc round the offside boundary before he 'put the lap on him' and swept a ball round fine on the leg side. There was no one else to go – slip had retired to the covers – so off went Andy, head down, elbows out, pads flapping, and chased that hit all the way down to long leg. Once he caught the ball, a bare yard from the long-leg boundary, he had little enough wind left for the throw-in, and I like to taunt him with the – untrue – allegation that the batsmen had time to run a five. I have never seen any other wicket-keeper so far from the wicket, except on his way out of the pavilion: not many of them would have gone at all. Andy did, without question: he always would, he is that kind of player.

Statistics do not always do justice to a trier. Andy is not a great batsman. He might have looked better if he had not played his innings in a side with a Hammond, a Barnett, a Graveney, an Emmett, or a Milton: better players than he would look journeymen batsmen in such a setting. He has, however, scored his thousand runs in a season. He did it in 1947 when, even immediately after the loss of Hammond, Gloucestershire made such a strong bid for the Championship. He scored twelve hundred runs. His average, certainly, was only in the lower thirties, but figures do not tell all the story. Fourteen times that season he was one of the two highest scorers in the Gloucestershire innings, usually on bowlers' wickets when Gloucestershire were struggling. As a batsman, he is a fighter, with the knack of coming off when he is most needed, the kind of batsman for whom a captain is most grateful.

The reference books will tell you that Andy Wilson comes from Middlesex, but he obviously belongs to Gloucestershire. That comfortable, dumpling figure and rosy face, the countryman twist of his cap, the broad grin, the plodding good cheer and determination he brings to the job he does so well because he likes it – all these things establish him in the West Country which has become his home.

Remember that game against Sussex at Hove, late in August of 1947, when Gloucester had to win to stay in the Championship hunt. Four wickets were down when the left-handed partnership of Crapp (79) and Wilson (73) doubled the score, and put their side in the fight. Yet Gloucester began their second innings 133 behind. Andy Wilson scored 96 – more than a third of his side's runs; he scored them pawkily until the end, when his supply of partners was running out. It was, I feel, less the disappointment of missing his own century than the knowledge that Gloucester had not enough runs on the board that grieved him when Billy Griffith caught him off Nye.

You learn a lot about a man when you are out in the field with him six hours a day for most of the summer; and county cricketers really know one another. Up and down England, I do not believe you will find a cricketer who does not like Andy Wilson – nor one who does not wish him well in his benefit year. Gloucestershire cricket owes him a good benefit because, leaving aside his undoubted skill and courage, he has always given that extra ounce which is not compellable from any man, but which Andy gives as second nature because he lives for the game.

*Stump High! Cricket Miscellany (ed. A. E. Wilson, 1953)*

# Not One to Cover

'Not one to cover' is a seriously cautionary comment in more circles than one. In cricket it is the batsman's warning to his partner that the fieldsman at cover-point is too good for them to expect a single from a stroke in that direction. Cover is potentially the villain or the hero of any fielding story. His specific task is to nullify the most romantic of all strokes, the cover drive: on the other hand, he has the opportunity to be the most spectacularly graceful fieldsman in the game.

Strictly speaking – certainly in the firm opinion of any captain who does not himself field in that position – there should *never* be one run from a stroke to cover. Yet, in practice, there often is. Jack Hobbs – who understood the tactic so well because he fielded there himself – used to 'bait' the opposing cover point. First he would play a series of checked strokes to him: hit hard the ball would reach the fieldsman too quickly to allow a single: but 'checked' – played gently – there was time for the batsmen to run one while it was travelling to him. Then, having lured him in too close, Hobbs would unleash the fully powered stroke, placed wide of him and too fast to be stopped, for four runs. It was a joke Jack always appreciated, but cover-points never did.

Cover does, of course, make catches – skiers and horribly awkward swirlers from mishits, and stinging skimmers from full blooded drives only fractionally mistimed – but he is predominantly a run-saver. Nyren, speaking from the wisdom of the Hambledon cricket of almost two hundred years ago, wrote that the fieldsman posted 'to cover the middle wicket and point' needed to know 'the exact spot where the two runs may be saved, and that where the one run may be prevented' – the perfect posing of a problem no one has ever managed to solve all the time.

Nevertheless, for the man eager in temperament and fast on his feet, it is the most exciting of all positions: he could probably excel in the deep but, at cover, the challenge is not to save the four or the two, but to save the one: he is as deeply involved with every ball bowled as any close catcher, for even the defensive stroke which trickles the ball out on the off side may give the chance of a quick single in his direction.

Nyren says he must 'play from the pitch of the ball, and the motion of the batsman so as to get the start of the ball' and 'learn to judge the direction in which the batter, by his position and motion, will strike the ball, and whether high or low, hard or gently, and before it is struck, he should be off to meet it.'

There is never 'one to cover' against a man who meets that demand. The first of them was Vernon Royle, good enough to play for Lancashire in 1873 straight from school while, as an attacking bat, he once finished second in the Lancashire averages: but his great fame was as a cover-point. He was ambidextrous, vitally important there since the right-hander's cover drive always tends to curl to the left. The enduring tribute to him was reported from a Roses match. Tom Emmett, that shrewd Yorkshire character, was batting when his partner pushed a ball out to cover and called for a run. 'Nay, nay' said Tom, indicating Royle. 'Woa, now, there's a policeman theer.'

Many of the finest cover-points, because of their speed of reaction and certainty of hand, have been translated and posted close to the wicket, like A. O. Jones – who invented the gully position – Percy Chapman, Patsy Hendren and Keith Miller. But Gilbert Jessop, the legendary hitter, who also opened the bowling for England against Australia, fielded there all his life and C. B. Fry, in his analysis of the playing methods of the great, picked him as the pre-eminent fieldsman. Jessop was stockily built and, crouched in anticipation, he was valuably near the ground. As he moved in to pick up, his right arm was in position to swing back and his left foot was lifted so, the instant the ball entered his hand, he was ready to throw in. His throw involved no hint of the 'wind up' which gives batsmen the crucial extra moment of running time. He saved the fractions of a second, so often decisive in a run-out, by throwing from the elbow down, largely by a flick of the wrist, so that the running batsman, accustomed to the often laborious mechanics of the throw from the deep, was beaten for speed.

From the deep, however, Jessop employed a different, more shoulder-powered, but still low, throw. In 1905, the Australians played Surrey at The Oval on the same three days as were allotted to the Middlesex-Gloucestershire match at Lord's. In the county game Middlesex were soon in trouble on a bad pitch and Gloucester, captained by Jessop, took an advantage by the end of the first day. On the second day the then Prince of Wales – President as well as landlord of the Surrey club – and his two sons arrived to watch play at The Oval in the afternoon, soon after the county began their second innings. It had been arranged that W. G. Grace should sit with His Royal Highness, as well as the Chairman, Lord Alverstoke and, since Surrey were batting, Lord Dalmeny their captain joined the company. Late in the day Hayward struck a ball wide of mid-on to the boundary in the distant – Harleyford Road – corner of the ground, a vastly long hit. Suddenly the ball came back out of the crowd in a fierce, low arc, plumb into the wicket-keeper's gloves. 'Middlesex must have lost' said 'W.G'. 'How do you know that, Doctor?' asked Dalmeny. 'Only Jessopus could have thrown that ball' answered the 'Old Man'. He was right. Jessop, unable to bat because of a knee injury, had left the rest of the Gloucestershire side to make the 14 runs they needed to beat Middlesex and gone to take a sight of the Australians. His cab put him down at the Vauxhall corner gate and he walked in just as Hayward's stroke took the ball into the crowd: and, to W.G. at least, the arc of his throw was unmistakeable. We may hope the heir to the Throne was suitably impressed by the 'Old Man's' expertise.

In that match at The Oval, Jack Hobbs opened the innings for Surrey. The critics of the time, though impressed by his batting, criticized his apparent slackness in the field and, always a model professional, he set out to rectify the fault. Quick-footed, neat and controlled in movement, intelligent in approach, within a couple of years he made himself into one of the finest cover-points in the history of the game – so that there was never 'one to cover' when Jack Hobbs was there. For a time, however, he 'kidded' batsmen that there was. He would move in slowly, allow them to take a few runs and then, as they assumed the single, he pounced. In eleven matches of the 1911–12 tour of Australia, he ran out fifteen batsmen from cover. His accuracy was such that, under pressure and with only one stump to aim at, he would whip all three out of the ground.

As a rule, though, he did not take that risk of overthrows: if the minutest margin of time was left to him, he threw not merely to the wicket-keeper, but slap into his gloves. His friend Herbert Strudwick, who for years kept wicket in the same Surrey and England sides, said, 'Jack threw so hard that, if I hadn't taken it, it would have smashed my ribs: at first I used to be a bit alarmed until I realized that it was always going to hit my gloves just over the stumps.'

As the years went by Hobbs ran out fewer opponents: one could observe those he did bring off, his catches and his stops, no one could count the number of runs his reputation saved, runs batsmen *might* have taken but did not dare to attempt because Hobbs was there.

In the days before bowlers set out to close the off side, when the old masters of slow left-arm tempted batsmen to drive into the covers, the post of cover-point was even more highly specialized than now. Indeed, Middlesex thought it worthwhile to include S. H. Saville for his cover fielding alone: and Jim Hutchinson, whose career batting average was under 19, and who was a negligible bowler, held his place in the Derbyshire eleven for a·decade for his value.

Some great men fielded there occasionally. Sir Learie Constantine, surely the greatest of all fieldsmen, was often needed for his close catching but he was pre-eminent at cover point as anywhere else.

The classic Australian cover was Syd Gregory whose successors were Tommy Andrews and, briefly, before he moved to short leg, Victor Richardson. But their cricket produced a whole succession of players whom memory recalls as all of the same physical mould, of no more than average height, wide shouldered and tapering down to neat, quick feet: all of them would run and pick up into the long, low accurate throw which marks the great Australian outfields – men like Vernon Ransford, Johnnie Taylor, 'Nip' Pellow, Sir Don Bradman, Neil Harvey, Jack Fingleton – all of whom fielded at cover often enough to demonstrate outstanding ability.

Other leading Englishmen in the position between the two wars were Percy Chapman – with the dual advantage of being left-handed and having the strength and timing to throw accurately and fast when off balance, but who soon became a specialist at silly-point – Eddie Paynter, Jack Davies and the bubbling Jack Stephenson, an entertainment in himself. At one point in the middle thirties Middlesex, for the slow left-arm and leg-spin bowling which they always favoured, could set an arc of superb cover fieldsmen – George Hart, Joe Hulme, Walter Robins and 'Tuppy' Owen-Smith – from short third man round to extra cover, and still have John Human in reserve and the elder master, Patsy Hendren, standing at slip.

In the post-war years the standard has been maintained by Cyril

Washbrook, unmistakeable as he prowled the covers, cap tilted, shoulders hunched and wary; Reggie Simpson, slim, poised and graceful; the Indians Gul Mahommad, Adhikari and Gaekwad; Athol Rowan of South Africa, Martin Donnelly and Brunty Smith, New Zealand; Alan Rees of Glamorgan and, when he could be spared from the near position, 'Tiger' Pataudi.

Now, though cover-point is no longer considered so important as twenty years ago, and when cricket standards are said to be deteriorating, the game has produced two men as fine as any who ever filled the position: arguably indeed, the greatest. Colin Bland, the Rhodesian, has so studied and practised the movements of stop, pick up and throw that he seems to blend the three in a single ripple of movement, and his accuracy is amazing. The West Indian, Clive Lloyd, hardly looks an athlete for he stoops and shambles: but he moves like a great cat and throws, on balance with whip, off balance with a kind of push, so that he is as fast in reaching and returning the ball as anyone we have ever known.

Still the wise batsmen must often say to his partner, 'It is not one to cover'.

*From 'Cover', the Magazine of The Provincial Insurance Co Ltd*

# The Bowler's Craft

*July* 1954. If a cricket ball is new and shining, the seam is held between the first and second fingers at a particular angle and the ball delivered at brisk pace with a loose wrist, it will swing as it passes through the air.

The method is not new. Noah Mann was said to deliver the ball made by his fellow Hambledonian, the cobbler John Small, with 'a curve all the way'. Sixty years ago, the late George Hirst discovered that the same power lay within his native method while, simultaneously, J. B. King of Philadelphia was acquiring it from the baseball pitchers. So, in this century, the bowlers of medium or faster pace who have chosen to toil but not to spin have been in a majority.

It was in the twenties that the late Fred Root achieved perfect control of 'late' swing. A delivery from him would come down on the line of the middle-and-off stumps until a bare couple of yards before it pitched. Then it would dive away to leg like a boomerang so that the groping forward stroke edged it to the hands of the short-leg fieldsmen. He compelled a stroke by the employment of the alternative delivery which went straight on to hit the off bail: few batsmen in the world could distinguish between it and the inswinger.

The smaller ball, the quality of the seam-stitches and the increasingly frequent replacement of the ball brought Root many followers not all of whom possessed his quality of positive attack.

The particular craft they discarded had been developed by some great earlier hands. Spofforth experimented with great pace and with swing, but he satisfied himself most when he bowled the off-break at such a pace that the ball would pitch on the off-stump and hit the leg.

In the wet summer of 1907, Tom Wass and Hallam bowled Notts to the County Championship. Few would believe, until they saw, that Wass bowled fast leg-breaks to five slips and a wicket-keeper standing back. The price to him of that great season was that, for the last twenty years of his life, his third and fourth fingers were inextricably wedged in the palm from cutting the ball out beside his middle finger.

Shaw, Attewell and their fellow disciples of length-bowling, too – men who minutely cut or spun the ball, varied its pace and flight within the limits of machine-accuracy – preferred the certain purchase of the worn ball.

Now comes the Pakistani, Fazal Mahmood, who opens his team's bowling as a 'swing bowler' but is happier when the skin of the match ball has been roughened by bat-stroke and the ground to enable him to cut two fingers down its side so that it breaks either way from the pitch.

As he bowls round England this year, he will recall to many a cricketer the greatness of those players of the twenties who, without help from pitch, wind or swing, denied rest to the weightily majestic batting of Notts, Surrey, or Yorkshire on the merciless pitches of Trent Bridge, The Oval and Leeds. There, where nature and the groundsman had conspired to create a batsman's paradise, such bowlers as Geary, Kennedy, Macaulay laboured to make the ball deviate from straight until corns hard as flints grew on their strong and artful fingers.

They could not hope conclusively to beat and bowl the great batsman in a defensive stroke. Their aim was, by minute variations of pace and length – as fine as the checking of a ball by following through on to a bent leg – to deny the batsman the comfort of playing the ball in the middle of the bat. Sooner or later he would make the infinitesimal error which is the difference between a stroke hit straight along the ground and the ball sent that bare catchable inch off the ground. It was not an art apparent from the seats around the boundary, but even from there it was implicit in the respectful approach of batsmen who might otherwise have been riding a whirlwind of runs.

In 1946 Alec Bedser was a swing bowler. The gift is not hard to command: but he added to it a fire which batsmen felt. To play his bowling is to bruise the flesh between thumb and index finger with the jolt upon the bat of a delivery which comes upon the bat fractionally earlier in the stroke than the normal sense of timing promises.

War had denied Bedser the slow and stern groundstaff apprenticeship which produces practised cricketers with unhurried care. He had to add craft to his gifts on the field of Test play, back the spear of late swing with the steady sword-play of bowling which changes course off the pitch. Only then did he become a complete bowler.

Now he is not merely a bowler for fast wickets. The pitch which suits the spin bowler also suits Bedser. His leg-cutter bowled off the top of the second finger is, in effect – and technically in all but the requisite of third-finger spin-application – a fast leg-break. Indeed, on the slow wicket which is beginning to crumble, his greater pace makes him a more effective bowler of breaks than the pure spin bowler.

For Bedser, however, there was the encouragement of frequent wet English wickets from which the cut ball turns like a whiplash. For Fazal, the matter was less simple on the granite-like pitches of Pakistan and with little of the English background of age-long practice with its many teachers and examples. Perhaps there is no clearer proof of that legacy of tradition and craft which passes with the adoption of cricket than this skill in the hands of a bowler in the youngest of Test-playing countries.

*The Spectator*

# When 'Demon' Spofforth Was Top of the Derbyshire Averages

No other kind of bowling has had quite such an up-and-down history as the off-break. Its practitioners have tended to flourish or labour almost as much according to the time when they bowled as in relation to their ability.

The early right-arm – underarm – bowlers tended, naturally, to spin from leg. The first recorded off-spinner was one Lamborn, whose Christian name is unrecorded and who was known as 'The Little Farmer'. A simple countryman, no batsman or field, he learnt his craft while minding his father's sheep, when he would set up a hurdle and bowl away at it for hours on end. When he first appeared for Hambledon in the 1770s he made an impression which Nyren recalled vividly fifty years afterwards:

'He had the most extraordinary delivery I ever saw. The ball was delivered quite low, and with a twist; not like that of the generality of right-handed bowlers, but just the reverse way: that is, if bowling to a right-handed hitter, his ball would twist from the off stump into the leg. He was the first I remember who introduced this deceitful and teazing style of delivering the ball. When All England played the Hambledon Club, the Little Farmer was appointed one of our bowlers; and, egad! this new trick of his so bothered the Kent and Surrey men, that they tumbled out one after another, as if they had been picked off by a rifle corps. For a long time they could not tell what to make of that cursed twist of his.'

Succeeding underarm bowlers – from William Lambert to 'Old Clarke' – used the off-break as a variation: but it is interesting that, in this century, G. H. Simpson-Hayward, known as 'the last of the lob bowlers', relied almost entirely on the leg-spinner: his off-break was much slower and indifferently controlled.

The roundarm bowlers all tended, from the very nature of their actions, to bowl an undercut off-break but most of them were of medium or even fast pace.

The Australian, F. R. Spofforth – 'The Demon Bowler' – was almost purely an off-spinner, but of varying speeds. He himself said, specifically, that he tried to adjust so that, according to the pace of the pitch, he spun enough to turn from the off stump to the leg. Incidentally he must be the only Australian Test player to head the Derbyshire bowling averages: he played a few games for the county between 1888 and 1890 and in the last of those seasons took 42 wickets at 11.36.

With the establishment of overarm bowling, most fast bowlers – rubbing the ball in the dirt in a way that would horrify their modern descendants – strove to bowl the off-break – or break-back as it was called – and so did most of the fast-medium and medium 'length bowlers' who employed what is now called the 'cutter'. The leading spin-bowlers of the period 1880 to 1900 were leg-breakers or left-arm. The first of the modern type of slow off-break bowler was Ted Wainwright of Yorkshire who emerged in the late 1880s and who spun prodigiously on helpful wickets but was too erratic to succeed on good pitches and influenced much subsequent selection by failing in Australia.

Schofield Haigh, of Yorkshire, and then Jack Crawford – the schoolboy genius who turned on Australian pitches where no one else deviated from straight – continued in the new century to push the off-spinner through at quite lively pace and Fred Tate, father of Maurice, was at least slow-medium.

But 'Razor' Smith, the thin Surrey player who bowled himself to exhaustion when he took 247 wickets in 1910, was genuinely slow: he was something of a freak since, on wet wickets, for a reason he never understood, his intended off-breaks often went sharply the other way!

Jack Newman, of Hampshire – though he was often called upon to open with medium outswingers – was a legitimate slow off-spinner: but he lost many wickets – lbw – through his habit of following through in front of the umpire.

These were, however, by modern standards, 'old fashioned' in method: in an age of, predominantly, off-side play, they bowled largely to hit the middle or middle-and-off stumps.

Newman continued an effective bowler into the twenties, when he and the Gloucestershire old hand, Percy Mills, were joined in the first great harvest of off-spin, by George Macaulay – Yorkshire – whose pace was often medium, Cecil Parkin, of Lancashire – basically an off-spinner but who bowled everything else as well – Leslie Townsend of Derbyshire, who was brisk in pace, Vallance Jupp, of Northants, who spun viciously, Peter Jackson, Worcestershire, Ewart Astill, Leicestershire, Sam Staples, Notts, and Reg Sinfield, Gloucestershire.

The beginning of the great period of off-spin can be fixed definitely at 1929. Then Tom Goddard, who had not succeeded in his earlier years as a fast bowler, returned to Gloucestershire after a year on the staff at Lord's during which he was turned into an off-spinner. That remarkable captain B. H. Lyon studied him and planned a field for him with three – or even four – short legs close up to the bat. Goddard wrapped his huge forefinger round the ball and, giving it a savage twist, took 173 wickets (at 15.15) in the season. The new method of attack was launched.

We must link with Goddard, J. C. Clay, who played for Glamorgan from their entry into the Championship in 1921, first as a fast bowler, subsequently as a leg-breaker and finally as the best off-spinner the game had known until then. His spin was sharp but his variations of pace, arc and length so controlled, and so well concealed that some of the best batsmen in the country accounted him the most difficult bowler they faced. In 1948, at the age of fifty, he was a major force in Glamorgan's first Championship win, and retired a happy man.

Climate and pitch conditions conspired gradually to make the off-spinner the major slow bowler of English cricket, outnumbering slow left-arm and, after the war of 1939–45, pushing the leg-spinner almost out of the game. Every county had at least one – Glamorgan and Yorkshire sometimes two, or even three – employing them as economic stock bowlers on good wickets, killers when the ball turned.

Such concentration on a single department of the game as went on in England in the post-war years – South Africa, with Athol Rowan and Hugh Tayfield, is the only other country to develop major bowlers in this kind until the West Indian, Lance Gibbs – was bound to produce a player of world stature. He appeared in Jim Laker; more hostile than

John Clay, a tighter bowler with even more variations, he rose to something near perfection in 1956.

In that summer, on helpful – but not impossible – wickets, he reduced an apparently strong Australian batting side to the abject. He twice took all ten of their wickets in an innings; in the Old Trafford Test had the amazing figures of nineteen wickets for 90 runs and, in the complete series, 46 at an average of 9.6. That was the high summer of off-spin – and it was tragically short. Only a year later, in 1957 – a move directed ostensibly against the 'negative' bowling of the inswing and 'inslant' – was introduced legislation limiting the number of leg-side fieldsmen to five. So the off-spinner who, on a turning wicket, had the skill to attack with four short legs, was no longer able to do so.

Batsmen had already set out to break his dominance by the sweep, the pulled drive and the 'lap'. Now, since his fifth man could not cover long leg, square leg *and* long on, they could hit their way through or over his leg trap, into the vacant spaces while one – or even two – fieldsmen were compelled to stand useless on the off side.

So the off-spinner was legislated into relative impotence, denied the field setting his skill demanded. Today, he is back where he was thirty years ago, striving to develop fresh tactics to overcome his handicap. But, for him above all – who has been hit so often 'with the tide' – that tide must, surely, turn again, one day.

*Edwin Smith Testimonial Brochure*, 1966

# Talking of Leg-Spinners – and Kent

There is no more certain sign of a prewar English cricket-follower than his belief in leg-spin. All round us the postwar generation of tight cricket disciples wags its head sadly at the very thought: 'Of course, a Benaud or an O'Reilly, that would be different; but, really you know, you cannot use a leg-spinner in these days of bonus points and batsmen who just wait for the bad ball'. It is, alas, little use to point out to them that Benaud, in a single afternoon, won the 1961 Test rubber for Australia – and that Benaud only became a good bowler by bowling – and bowling, and bowling. It is a vicious circle: modern English leg-spinners do not bowl enough to bowl well.

Nevertheless, the elders remain firm in their conviction that leg-spin is an effective cricket weapon. They are, indeed, at times apt to overplay their hands in their enthusiasm. So, when the news went over the cricket bush-radio that Kent were introducing a new leg-break bowler, David Baker, in 1961, he had some fervent supporters before he even turned his arm in county cricket. When he knocked down some Yorkshire wickets – always the favourite targets of English leg-breakers – he had even more friends. The snares and dangers that lie in the path of science-fiction heroes are nothing by comparison with those ahead of the man who tries to bowl leg- and googly-spin in modern English cricket. So to prophesy a great future for Baker would be even more unwise than in the case of a young batsman or fast bowler with less than a dozen matches behind him – and that would be rash enough.

But at least it is in his favour – if tradition means anything – that he plays for Kent, the county that has, for years, been the stronghold of the 'leggie'. Why, it is not so long ago that, in August, when 'Father' Marriott was free from his teaching duties at Dulwich to take the end opposite 'Tich' Freeman, Kent kept the two of them on for hours.

Perhaps, in a way it was a Kent bowler – the fantastically unlucky Doug Wright – who, with the Australian, Bill O'Reilly, put really slow leg-spin out of fashion. No one ever truly finger-spun the leg-break and googly so fast as Wright before: it will be remarkable if anyone ever does again.

On the theme of leg-break bowling, however, cricket history leads us back even further in Kent's history – to that remarkable figure, D. W. – 'Daddy' – Carr. He is, of course, now something of a 'quiz question' player, who was picked for England in his first season – 1909 – when he was thirty-seven years old. But he had appeared in *Wisden* long before that. In 1891, as an undergraduate at Brasenose, he played in the Oxford Freshmens' match, which was much interrupted by rain; he went in at number four – and scored four – and, bowling eighteen overs in one innings, took three wickets – including that of M. R. Jardine, the University captain – for 27 runs. He was then picked among the sixteen Freshmen against 'The Twelve' and took no wickets for 17 runs. Those figures, combined with a knee injury, virtually ended his University cricket career.

So, until he was approaching middle age, his cricket consisted of some steady medium-paced bowling and occasional middling innings in Kent club cricket, notably for The Mote and the Band of Brothers. In 1905–06, the 'new' South African school of googly bowlers, developing Bosanquet's trick, became a force in world cricket by beating England. In 1905, Douglas Ward Carr had begun seriously to experiment along those lines: and he profited from watching the South Africans when they displayed their method – slightly less successfully than they had done at home – in England in 1907. C. B. Fry, indeed, described Carr as much like the South African googly bowlers in method.

He had considerable success with his new bowling in Kent club cricket in 1908. But the county were very powerful in 1909 (in fact, they won the Championship) and their bowling was so strong that Fielder, Blythe and Woolley rarely needed the already available assistance of Fairservice and Humphreys. So it was understandable that they hesitated to drop an established player for a thirty-seven-year-old leg-break bowler whose batting and fielding were relatively undistinguished and who, in any case, had to take leave from his teaching to play. They compromised by giving Carr a game against Oxford University at the end of May: he seized the chance to take seven wickets for 95 in the match: an extremely impressive first appearance in first-class cricket. Even that performance, though, was not sufficient to win him a place in Kent's Championship side. But 1909 was the year of an Australian visit. In those days there was not an overseas tour every year, and many of the counties did not wholly approve the disruption of their domestic cricket. So the selectors announced that, since leading players were being taken from the counties for five Tests, the sides for the Gentlemen v Players matches at The Oval and Lord's would be picked from players not wanted for county matches. But for that circumstance, D. W. Carr's career might have been altogether different, and far less sensational. He was chosen for the Gentlemen at The Oval, where he took the wickets of the first four batsmen in the second innings of the Players. That carried him into the Lord's match, which began a day later, when he distinguished himself by taking the wickets of J. T. Tyldesley – twice – and Tom Hayward.

His first-class cricket career now consisted of three matches, spread over seven weeks; and he had not yet taken part in a County Championship match. His bowling figures were:

|  | Overs | Mdns | Runs | Wkts |
|---|---|---|---|---|
| For Kent v Oxford University | 20.5 | 2 | 65 | 5 |
| at Oxford, 27, 28, 29 May | 12 | 1 | 30 | 2 |
| For Gentlemen v Players | 17.3 | 1 | 58 | 3 |
| at The Oval, 8, 9, 10 July | 22 | 3 | 80 | 5 |
| For Gentlemen v Players | 25.3 | 4 | 71 | 6 |
| at Lord's 12, 13, 14 July | 16 | 1 | 57 | 1 |

In those three matches his bowling had made such an impression that, with the Test rubber in a critical position – Australia led by two wins to one, with two to play – he was summoned as one of the twelve English players for the Fourth Test at Old Trafford. But on the morning of the match he was the one left out of the final eleven because – as he was subsequently to recall – the pitch was considered too soft for his bowling to be effective.

At last he was put into the Kent first team and in three matches he had these figures: six for 85 v Essex; eight for 106 v Middlesex; six for 99 v Hampshire.

He was one of the thirteen called to the Fifth Test and, after a first-class career of precisely six matches, he opened the bowling for England against Australia. He bowled S. E. Gregory at 9; had M. A. Noble lbw at 27 and W. W. Armstrong lbw at 55: so, with Australia 55 for three, Carr had taken all three wickets for 18. He was the only English bowler – though S. F. Barnes, Jack Sharp, Frank Woolley and Wilfred Rhodes were in the side – to trouble the Australian batsmen on a perfect batting wicket. But, to the displeasure of the critics, A. C. MacLaren kept him on for over an hour and a half – the longest spell he had ever bowled in first-class cricket. That error, and his earlier decision to omit the fast bowler, Buckenham, for Sharp, probably cost MacLaren the captaincy: he never played for England again. As was to be expected of one of his type, Carr lost his nip through being bowled too long and his eventual figures, in the Australian total of 325, were five for 146. In the massive Australian second innings of 339 for five on a still good pitch, Carr had two (Armstrong and Victor Trumper) for 136.

That was D. W. Carr's first and last Test match; but he remained an extremely effective bowler. In five more Championship matches that season for Kent he took thirty-one more wickets, with twelve for 116 against Somerset and seven for 38 against Leicester. But he probably was happiest to play a major part (with four for 27 and four for 78) in Lord Londesborough's XI's win against the Australians at Scarborough.

In 1909 D. W. Carr was a preparatory school master; a thickset – indeed, well-covered – man. In subsequent years he was at some pains to take off weight, and he appeared for the season of 1910 markedly slimmer than in the previous summer. He had a pleasantly humorous face and an amiable, even benign, manner; not easily ruffled, he was an equable bowler who took punishment without losing confidence or his length. He was pre-eminently, for a leg-spin bowler, accurate: far more so than his predecessor, Bosanquet who, however, probably spun the ball more. Carr tended, in the modern idiom, to 'push it through', bowling faster than many of his type, relying on his good length – rather than flight – and the concealment of his googly, to beat batsmen. If he did not turn the ball prodigiously, his bowling bounced quickly off the wicket and his spin was sufficient to beat the bat. Indeed, throughout that first season he impressed even more by the number of times he beat the best players so completely as to go unrewarded than by the substantial number of wickets he took.

Each summer up to the First World War, he became available for Kent as soon as the school term ended and regularly played in their nine or ten August matches – of which his bowling regularly won at least two – averaging fifty wickets a season.

For Kent in Championship matches he took: 31 wickets at 14.21 in 1909; 60 at 12.16 in 1910; 55 at 16.46 in 1911; 49 at 9.59 in 1912; and

47 at 18.55 in 1913. In those five years, Kent were three times County Champions, once runners-up and once third. Carr had unusual success on the soft wickets of the August of 1912, which must have made his omission from the Fourth Test of 1909 – because the ground was soft – seem extremely ironic in retrospect.

At the end of July 1914, D. W. Carr joined the Kent side for the match with Surrey – who were ahead of them in the Championship – at Blackheath. Jack Hobbs – the first true master of the googly bowlers – and Tom Hayward put on 234 in less than three hours for the first wicket; Surrey made 509, and Kent were never in the match with a chance. D. W. Carr bowled 28 overs and took no wickets for 134 runs. *Wisden* remarked baldly, yet poignantly, at the end of its report on the match: 'Carr bowled with so little of his customary skill that he did not assist Kent again.'

That was, in truth the end of 'Daddy' Carr's first-class career: statistics show that, in snatches of five seasons between May 1909 and August 1914, he took 334 wickets at an average of 16.84: and scored 425 runs at 9.04. But he is remembered because, virtually unknown – not even considered for a county cap – and thirty-seven years old, he was picked for England against Australia and succeeded. He relished the joke, for he was a humorous man. He also relished 'Shrimp' Leveson-Gower's story of a day – in 1926 – when A. W. Carr was chosen as captain of England. The news was communicated to that great autocrat of Kent cricket, Lord Harris, whose instant response was, 'Carr – ah, Carr – a bit old, but Kent – we can't go wrong there.' At that time 'Daddy' Carr was fifty-four years old. He died, in Sidmouth, in 1950, at the age of seventy-eight.

To revert to David Baker – he has already bowled a hundred more overs of leg-breaks in first-class cricket than D. W. Carr had done when he opened the bowling for England against Australia. But then, Baker has more time to spare. Sadly, he is likely to need it.

*Kent CCC Annual*, 1962

# The Disappearing Wrist-Spinner

*April* 1964. The virtual disappearance of the wrist-spinner from English first-class cricket has been lamented for years without, so far as one can observe, any effective action being taken to prevent it.

To define him, the 'wrist' – or 'wristy' or 'unnatural' – spinner is a right-arm bowler of leg-breaks or a left-arm bowler of off-breaks, with or without the respective googly. The species flourishes in Australia,

New Zealand, India and the West Indies, but in England has been all but exterminated by finger-spinners, in-swingers, green wickets and an epidemic of bonus points.

While this decline is often remarked, it may be that its extent is not fully appreciated. Statistics are not always the most effective yardstick of cricket, but in this case the figures are both striking and incontestable. In 1946, in County Championship cricket, 23 wrist-spinners from 13 counties were given a modicum – 70 overs – of bowling during the season. In 1963, the figure was nine bowlers from six counties. In 1946, five of them bowled more than 700 overs and another four over 400. In 1963 only T. Greenhough bowled more than 500 overs (565) and only two more, R. W. Barber and R. Hobbs, as many as 300.

The same situation, of course, has been reflected in Test selection. Here the figures are not quite so obvious. Thus, F. R. Brown was at his greatest as a leg-spin bowler, but undoubtedly his choice for England between 1949 and 1951 was based largely on his captaincy and certainly through that period, and at Lord's in 1953, his bowling *in Tests* was largely medium-pace 'seam-up' to a defensive length. Again, J. Wardle was primarily an orthodox slow left-arm bowler; but in four Tests – one in Australia and three in South Africa – he employed almost entirely the 'Chinaman' (which he probably bowled as accurately and deceptively as anyone has ever done). Conversely, Denis Compton's usual method was the 'wristy' left-arm spin but his major Test spell – at Cape Town in 1949 – was bowled entirely in 'orthodox' fashion. John Ikin was reckoned a useful leg-break bowler: that ability was a considerable factor in his selection for the Australian tour of 1946–47: but he bowled, on average, less than five overs in each of his eighteen Tests. Of others, notably K. Barrington – first engaged by Surrey for his leg-break bowling – R. Subba Row, D. B. Carr, M. C. Cowdrey, and Sir L. Hutton, their Test careers bear virtually no trace of the fact that they have trafficked in wrist-spin: though Hutton was once – at Leeds in 1948 – thrown into the firing line to see how much of his occasional skill he could produce at the crucial stage of a Test.

All this said, by figures accurate enough to make their point fairly, between 1946 and the end of 1963, England took part in some 156 Test matches: in those matches they made 67 selections of wrist-spinners *qua* wrist-spinners. In the nine years from 1946 to 1954 there were 50 such selections (of five players of whom D. V. P. Wright made 25 appearances) while in the second period, 1955–63 – of the same length but which included more Tests – there were only 17 such selections (of three players, including Wardle on the four occasions noted earlier).

In the post-war period, the attitude of selectors on all levels and of most players – *in England* – was that the leg-spinner, unless he could produce the bonus of a thousand runs a season plus good catching, was a luxury.

This antipathy has been reflected in the production of wrist-spinners. Of those who have achieved Test selection, Wright – whose unusual pace lifted him far out of the normal run of his kind – F. R. Brown, R. O. Jenkins and Peter Smith were developed in pre-war cricket while E. Hollies and E. Leadbeater both made spin second to accuracy – they were 'rollers' rather than really vicious spinners. Perhaps most significant of all, Wardle, despite his great gifts for wrist-spin, was usually preferred as a finger-spinner of which our cricket had plenty. Thus Greenhough – for all his tendency towards the googly rather than the leg-break – Wardle (when allowed) and R. W. Barber emerge as the only wrist-spin bowler English cricket has developed to Test level in the eighteen seasons since the Second World War. Were conditions unsympathetic to the method? This is not proven. The Australians, J. E. Walsh, B. Dooland, G. E. Tribe and, to a lesser extent, C. L. McCool, J. Pettiford and K. Grieves, were all successful in county cricket: so was G. Goonesena from Ceylon and the New Zealander, W. E. Merritt.

The decline in our domestic wrist-spin has not merely deprived England of an extra attacking edge of obvious value on hard wickets such as prevail in Australia, West Indies, South Africa, India and Pakistan – but it has left our batsmen constantly short of practice, and often deficient in technique against it. Yet the warning was plain in the immediate post-war Test cricket when, in the space of some six or seven years, England were sorely troubled by C. L. McCool, W. G. Ferguson, J. Iverson and S. G. Shinde – all leg-spinners who took ten or more wickets in a Test series against England – even if we exclude Ramadhin as being basically an off-spinner who employed a leg-break for occasional variety.

More lately we have seen them embarrassed by S. P. Gupte and C. Borde even on the good wickets of India while, in 1961, Richie Benaud won the Manchester Test and the rubber in a single spell of leg-spin.

Still, from time to time, the young leg-break bowler springs up in England to baffle batsmen in the nets. The list is a long one; but it would be almost cruel to name the young men who, in the last decade, have tempted their coaches to believe a new match-winner had been found. The next news has been that the lad has drifted out of the game without ever having had the chance to prove himself as the traditional leg-spinner did, with a long spell of bowling, taking punishment, buying his wickets but – and Wright was an impressive example of this fact – taking his wickets more quickly, in terms of overs-per-wicket, than any other kind.

Now we have a new 'white hope' in Robin Hobbs of Essex. Strangely enough Essex, sometimes accused of defensive strategy, have given wrist-spin a far greater chance than most other counties since the war. In 1946, for instance, they sometimes used three of them – T. P. B. Smith, F. H. Vigar and R. Taylor – in a single innings. They persevered many years with W. T. Greensmith and brought back Dr C. B. Clarke.

Now they have encouraged Hobbs who, in conditions which seemed like heaven to him – the mat in East Africa and the hard wickets of Jamaica – has made a deep impression during this past winter. These were, certainly, minor tours, but his ability – in those conditions – was unmistakeable. He is more accurate than most of his kind, especially if we consider his considerable spin; he takes punishment philosophically, is not afraid to attack and, if he does not command a marked googly, has adequate variety in the shape of a top-spinner that whips through very quickly. Hobbs is a devoted leg-spinner: he has bowled nothing else since he first started to play cricket – indeed, he says he cannot bowl an off-break. He is at times a brilliant outfield and he might yet make a useful, forcing bat – important assets if he has to work his passage until times – and pitches – change.

Meanwhile he seems fated, especially in his own county, to find hard or dusty wickets a rarity. More often the ball will come to him still shiny, because of the lush green outfield, giving him no true finger-purchase for the effort to wrest turn from an equally grassy pitch. Perhaps he should be given a nice bare, fast net and left to practise on it throughout the English summer to keep him in trim to go automatically on all England's overseas tours. If such a suggestion seems pure Alice-in-Wonderland, that is merely a reflection of the circumstances that produce it. *The Cricketer*

# Rhythm in Action

The secret of power is timing; that is why the great cricketers – hitting, throwing or bowling – have impressed us not only by their power, but by the rhythmic beauty of their movement.

When Frank Woolley's body fell with lazy elegance into the line of his stroke, the ball left his bat at surprising pace. When Neil Harvey returns from the boundary, he seems to do little more than wave his arm. Perhaps, indeed, a bowler's action can be the most poetic motion in cricket. Maurice Tate had been a slow bowler until that day in the twenties when, wearied of bowling at Philip Mead's unnaturally broad bat, he suddenly gathered himself and sent down the first of the deliveries which were to make him the greatest fast-medium bowler of his time – perhaps, indeed, of all cricket. His father before him had a sound, flowing action; and Maurice's own slow delivery had been basically right. This new action, however, was the ideal; it was a natural, unpremeditated unity of arms, body and feet. The result was bowling which leapt from the pitch in defiance – all but contradition – of the laws of timing.

Pictures crowd into the memory of great bowlers; some – like Clarrie Grimmett and even Bill O'Reilly – violated all the instructions, but were great nevertheless: the word, however, is *nevertheless* they were outstanding *despite* poor actions, not *because* of them.

Two fast bowlers came back to mind. The first is Ted McDonald, the Australian Test player who subsequently went to Lancashire. He came up to the wicket like a sprinter and then, at top speed, his arm came over, hostilely high and the ball seemed to bounce like a tennis ball. The second was Harold Larwood, with the fierce, accelerating run-up, his arm at delivery straight as a guardsman's back, to compensate for his lack of height and make his bowling rear threateningly from the pitch. Then there were the two left-armers, Bill Voce, applying all his beefy power, and 'Nobby' Clark of Northants, whose whole body seemed to whip as he sent down one of the most dangerous pace deliveries of modern cricket.

There was, too, a strange, jazzy rhythm about Doug Wright's bounding, leaping run: sometimes – indeed, sadly often – it went wrong; but when it was right it imparted a sinister arc to a deadly leg-break. We are reducing our pace – down to Wilfred Rhodes, with his sidling delivery from which the left-arm spinners seemed to float down in a gentle curve, ideal for hitting. There lay the secret of his deception; the attribute called 'flight'.

Most facets of cricket can be instilled by instruction; sometimes flaws can be eradicated; but there has never been a substitute for the natural action which makes great bowling handsome at its most hostile.

*Cricket Spotlight*, 1958

# 11

# Pieces from the Papers

## It Occurs to Me . . .

It occurs to me that a poor South-country man ought never to think that he knows anything about Yorkshire or Yorkshiremen.

I walked into Headingley for the Leeds Test match with the air of one who knows his way around the place. There he was, at his bookstall immediately inside the gate – Smithy. As usual, his cricket shirt was open at the neck, his white coat was catching the breeze, his hair was swept back to the neck-line as sharp as a razor slash.

'Hullo, Smithy,' I said, anxious to convince myself that I was not in strange country, 'how are you?' Then, as I noticed a sunburn on him that would have turned a Riviera lifesaver green with envy: 'Have you been having some sun in Yorkshire – or where did you get that sunburn?'

'Australia,' he said with a grin.

Now, Smithy sells newspapers and sporting magazines at the Yorkshire cricket grounds. He played cricket as hard as any other Yorkshire boy until he was fifteen, when he was so ill that he never caught up with the other boys again.

He was apprenticed to a plumber, but he wanted to be in cricket, so he started selling newspapers at the cricket grounds round his county – Leeds, Sheffield, Hull, Scarborough, Huddersfield.

It was last summer that Yorkshire matches and even Tests in Yorkshire stopped being enough for him – he wanted to go to Australia. Mrs Smith decided him to go by saying that it was a good idea. He sold the van and the tools which were the stock in trade of part-time winter plumbing business for £100, left his wife the newspaper round to keep her and the two children for the winter and bought a ticket to Australia on the Strathaird.

Arthur Smith, from Leeds, landed in Perth, Western Australia with a small trunk, an overnight case, £15 and 200 copies of Len Hutton's benefit booklet. He off-loaded the booklets, left his trunk in Melbourne and set off. How he was going to sleep, eat, travel, get into cricket grounds and above all get back to England in the following spring were matters of faith and hope, but not of charity.

He could sell newspapers in England, couldn't he? He wanted to see the MCC's matches in Australia and, to that end, by heaven, he could sell newspapers in Australia. He could sell souvenirs of the touring team – if he could find the souvenirs and the people who produced them – and if he could persuade them to let him have a stock of them.

The tour rolled on. Sidney Barnes, toughest and most businesslike of Australian cricketers, drove Smithy from Towoomba to Sydney. That trip apart, he flew once, otherwise he took the local transport to the end of the main street and thumbed his way to the MCC's next port of call.

Things were not always easy. So far from money piling up for the return trip to Mrs Smith and the next Yorkshire season – at Canberra he had to sleep in the bus shelter and twice he slept on park benches.

He saw those Test matches and, when an English player – particularly his fellow-countryman, Len Hutton – did well, he could afford to be proudly an Englishman.

In Australia evening newspapers cost threepence each; the seller's commission is twenty-five per cent. But in Melbourne paper-sellers are not allowed to sell inside the ground. So Smithy had to sell his papers outside and buy his way into the ground until the next batch of papers arrived. While the MCC side was in Tasmania Smithy sold papers outside Richmond Station at Melbourne and slowly the £100 built up.

He never had a drink or a cigarette all through that tour. His story spread round Australia and six broadcasts helped to fill his shrewd Yorkshire wallet.

As Len Hutton broke records so did his fellow-Yorkshireman Smithy – on the second day of the Adelaide Test with 1224 newspapers sold in a single day.

He bought his ticket home, presents for his family and friends and landed at Tilbury in time for the new cricket season with £7, a shy, sharp smile and a terrific layer of sunburn to prove that he had been from Leeds to Australia for a cricketing winter.

If you want another proof ask Mrs Smith behind his stall at Headingley whether she is the wife of the man who went from Leeds to Adelaide and back and, if she is not forced to tell you that her husband is too busy to be interrupted, she will be proud to introduce you: I suspect that Mrs Smith is also fond of cricket.

*Evening News (Periodic Series* 1951–54*)*

# I Shall Dine with a Legend

*June* 1951. Next Saturday I go to dinner with a legend. The occasion is the celebration of the eightieth birthday of that fabulous cricketer – 'the fastest bowler who ever lived' – Charles Kortright, of Essex and the Gentlemen of England.

There are those who would argue that the Australian Ernest Jones was faster and others would propose Neville Knox, of Surrey. We cannot assess their pace as we cannot compare the round-armed might of Alfred Mynn in the 1840s with the up-reaching swing of Larwood ninety years later. Therefore we shall be wise to accept tradition, for tradition in these matters is usually right. And tradition has labelled C. J. Kortright as the fastest of all bowlers.

Most convincing of all, perhaps, 'Korty' fills the bill perfectly as a man. Born to a comfortable, private income in an age more expansive than this generation can ever know the world was his oyster. He could do anything he liked, and he decided to be a fast bowler. It was a prodigal expenditure of his thoroughbred physique, but for him it was worthwhile. He played county cricket, on and off, for fourteen years, but his great fast-bowling reputation is based on six summers of pace so furious that no man could have maintained it longer.

In that short spell he made himself one of the immortals of the game.

Kortright bowled in the classic manner to a length on, or around, the off stump, challenging the batsman to cut a ball of such speed. He has little time for the modern talk of 'swing' or 'swerve', but his fingers bear the marks of the corns he raised by whipping in the ball that 'went with the arm', or tearing off his murderous break-back.

He once bounced a ball off the deadest of Leyton wickets to plant a giant bruise on the stomach of Dr Grace himself. He played hard, but he had his own strict standards of cricket, and taxed Lord Hawke outright – on one of his Lordship's own Yorkshire grounds – when he felt that all was not as he would have it.

He was convinced that a certain Lancashire bowler threw, so he told their captain what he proposed to do. Then, in the middle of the Lancashire innings, he ran up to the crease, stopped, and perpetrated a bare-faced throw – to prove that the umpire would not notice it!

He is still as uncompromising in his attitude to anything he thinks unreasonable or unfair, and characteristically unflinching in face of the ailments which beset a man of his age. His birthday was, in fact, a month ago. He celebrated it quietly with a few of us in talk over tea. Because he retains the true courtesy of his own period the date of this celebration dinner is related to the convenience of as many as possible of his friends, rather than to his actual birthday.

Talk to him – who is, himself, cricket history – and a half-forgotten age of the game comes to full and fully recollected life.

Ask him of that burning July day of 1898 when the City streets were blocked by cab-horses which had collapsed in the heat. That morning 'Korty' went to Lord's to play for the Gentlemen against the Players in W. G. Grace's Jubilee Match. In that heat he bowled from the start of play to lunch at, says *Wisden*, 'tremendous pace'. At the end, batting number eleven, he joined W. G. Grace and scored 46 of their last-wicket partnership of 78.

The two failed by only one minute to save the match, and then they walked in together from the wicket, those two timeless cricketers – W. G. Grace, the greatest of them all, and Charles Kortright – the fastest bowler who ever lived. *Evening News*

# Worcester Was our Symbol

*April* 1980. On 3 May 1946 a new chapter of cricket history began. Twenty-two cricketers of Worcestershire and India wrote its opening words with the match which started postwar first-class cricket. They did so in the traditional fashion of the touring side showing their initial paces in the manner established in the 1930s when Don Bradman habitually – and as he was to do again two years later – announced himself with a century.

The return of peace had different meanings for different people; of course the returning to families, homes and everyday life were the main ones. For many, though, lesser matters assumed considerable importance. Later generations must find it hard to appreciate quite the extent of the nostalgic attraction of cricket; as a symbol of returned normality for the war-weary. Nostalgic it was then, and nostalgic now in recollection of those shaded days of gratitude for the living, grief for the dead, the present and the absent of so many fields.

The New Road ground at Worcester, remembered as a place of bowlers' sweat, and easy runs before the war, was bleak that Saturday morning. Dominated by the Cathedral and lying in the arm of the Severn, it is the most felicitous of grounds in the sunshine, but now dark under the cloud, it was swept by a bitter gale howling across from Diglis. Yet such was the attraction of cricket renewed that over 8000 people – as large a crowd as any local could remember – many of them huddled into 'demob' coats, filled the ground.

Most of the Indian team had never seen England before. They had practised for a day only, in muddy nets at Lord's, and made a horribly uncomfortable journey from London in a coach which lost its way through the Midlands and deposited them at their hotel at three in the morning before the match. Few of them had ever played cricket in so low a temperature; and the bowlers, at least, must have contemplated with some pleasure the prospect of a day in the warmth of the dressing-room while their batsmen established a position, awaiting an improvement in the weather.

When their captain, the Nawab of Pataudi – a prewar batsman for Worcestershire and England – won the toss, however, he asked Worcestershire to bat. So only the five left out of the side sat, overcoated, round the pavilion stove as a shivering, multi-sweatered team plodded out into the field closely followed by the opening batsmen. Together they produced a convincing overture to the game's revival.

The heavily built Bengali, Shute Banerjee, lumbered up and bowled the first ball, which bounced sluggishly off the pitch. Singleton let it hit his bat and the first 'real' cricket match in England for six-and-a-half years had begun. Sandy Singleton and Dick Howarth were regarded as allrounders, bowlers who batted in the lower half of the order, in the days before 1940. Now, though, in the manner of men unaccustomed to enough time for long innings, they let the bat swing through healthily. According to the faded notes in an old book they put on 61 before a major Test cricketer of the future announced himself.

A bustling light-heavyweight, limber, well-balanced, quick in reaction, Vinoo Mankad was an astute, natural, allround cricketer. As a slow left-arm bowler he was already accustomed, through the heavy labour of stock bowling on the plumb wickets of India – where batting was the aristocratic portion – to spinning until his index finger bled to derive the degree of break that might disturb a good batsman.

Now he prised enough turn out of the heavy Worcester pitch, only lately relieved of the Severn floods, to beat Dick Howarth's stroke on the outside and hit his off stump. Lala Amarnath, a most immaculate medium-pace swinger; Sarwate, who bowled the leg-break and off-break but no googly; and Shinde, the long-armed leg-spinner, performed their duties with chilly responsibility.

Singleton batted with confidence and some aggression; Eddie Cooper pawkily correctly; 'Doc' Gibbons with his invariable air of ease and Reg Perks lustily. Mankad, though, had the measure of them all. Four for 26 off twenty overs presaged performances to come. Gul Mahomed at cover-point was brilliantly explosive; and Worcestershire reached as many as 191 largely because hands unaccustomed to such cold could not hold all the catches offered.

None of the watching faithful, though, was disposed to be critical; only grateful. When the Indian innings began, Perks, tall, wide-shouldered and strong, a picture of times gone, swept up on his long run and, slightly square-on by purist standards, but still menacingly, bowled faster than the pitch seemed to promise.

Weather had denied him any net practice and he was burning to bowl again. He had reached his peak in 1939. In the final Test – against the West Indies – of that last prewar season he took five for 156 in their total of 352, and always swore nine catches were dropped off him.

He was a cricketer of gusto; labelled fast-medium but at times capable of considerable pace and a fearsome bouncer. Dick Howarth's subtle flight and left-arm spin accounted for Mushtaq Ali and Amarnath before Perks bowled Vijay Merchant with a sharp inswinger which pitched middle and leg and straightened; a murderous ball; lbw.

Rusi Modi, a tall, slim Parsee, reluctantly took off his heavy overcoat and walked out, grey with cold. The ball hit his modestly handled but meticulously straight bat with monotonous certainty. Gul Mahomed played his left-handed pranks; the Nawab of Pataudi – senior, of course – batted with the assurance of old; Mankad was businesslike. India scored one more run than Worcestershire in an hour longer.

The Monday crowd, smaller than that of Saturday but equally determined to enjoy themselves, despite the north-easter, had the finest entertainment of the match. Did Singleton and Howarth really start the second Worcestershire innings on a slow wicket with a stand of 146 in an hour-and-a-half against a front line touring attack?

Upon the word of an eye-witness they did. Howarth, indeed, made 105 in only a few minutes more than two hours. Determinedly deliberate, he considered his cricket; and concealed the extent of his anxiety about it. A year later he took a wicket – of the South African Denis Dyer – with his first ball in a Test match.

He scored a second century against the 1946 Indians at the end of their tour – a spectacular 114 for Leveson-Gower's XI at Scarborough. In the same match, he took four for 38 in their first innings and in the second, during a splendid spell of only ten overs, four for 12, and had the game in his grasp when his captain, Brian Sellers, in an inexplicably ham-handed decision, took him off.

He brought him back too late before the rain came to save the match and robbed Howarth of the rare feat of a century and ten wickets in a match. Dick could catch too, and he read a game better than most. His relaxed air was deceptive; he bowled with quite remarkable stamina in the injury-shackled England side in West Indies in 1947-48. Cruelly crippled in recent years, he still followed Worcestershire cricket closely from his shop and house across the bridge from the ground. He died only a few days ago.

Gibbons made another poised and accomplished innings; Roley Jenkins, eagerly acquisitive, came by 35 invaluable runs. Otherwise Mankad again sunk his teeth into the innings; Shinde gave his leg-breaks – and a googly which stunned Syd Buller – air and much twist. Those two dealt with the rest of the batting.

So India needed 284 to win and, since Mushtaq Ali had strained a leg muscle, Mankad opened with Merchant. Peter Jackson, the off-spinner who doubled as new-ball bowler of slow-medium out-swing, bowled Mankad before the innings settled.

Merchant, compact, imperturbable, infallible punisher of the loose ball, proceeded to make a fifty so efficient he might have batted all his life in poor light on damp English wickets, and India were winning when Howarth beat him through the air for an lbw. Amarnath hooked a short ball from Perks into his face, retired bleeding, returned and mistimed a ball from Singleton who, with Perks and Jackson, worked down the batting until 177 for seven.

Banerjee came in to partner Modi, who, looking even colder than on Saturday, was languidly but utterly sound; bat all middle. They put on 78 cheerfully authoritative runs before Singleton pushed an off-break through too briskly for Modi. Still Banerjee thrashed on with supreme confidence. He was the biggest member of the team; a cheerful extrovert; given to conversation and jokes in the field, prone to little impromptu dances.

A few minutes before tea on the following Saturday, in the touring side's match with Surrey at The Oval, he and Chandu Sarwate came together at 205 for nine. Neither had scored.

By 12.30 on Monday, when Parker bowled Bannerjee, they had put on 249 in the highest last-wicket stand ever made in England; and the only occasion in cricket history when numbers ten and eleven have both scored centuries. Moreover, while there may have been two or three, but no more, in streaky strokes, the partnership was chanceless. Both had opened the innings in India; but they did not, happily for the peace of mind of English bowlers, often thus contradict the batting order.

Back at Worcester, Sarwate was soon gone, but Bannerjee thrust on in a genuine attempt to win, which brought the casuals from the bars and ended only when Perks, in characteristic indignation at tail-end impertinence, came back to bowl him with a convulsive yorker.

Worcestershire and, it should be said, the weather – had beaten the touring side by 16 runs.

If some of the players were six years out of match practice, it was splendid overcoated entertainment. Any man is entitled to remember the first match he ever reported.

This, though, was an historic occasion and, only partly through euphoria, there were many to applaud and few to complain. It was the beginning of a brief Indian summer – with 1947 as its climax – for English county cricket. In some ways it had never been quite so deeply relished before.

In many ways an age has passed in the thirty-five years since that match. Eight – or is it nine? – of those who took part are now dead. They are immortal, though, in the memories of many of that rapt, gale-harried, crowd of 1946.

For this cricket romantic, the players he watched as a young man do not even age. Indeed, they always bat or bowl as well as – or better than – they ever did, watched through the summer-tinted spectacles which are the eyes of youth. *The Guardian*


# When Laker Towered over Park Avenue

*April* 1980. The English cricket spectator is at heart partisan. He relishes rivalry, the older and more local the better. For that reason the technically finest domestic cricket matches, Test Trials, rouse little excitement and rarely attract appreciable crowds. Thus only a few people have watched some outstanding performances.

In 1923 Maurice Tate, hitherto primarily a batsman, but a run of the mill county off-spinner, suddenly emerged, at the age of twenty-eight, as the greatest of all fast-medium bowlers. The change was bred out of sheer frustration. At the end of July 1922 he had bowled long and unavailingly to that obdurate left-hander, Philip Mead, when, from his ordinary off-spinner's run he had released a faster – much faster – ball that bowled him. He began 1923 in that new style; there was no touring side in England that summer and so two Test Trials were played and Maurice Tate bowled himself into both of them.

Nearer today, in the Worcestershire Trial of 1974, Geoffrey Boycott scored a century in each innings by a technique as virtually flawless as even he has ever achieved. It is sometimes forgotten, too, that, in the same match John Edrich, without a mistake, almost emulated him with 106 and 95.

Yet it's doubtful if any of those performances were more outstanding than Jim Laker's in the Test Trial of 1950. He had been blamed – and, indeed, had been inclined to blame himself – for England's failure to beat Bradman's Australians in the Headingley Test of 1948. In fact, though, the late decision to leave out the second spinner and the missing of seven chances (three from Bradman off Laker) were powerful contributory factors.

His talent was unquestionable. During the war, stories had come back to England of the young off-spinner playing Services cricket in Egypt whose spin was such that the batsman at the non-striking end heard the ball buzz as it left his fingers. With peace, post-war cricketing England saw him, like Trueman a year or two later, as something of a symbol of the new age of the English game. Indeed, he was chosen for the arduous 1947–48 tour of West Indies after only fourteen first-class matches.

So, although finger-spin is traditionally associated with wide and deep experience of the craft, he had to take some technical short cuts. He had, though, never compromised in the matter of spin or length. After Headingley he was dropped from the team for the Fifth Test; was not taken on the South African tour of the following winter and was chosen for only one of the four New Zealand Tests of 1949.

So he had a place to win when he was picked for the 1950 Test Trial at Bradford. That is one of the most honest cricket pitches in the world. In normal conditions it is a fine wicket for strokemaking; but, after rain, drying conditions will stir it into a true 'sticky'; as both the 1948 Australian and the 1950 West Indian sides discovered to their alarm in their games with Yorkshire.

The two teams included five of the young University batsmen – Hubert Doggart, Peter May, John Dewes and David Sheppard from Cambridge, and Donald Carr of Oxford who had been making so many runs on good wickets, especially those at Fenner's. The nominated twelfth man was the Hampshire opener, Neville Rogers, always a skilful player of off-spin and who, four years later, carried his bat for MCC against Surrey at Lord's when Laker was at his most destructive. Although two of the original selections dropped out, however, replacements were drafted in, and Rogers remained twelfth man.

31 May 1950 was a chilly day in Bradford with a scattered crowd taking shelter from the wind on the Park Avenue ground, only five miles from Shipley, where Jim Laker was born. He had been noticed and coached by Yorkshire as a promising batsman for Saltaire before the war but, after he left to join the army at the age of eighteen, he never returned to the county. Now, his father and mother were dead; he was established in the south; and an elderly aunt was his only remaining relative in the district.

It was argued afterwards that, if the match was to be of any value to the selectors, the pitch should have been covered, or England, instead of the Rest, should have batted. The wicket, though, had been left open to the rain and now it was drying under the influence of wind and fitful sunshine; while the England captain, Norman Yardley, could also regard himself as on trial. So, lacking any instructions from the selectors to the contrary, he put the Rest in to bat.

Jim Laker went out to look at the pitch, recognized its character; and knew precisely what he had to do. Yardley kept on Trevor Bailey and Alec Bedser long enough to dispose of David Sheppard before he called up Laker, who set an attacking leg-side field, went round the wicket and pitched length and line at once.

Never a demonstrative cricketer, he was now in his element and at his most noncommittal. Tongue in cheek, he strolled back to his mark at his characteristic constabulary gait; looked up to the sky as he turned and then jogged the approach he used artfully to vary, constantly changing the number of steps so as, often, to defeat the batsman's timing.

Although Laker was a master of flight, he understood only too well that he did not need it now. He gave the ball little or no air, the batsmen no time to move out to him. Only Don Kenyon shaped remotely convincingly at him. The young men relied on the forward defensive push, but it was not enough. The ball leapt and turned spitefully. In his first over Hubert Doggart and Peter May were picked up at short-leg and still not a run had been scored from Laker when Donald Carr went in the same way.

Faced with a dilemma when Eric Bedser came in at number six, he could hardly fail to give his county team mate a friendly 'one off the mark' and wheeled up a full toss. Eric carefully pushed it to mid-on where his brother Alec had thoughtfully moved four or five yards deeper than necessary, and took a single. Kenyon, deceived by a ball which went with the arm, was caught at the wicket by Godfrey Evans; Eric Bedser lbw to one which hurried through; Dick Spooner and Bob Berry bowled 'through the gate', before Fred Trueman inside-edged a single and then was stumped off the returning Alec Bedser. To complete his morning Laker picked up a savage drive to catch and bowl Les Jackson.

Ten minutes before lunch the Rest were out for 27, the lowest total ever made in a representative match. For an hour and a half of perfect and hostile spin bowling, Laker's figures were fourteen overs; twelve maidens; two runs; eight wickets; bettered statistically only by the nine for two of a certain Gidean Elliott, once described as 'the fastest and straightest bowler in Australia' for Victoria against Tasmania in 1857–58.

The local boy had made good. No one from his youth was there on a working-day morning to share the moment with him: but the England team and the Rest batsmen who had been his victims formed up to applaud him into the pavilion, with unmistakably whole-hearted admiration.

In the afternoon Len Hutton played an innings of superb virtuosity against the pace of Len Jackson and Fred Trueman, the cut of Alec Bedser, the leg-spin of Roly Jenkins and the slow left-arm of Bob Berry. Although the wicket had eased a little, the spun ball still turned sharply but Hutton was at his masterly best, playing in complete sympathy with the break, seeming, indeed, to harness it to his stroke. Reggie Simpson made a typically poised 26 off the fast bowlers; Bill Edrich a determined 46; but Hutton's 85, before he became Trueman's only wicket of the match, was a masterpiece.

Bob Berry's five for 73 took him into the First Test but could not save the game for the Rest. Eric Bedser made a capable 30 and Spooner 20 but Eric Hollies, with six for 28, bowled them out a second time and, before lunch on the second day, England had won by an innings and 89 runs.

After that performance Laker could hardly be left out of the First Test against West Indies but his one wicket for 86, after injuring his hand while batting when Hollies and Berry bowled England to a win on the dusty pitch at Old Trafford, was not enough to keep him in the side. Overwhelmed by the batting of Everton Weekes, Frank Worrell, Clyde Walcott and Allan Rae, England were heavily beaten in the three remaining Tests.

No one who played with or against him would dispute that Jim Laker was the finest off-spinner, certainly of his own time, probably of any. Yet, amazingly, while England played ninety-nine Tests between his first and last appearance, he took part in only forty-six of them: went only once to Australia and once to South Africa.

His nineteen wickets against Australia at Old Trafford which surely will never be equalled and another 'all ten' against them for Surrey, of course, lay still six years into the future from Bradford. Then, in 1956, he took forty-six Australian Test wickets at 9.60 and virtually won the series by his own efforts.

He probably took equal pleasure from his figures in Australia in 1958–59. A number of the Australians believed that the English pitches of 1953 and 1956 had been 'cooked' for him; and several declared they would murder him on their own pitches. He took immense tactical thought before he went on that tour. Although the cruelly arthritic finger which eventually ended his career prevented him playing at Adelaide in an England side beaten by four matches to none, he bowled more overs, took more wickets and had a better Test average than any other English bowler. That gave him immense, though unspoken, satisfaction.

Reminded of the Bradford eight for two, he recalls with a wry grin the question of a local reporter: 'Are these your best bowling figures, Mr Laker?'                                                        *The Guardian*

# The Taming of Ram and Val

*April* 1980. The balance of international cricket generally changes slowly. Only rarely do spectators see the history of the game reshaped under their eyes within hours rather than years. Yet that happened twice in a decade of England–West Indies Test matches.

When John Goddard brought his side to England in 1950, West Indies had never won a Test match – let alone a series – in their three tours of England. The fact that they had never lost a rubber in their own country, where they had won two and drawn one, was not widely realized by a public which had barely heard of, and never seen, Everton Weekes, Clyde Walcott or Frank Worrell.

Certainly, even the cricket buffs of England knew nothing of the two young spin bowlers, Alf Valentine and Sonny Ramadhin who had played only two first-class games each before they were chosen for the tour. There was little apparently to disturb the general complacency – or blissful ignorance – when England won the First Test, played on an explosive dust-heap at Old Trafford.

In order to adjust the imbalance between bat and ball, the groundsman there had been instructed to use less hose and roller. Now, after a week of baking sun, the finger-spun ball leapt off a length. Indeed, Valentine, slow left-arm, often made it bite so sharply as to fly over the shoulder of even as tall a wicket-keeper as Walcott.

Valentine, in his first Test, took the first eight English wickets, his second eight in an innings on the ground that week (eight for 26 against Lancashire). England were lifted from the ignominy of 88 for five by a daring innings of 104 by Godfrey Evans and a dogged 82 by Trevor Bailey. The spin bowling of Eric Hollies and Bob Berry – seventeen wickets between them – gave England a comfortable win by 202 runs, to the apparent surprise of none.

So, to Lord's where, although the left-handed Allan Rae held their innings together with a patient 106, a West Indian total of 326 seemed no great cause for concern on a true batting pitch. Surely enough, in the first hour, Hutton and Washbrook made 43 for the first wicket against

Prior Jones and Hines Johnson without undue alarm when Ramadhin and Valentine took over the bowling.

Ramadhin, a tiny, neatly made Trinidadian of Indian and West Indian extraction, bowled mainly off-breaks but, from needle-strong fingers, he delivered a leg-break without observable change of action. The two differed in arc and some, Jim Sims for instance, could 'pick' the leg-break infallibly from sideways on.

Like S. F. Barnes – of vastly different physique and pace – he spun the ball from between the stretched index and middle fingers. In frequently poor English light – especially at Lord's where there was no sightscreen at the Nursery End – batsmen found it impossible to read the turn of the fingers in the quick wheel of the fully sleeved arm.

The perpetually smiling Valentine, from Jamaica, plodded up as if his boots were filled with lead, and gave his orthodox left arm such a fierce wrench that his calloused spinning finger frequently bled. At first he was almost slavishly unvarying, pushing it through at slow-medium, with little subtlety of flight. He became skilled, though, in the use of the ball which went with his arm and, sparingly used, often proved effective.

Twenty-three runs came off their first six overs before they suddenly took a grip on the play with five consecutive maidens. Hutton was clearly resolved to hit Valentine off; three times he went down the pitch to him only to check his stroke. The fourth time, Valentine bowled wide and short – and Walcott could take his time about the stumping. In the next quarter-hour to lunch, Ramadhin and Valentine bowled seven overs and four balls to Washbrook and Edrich without a run being taken from them: at lunch England were 62 for one.

The afternoon play was a cruel awakening for the Lord's crowd. Perhaps the nearest experience of the kind in this country was that of the soccer defeat – England's first by a foreign team on a home ground – by Hungary in 1953. Then, as now, the opposition was manifestly and dishearteningly superior.

Valentine was at his mark waiting to bowl when Edrich took guard in the afternoon and played his second ball for a single. He did not score again for almost an hour. Washbrook drove Ramadhin for four and then, moving down to repeat the stroke, was beaten by an off-break and stumped. Doggart, all at sea with Ramadhin, was lbw to a leg-break which straightened; 60 for no wicket had become 74 for three.

Parkhouse of Glamorgan, the in-form batsman of the season, came out to partner Edrich and, as the crowd's incredulity gave way, first to anxiety and then to acute tension, those two played back eight consecutive maidens before Edrich dabbed Valentine for a single. Parkhouse, faced at last by bowling he could 'read', swung cross-batted and was bowled.

Edrich hoisted a signal of defiance with a four off Ramadhin before he and Yardley were clamped in a run of six maidens by bowlers who bustled in eagerly to bowl their overs at a rapid rate. An infinitesimal flurry of six runs and Edrich, drawn cruelly forward by Ramadhin's dipping leg-break, edged to Walcott who had had space, too, to have stumped him. The scoreboard showed England 86 for five, last man eight. Still the two spinners wheeled away, attacking so fiercely and accurately as to contain as well as threaten.

Ramadhin bowled Evans; Valentine dealt with Yardley and Jenkins; Ramadhin bowled Bedser; but Wardle swung his bat for a hectic 33 until Goddard brought back Jones to break the last-wicket stand by having Berry taken at slip. In four hours ten minutes England were put out for 151; and, in an hour less, Ramadhin (five for 66) and Valentine (four for 48) had bowled between them 88 overs; 55 of them maidens.

Towering above even such amazing figures, the giant fact was that, even on a good batting pitch, the English batsmen had been baffled and beaten. Walcott made 168 not out, Weekes 63, Gomez 70 and Worrell 45 in West Indies' 425 for six when Goddard's declaration left England 601 to win. Washbrook (114), with high professionalism (he treated Ramadhin strictly as an off-spinner), and Parkhouse, who played his own stroke-making game, put on 83 for the third wicket, but England were 218 for four at the end of Monday.

On Tuesday, as West Indians from all over London and further afield gathered on the Nursery End stands, Ramadhin and Valentine took afresh their strangling grip on the batting. The last six wickets went down for 56 runs. In the second English innings, they sent down 143 overs; 90 maidens and took nine wickets for 165 runs. West Indies had won, handsomely and historically, their first Test in England by 326 and their supporters flooded across the ground in such a carnival of triumph, joy and calypsos such as Lord's had never known before.

By the time they reached Trent Bridge they were known all over England, not only for their bowling but, even among the non-sports-minded, for the calypso 'Cricket Lovely Cricket' that 'Lord Beginner' had composed in their honour immediately after the Lord's Test.

Yardley took first innings and, on a 'green' first-morning pitch, England, without Hutton, his chosen deputy, Harold Gimblett, Denis Compton and Edrich, went down before the seam bowling of Jones and Johnson for 223.

As the pitch eased, West Indies (Worrell 261, Weekes 129) took a lead of 335, and also relishing the improved conditions, Simpson, Washbrook, Parkhouse and Dewes all made good scores after their first-innings failures. 'Ram' and 'Val', as they were now tagged, worked harder than ever: 173.2 overs; 74 maidens; eight wickets for 275 and the West Indies won by ten wickets.

They laboured again at The Oval where Hutton carried his bat through the first English innings with 202; but, even then, 344 left them 159 behind. In the second innings Hutton could not save them: all out for 103 (Ramadhin and Valentine fourteen for 261 in the match). They were beaten by an innings and 56.

Altogether in the four-match rubber the spinners' figures were: Valentine 422.3 overs, 197 maidens, 674 runs, 33 wickets; Ramadhin 377.5 overs; 170 maidens; 604 runs; 26 wickets. The other eight bowlers took eighteen wickets between them.

In the tied series with Len Hutton's team in West Indies in 1953–54, Valentine (seven wickets) was less successful but, even in that bright light and on hard wickets, the puzzle of Ramadhin remained unsolved. He had twenty-three wickets – no other West Indian took more than eight – and was the effective match winner in the First and Second Tests.

The story of 1950 promised to be repeated when the pair returned in 1957 and, together or singly, killed off the batting of Worcestershire, Northamptonshire, Oxford University (Ramadhin thirteen for 48), Cambridge and Yorkshire before the First Test at Edgbaston. There, Valentine, despite his successes against the counties, was left out and the supporting spin came from Denis Atkinson, Garfield Sobers, and Collie Smith.

Roy Gilchrist, a bowler of fiery speed, had Brian Close caught at the wicket before Goddard called up Ramadhin. Like the re-run of a well-remembered film, he baffled one English batsman after another. There was no one quite so relentlessly efficient as the Valentine of 1950 at the other end: but Ramadhin hardly needed anyone. While 92 runs were scored, the next seven English batsmen – Peter Richardson, Doug Insole, Peter May, Colin Cowdrey, Trevor Bailey, Tony Lock and Jim Laker – puzzled, at times baffled, were probed and beaten by his cunningly flicked spin. Occasionally the off-spinner, more often the leg-break, turned: he seemed to take most of his wickets with the ball that went quickly through while the batsmen on the back foot played for the turn.

Certainly he was not the same bowler as in 1950; his arm action had changed noticeably. There was none, though, to fault the man who had taken seven for 49 and England were all out for 186. Again in ponderous recall of 1950, Walcott and Worrell batted commandingly: so did the young Sobers, while the boyishly joyous Collie Smith – all too soon to be tragically killed – scored a century in his first Test against England. A total of 474 gave them a lead of 288 with half the afternoon left on Saturday.

A cautious start by Peter Richardson and Brian Close was ended, and all the old torment repeated, when at 63 Richardson guessed wrongly at Ramadhin; and, in his next over, Insole was bowled by an off-break. Close, handicapped by a bruised hand, and May, saw out the day at 102 for two, but the exultant reaction of the many West Indian spectators reflected the course they and the English supporters expected the game to take.

That evening, and again on Sunday, some extremely knowledgeable former and current English cricketers discussed the crucial question of Ramadhin at considerable length. Bill Bowes, once a Yorkshire and England fast bowler, by then cricket correspondent of the *Yorkshire Evening Post*, was one convinced that Ramadhin's now psychological as well as technical advantage could best be countered by treating him as an off-spinner and playing forward.

To accept the plan of campaign was one matter, to implement it, another. After a quarter-of-an-hour of Monday, Close edged Gilchrist to slip; Cowdrey came in to May; and Ramadhin began to wheel his arm. Cowdrey played massively forward; all care, left pad and patience. From time to time May rolled out a stroke commanding enough to keep the field at arm's length but the two were almost painfully watchful. Gradually they grew into assurance but they never relaxed their extreme watchfulness against Ramadhin. To be sure, Worrell did not bowl at all in the English innings and Gilchrist, too, was injured. Nevertheless, with Atkinson, Sobers, Smith and himself available, Goddard certainly bowled Ramadhin too much.

As the huge partnership between May and Cowdrey grew, changing the shape and mood of the match, Ramadhin himself began to look puzzled. His frustration grew as he rapped unavailingly against Cowdrey's outthrust left pad.

England were by no means safe but gradually it dawned on everyone there that, not simply this match, but the series and, perhaps the entire mystery of Ramadhin, were being resolved. Ramadhin's figures on that historic Monday were 48 overs; 20 maidens; 74 runs; no wickets. After Close was out in the first half hour, no wicket fell all day. May moved comfortably past his unavailingly against Cowdrey's was 78 at the close of play; and England 378 for three.

When play restarted on Tuesday, they were no more than 90 ahead: their position still critical. So the two batsmen continued down the morning; Cowdrey reached his century in only a little short of eight hours but then, as the situation eased, he played more freely. When he lofted Smith to the substitute at long-on, he and May had put on 411, a Test record for the fourth wicket. A few brisk runs with Evans and May declared. He had seen the score from 65 for two to 583 for four; his 285 was the highest score in postwar Test cricket; and he had made a game which had seemed lost, safe for England.

Crucially, even historically, Ramadhin had at last been mastered. With no reward since the wicket of Insole on Saturday afternoon, he had the greatest number of balls (588). *The Guardian*

# Year that the Counties Played on . . .

*October* 1983. The 'first-class averages' used to apply to matches in which a majority of the players were of first-class status. Now they cover the three-day Championship and five-day Test matches which the county players themselves regard as 'businesses'.

Indeed, the county figures take no note of the over-limit matches, although last summer the top cricketers took part in fewer Championship games than – outstandingly – the World (Prudential) Cup, the John Player Sunday League, the NatWest Bank Trophy and the Benson & Hedges Cup – the competitions where, even at international level, there is no true regard for the professional criteria which allow a batsman to build an innings and demand that a bowler attacks.

It cannot be said too often that, while over-limit cricket is an entertainment – and has proved a financial lifeline to the counties – it is not the real game. That may be proved by the single fact that in over-limit play a team does better to restrict its opponents to 100 runs for no wicket than to bowl them out for 101.

The English summer of 1983 saw seven visiting countries here for the World Cup and, in the county game, the now significant number of overseas players imported by the counties – a substantial proportion of the West Indian Test side, a few Pakistanis, and, increasingly, South Africans.

It is revealing to look back to the last season of 'pure' County Championship cricket in 1927. True, a New Zealand team toured England that year, but they played no Tests and the main fixtures of the summer were the Test Trial matches and Gentlemen v Players. The Championship was based on as many fixtures as the counties would, or wanted to, arrange.

Points were awarded; eight for a win; five for a first-innings lead in a drawn match; three to the side *behind* on the first innings in a draw – ! – four to each side in a tie, and four each for a game in which there was less than six hours' play and no decision on first innings. The order was decided on percentage of points gained to maximum possible.

Yorkshire, Lancashire, Notts, Sussex and Worcestershire had fixture lists of 28 matches; others between 26 and the 20 of Middlesex and Derbyshire.

Competition for the title was extremely close; indeed it went for decision to the final match, when Nottinghamshire had only to avoid defeat by Glamorgan – who had not won a match all season – only, in the most amazing result of the summer, to lose by an innings.

The Yorkshire fixture list, including three games outside the Championship, did not allow their players a single day off (apart from Sundays) between 4 May and 2 September. Although one of their matches was abandoned without a ball bowled, still eight of them appeared in 30 or more; three others in 26, 28, 29.

In an attempt to help bowlers and reduce the dominance of batsmen the wicket was made an inch higher and an inch wider. The size of the ball was reduced to between $8\frac{3}{16}$ and nine inches in diameter. Individually, though, Walter Hammond, who had been prevented by illness from playing at all in 1926, returned to score 1000 runs in May. Philip Mead of Hampshire became the fourth man to score a hundred centuries. Alf Dipper of Gloucestershire played 53 first-class innings; 'Dodge' Whysall of Nottinghamshire and Jack Russell of Essex, 50. Eleven men scored more than 2000 (Hammond 2969 at 69.04); and Douglas Jardine, with only 14 innings, was top of the averages with 1002 at 91.09.

Among the bowlers Charlie Parker – like this season's hard labourer, Norman Gifford, slow left-arm – sent down 1727 overs; Maurice Tate, at lively fast-medium, 1569; and 11 others, more than 1000. Effectively top of the bowling was Harold Larwood, with 100 wickets at 16.95 before he suffered an injury so serious that his entire future seemed in jeopardy. Included in the averages were George Cox of Sussex at 53 and Percy Perrin (Essex) 51.

After a splendid start with bright sun and fast wickets (in May five different batsmen scored two centuries in a match) the summer became desperately wet: 97 whole days were lost, five games were completely rained off. So, in the absence of Test revenue, few counties made a profit but still the editor of *Wisden* could note that: 'Thanks to increased membership most of them could meet their troubles more or less satisfactorily.' In our times, of course, the loss of a single season's Test income would leave a majority of the counties bankrupt.

At the end of the summer the Yorkshire committee named Herbert Sutcliffe as county captain for 1928. At once two different partisan groups protested, one at the idea of appointing a professional, the other at his choice in preference to Wilfred Rhodes (now forty-nine). The problem was resolved by Sutcliffe, who cabled from South Africa expressing his pride at the honour, but declining to undertake the office, while declaring his willingness to serve under any other captain. Captain W. A. Worsley was appointed instead.

Most interestingly by present-day standards, at the end of the New Zealander's tour, Cecil Dacre, a splendid attacking batsman with the tourists, approached Gloucestershire – his father's native county – with a view to playing for them. The editor of *Wisden* observed sternly: 'It is satisfactory to learn that the first steps in this arrangement did not come from Gloucestershire.' The regulations of the time, however, required Dacre to qualify by residence – until 1930.

In the previous year at The Oval, England had won The Ashes from Australia; and there was a splendid wealth of talent in the country. In the Test Trial at Lord's, the England side was: Jack Hobbs, Herbert Sutcliffe, Charlie Hallows, Walter Hammond, Frank Woolley, Vallance Jupp, Douglas Jardine, Maurice Tate, Harold Larwood, 'Tich' Freeman, Walter Livsey. They made 461 for six declared. The Rest were: Andrew Sandham, Percy Holmes, 'Young' Jack Hearne, Patsy Hendren, Lou Bates, Errol Homes, Leslie Ames, Guy Jackson, George Geary, Frank Sibbles, 'Nobby' Clark.

All of them except Bates, whose attractive 49 was highest score but one for the Rest; Sibbles, their most successful bowler; and Livsey, who allowed only eight byes in the two innings of the Rest, and who was robbed of a Test place by illness, eventually played for England.

Somewhere between the two lies reality, and the ideal English cricket season; but who shall say where? *The Guardian*

# Dear Old Ken

It was the last day of the match: of course, it would be. The game had run until well after six: of course it would. The piece was difficult to write: of course it would be. The car would not start: of course it would not. Lifting the bonnet was like flying a flag of distress; apart from the radiator cap and the old gauge, what it revealed was meaningless.

The consequence – abandoning the damned thing until a local garage – probably not to be contacted until next day – could collect it; then waiting while it was repaired, making arrangements to collect it; and a Test match lay only a day ahead – piled heavily on the skull. Then, all at once, a cheerfully semi-cockney voice lifted the depression with 'Hulloh, mate, what's wrong then, eh, won't she go?' It was Ken Barrington, rolling along with his bag; all toothily cheerful grin.

'You don't know too much about it, do you?'

'No – nothing, Ken.'

'Move over, then.'

Apart from human beings, cricket was by far his first major enthusiasm but motor cars were unquestionably the second. There followed a description of that particular car, its engine, its shortcomings – and merits – and an examination of what seemed to be the present problem. A nearby bench was requisitioned as a resting place for screws, nuts, washers and the other objects gradually exhumed from the innards of the mechanism. The light began to go.

A suggestion that it would be a good idea to ring the AA or a garage met with – 'No, don't worry; by the time they get here I shall have it done.'

The light failed: a torch was produced. Car owners humbly brought beer from nearby bar. Beer ignored by now deeply involved mechanical investigator.

It took a solid hour and a half; then, face suffused in 'triumph, the technician tugged the starter wire and everything burst into action. Then the beer could be poured down with the air of one who had earned it. Would he come into the pub, have 'the other half' and wash the oil off his hands. Already, though, he was swabbing off the grime with a cloth and petrol. No, no, it was too late, and he far to go – further, in fact, than the beneficiary of his skill. *Please*. No, another time, perhaps. Spluttering, respectful gratitude; *so* grateful; what *should* I have done without you? What can I do? 'Nothing, just don't give it another think, mate.' Kind as they have ever come: there were better batters – but not many if they were playing for your life – but, surely, none who was so well liked by so many. Dear old Ken.                                   *The Guardian*


# Back to Cricket's Second Base

The peripatetic cricketers of *The Guardian* do well to go to America. The first 'local' cricket recorded outside Britain was in America, probably in 1656 (New York); certainly in 1709 (Virginia).

The first English cricket team to go overseas was taken by George Parr to Canada and the United States in 1859.

It was an extremely strong one of twelve professionals (eleven to play and one to stand umpire) who won all their eight matches – all against odds – and played some exhibitions. In the second innings of the match with a United States XXII, Caffyn took sixteen wickets for 24 runs. Wisden, against XXII of the United States and Canada, took sixteen for 14 and thirteen for 43.

The touring players were contracted for £50 a man but, although the last match, at Rochester on 21 and 24 October, was played in heavy snow, attendances were so good that they were eventually paid £90 each.

On the way from Canada to New York the side was taken to see the Niagara Falls where John Jackson, the Nottinghamshire fast bowler, being told that 1,500,000 gallons a second flowed over the Falls, said, 'Ay, ah wouldn't dispute it; ye see theer's nowt to stop it.'

It seems that plans were made for another team to visit the United States in 1861. The outbreak of the Civil War precluded it and by the end of it, baseball – so much simpler for soldiers to play in open country – had become the national game of America.

So the second English party to America did not go until 1868. Captained by Edgar Willsher of Kent and playing entirely against odds, it won five of its six matches; the other was left unfinished through rain.

The touring side's pace bowlers proved all but unplayable. Willsher – 'left armed; fast and ripping round-armed with a twist from the leg to the off' – had analyses such as eleven for 27, fourteen for 23; George Freeman, of Yorkshire, whom both Richard Daft and W. G. Grace described as the best fast bowler they ever played against, took twelve for 27, twelve for 12, fourteen for 15, and thirteen for 9; George Tarrant-Wood, who always played as George Tarrant (only 5 feet 7 inches and 9 stone 7 lbs – 'a spare-built man, though strong, a very fine fast round-armed bowler'), took twelve for 16, when at last he managed to get on.

The pitches were poor. That at Boston was described as 'the most "duffing" one ever seen; the wicket was laid with thick, coarse, grassy turf with holes in it big enough to lose the ball'. Much of the opposition, though, was also poor. XXII of Canada, for instance, were beaten on the first innings by extras alone; Freeman and Willsher put them out for 28; and the Canadians bowled thirty wides; they must have been grateful that rain washed out the match.

Prophetically, the strongest opposition came from Philadelphia, soon to become the major centre of American cricket; already their XXII were 'All but one native-born Americans'.

They included four Newhall brothers, of whom Charles took eight for 57 and six for 30. He bowled fast, deliberately and consistently short – what he called 'rib roasters' – with the effective variant of an extremely accurate yorker described as 'Charlie's white alley'. His quality is indicated by the fact that, of the 159 wickets credited to Philadelphian bowlers against ten 'foreign' teams between Willsher's in 1868 and Roller's in 1886, Charles Newhall took 80; an amazing proportion.

In 1873, R. A. Fitzgerald, the secretary of MCC, raised a twelve-strong amateur side which, with some outstanding cricketers, including W. G. Grace, was unbeaten in its nine games. Their travelling expenses were paid and hospitality was provided, frequently to banquet standard; while *Scores & Biographies* notes, blandly enough: 'For each match, each gentleman cricketer received from their opponents 600 dollars in gold.'

It affords an ironic comparison with the professionals' £90 for an entire tour, and may explain the fact that all twelve amateurs took part in several fixtures. S&B records, too, that 'Mr Grace, as usual, showed he far outshone all other cricketers past and present; he was unwell for some time, but his play continued wonderful.'

It seems to have been an extremely convivial tour and Fitzgerald wrote a Victorian period-piece account of the tour called Wickets in the West. He observed of one match, 'The spirited New Englanders did their best to win and nearly won. We are of opinion that, with one or two exceptions, the Twelve did their best to lose, and nearly lost.' W. G. Grace was the figurehead of the tour and was in constant demand to make speeches.

His first consisted of, 'Gentlemen, I beg to thank you for the honour you have done me. I never saw better bowling than I have seen today and I hope to see as good wherever I go.' It proved popular with an audience impatient of long speeches, and he retained it throughout the tour, simply substituting for 'bowling', 'fielding', 'ground', 'batting', 'good fellows', 'ladies', and, at the last, 'oysters'.

He was only once in difficulties, replying to a speaker who had referred at some length to the three Graces; W. G. regretted that his sisters were not there to reply for themselves.

Despite the growing popularity of baseball, cricket in the United States flourished; and received many visitors. A number of Australian sides returned home by way of America. In their matches with them, Philadelphia achieved an honourable draw against D. W. Gregory's side of 1878 which had beaten MCC. They beat the – extremely travel-weary – 1893 team; lost a three match rubber to Trott's 1896 team by two–one.

The 1932 Australians, including Bradman, met strong Illinois Association sides (cricket has been played in Chicago since 1876). In four innings against XVIIIs of Illinois, Bradman was put out for 4, 6, 13, and 41.

A team from Ireland toured the United States in 1879; another from West Indies in 1886. Between 1884 and 1908 the Gentlemen of Phila-delphia came to England five times, meeting strong opposition in matches accepted as first-class.

Their outstanding player was J. B. – 'Bart' – King, accounted the finest of all American cricketers and described by Sir Pelham Warner as 'one of the greatest bowlers of his or any other time'.

On the Philadelphian tour of 1908 he was top of the English first-class averages with 87 wickets at 11.03. Tall, strong, fast-medium in pace, he bowled most dangerously a late inswinger; and he was an immense competitor.

In a match between his club, Belmont, and Trenton, the opposing captain missed a train and arrived only in time to bat at number eleven. Apologizing, he averred his team would not have been in such a plight if he had been there earlier. King heard him, and ordered his ten fieldsmen off the field. As an afterthought he called back one man and posted him twenty yards behind the stumps and four paces to leg. Asked why he wanted a fieldsman there he answered, 'He's not a fieldsman; he is there to pick up the ball and return it to the umpire'.

Surely enough the first ball hit the leg stump and rolled to the non-fieldsman, who discharged his appointed duty. On another occasion, against a side which had lost seven wickets, King sent off all his fieldsmen except the wicket-keeper and took the remaining three wickets in four balls for no runs.

Lately some good cricket has been played by West Indians who have come to New York to work. The last major 'native' development occurred in Hollywood.

Sir Aubrey Smith, C. A. Smith to *Wisden*, was known to the cricketers of his time as 'Round the corner Smith' because he bowled his fast-medium from a slanting approach, appearing surprisingly from behind the umpire.

He played for Charterhouse, Cambridge University, Sussex and the Gentlemen; captained Sussex, Shaw and Shrewsbury's 1887–88 team to Australia and the English side which, in 1888–89, played what was later accepted as the first Test matches in South Africa; and then stayed on to captain Transvaal against Kimberley in the first Currie Cup match.

He made a reputation as a stage actor in England and then, to the delight of producers and casting directors in Hollywood, made a world reputation in films as the personification of the patrician Englishman.

Not in emphasis of that reputation, but out of enthusiasm, he founded the Hollywood Cricket Club in which he was joined by Ronald Coleman and others of varying acting and cricketing ability.

In this atmosphere the *Guardian* cricketers should prosper: watch them: they should watch themselves.

*The* Manchester Guardian *Cricketer*

# This English Summer
# Fails to Save Australians

28 *August* 1968. No Test match in England has gone to such a dramatically close finish since Hirst and Rhodes won Jessop's match of 1902 on

the same Oval pitch where England yesterday beat Australia by 226 runs with a bare five minutes to spare. So the rubber is tied: Australia have retained the Ashes, but England have found some compensation for the frustrations of Lord's and Edgbaston.

Only a little earlier, though, it had seemed that, for the third time in the series, rain which wiped out the afternoon's play had destroyed England's winning position and, even half an hour from the end, Australia looked safe. Cowdrey, however, drove on into the extra half hour and amazingly – for there was nothing in the pitch to account for it – the last five Australian wickets fell in 31 minutes before a small but intent, tense, easily irritated, but eventually delighted crowd.

Inverarity, rising above anything else he has done on the tour, was the core of the Australian resistance. First in, last out, he was cool and steady to the end. For England, Underwood – sympathetically captained by Cowdrey – took seven wickets for 50 in his best Test bowling performance in strategy and effect as well as statistically.

The pitch, before the storm, was generally as gentle as on the four preceding days: but the spinners could turn, though only slowly; there was no pace or movement for the faster bowlers. At the pavilion end, however, there were a few worn spots about Underwood's normal length from which the ball would both lift and turn unnaturally. After the rain, which bound up the earlier spots, it was even easier – mild in pace and giving no observable turn.

The morning play broke rapidly into action. Inverarity played Snow coolly and, surprisingly for one with such a pronounced onside bias, cut him perfectly for four. With Lawry and Redpath out overnight, the English players must have seen Chappell as the chief obstacle to their progress. He had failed in the first innings, but never twice in any previous Test of the series. He had made only one scoring stroke, however, when he played back to Underwood instead of forward, as is his defensive habit, and was lbw.

Walters, playing 'off the pitch' as they say, made some rapid late adjustments, but few batsmen would have survived the ball from Underwood which pitched on a spot in line with the stumps and spat up and across him, took the outside edge and gave Knott a sharp chest-high catch.

Twenty-nine for four read like the beginning of collapse but Inverarity – playing studiously straight, bat beside pad and with an air of calm purpose – and Sheahan – less at ease, but correct and careful – applied themselves to occupation of the crease.

For Underwood, Cowdrey set a quite remarkable field of two slips, gully, silly-point, silly mid-off and, on the leg side, two, sometimes three, short legs all within four yards of the bat: all brave men, likely to have an intimidating effect on the batsmen but perhaps a little too close to be reliable in catching. Illingworth was content with two short legs, silly mid-on, slip and gully as he wheeled away for less than one run an over.

Inverarity, intent on guarding the line of his stumps, kept neatly out of trouble from the ball which, once in most overs from Underwood, turned and leapt; while Sheahan played some bold strokes in an attempt to break up the close field. They had endured almost an hour – and Inverarity had survived a sharp chance to Dexter, perilously close at silly-point – when Sheahan, attempting to break away from Illingworth's tight rein, pulled him and was well caught, low down on the run at mid-wicket, by Snow.

Jarman, quick in footwork and determined, played back hazardously but effectively to Illingworth and stayed with Inverarity until, two minutes before lunch, the thunderstorm broke. At that point Australia, 86 for five, were 265 behind and 210 minutes remained for play.

When, after a remarkable mass effort by the groundstaff and some fifty volunteers, the ground was fit for play, it was a quarter to five and the only possibility of a finish seemed to lie in freakish behaviour of the wet pitch. It was, however, deeply soaked and there was no sun to form a top crust that the spin bowlers might use.

No one bowled two consecutive overs of the first five from the pavilion end. For Underwood at the other, the entire team except the bowler stood virtually shoulder to shoulder in the close-catching positions: for Illingworth there was a single man saving the one. Inverarity played with admirable aplomb, Jarman a little more anxiously; once or twice one of the close fieldsmen dived forward in the attempt to snatch up a ball lofted a few inches from the bat before it touched the ground. But gradually England's hopes of winning were fading: only Cowdrey went questingly on, unable to believe that the weather could thwart him again. D'Oliveira was the fifth bowler and the sixth change in forty minutes: he floated a ball gently away from Jarman's forward stroke to hit the off bail and at once Cowdrey brought back Underwood in his place.

Underwood could not turn the ball as he had done in the morning but he worked away, varying pace, length and line. His second ball to Mallett topped and flew to Brown at forward short leg. In gradually mounting tension, McKenzie pushed forward and Brown, diving at short leg, caught a ball which was never more than a couple of inches from the ground.

Twice Illingworth found the edge of Inverarity's bat with the ball which went with his arm, but each time it flew untouched between wicket-keeper and slip, and now – with twenty-five minutes left – he and Gleeson set out sensibly to save the game, occasionally forcing through the close field, contriving that Inverarity had most of the bowling. Eventually, however, Underwood – bowling round the wicket – pinned down Gleeson, who proceeded to play him with his pads: Underwood switched to over the wicket, but Cowdrey waved him back to the other side and with his next ball he bowled Gleeson off stump. Ten minutes remained when the last man, Connolly, came out to Inverarity. Five minutes passed: still the fieldsmen stood in two unbroken ranks and at last Underwood made one straighten and Inverarity, for once picking the wrong line, was lbw.

The game was won and lost: the crowd swarmed happily round the pavilion, players came out and waved and went, and another England–Australia rubber with its unique quality of cricket history was over.

The Horlicks awards made after the match were: Man of the series – John Edrich; Australian batsman of the match – Bill Lawry; Australian bowler of the match – Alan Connolly; English batsman of the match – John Edrich; English bowler of the match – Derek Underwood; special award – the outstanding fieldsman of an outstanding fielding side – Paul Sheahan.                                                                    *The Guardian*

# Glamorgan Win the 'Fifth Test' at Swansea

*August* 1968. Wales won – and Australia lost spiritedly. The chronicles of the game will record that Glamorgan beat the Australians by 79 runs at Swansea yesterday, but the thought in the minds of those who were there was crystallized by the Glamorgan player who said, 'Well, we've won the Fifth Test. Can England win the Sixth?'

A simple, complete phase of the game was played out in the day, in which Australia began their innings needing 365 runs to win with a possible six-and-a-half hours in which to make them; and it was an essential ingredient of the interest and excitement that they did, unmistakably, set out to win. Indeed, at one point it was apparent that the task was within their powers, and the outstanding individual performance of the day was Sheahan's courtly innings of 137.

Another large crowd completed by far the largest attendance at any Australian match of the tour apart from Tests and, at the moment of Glamorgan's triumph, emerged as a choir of balanced harmony. Their team's cricket, too, was harmonious, a complete team effort, admirably directed by Don Shepherd and constantly dramatically expressed in superb fielding.

The fall of the first wicket set the tone of the day. Redpath had already narrowly escaped being run out by a return from Rees before he set off for another hasty single to the same fielder who ran him out with a direct underarm throw to the wicket. Nash produced the best ball of the day for Inverarity; it swung into him and, as he made to force it through the onside field, it moved back off the seam and hit the top of the off stump. There is no answer to that.

At this point Sheahan came to join Cowper and the day entered its decisive phase. Shepherd took the pavilion end, maintaining his characteristically immaculate length and line, while Brian Lewis bowled his sharply spun off-breaks opposite him, into the more responsive end of the still slow wicket. Cowper played with cool poise, assessing each ball shrewdly and finding opportunity to take enough fours through the offside field to keep Australia comfortably level with the demanded scoring rate. Sheahan, who has been more out of luck than out of form, absorbed some of his partner's steadiness, the partnership grew in assurance and style, and it moved at a run a minute to 116. Then Cowper, who had handled both bowlers without hurry or difficulty, was tied down for four overs and, suddenly irked, swung both across the line and against the spin of a ball from Lewis and skied it so steeply that Eifion Jones had time to walk up from behind the wicket to make the catch.

From that moment Sheahan *was* the Australian innings; but it always seemed unlikely that he would find enough enduring partners to achieve his team's now distant objective. He swept two sixes backward of square leg and reached his century with a full flowing drive which carried the long-on boundary. But most of his nineteen fours came from cover drives made in the manner his Australian admirers forecast. It was such an innings as should re-establish his faltering confidence.

Joslin drove at the gap through mid-off only for the bowler, Lewis, to close it and make the catch. Jarman was all aggression until he pushed forward to Shepherd and gave a typical short-leg catch to the prehensile Roger Davis. Hawke was caught driving and Gleeson, unsettled by a wide turning off-break, pushed up the next ball to short leg. Mallett was run out attempting a quick single to complete Sheahan's century and Sheahan himself, striving for even faster runs, drove a steep return catch to Walker. Connolly and Renneberg, in a late, semi-serious flurry, drove off Lewis, weary of his thirty-two consecutive overs, and just before four o'clock Walker bowled the last ball of the match which Renneberg hit straight to Majid at cover.

Then came the song, champagne – on ice since the morning – and then more song, still welling up from the bar below more than an hour afterwards. Glamorgan have beaten the Australians before; indeed, they have beaten a touring side of every Test playing country. But still, each time they do it, it is a Welsh occasion which sweeps up even an Englishman in its surging exaltation. *The Guardian*

# Everyday Cricket in Distilled Form

*April* 1969. Middlesex beat Yorkshire by 43 runs at Lord's yesterday in a splendid advertisement for the over-limit cricket of the Sunday League. The batting of Parfitt, and in a fine Yorkshire rally, Wilson and Binks, the bowling of Old, Wilson, Connolly, and – decisively – Price, plus the fielding of both sides made a superb afternoon's entertainment. Ultimately the breakthrough by Price with able backing from Connolly proved too deep even for Yorkshire's traditional powers of recovery.

This match gave all that can be reasonably asked of the players in this competition of high hope. No batsman can bat, no one can be in the field, for more than about two hours; no bowler can run up more than fifteen yards or bowl more than eight overs. So every player can concentrate the strength that in normal county cricket he would eke out over eight hours or perhaps thirty overs. The end product for the spectator is everyday cricket in a distilled form; not perhaps so profound as the county game but intensive and highly keyed. Those who expected to see a contrived finish with a result achieved only in the last possible over are likely often to be disappointed. If, however, they are content with a hard match played to a finish within a single afternoon, this is their ideal.

The only disappointing aspect of a sunny day was a meagre crowd – only 2400 paid. This cricket is sufficiently fine entertainment to do more than pay its way. Perhaps potential spectators are waiting to be convinced. There was a counter-attraction at The Oval but London ought easily to support two matches of this quality.

Middlesex were 8 for two wickets before Parfitt, batting realistically and taking calculated risks, and Radley, snatching every opportunity to make scoring strokes, carried them to 63 by the nineteenth over when Parfitt was well taken by Hutton tumbling at mid-off.

Close's field placing was shrewd and, though two difficult chances were dropped, the standard of fielding was high. Importantly, Wilson and Balderstone demonstrated that the spin bowler is not necessarily uneconomic in this cricket. Titmus, Hooker, and, even more valuably, Jones made their contributions but Middlesex can hardly have regarded their 137 for eight wickets as a commanding total.

It was proved so within five overs when Price – who also contributed an alert run-out – and Connolly cut down the Yorkshire batting to 10 for four. Briefly Hampshire and an anxious Balderstone put a bold face on the situation but when Hampshire drove Price to Jones at mid-on, Yorkshire had no batsman left of the stature to play a match-winning innings with 112 needed from the thirty overs. Balderstone went at 26 for six in the fifteenth over and at such a juncture most sides would have faded modestly into the evening.

Not Yorkshire, though. Binks batting determinedly and with genuine acumen and Wilson, picking the right ball to hit with more than usual care, put on 48 for the seventh wicket before, at 74, Hooker bowled Binks and Hutton with consecutive balls. Even then Wilson – he hit three sixes and was once grotesquely dropped – maintained the asking rate of five runs an over, carried Yorkshire to 94 and the glimpse of winning; only then did he mistime a drive and Smith at long on caught him. Jones finished a useful day for a second eleven player with a magnificent caught and bowled. There can be little doubt that every spectator at this match went away persuaded of the entertainment value of the Sunday League. *The Guardian*

# Lord Constantine

## *Spectacular All-round Cricketer and Racial Equality Campaigner*

2 *July* 1971. Lord Constantine, MBE, the spectacular and popular West Indian all-round cricketer, the greatest of all fieldsmen and an effective campaigner against colour prejudice, died in London yesterday. He was sixty-nine. To a wide public in the 1920s and 1930s he was the personification of emergent West Indian cricket and he used his standing as a games-player with judicious dignity to further the causes of political independence and social equality for his people.

He was born in Diego Martin, near Port of Spain, Trinidad, on 21 September 1901, the son of Lebrun Constantine – 'Old Cons' – a sugar plantation foreman who was a member of the West Indian teams which toured England in 1900 and 1906, and the first West Indian to score a century in England. Family practice with his father, his uncle, Victor Pascall, a slow left-arm bowler for Trinidad, and his mother keeping wicket, early instilled cricket into the younger Constantine. But obvious natural aptitude and keen fielding, rather than any outstanding figures, won him a place in the Trinidad team in 1921. He had played in only three first-class matches when he was told to be ready to join the 1923 West Indian side for England. On that tour, apart from a brave innings of 60 not out in a total of 97 against Derbyshire, he made an impression only by brilliant fielding at cover-point. During the next five years in the West Indies, however, unremitting practice made him a genuinely fast bowler and a sure slip fieldsman while, through his fine eye, natural timing and speed of reaction, he became an explosive, if inconsistent, attacking batsman. Those years of application bore fruit in England in 1928.

In the three Tests of that summer – the first ever played by West Indies – he achieved no more than five wickets and 89 runs: but on the tour he became the first West Indian to perform the 'double' of 1000 runs and 100 wickets in a season.

Above all, a single match established him and his country's cricket in English public imagination. At Lord's in June, Middlesex batting first, declared at 352 for six wickets and put out the West Indians for 230 in which only Constantine, with 86, scored more than 30. In the Middlesex second innings Constantine took seven wickets for 57. West Indies, needing 259 to win, were 121 for five, and apparently losing, when Constantine went in. He hit with such force that one straight drive broke the finger of the bowler, Hearne, and went on to strike the pavilion rails and fly up into the seating. Constantine scored 103 out of 133 in an hour, and won the match for the West Indians by three wickets.

From that day until he retired from all play some thirty years later, Constantine attracted crowds as few other cricketers have ever done. In 1929 he was engaged by the Nelson club and except in 1939, when he joined the West Indies team in England, he continued as a League professional with considerable success for Nelson, Rochdale, Bootle, Crompton and Windhill until 1948.

For some years he bowled at such pace that he was menacing to the best batsmen even on good wickets. Of little more than average height, wide-shouldered and long-armed, he took a short, lively run and bowled off a fine leap with a high action and a full follow-through. He developed many variations, including a well disguised and controlled slower ball, which was often a leg-break or googly and, as he grew older, took many wickets by guile and accuracy. In the deep field he made catches that seemed far beyond his reach, swooped to pick up at full speed with an apparently boneless ease and his throwing, on or off balance, was strong and accurate: while close to the wicket his catching was bewilderingly quick and certain. As a batsman he was prepared to attack any bowler; he cut, pulled, hooked and drove exuberantly, produced some remarkable, spontaneous strokes to counter the unexpected and some blows of phenomenal length. The essence of his cricket was that by batting, bowling or fielding he might win any match from almost any situation.

Before he left the West Indies Constantine had, in the words of his fellow Trinidadian, C. L. R. James, 'revolted against the revolting contrast between his first-class status as a cricketer and his third-class status as a man'. Professionalism enabled him to settle in England to study law and to argue the causes of West Indian self-government and racial tolerance. In many Lancashire towns where he played cricket there were children who had never before seen a coloured man; and, by speeches and lectures, and the publication of pamphlets, he did much to foster understanding of his people's problems. He and his wife fitted happily into Lancashire life and in 1963 the freedom of the Borough of Nelson was bestowed on him.

In eighteen Test matches for West Indies between 1928 and 1939 he scored 641 runs at an average of 19.42 and took 58 wickets at 30.10. These are unimpressive figures but, at Georgetown in 1930, his nine wickets for 122 linked with Headley's two centuries to give West Indies their first win in a Test match: and in his last Test, at The Oval in 1939, he took five English first innings wickets for 75 and then scored 78 out of 103 in less than an hour. Because he spent so much of his career in the leagues, he played only 194 innings in first-class cricket; scored 4451 runs and took 424 wickets. Figures, however, cannot reflect his aggressive approach, tactical acumen or his quality as an athlete, entertainer and match-winner, nor prove the fact, which his contemporaries never doubted, that he was the finest all-round fieldsmen the game of cricket has ever known.

He remained in England during the Second World War. From 1942 to 1947 he was a Welfare Officer, with particular responsibility for West Indian workers, in the Ministry of Labour and National Service, and received the MBE for his services. In 1944 he took action against The Imperial Hotel, London for 'failing to receive and lodge him' and won the nominal damages he sought.

In 1954, after a long struggle, he passed his Bar Finals and was called by the Middle Temple in 1954; he became an honorary Master of the Bench in 1963. He published his book *Colour Bar* in 1954. When he returned to Trinidad in 1957, he was called to the Bar there and elected as a People's Nationalist Movement member for Tunapuna to the first Trinidad Legislature, in which he became Minister of Works and Transport. Disillusioned by politics, he did not stand for re-election in 1961 and in the following year was appointed High Commissioner for Trinidad and Tobago in London, a post he held until his resignation in 1964, after trying to help to solve difficulties in Bristol when busmen were said to be operating a colour bar. He subsequently practised in the English courts, wrote and broadcast on cricket, and, in 1966, became a member of the Race Relations Board. He was knighted in 1962. In 1967 he became Rector of St Andrews University; in 1969 he became a life peer. He was also a governor of the BBC.

A man of quiet manner, religious conviction and high principles, Constantine was popular on all the levels at which he lived and worked. He married, in 1927, Norma Agatha Cox: they had one daughter.

*The Times*

# 12

# Elderly Reflections

## The Watson–Bailey Epic

*March* 1980. Some in the Press-box thought it would all be over by lunch; others gave it until three o'clock. No one thought it could run anywhere nearly all day in this fine weather; certainly no one gave anything for England's chance of winning, or even saving, the game against Hassett's powerful Australian attack. It was Tuesday, 30 June, 1953. The night before, England, set 343 to win, had lost the wickets of Kenyon, Hutton and Graveney to Lindwall and Johnston in less than an hour. Watson, coming in at number five, had been dropped once and had given another half-chance in a single over of Ring's leg-spin, turning in awkwardly from the worn patch outside the left-hander's off stump. So, on the last morning, at 20 for three, they wanted 323 from exactly the same seven wickets as had fallen in 93 minutes for 81 runs on Saturday afternoon when the pitch was much less worn.

On the first four days the crowd had massed densely up to the boundary ropes. Now the grass was bare; spectators were scattered about the seating; the atmosphere devoid of the tension of the earlier phases. The applause was splutteringly formal as Denis Compton, at his cheerful shamble, and Willie Watson, tall, fair-haired and composed, walked out to pick up the innings. Difficult as it may now be to believe, Compton had had such a short time of it since 1950 that he was playing for his place; for Watson it was his first Test against Australia.

With portentous care they saw out a dozen overs of Ray Lindwall – master craftsman among fast bowlers – and Bill Johnston, dealing in almost everything between slow finger-spin to lively swing and cut from a considerable height and the awkward angle of the left-armer. Then Hassett, determined to keep them under pressure, hustled up both his leg-spinners. Ring bowled Watson a probingly accurate maiden over, pitching in the dust on his off side. Benaud was less accurate and, in a single over, Compton hit him three times with increasing power through mid-off for four. Johnston returned. Ring spun into Watson, whose forward stroke only half-trapped the ball between bat and pad; as it rolled agonizingly on he kicked it away adroitly, as became a soccer player, from no more than six inches short of his stumps.

At half-past twelve, Ron Archer, the Australian twelfth man, came down the pavilion steps with a tray of drinks only for Hassett, with a single, sharp, cutting gesture, to send him back. He wanted no interruption in the process of winning the match. Surely enough, ten minutes later, Johnston dropped a brisk cutter on the edge of the worn patch; it straightened and kept low enough for any batsman; and Compton was lbw. That, it seemed to everybody, was the decisive blow. Nearly five hours to go: and, as Bailey walked out, someone observed that, in nine innings against Australia, his highest score was 15, his average less than eight.

This situation was to prove his element; and to establish him as an effective Test cricketer. There was no pressure upon him to score runs (only a lunatic could contemplate England forcing a win against such opposition). So Bailey could concentrate upon the stubborn defence which was to characterize him in cricket history. He plunged religiously forward, pad first, bat following closely in the prod which, Keith Miller once said, haunted his dreams.

Watson now settled to his innings. He was always a calm, almost aloof, but handsome batsman; purist in style; poised, upstanding, virtually incapable of an ugly stroke. Some said he was not sufficiently competitive; but, at all games (he was one of the last double, cricket-soccer, internationals), he was a cool thinker. Upon opportunity he struck hard; driving away the close fieldsmen who might catch him off the ball which lifted from the dust. Both batsmen treated Miller with such respect that his four controlled and fast overs yielded only one run. As the batsmen walked in to lunch – 116 for four – one small section of the crowd let out a sudden, perhaps intuitive, burst of quite excited applause.

Soon after lunch, too, with England 227 short of the statistically possible win, but four hours short of the unlikely draw that was their highest objective, the bush telegraph sent the news of resistance through London, and the ground began to fill. A few minutes before three Hassett took the new ball. There to use it were the now legendary Lindwall and Miller; destroyers of the England batting of 1946–47, 1948, 1950–51, reinforced by Davidson and Johnston.

Ever since 1948 these two had possessed the almost hypnotic power to chill an English crowd into awed silence. It happened again as Lindwall slowly furled his sleeve and tapped his foot like a stallion pawing the ground. All day Watson had been growing in stature; making his strokes with a lack of hurry which argued that the bowling was not fast. Five fierce overs for five runs and a shattering blow on Bailey's determined bottom hand, and Hassett allowed Archer to bring on drinks. Another five overs, rising to crescendo, from Lindwall and Miller; the odd bouncer flogged out of the reluctant Lord's wicket; another thunderous blow on Bailey's knuckles. Altogether ten overs for only nine runs; but no wicket. Slowly, as two of their batsmen resisted the arch destroyers, the crowd sensed that England might, historically, save the game. Increasingly often, survival through a testing over produced a slightly feverish burst of applause.

At tea Watson and Bailey were still there; the wildest hope of an England win snuffed out by Lindwall and Miller but only an hour and 55 minutes from the honourable safety of a draw. Gradually acceptance of defeat gave way to anxiety, to hope, to shaky, illogical, but spirited confidence.

Look, though, at the batting to come – Freddie Brown, Godfrey Evans, Johnny Wardle, Alec Bedser, Brian Statham; all so desperately vulnerable to such pace as this that they could be swept away in ten minutes.

Hassett threw in Miller (five overs for seven runs) and Davidson (five for eight) at their highest pace; saving Lindwall, it was later argued, to sweep away the rest, once breakthrough was achieved. It was almost half-past five when Watson swung Ring with the spin over Benaud to square leg for the boundary that brought him a century in his first Test against Australia. The crowd stood to him in applause, at once admiring, incredulous, affectionate, grateful; it was a greeting for an emperor. He had played one of the epic innings of Test cricket, flawless since the initial gropings of the fourth evening. Then Ring did it again and Hole, at short leg, took the catch off bat and pad. Forty minutes remained; Freddie Brown came in and drove savagely at Ring.

Walking down from the commentary box a sudden thought led past the England dressing-room to one of the huge, deep, Lord's baths where Willie Watson lay deeply relaxed.

'Oh, *bloody* well played Willie.'

'Thanks; wish I could have stayed – don't go – have you got a cigarette?' He took it, and a light; inhaled deeply. Len Hutton came in; took the other chair. 'Sit down.' Hurried sorties to the balcony saw a couple of lusty swings by Freddie Brown; rebuked by two scowling shakes of the head by Trevor Bailey. Back to the bathroom: the listening silence was broken by a sudden burst of applause; and Len's quick, agonized 'Trevor's out.' A few moments later, Bailey himself came into the bathroom, sweating, weary, eyes darkly sunk, face deeply lined as that of one in a fever. He and Watson exchanged nods; then: 'Sorry skip' and, more of a sob than an oath, 'Silly shot – straight to cover.' Len dismissed the apology with a quick scratch of the head.

'How long?'

'Half an hour.'

'Has he brought Ray on?' (In retrospect that was the decisive issue). A quick foray – 'No' (and he did not). The tension in the bathroom became too much. Or was it worse than Freddie Brown's boundaries and edges? Three minutes remained when Hole caught him at slip off Benaud. So four balls of the last over left at 282 for seven; Australia could still do it.

They did not; Wardle kept out of trouble, and he and Evans walked in at the end of, surely, the epic rescue operation of all Test cricket. England had been given the chance to win the Ashes and, at The Oval, they did so, after nineteen years. By then, though, the English selectors had dropped Willie Watson, who at Lord's had so gallantly and handsomely created the opportunity. Selectors may overlook greatness; history does not.                      *Wisden Cricket Monthly*

# Brearley

## *Has There Been a Better Captain?*

*October* 1981. When the selectors invited Mike Brearley to continue as captain of England for the Oval Test, they honoured a considerable achievement. Primarily and amazingly he had led England from one (imminently two) down against Australia to three-one up. The Ashes had been won (or retained, according to your point of view) by the most vividly exciting three consecutive wins in the history of Test cricket.

So Brearley is the only English captain to equal – even to approach – the record of Sir Donald Bradman in winning eleven Anglo-Australian Tests. W. G. Grace scored eight in five series; no one else is in competition.

If England had won at The Oval, Brearley would have stood alone; which, to his cool mind, probably would seem more than his due. Yet it is difficult to believe that there has been a better captain – *qua* captain – on either side. An England selector once remarked: 'This man is as good a captain on the field as "Illy" – and I have no higher praise than that; off the field, he is far and away the best we have ever had. If only he could get some more runs there could never be any question about him.' Since then Brearley has undoubtedly become a better tactician. He has never been dropped from that office for his school, university (two centuries against Oxford), county (two outright Championships and one shared: one Gillette Cup win) or country. Up to The Oval, he had captained England in thirty Tests against all countries: they had won eighteen, lost four: and taken seven rubbers, lost one, drawn one.

It is not crucial to his captaincy that he got a first in Classics and a two-one in Moral Sciences at Cambridge; indeed, it is more relevant that, while studying to that level, he contrived to score more runs (4068) for that university than any other undergraduate. It is not essential that he came first in the top grade of the Civil Service entrance examination; nor that he researched and lectured in philosophy at the Universities of California and Newcastle. Those aspects of his life indicate an extremely keen brain and a high quality of thinking; they might, however, indicate no more than an impractical intellectual. It is more significant that, in recent years, he has studied psychoanalysis; and that he cannot take the English team to India this winter because he will be starting a three-year course on the subject. Most revealing of all is his planned career in psychiatric group therapy.

His main characteristics are the ability to assess himself objectively; the automatic sympathy for – and virtual need to study – other people; and, finally, an immense mental hunger. Often – indeed, generally, and quite lately – highly gifted cricketers' play has been thrown out of gear by the demands of captaincy: that they should think of, and for, other players. Cricket, especially top-class cricket, is a lonely game; individually successful cricket must, quite essentially, be selfish. When they are not batting or bowling, many players like to relax in some undemanding fielding position. For Brearley, though, that would be mental starvation; his brain demands fodder. Without captaincy – that of England or Middlesex – sheer boredom would have driven him from the first-class game by now.

Many people set out to motivate others; often as the best way to their own success. Mike Brearley, however, instinctively studies other people; if that enables him to fire them to the greater effect of the team he leads, that is an inner, as well as a material, reward.

He is handsome in a fresh, boyish way; has an honest face, impeccable manners; dresses neatly but not elaborately; he went to a public school, Cambridge University, and plays his county cricket from Lord's. Those superficial facts deceived the Australian Ockers and, in England, the orc-yobs and mosters, to regard him as an affected member of the privileged class: and to treat him with all the viciousness of the mob. He accepted that treatment with quiet contempt, not bothering to argue that it was quite undeserved.

His father, a schoolmaster, played once for his native Yorkshire before he moved to London, and twice for Middlesex afterwards. Mike won a scholarship to the City of London School; and then to St John's College, Cambridge. He was born and lived in the county of Middlesex. He has never, though, been an Establishment man in cricket or any other field. He supported David Sheppard in his opposition to MCC on the D'Oliveira-South African issue in 1968. When the Cricketers' Association were refused a share of broadcasting and television revenue for the players, he was among the first to advocate protest; and the progressive action which persuaded Lord's to acquiesce. He, too, saw more clearly than most that the Packer affair could not be allowed to split the game; advized against the official desire for retribution and, to the last possible moment, opposed the banning of those who joined World Series. He commands much loyalty because he has always fought for his players' rights – and they know it.

He has a strikingly open mind; but a firm set of standards. Much of his strength as a captain lies in the fact that cricket is not the be-all and end-all of life for him. Indeed, he played no first-class cricket in 1966 or 1967; and only in the latter half of the following three seasons. One is reminded of C. L. R. James's text, in that fine book *Beyond a Boundary*: 'What do they know of cricket who only cricket know?' Brearley has always been able to stand back and look at cricket and cricketers as from the outside; few involved at Test level have had that capacity.

On the other hand, it may be argued that his near-separation from the game in those formative years after he came down from Cambridge, between twenty-four and twenty-eight, precluded the full technical maturity which might have redeemed his immense early promise. After all, in 1964 he was elected Young Cricketer of the Year by the Cricket Writers' Club; captaining MCC Under-25 in Pakistan in 1966–67, he scored 312 not out in a day against North Zone; and headed the averages with 132.16, well ahead of Amiss, Fletcher, Ormrod, Abberley and Richard Hutton. In 1975 only Boycott among English batsmen bettered his figure of 53.41: and his first three Test caps were won solely as a batsman. We may note, too, that his batting average this season – 43.45 – up to the selection for The Oval, is that of a successful county batsman.

In all Tests, though, his figure is only 22.89 (though his 52 catches, mostly at slip, are a bonus); in his first three Tests of this series, a mere 15.

Technically, he is correct enough, and unflinching against pace, perceptive against spin; and has held out long enough against hostile attacks to prove that he has more than the germ of the matter in him. Often he seems determined to make over-certain. Without doubt, he is a thinking cricketer; yet it must be possible that those lost seasons of his twenties might have made him a more instinctive batsman; and the instinctive player is always likely to be that crucial fraction of a second quicker in reaction than the thinker.

To his immense credit, his behaviour, general demeanour and, for that matter, his batting, were never more impressive than in the only rubber he lost, that of 1979–80 in Australia. England were beaten in the three-match series three-nil: a result Greg Chappell thought as unfair as the five-one the other way in 1978–79.

Brearley was charged with the onerous duty – which should never have been imposed upon a captain – of publicly restating the TCCB's refusal to accept the terms, specifically designed for the Packer television 'spectaculars' – wearing striped gear, using a white ball and employing fielding circles. If that was necessary – as it ought not to have been – it was the manager's task.

In the event it made Brearley initially unpopular and the Ockers soon climbed on his back: the Australian manager, John Edwards, said they made him ashamed to be an Australian. Nevertheless, despite their screamed hate, and in face of an attack including Lillee, Thomson and Dymock, he kept England in the First Test with a four-hour 64, substantially top score of the first innings.

At Melbourne, against Lillee, Pascoe and Dymock, his 60 not out preserved England's chances when the middle order collapsed. He averaged a game 34.20 for the series.

He has, though, always been anxious – almost certainly over-anxious – to prove himself as a batsman at Test level. Had he played under J. M. Brearley, his captain might well have given him the reinforcement he needed to live up to his full ability in Tests. A case, we may assume, of 'Physician heal thyself'.

Personable, humorous, convivial, and friendly; yet Mike Brearley is a serious man, in that he does not care to waste good contemplative time. His courtesy should never be mistaken for lack of decision; the smile conceals, at need, an inflexible will. He will hardly want to return to Test cricket. A season or two, if that, with Middlesex and he will turn to his domestic life and a fresh career. Mike Brearley has served English cricket well, led it to successes probably beyond its deserts. Unhappily his captaincy – happy in itself – is not of a type that can be taught nor, except in the rarest – apart from this case unknown – circumstances, is it natural in cricketers.

*Wisden Cricket Monthly*

# New Zealand Power

*April* 1983. The New Zealand cricketers have always been welcome visitors to Britain. Once the cynics might have attributed that to the fact that they invariably lost to England. That, though, can no longer be adduced since they beat England at Wellington in 1978. Indeed, they gained the right to take on the world when they beat Australia at Christchurch in 1974; they have now beaten all their Test opponents and they emphasized their standing – at least for those who accept the criterion of the limited-overs game – in the recent World Series Cup competition in Australia. Then they had the ill-luck to go into the finals without Richard Hadlee, one of the finest fast-bowler allrounders in the game, who was injured.

There the weakness in New Zealand's representative cricket has generally lain; not in the quality of their best players but in their numbers. Producing a side capable of taking on the other cricketing nations is a considerable achievement for not merely the smallest Test-playing country but one which, with a population of 3,160,000, is smaller than even a single city of each of the others, except West Indies and Sri Lanka.

The cricket relationship between Britain and New Zealand, diagonally distant across the world, has been surprisingly good, especially by comparison with the attitude of Australia. England have consistently sent out touring teams, despite the distance and economic difficulties. After the tiring tour of Australia the continuation to New Zealand for, often, three Tests and a few other matches must often have seemed Pelion piled upon Ossa to weary English cricketers. Those visits, though, have invariably been friendly and enjoyable – at least, ever since 1877, when poor Ted Pooley of Surrey was arrested and, when he should have been keeping wicket in the first Test every played between England and Australia, was languishing in Christchurch gaol.

Australia, on the other hand, has appeared a poor – even contemptuous – neighbour. In 1929-30 England sent the team under Harold Gilligan which, on 10 January 1930, at Lancaster Park, Christchurch, ushered New Zealand into Test cricket with the first of a four-match series. England and New Zealand had already played twelve Tests in four series before Australia sent Bill Brown's party on a four-week, one-Test tour in 1945-46. The two countries did not meet in Australia, however, until 1973-74: and in a return rubber – played, all but incomprehensibly, after so many blank years, in the same season – New Zealand achieved their first win in only the sixth match between the two. It was a hard-fought game; decided by Turner, who scored a century in each innings; Richard Hadlee (seven for 130), his brother

Dayle (five for 117), Richard Collinge (five for 107) and some fine catching. Unhappily the New Zealanders had to endure a degree of 'sledging' – the current term for abuse and obscenity directed at opponents – which nearly marred the national celebrations of their triumph, and still rankles with some of them. Glenn Turner is an extremely independent-thinking man; and certainly the only Test cricketer to be married twice on the same day. By immense thought, and initial concentration on defence, he lifted himself from an ordinary to a world-class batsman, and his career certainly ought not yet to be ended.

A few Australian teams had been there before: though never for a Test match. In 1905, for instance, Darling's side sharpened up for their English tour with six matches (two against odds) there. They won four of them by an innings and drew the other two. *Wisden* – in a two-page 'summary of the matches, together with the batting and bowling averages' – contrived never to mention the name of a single New Zealand player.

Tradition recalls, though, that at Auckland the doughty Bill Stemson, opening the bowling for the local XV, knocked out Victor Trumper's leg stump with his first ball – at the very moment that the umpire called 'no-ball'. Stemson, like the Hon. Frederick Beauclerk bowling at Tom Walker of Hambledon a century and a half before – 'off went his hat . . . dash upon the ground.' Trumper continued to make 92: better than his average for the tour, which was 89.66.

New Zealand have progressed far since the day in 1914 when Victor Trumper scored 293 in 180 minutes against Canterbury; and particularly since the Second World War. Several of their inter-war players came into the English county game. Stewart Dempster, who captained Leicestershire from 1936 to 1938, was an extremely accomplished opening batsman; immaculately straight in defence, a powerful driver and a product of his time in the strength of his onside play. In a New Zealand team of all periods, he would go in first with Glenn Turner. Bill Merritt played several seasons of league cricket for Dudley and, with Ken James the wicketkeeper, for Northamptonshire. Merritt spun the leg-break and googly very sharply, if not particularly accurately; on his day, though, he was almost unplayable. On the 1931 tour, for instance, he amazed some knowledgeable critics when he took the new ball in the second innings of an extremely strong MCC batting side and, making it loop and turn, took seven for 28 to give New Zealand an innings win.

Tom Lowry, the Cambridge Blue and capable wicketkeeper/batsman who captained the 1931 team to England, also turned out for Somerset. R. C. Robertson Glasgow used to declare that he qualified on the grounds that he was born in Wellington; and no one ever asked him whether he meant Wellington, Somerset or Wellington, New Zealand.

The touring team of 1949 was exceptionally well-equipped in batting.

That fact decided the outcome of the rubber. When the fixture list was first drafted they were offered three four-day Tests. That astute accountant, Walter Hadlee, pointed out that such a programme would involve six blank – and therefore uneconomic – days at the best part of the summer; and he opted for four of three days each. When that was agreed, he remarked drily, 'There is not much doubt that our batting is good enough to draw all four of them.' And it was so.

That side included the finest left-hand batsman of the post-war era in Martin Donnelly. Short, neat, quick on his feet, able to dominate the best bowling by controlled aggression and a wide range of strokes, he prompted C. B. Fry to the comment that no left-hander of his time was better. Wally Hammond said laconically that he was 'one of the few really great ones'. That was high praise indeed; but justified. He had toured England with their 1937 team when he was only nineteen and played some courageous defensive innings in a losing team. After the war he took a post-graduate course at Oxford and joined the touring party of 1949. His 206 in the Lord's Test, still the highest score for New Zealand against England, was a masterly performance, with twenty-six fours and absolutely flawless until he passed 200 and started to take risks. He captained the University; but when, after a few games for Warwickshire and one for Middlesex, he took up a business appointment in Australia, he was much missed at many levels. He was, too, a brilliant rugby stand-off, capped for England while he was up at Oxford. In addition he was a man of much personal charm; an easy, relaxed manner, and a sense of humour which ranged from the dry to the zany.

If Donnelly was the finest left-hander of the era, his fellow New Zealander, Bert Sutcliffe, must challenge Neil Harvey for the next place. Splendidly athletic, an upstanding fluent strokeplayer, he had been in first-class cricket less than three years when he came with Walter Hadlee's team to England. Yet only Bradman among visiting batsmen had ever bettered his aggregate of 2627 runs (at 59.70) on that tour. He scored over 50 in five of his seven Test innings; Donnelly in five out of six. Indeed, that 1949 side made even more runs than Bradman's powerful Australians of 1948. Neither were Donnelly and Sutcliffe alone; Mervyn Wallace all but achieved the feat of a thousand in May. When they beat Surrey at The Oval, Walter Hadlee played an innings of consummate skill: 119 not out in a total of 249 against Alec Bedser bowling his leg-cutters explosively on a dusty wicket.

That was the first tour of John Reid, the strong man; only twenty when he reached England, he scored 50 in his first Test innings and went on to a career total of 3428 runs in Tests. At one juncture he held the New Zealand Test records of scoring most runs, most centuries, taking most wickets, holding most catches, playing in most matches, and captaining most often. He set the record by appearing in 58 and captaining in 34 consecutive Tests. A useful fast-medium bowler, he frequently kept wicket; and was an outstanding fieldsman anywhere. A mighty driver and hooker, his fifteen sixes in an innings for Wellington against Northern Districts (1962–63) has never been equalled. He batted with great courage and determination, especially during the 1950s in a series of weak teams which he often seemed to carry on his shoulders.

A representative New Zealand side which began its batting with Turner, Dempster, Sutcliffe, Donnelly would trouble any bowling side whether they followed them with the doggedly and valuably resistant Bev Congdon or Geoff Howarth (another to score a century in each innings of a Test). Then would come the allrounders, John Reid, the other strong man, the tall, combative Bruce Taylor, and, of course, the highly talented Richard Hadlee. With Botham, Kapil Dev and Imran Khan, Hadlee completes a remarkable current vintage of allrounders. Spin bowling had generally been New Zealand's weakness; but a good selector will settle for their best – Hedley Howarth, a class slow left-arm bowler who played too little cricket, and Bill Merritt (just ahead of Roger Blunt, who was the better bat). The irrepressible and lightning-fast Frank – 'Starlight' – Mooney or the tragic Ken Wadsworth would keep wicket – if a specialist was chosen.

It is tempting, though, in that 'all-periods' team, to play John Reid as wicketkeeper and bring in an extra batsman or a pace bowler in Jack Cowie or Dick Motz, both immense triers at right-arm fast-medium; or the slightly quicker Richard Collinge to impart left-arm variety. On the other hand, remembering how well Reid bowled when the side was in trouble, his versatility in bowling, fast-medium outswing or, on a favourable wicket, off-cutters, and his fine close catching, the specialist goes in.

So the team, in batting order, would be Stewart Dempster, Glenn Turner, Bert Sutcliffe, Martin Donnelly, Geoffrey Howarth or Bev Congdon, John Reid, Bruce Taylor, Richard Hadlee, Frank Mooney, Hedley Howarth, Bill Merritt. They would be talented, entertaining and generous opponents; and extremely good company.

*Wisden Cricket Monthly*

# Into the Unknown

*June* 1980. It is doubtful if there has ever been a purely objective preview of a cricket season. The follower of the game is essentially subjective, deeply concerned with loyalties, both team and personal;

swayed by inclinations as basic as a bias towards either batsmen or bowlers in general; sense of values; nostalgia; and simple taste for a specific form – Test, three-day or one-day – of play.

So to look forward to one's last season is to peer ahead through bi-focal lenses formed of prejudice and sentiment; willy-nilly applying the values of one generation to the events of another. Cricket is a personal matter: as different in its significances and qualities as the people who follow it. In a lifetime we look forward to many seasons, their importance varying with our age and experience. To look forward knowingly to one's last summer in the game, though, is a personally unique experience in which the demanding and the generous are intermingled. Many people never know their last season on their own level of the game is beginning, nor do they always reach its end. Sir Jack Hobbs, for instance, persuaded against his judgment to continue with Surrey, scored the only century made against Lancashire, the champions, at Old Trafford in 1934. A few days later, the Oval crowd barracked him for misfielding a ball at cover. He, one of the greatest of all fieldsmen in that position – did he not run out fifteen Australian batsmen over there in 1911–12? – could not stomach the indignity and he never played there again: and retired soon afterwards. Maurice Tate, the finest English bowler of his generation, was still an extremely capable county cricketer in July 1937, when the Duke of Norfolk peremptorily sacked him, as at the end of the season. He was dropped; had to be recalled, and in the last month of the season demonstrated the extent of the error as leading bowler, taking more wickets than all the other Sussex pace bowlers put together before he walked out of the ground where he and his father had grown up to eminence as players; and where the Tate Gates now stand in his memory. Many others of some standing, as well as lesser men, are unaware of the end until they are simply, but finally, dropped.

The classical story of cricketing retirement is that of Patsy Hendren who, asked why he was retiring, replied: 'Because you said that.' 'What do you mean?' the questioner pressed. 'I'm going while you still ask why; I'm not waiting until you ask why not.' (After thirty years in the first-class game, perhaps the decision was not too difficult.) There is a time for us all, if we live long enough, to make our exits with dignity rather than linger too long on the stage.

The summer of 1980 is a special one. Five Tests against arguably the greatest of all West Indian sides – if it lacks the balance and spin of the 1950 team with Ramadhin and Valentine, its four-man pace attack is unmatched in the history of the game – offer English cricket a contest it will be hard put indeed to survive short of heavy defeat. The game against Australia, the centenary of Test cricket in this country, will be marked, for financial reasons, by a match at Lord's, although the original fixture was at The Oval. It will be regarded by the Australian players as a matter of dignity to win, for they still smoulder with resentment at the defeats inflicted on their team in the absence of the Packer men.

England face these matches with a team well beaten last winter when the batting was not of Test class; and which now finds its pace bowlers ageing, in the case of Willis, or, like Hendrick, of suspect fitness; its spinners, including even Underwood, reduced in potential by the new ruling on the covering of wickets at all times when play is not in progress.

Every English cricket-follower's hopes must be for the maturity of the many young batsmen in the game. Already it is possible to see a fresh generation of pace bowlers growing up. The spin, with Underwood, Emburey, Pocock, Edmonds and Miller all highly capable, can take care of itself. The main anxiety lies in the search for batsmen. The development of many of the most promising seems most disappointingly arrested. The fault lies less with them than with the present shape of the game. The introduction of three one-day competitions and the 100-overs limitation (most stupidly and pig-headedly retained at the TCCB spring meeting) conspire to reduce their opportunities of building an innings in the traditional fashion to half those enjoyed by previous generations. The one-day game provides lively and concentrated entertainment; and it has lifted the standard of our outcricket to heights of excellence barely envisaged twenty years ago. On the other hand, it strikes at the foundations of the craft of batsmanship fostered by three-day county cricket, for which there is no true substitute. Perhaps the risk was consciously taken; it would be difficult now to put back the clock; and impossible for the game to exist without the sponsorship attracted by the over-limit form. So the emergence of these unquestionable talents must be awaited with even greater patience than in the past.

While a fine summer and a revival in English Test cricket are major hopes, and the spectacular strokemaking and fast bowling of West Indies and the arrival of Australians new to everyone will make for fine watching, everyone has his own personal taste.

My own is for county cricket in three-day matches. After thirty-five years, every look forward, however determined, must involve comparison with the past. Even the three-day pattern is not what it was. The John Player competition stimulated both interest and finance but it took away the county cricketer's away-match Sunday. There were generally five or six of them in a summer. Everyone got up late and, over the newspapers and talk of the previous day's doings in their own match and those reported, breakfast was a leisurely, long drawn-out affair; in retrospect, generally regarded tolerantly by hotel staffs. Now the frequent interruption of Sunday travel has made the midweek fixture the coherent occasion.

For the writer this last season as commentator and reporter, in a world unlike any other, leads into the unknown.

As a farewell to the familiar scene, the anticipated delights of the summer lie in Championship cricket – Schweppes' sponsorship was a most sympathetic gesture – at such places as Taunton, Hove, Bath, Worcester, Cheltenham, Southampton, Bournemouth. There, among quiet and ruminative crowds; where one can hear the batsmen calling; the bowler's grunt of effort; the smack of ball into hand or glove; feel the thud of the chasing fieldsman's feet; a man is close indeed to the game and the players in a way that never occurs in any other country or any other major spectator sport – at a football match, for instance, the spectator feels cut off – not even at a Test match nor on such grounds as Lord's, which are remote in feeling.

In such a setting, the outsider shares the atmosphere of cricket. The sounds, too, are as evocative as they are peculiar to this facet of the English scene; the murmur of conversation; the hush as the bowler moves in at a crucial stage; the appreciative clapping prompted by a pleasing stroke; the sharp half-gasp, half-killer-shout that greets the fall of a wicket; the sigh at a dropped catch. The initiate can identify them all with his eyes shut.

At Bournemouth, the batsmen walk out from the dressing-rooms over the spike-splintered floorboards, through the drinkers in the members' bar to the crease; and, after play, repair to the marquees on the boundary edge; at Hove, Taunton, Bath and Southampton, they walk down between the seats from which their friends or relations can wish them luck; or, on the way back, commiserate with them *sotto voce*.

For this year that will be the main hunger: for the rest of my life the abiding nostalgia.                    *Wisden Cricket Monthly*

# Alderney Elysium

*September* 1982. The idea was the Editor's. 'Alderney is not exactly deserted,' he said, 'but why not pick a desert island cricket team?' That, we decided, did not necessarily mean the strongest or the finest eleven; but the one the selector would most enjoy watching. A twelfth man is allowed, and he will play: one of their side will undoubtedly pull a muscle: if not, under our unstringent rules – nothing so strict as laws – they will all play.

The choice involved a pleasant dinner of discussion and reminiscence and the eventual team – in batting order – was Sir Jack Hobbs (Surrey and England), Wilfred Rhodes (Yorkshire and England), Vivian Richards (Antigua, Somerset and West Indies), George Brown (Hampshire and England), Keith Miller (New South Wales and Australia), Ted Dexter (Sussex and England), Mike Brearley (Middlesex and England), Ian Botham (Somerset and England), Lord Constantine (Nelson, Trinidad and West Indies), Jim Laker (Surrey and England), Doug Wright (Kent and England), Wesley Hall (Barbados and West Indies). There were, too, a number of near misses; some left out only because there are eleven and not twenty in a cricket team. Some comfort is to be derived, too, from the fact that, not quite by cheating, it is possible to include on the other side a few cherished cricketers who have positively appeared for Alderney.

The problem, it must be feared, would be not merely the pitch – matting over asphalt – but the outfield. The landscape of The Butes, despite the voluntary – indeed, compulsive – efforts of Ian Waterfall, is pure bump, tuft, ridge and furrow. It is overcome only by the intrepid James Bardwell who, though now in his seventies – paying a vice-president's subscription and acting as treasurer– contrived to be impassable at mid-off by simple, but heroic, dint of interposing his unpadded shins in the line of the ball. Perhaps the States will turn a steamroller over it; at the same time they might lay a reliable artificial pitch. For desert island purposes, though, all will be ideal.

There has never been any deficiency of refreshment and it is unlikely to befall us now. There will be no shortage of comfortable changing and shower facilities in hotels no more than a half-length throw-in from the ground; and simple toilet and gear adjustments can be made in the pavilion/shed.

There will be, too, a sufficient supply of amenable umpires who will not interrupt the spectators' pleasure by giving out a good batsman in full cry; nor denying a bowler the reward – even if it has to be deferred – of a great delivery.

Neither will Alderney be deficient in ability. Their innings will be opened by Roy Marshall (Barbados, Hampshire and West Indies), that splendid striker, who once drove a ball so far off the plateau which is The Butes that it was never seen again. Of course – and whatever carpers may allege – *if* it pitched at the right point in the road beneath, it *could* have bounced into the sea. Did not Ted Alletson hit one from the Hove ground on to the beach? (At least it was found there.) Leo Harrison, who scored the first post-war century on the ground and also stumped a batsman and replaced the bail before the victim could turn round, will keep wicket. No match without him would be quite ideal for this selector.

Frank Tyson, who once demonstrated his pace – in the prudent absence of a batsman – with an awe-inspiring delivery which pitched on a length and hit the pavilion amidships without bouncing again, will be the sharpest edge of attack. No one who recalls the gasp that went round English – and Australian – cricket grounds in the mid-1950s as spectators first saw him propel a cricket ball, will deny his right to be admitted to this august company.

That game, safe-handed trier, Ken Suttle of Sussex, is another old Aurignac to add to the island strength; while the local stalwart, Joe Harrington, in turn fast bowler, slow bowler, opening bat, wicketkeeper and umpire over thirty-odd years, must never be left out of his native side.

In the absence of Ray Parkin, who shamefacedly admits to tearing a cartilage at tennis, the captaincy of the island will devolve – not quite so effectively on a perfected pitch and outfield as of old – on Michael Packe. He scored fifties for Cambridge without getting a Blue, captained Leicestershire; was a major in the First Airborne (with Hugh Bartlett and Billy Griffith) during the war, wrote a history of that unit, and the authoritative life of John Stuart Mill. His intellectual and conversational contribution also will be considerable, and will, to a degree, compensate for the influence of Mike Brearley on the visitors.

Time to examine the main selection: Jack Hobbs must come first in any team; not merely because he blended perfection of execution with complete ease of style; but also because of his generosity of spirit. How many leading batsmen of today can laugh when they are out; or turn to the bowler who has 'done' them with a googly and say 'Well bowled'? Jack will be relaxed and modest; but everyone present who ever tried to hit a ball with a cricket bat will watch him with profound admiration. He stands alone among batsmen.

Wilfred Rhodes will go in first with him. As Sir Jack once said, 'he was not so good a batsman as Herbert (Sutcliffe) or Tom (Hayward) and he wasn't really quick on his feet; but he was the best runner I ever batted with.' In their brief reign before the First World War those two were the finest pair between wickets the cricket world has ever known: with no more than a nod – sometimes not even that – they took singles from dead-bat strokes, and with such audacity and impunity as often to 'throw' the opposing bowlers psychologically. Wilfred must play, too, for his bowling. He did not merely take more wickets – 4187 – than anyone else ever did in the first-class game, but his approach and delivery swing were a unity of sweet rhythm; and the arc of the ball continued a line of utter blandishment; but, in its very curve was art, and the cunning of a master craftsman.

Vivian Richards of the patrician nose, high-pointing cap peak, immaculate shirts and a feline grace of movement, is modern cricket's reply to the great strokemakers of the past. Excitingly capable of hitting extremely hard, he is, as was said of Joseph Guy over a century ago, 'all ease and elegance, fit to play before the Queen in Her Majesty's parlour'. All that and humble and loyal enough to try desperately hard for his side; and big enough to smile in failure.

George Brown must play, not merely as a true allrounder – who excelled as batsman, bowler, wicket-keeper, close and deep fieldsman – but probably the most consistently violent and clean striker anyone now alive has ever seen. He was remarkably capable of summoning all his immense strength and hitting a cricket ball with all of it. Not even Peter Marner – whom he keeps out of this team – could match him in that direction. On the rare occasions when George kept wicket – almost solely in Test matches – he stood up to fast bowlers wearing only his tattered motor-cycling gauntlets; he could throw huge distances and catch faster than the eye could follow.

If anyone of later years is to compete with George Brown as a spectacular all-round cricketer it must be Keith Miller; masterly fast-medium swing bowler, capable at will of extremely high pace – or able to toss in a perfect-length googly; gloriously long hitter; and happily acrobatic slip catcher. Most convivial of cricketers.

Hereabouts must come Ted Dexter, an echo in our time of 'The Golden Age', the upstanding, peremptory strokeplayer, with an impulse to master; and, at heart, a contempt for caution. All but incapable of an innings which was not both handsome and competitive.

There have been many fine fieldsmen, but never a greater than Learie – Lord – Constantine: indeed, never one nearly so great. He had, of course, immense physical advantages; long arms, perfect balance: lithe as a panther, he might have been made of toughened rubber and steel springs. He sprinted at immense speed, bent, picked up, and threw in with a flowing and finally convulsive twist of his body: and the throw was absolute in its speed, length and accuracy. Close to the bat, although he never started too soon, his speed of reaction was such that he covered amazing distances to make catches while others would still have been waiting to pick up the line of the ball; and he was utterly prehensile. He concentrated fiercely; and, devoted and loyal, always kept himself perfectly fit. He won matches as fast – and slow – bowler, or attacking batsman. With Nelson he lifted the standing of the coloured cricketer and of the league professional to impressive heights, and, though he played purposefully, he was superbly entertaining.

Mike Brearley plays because he adds virtually a fresh dimension to a game by captaincy which is at once shrewdly penetrative and humanly perceptive, sharply observed and rapidly assessed. His is as acute an intellect as any the game has known but those who label him simply an intellectual fail to appreciate a warm humanity.

Here, too, he provides a buffer between the explosives; and is followed by, and could, with advantage to both (pun only half intended), bat with Botham. Botham is chosen because no one has ever reacted more gigantically to the challenge of a match. Perhaps he has batted or bowled in pedestrian fashion but if so he has not noticed it; and neither have the spectators. Ian Botham is, above all, in our day, the man to watch.

Jim Laker has always been a most absorbing bowler to watch. It was old William Lillywhite who said, 'I suppose if I was to think every ball, they'd never get a run'. By that standard it is surprising that anyone ever scored off Jim Laker. His mastery of technique – length, flight, spin, line, variation, change of pace – was complete. Above all, his mind was – is – never still. Perpetually active; shrewd, questing, probing, his subtleties are often missed by the batsman a mere pitch-length away. So there is little hope that the ringside spectator will perceive them; but he will see their result in what happens to the batsman. It was a cricketing education to watch Jim bowl.

With Doug Wright, we return to the high explosives. At the end of his swift, bounding run, he bowled leg-break or googly at an unusually high speed. He could have his off days; but no one else in our time – or probably in any other – had comparable ability to bowl a blind-length leg-break which would knock out the stumps of a well-set and top-class batsman.

It was fortunate for all cricket followers that television was invented in time to show us all Wesley Hall bowling. He had the most splendidly athletic – and, to many batsmen, quite terrifying – run-up – charm flying from his neck on its gold chain – and final eruptive heave to deliver a truly fast ball.

We must not miss a ball of this Elysian entertainment. If the duration of the match were all time, that would not be too long for a cricketer.

*Wisden Cricket Monthly*

# Index